SODOMSCAPES

Sodomscapes

HOSPITALITY IN THE FLESH

LOWELL GALLAGHER

FORDHAM UNIVERSITY PRESS

New York 2017

Fordham University Press has no responsibility for the
persistence or accuracy of URLs for external or third-party
Internet websites referred to in this publication and does
not guarantee that any content on such websites is, or will
remain, accurate or appropriate.

Fordham University Press also publishes its books in a
variety of electronic formats. Some content that appears in
print may not be available in electronic books.

Visit us online at www.fordhampress.com.

Library of Congress Cataloging-in-Publication Data
available online at http://catalog.loc.gov.

Printed in the United States of America
19 18 17   5 4 3 2 1
First edition

This is for my mother,
Bernadette Marie Collette Gallagher (1912–2014).
May her memory be for a blessing.

To my sister, Alice Osborne.
I carry you in my heart.

CONTENTS

Color plates follow page 112

PREFACE: ENTERING SODOMSCAPE

> Then the Lord rained on Sodom and Gomorrah sulfur
> and fire from the Lord out of heaven; and he overthrew
> those cities, and all the Plain, and all the inhabitants of the
> cities, and what grew on the ground. But Lot's wife, behind
> him, looked back, and she became a pillar of salt.
>
> —GEN. 19:24–26[1]

Mon amie, il faut que je parte.	I must leave, my dearest.
Voulez-vous voir	Would you like to see
l'endroit sur la carte?	The spot on the map?
C'est un point noir.	It's a black dot.
En moi, si la chose	Inside me, if things
Bien me réussit,	turn out well,
ce sera un point rose	there will be a pink dot
dans un vert pays.	in a green country.

—RAINER MARIA RILKE, "Départ"[2]

September 12, 2000, Ein Bokek, Israel. I have arrived at the Dead Sea, in search of Lot's wife.

Things have not turned out well. I had forgotten that the most important word in Rilke's poem is the conjunction *if*, the indiscriminate and thus always faithful messenger of contingency. The black dot on the map has not become a pink dot in a green country. The legendary image of a mortified landscape is what I expected to find, having apparently forgotten the observation, documented in virtually every travel guide book in recent circulation, that the unusual geological features of the region—the hypersaline lake and the seven-mile salt ridge called Kashum Usdum—now share space with a sprawling industrial and consumerist complex. A further impediment arose at the time of my visit. Because of structural renovations on the southbound highway along Mount Sedom, the solitary road sign directing tourists to the salt pillar had been temporarily removed. Without the visual index, the designated escarpment yielded something I was not looking for. What appeared instead of the fabled remnant was the breakdown of a Gestalt principle: nothing less than the dissolution of figure into the blankness of ground.

Help was eventually at hand, in the form of an impromptu archive of photographic images hastily pulled together from a circuit of concierge desks and souvenir shops in the vicinity. The resulting collation of landscape and archive finally produced the likely candidate (fig. 1). The photographic testimony to the object that tourists are directed to find at Mount Sedom no doubt speaks to the claims of fanciful antiquarianism or literal-minded piety, but the salt outcrop has virtually nothing to do with Lot's wife. My excursion through the Dead Sea region has supplied a different perspective. The more provocative remnant of Lot's wife resides not in the geological artifact that tradition has settled upon, but instead in the scattered expressions of the biblical figure's narrative conundrum—the porous interface of motion and stasis. This piecemeal rendering of the legendary topography of Sodom is not locatable on a map. Instead, it is hidden, and on the move, in plain view.

Let me put this another way. The essence of Sodom, and not least the enigmatic face given to Sodom by Lot's wife, belongs to an *elsewhere*, driven by the sense that localized determinations of commemorative practice capture neither the conjectural nor material grounding of the conjured place or event. This *elsewhere* belongs to the mutating syntax and roving provocation of what I call Sodomscape. The key to the notion derives from the linguistic components gathered to produce the term. For all the suppleness of its applications, the word *Sodom* adheres to the stabilizing properties of a proper noun. As such, even when it is coaxed into adjectival variants, the word harbors the collector's dream of a stilled cabinet of knowledge, where questions are brought into the beautiful composure of the possessed fact, the statistical datum, and the type of domesticated wonder incarnated by the inert "piece of the pillar" that met Georg Christoph Stirn's curious gaze as he toured the Anatomy School in the Bodleian Quadrangle in 1638.[3]

The addition of the suffix *-scape* silently changes all that. Derived from the Germanic root *skap*, the suffix has an etymological twin that more clearly conveys the sense of composure just described: *-ship*, which invokes settled or typical attributes of a condition or state of being.[4] Friendship. Hardship. Connoisseurship. Landscape, the most commonly used word in which the suffix *-scape* appears, touches on a neighboring semantic region by conjuring an aesthetically gratifying vista: scenic composure. But landscape also instills a certain discomposure, a kind of metabolic energy harnessed by the suffix's root sense: to create, install, or bring into being. Landscape therefore holds two seductions in precarious balance. It is, one might say, the unnervingly perfect host, because it sustains both the docil-

Figure 1. Pillar of Salt, Mount Sedom, Israel. Photo courtesy of Jay H. Geller.

ity of harmonious composition and the sheer eventfulness of the moment of onset or emergence, the *dérive* or drift into something that has not yet settled into place.[5]

Sodomscape captures the precariousness of the double seduction, and it does so through the particular homonymic tincture that the noun *Sodom* adds to the suffix *-scape*. Because notions of flight, exile, and exposure are deeply ingrained in Sodom's semantics, the converted place name reminds us that the soundworld of *-scape* also hosts two coincident senses of the noun *scape*: as variant of the nominative form of *escape*, and as back-formation of *landscape*.[6] Though it does not mention Sodom, Jean-François Lyotard's essay on landscape's unnerving solicitations captures the train of

thought just described. Provocatively titled "Scapeland" (in both the original French and the English translation), Lyotard's causerie also presents a
threshold into the itinerary pursued in this book.

"Deserts, mountains and plains, ruins, oceans and skies"—all phenomena conventionally associated with landscape.[7] This topography, however,
is not essential to the strange alchemy that the sensation of landscape produces. For Lyotard, the etymological root of the French word for landscape, *paysage*, draws us outside the naturalized purview of what may be
said to count as landscape: "It used to be said that landscapes [*Paysages*]—
pagus, those borderlands [*ces confins*] where matter offers itself up in a raw
state before being tamed—were wild because they were, in Northern Europe, always forests. FORIS, outside. Beyond the pale [*En dehors de l'enclos*],
beyond the cultivated land, beyond the realm of form."[8] The intuition preserved in the word *pagus* is that any place, any scene—whether rural or urban, indoors or outdoors—may metamorphose into a "scapeland:" "even
the cacophony of the Place de la République," Lyotard observes, "can become a landscape at 5:30 PM on a winter's day, when it is choked with thousands of jammed vehicles."[9] Landscape's indiscriminate generosity turns
on one precondition, which also makes itself felt as the unfailing result of
what comes to be apprehended as landscape: "ESTRANGEMENT [*dépay-
sement*]," separation from the familiar contours of place.[10]

"If place is cognate with a destiny," as Lyotard suggests, then landscape
draws one into an estranging experience of "a place without a DESTINY."[11]
Sodomscapes expresses the intent to take Lyotard at his word and to see
where this may lead. For Lyotard, the intuition leads at one point to the
edge of the Genesis text: "In order to have a feel for landscape you have
to lose your feeling of place. A place is natural, a crossroads for the kingdoms and for homo sapiens. The mineral, vegetable and animal kingdoms
are ordered by knowledge, and knowledge takes to them spontaneously.
They are made, selected for one another. But a landscape is an excess of
presence. My *savoir-vivre* is not enough. A glimpse of the inhuman, and/
or of an unclean non-world [*l'immonde*]."[12] The mention of homo sapiens
and the three kingdoms (*règnes*) makes it clear that Lyotard has Linnaeus
on the mind. This makes perfect sense, given the stature of Linnaeus's
contribution to the modern scientific "feeling of place" as a taxonomic
grid filled with objects that conform to designated morphologies. It bears
recalling, however, that the virtual Ur-text of Linnaeus's *Systema naturae*
is the Priestly account of creation in Genesis, with its serene depiction of
hierarchical orders of the cosmos that are brought into being and sustained
in place by the correlation of naming and knowledge.

Lyotard wants to leave all this behind in his search for the essential, if counterintuitive trait of landscape as a "mark," not an "inscription" but "the erasure of a support." Indeed, the argument bids fair to take leave of the Linnaean system, for there is no discernible place in that system for the "excess of presence" unleashed in Lyotard's essay's textual arena. But the Genesis text is more hospitable. Its name for the estranging proximity of excess, the *immonde*, the unworldly dimension to the perceived world, is Sodom. Sodom is the essence of landscape. Its portal is the figure of Lot's wife, the inscrutable salt pillar, falling into the anonymity of space and time.

And the figure is portable.

SODOMSCAPES

Introduction: Figural Moorings
of Hospitality in Sodomscape

The Cleveland Museum of Art houses one of the most challenging treatments of the Sodom story in twentieth-century visual culture, Anselm Kiefer's multimedia work *Lots Frau* (plate 1). It is easy to miss the pale script spelling out "Lots Frau" in the painting's lower right-hand corner; yet, without it, the work hardly bears relation to either Sodom's biblical account or the art-historical archive. The inscription supplies only minimal clues, just enough so that the railway tracks and the postapocalyptic landscape eventually prompt recognition of the Sodom story's generic narrative elements—the drama of exile, the specter of annihilation. For viewers who are familiar with Kiefer's aesthetic and political preoccupations, these elements suffice to identify the painting as a piece of postwar traumatic memory work, imagining the Nazi death camps (more precisely, the apparatus of forced transit) as Sodom's anamorphic modern avatar.[1] Arguably, however, the painting's most perplexing formal feature is the conspicuous missing element—Lot's wife. There is no indication of the fleeing woman or the salt pillar. Paradoxically, this absence testifies to Kiefer's fidelity to the biblical source's narrative conundrums. Like the Genesis text, Kiefer's painting silently broods over two questions: what happened to Lot's wife, and who owns the story of what she saw in Sodom?

Sodomscapes: Hospitality in the Flesh pursues these deceptively simple questions in their continuing provocation across a range of genres and cultural locations, allowing us to observe Lot's wife's figural plasticity. In her surprising range of modes of appearance, Lot's wife proves a resilient witness to the hospitality crises lodged in the Sodom story. The stilled gesture of witnessing tests hospitality's conceptual limits by embodying the coiled tension between generative and hazardous dimensions of hospitality's welcome to the outsider or stranger. In this capacity, the biblical figure draws critical attention to its own unpredictable expressions and capacity as a mutating crucible of social, political, aesthetic, religious, and ethical concerns.

The first step in laying this itinerary's groundwork begins by returning to Kiefer's painting's touchstone, the biblical proof-text, Genesis 19, and its single straightforward message. Prompted by the "outcry" against Sodom and Gomorrah, divine judgment swiftly and totally annihilated the residents and surrounding territory of the Cities of the Plain.[2] Lot's wife turns back, and instantly transforms. Gone, yet strangely remaining. Her metamorphosis, an anomalous feature in the Abraham and Lot cycle, seems to exempt her from death. At the same time, it also seems to presuppose her death under the cover of a figural surrogate, whether an inorganic life form (a pillar of salt, after the Hebrew text) or a found artifact (a statue, after the Latin Vulgate).[3]

The biblical text withholds explaining Lot's wife's motive for turning toward Sodom, despite the divine interdiction against looking back.[4] The lacuna raises the question of whether the Sodom that Lot's wife sees corresponds to the domicile and ethos that precipitated the catastrophe, and as such places Lot's wife at the headwaters of a curious parting of ways in Sodom's cultural and critical legacies. To this day, the word *Sodom* retains charged connotations of perverse and death-bound sexuality.[5] It probably goes without saying that this legacy now shares space, awkwardly, with the more complicated stories told by biblical scholars, cultural historians, queer theorists, philosophers, and artists from across the gamut of aesthetic genres.

Broadly speaking, revisionist accounts have called attention to how Sodom's imputed sexual stigma functions as a figure for a deeper and less easily localized problem: rooted and clandestine forms of inhospitality.[6] This revisionist perspective thus discloses the conflict-laden process through which artists and scholars critically challenge and attenuate the stigma of Sodom's pernicious exceptionalism, enabling persons and collectivities identified with nonnormative erotic dispositions and sexual behaviors to claim voices, social visibility, ethical equipment, and political responsibility. This is not to say that the stigma of Sodom has been thoroughly demystified. Rather, the revisionist perspective reclaims Sodom as a resilient figuration of hospitality's inherent contradictions and challenges, in both its life-promoting and hazardous aspects.[7]

The encounters with Lot's wife that populate this book thus touch on the protocols of queer inquiry from a highly specific angle of vision. The conjectured memory of Sodom driving the backward turn of the fleeing woman does not so much discover untold regions of queer sexuality as it tracks an encounter that both solicits and resists the satisfactions of naming.[8] My engagement with queer inquiry therefore concerns less the bearings of affect and allegiance that inform social constructions of queerness, and more the fissuring and recombinatory energies behind received broad protocols of identity formation and affective attachment. I will return to this point. For the moment, I wish to emphasize what I take to be the essential provocation raised by Lot's wife's place in the Sodom story.

As mapped in these pages, the mutating appearances of Lot's wife's stilled moment of capture, her arrested flight, serve as a virtual window through which we may observe how the repeated desire to reclaim Lot's wife, across millennia and a wide range of art forms, renders the fabled pillar of salt (or statue) an apt figural laboratory for testing the bounds of hospitality's two faces—welcome and risk—in diverse cultural locations. I make two related claims here. On the one hand, journeying through the aesthetic, exegetical, and philosophical archive on Lot's wife advances a more nuanced appreciation of figural expression's intimate concern with the adventure built into the hospitality question—the unpredictable relation between host and guest. On the other hand, the same archive repeatedly conjures up the reverse, reminding us that the event of hospitality invariably relies on the resources of figural imagination and thought in the shared and uncertain task of building or sustaining an environment—a Sodomscape worthy of the name—in which mutual communication, responsiveness, and dwelling may begin.[9]

Figure, of course, has protean aspects, borne of the word's application across a wide range of philosophical, aesthetic, and rhetorical disciplines. For my purposes, the most appropriate and tractable response to this potentially unwieldy feature is not to undertake a systematic genealogy of figure, as such a project would make for a different book. Instead, as our itinerary into the archive on Lot's wife unfolds, shifting aspects of figural expression will be called into service for their heuristic value. That said, a brief look at the source words may for now suffice to indicate this semantic arena's broad contours. From the Greek *schema* (outline), the Latin *figura* designates the appearance of a form, as well as the image or likeness of an absent thing or event. With these functions, figure bears a kindred relation to the meaning-making operations of symbol and allegory. From the Greek *typos* (blow or impression), *figura* additionally suggests the temporal dynamism of an action or intervention. The Latin barbarism *tropus*, from the Greek *tropos* (a turning), introduces a further associative field, in which the action of figure picks up the rhetorical provocation of tropes. This provocation has two aspects, since troping deviates from linguistic and communicative norms even as it supplies expressive means to overturn the naturalized basis of norms (their homely character) and reach beyond the bounds of the familiar.

This book's specific wager is that figure's protean character supplies an indispensable resource for understanding how Lot's wife's mutating appearances constitute resilient and fluent "thought-things"—prompts for critical reflection on the moorings of the hospitality question.[10] Moorings, of course, refer to the instruments used to hold a vessel in place before voyage. Where hospitality is concerned, the figure of moorings serves two contrasting functions. First, it conjures a paralyzing impasse brought about by the convergence of contradictory imperatives. Second, it issues a silent summons to think through the impasse—not to dissolve its terms, but to think otherwise about hospitality's identifying marks and boundaries.

I take Jacques Derrida's ruminations on this provocative intertwining of two moments of onset—arrest and release—as an axiomatic reference point. Derrida's starkest rendering of the problem appears in the final pages of the seminar-lecture "Step of Hospitality/No Hospitality" [*Pas d'hospitalité*]: "We will always be threatened by this dilemma between, on the one hand, unconditional hospitality that dispenses with the law, duty, or even politics, and, on the other, hospitality circumscribed by law and duty. One of them can always corrupt the other, and this capacity for perversion remains irreducible. It *must* remain so."[11] The tensile strength of the scene turns on the fact that the "dilemma" stages a bewildering conflict between Emmanuel Levinas's thought experiments on ethical relation and Immanuel Kant's ethical system. Famously, Levinasian ethics depicts a harrowing event of self-dispossession and infinite responsibility toward the enigmatic singularity of the Other (*autrui*, "the personal other"). On its face, at least, Kantian ethics is more easily digested, if only for its apparent adherence to a hospitality "circumscribed by law and duty."[12] This is not to say, however, that Levinas voices the unconditional side of hospitality, while Kant voices the conditional, since both advocate an unremitting posture of ethical fidelity.

In essence, Kant's ethical system advances reason's self-regulating properties as means to disclose universal values and imperatives. Levinasian ethics presents something more discomfiting, in part because it is not a system, but rather a mode of witnessing. Levinasian ethics witnesses the random and unavoidable onset of a perilous encounter with the breakdown of knowledge frames that are based on instrumental codes of separation and immunizing distance. One of the master tropes for this encounter in Levinas's idiom turns on the elusive yet compelling appearance of the "face of the Other."[13] *Face* here refers not simply to what is available to vision and knowledge, but to what exceeds such protocols—an exposure that troubles the familiar contours of what it means to be in relation. Tellingly, the nature of the disturbance that Levinas describes finds expression in the idiom of hospitality. Entering Levinas's world means discovering the disorienting proximity between the rather appealing idea that "the subject is a host," and the deliberatively provocative depiction of where this leads: "subjectivity is being hostage."[14] Gift-giving morphs into an uncontrollable event of being given over to the unknowable.

This small taste of Levinas's language goes a long way toward explaining the clear and strident dissensus in Levinas studies over his ethical vision's political implications. As Richard Wolin points out, the suspicion lingers that in Levinas's work a "well-nigh unbridgeable chasm opens up between ethics and justice."[15] Observing that the words *host* and *hostage* in Levinas's idiom function as figural gestures rather than regulative concepts or empirical descriptions does little to neutralize allergic reactions to Levinas's thought. As you may guess by now, however, it is precisely this figural dimension that accounts for the recurring interest his writings will hold at later points in this book—not least for the guarded attention he pays to the Sodom story and the pillar of salt.

For the moment, I simply suggest that Levinas's figures of hospitality give body to his thought's guiding orientation, which stringently advocates vigilance against the false complacencies that follow from routinized habits of thought and action in any domain. When Levinas reminds us of the omnipresent call to "compare the incomparable," he is thinking foremost of shared philosophical legacies of justice (he calls this "the Greek moment in our civilization").[16] The same words, however, aptly describe the basic movement of figural thinking (without regard to the received distinction between biblical and Greek legacies). Levinas passes over this point, but one of the goals of my excursion into Levinas's contribution to the Sodom archive is to point up how his insights' figural traits give heft to his claim that the call for justice primordially arises from the everyday discrepancies and challenges that shape the rhythm of being in common with others. The call to "compare the incomparable" serves, in the first instance, as a reminder that the ethical relation is not an absolutely private affair or *folie à deux* in the delirium of infinite responsibility. To "compare the incomparable" means to recognize that there are plural expressions of alterity to contend with—and to dwell with.[17]

Derrida's debt to Levinas is famously complex and ambivalent, yet his insistence that the "dilemma" at hospitality's heart is "irreducible" carries an unmistakable Levinasian accent. Radical vigilance, however, is not the only factor. No less important is the unstated suggestion that while both faces of hospitality—conditional and unconditional—share "the capacity for perversion," the meaning of perversion does not remain constant. What looks like dereliction from one side may appear from the other as an unheralded chance at an otherwise unimaginable future. Derrida ventures a version of this conjecture in the eulogy he delivered at Levinas's funeral in 1995: "possible hospitality to the worst is necessary so that good hospitality can have a chance, the chance of letting the other come, the *yes* of the other no less than the *yes* to the other."[18] Derrida's cautious insight—his attunement to the fragile moment when paralyzing impasse may open onto unsought chance—captures the gist of the overlooked message held by the figure of Lot's wife in the interwoven scenes of encounter that appear in this book's chapters.

Road Map

The seven chapters ahead offer a virtual circuit tour of Lot's wife's exemplary appearances in the Sodom archive. Each chapter begins by looking at a visual artifact, chosen for its aesthetic insight into the transmuting character of the ethical questions that arise when received roles of host, guest, and stranger begin to encroach on each other. Chapter 1 examines one of the jewels from the studio of the Parisian illustrator Maître François, an illuminated page from a late fifteenth-century manuscript of Augustine's *City of God*.[19] Maître François's design affords the imaginative occasion to observe how the ferment of patristic and medieval practices of allegorical composition and reading comes within reach of the law of unintended consequences. The saturated panorama of the flight from Sodom shows how the allegorical mode's rich variance promotes established exegetical and proselytizing habits of looking at Lot's wife in Jewish and Christian biblical tradition. The scene, in other words, presents a pictorial digest of condemnatory judgments that survive to this day as stock interpretations of the legend. The pillar of salt stands for impenitent disobedience, prudential error, or the perils of curiosity: pick your poison. At the same time, the allegorical network's fluency discloses breaches in the compositional chains connecting text and meaning. In these dead spaces between the visible and the legible, the depiction of the abortive flight opens onto a glancing intuition of an ethics of hospitality founded neither in the sovereignty of the law nor the satisfactions of duty.

Chapter 2 lingers on Maître François's design, treating it as a future memory of pillar of salt allusions in Maurice Blanchot and Emmanuel Levinas's delicate yet fraught philosophical conversation about the ethical aptitude of artworks. The Sodom archive's figural suggestiveness guided Blanchot's and Levinas's shared predisposition to identify the primordial affinity of artworks with the disruptive urgency of prophecy. Though the allusions traverse several pages of mutual critique and accommodation between the two thinkers, the touchstone text is Blanchot's 1957 essay "Prophetic Speech," which declares prophecy's fidelity to an impossible future, which "one would not know how to live and that must upset all the sure givens of existence."[20] Thus situated, the pillar of salt's subliminal association with prophecy becomes the site of an ecumenical settlement between Blanchot and Levinas over the captivating aesthetic power of artworks. On this note, Maître François's image and the late modern moment of philosophical hospitality between Blanchot and Levinas speak to each other across centuries. Through different registers of discernment, the two scenes conjure the figure of Lot's wife as the material remains of a thinking beyond the limit of the phenomenal face of appearances and cognition, so as to give witness to the radiant and interruptive force of artworks' worlding and unworlding dimensions.

Chapter 3 treats the aesthetics of vanishing legibility—a perceptual technique associated in early modern visual cultures with the geometricized optics of linear perspective—as a lens for discerning varieties of survival equipment available to English Catholic communities seeking safe zones of habitation in the post-Reformation world's uncertain landscapes (in moral as well as geographical and political senses of the word). My focal point in the chapter concerns the controversial apostolic career of Mary Ward (1585–1645), the early modern "Jesuitress" whose pastoral ambitions provided the impetus for the eventual worldwide teaching and social justice ministry of two religious orders, the Sisters of Loreto and the

Congregation of Jesus. The institutional success of Ward's project, however, was not a foregone conclusion in the turbulent ecclesio-political climate of mid-seventeenth century Europe. In the decades following Ward's
death and the Roman Curia's denegation of her community, a narrative
sequence of paintings commemorating Ward's life and mission, the so-
called *Painted Life* (*Gemaltes Leben*), was assembled in southern Germany.
Commemoration, however, is not its sole purpose. The paintings' experimental iconography adds an edginess to the ensemble by launching an eschatological memory of Ward's legacy that doubles as a polemical gesture
of visionary survival. Transfigured markers of Lot's wife's dispossessed
condition are the key.

Through this warping gesture, the paintings speak predictively to the
complex legacy of biblical *figura* in late modern literary and theological
cultures. On the one hand, they confirm Erich Auerbach's cherished hope
in the ongoing adaptability of *figura* as a means of maintaining neighborly
proximity between past and present in historical realism's secular grammar. On the other hand, the paintings anticipate the keen interest that
Auerbach's contemporaries from the progressive *ressourcement* school of
Catholic theology would also develop in deploying *figura*'s resources as
a means of opening up more generous—more hospitable—pathways between Catholicism and modernity.[21]

Early in their history—at some undocumented moment in the eighteenth century—the fifty tableaus comprising the *Painted Life* found haven in the house of Ward's order in Augsburg. They remain there to this
day, incorporated into the rhythms of the local convent and school. Yet,
for the most part, they are functionally invisible as aesthetic interventions
in their own right. In more than one sense, then, the paintings and their
polemical provocation are hidden in plain view. This circumstance testifies
to the critically adaptive resources of anamorphic vision. Anamorphosis's
defining disfigurement may be found not only in the artwork as a techni-
cal compositional feature—think of the famous distorted skull that cuts
into the sumptuous scene of diplomatic hospitality in Hans Holbein's *The
Ambassadors* (1533)—but also in the shaping conditions through which the
artwork "speaks," becomes legible and eloquent. This extended canvas of
disfigured perception recurs with increasing edginess and daring in further
stations on our itinerary.

Consider, as chapter 4 does, the case of Russian avant-garde artist Natalia Goncharova (1881–1962). The panache of her costume and set designs for Sergei Diaghilev's 1914 production of the opera-ballet *Le Coq
d'Or* placed her on the cusp of Western celebrity. Earlier in her career, she

turned to the Sodom narrative for inspiration in creating an aesthetically eclectic visual manifesto. Chapter 4 examines the volatile assemblage Goncharova produced in *Salt Pillars* (*Solianye stolpe*, ca. 1909) for its radically innovative capture of the transmuted woman as a hallucinatory necropolis. Diverse painterly styles—Eastern and Western, abstract and representational—converge in an expression, at once unnerving and hopeful, of messianic cosmopolitanism. The messianic, with its electric grasp of the space between a "no-more" and a "not-yet," held great appeal for Goncharova, even though on its face messianic urgency would seem to make an uneasy companion to the more capacious time-space commonly associated with the cosmopolitan ethos.[22] Goncharova's painterly experiment, however, supplies the linking middle term. The strangely oneiric and mortified landscape of *Salt Pillars* assembles a prescient image of Hannah Arendt's notion of natality, which Arendt draws from Augustine's definition of the human as inherently endowed with the capacity for gratitude and the ability to begin again in the midst of uncertainty. Arendt's thoughts on the subject of natality are famously unfinished, but the tenor of her remarks both tempers and refines the merger of messianic and cosmopolitan instincts at work in Derrida's rendering of the hospitality question. So, too, does the aesthetic experiment in *Salt Pillars*. Put simply, the painting gives figural expression to what Peg Birmingham calls the "double *principium*" of Arendt's notion of natality, the turn toward new beginnings and givenness.[23] Through this gesture, *Salt Pillars* presents a patient attentiveness to the complicity of worlding and unworlding gestures in the rhythm of being with others.

Chapter 5 examines a different brand of convergence: the contemporary crush of industries populating the fragile ecosystem along the southwestern shores of the Dead Sea. The local tourism and hospitality industry rather inefficiently trades on the region's legendary association with the destroyed Cities of the Plain. But Sodom's contemporary face resides elsewhere, anamorphically extended across the southern reaches of the Jordan Rift Valley into the Negev desert. The hospitality industry's co-implication in the congested nexus of neighboring activities—nature reserves, spa clinics, radiology centers, pharmaceutical and cosmetic companies, as well as chemical extraction plants—presents a fully secularized avatar of the function that both Sodom and Lot's wife serve in the Genesis text. Like the biblical prototype, the commercial assemblage incarnates the two inseparable faces of hospitality, welcome and risk. As the Dead Sea region knows all too well, the contemporary expression of these two faces uncannily resembles the twin engines of biopower: the "capacity to foster life or disallow it to the point of death."[24] The notable symptom of this operation takes shape, perhaps surprisingly, in the region's robust invest-ment in the skincare industry—in particular, the therapeutic regimens for psoriasis, the disorder whose biosemiotic profile and biomedical history quietly point up the shared socio-ethical borders of community and im-munity in the figural mooring of Sodomscape.

Chapters 6 and 7 further explore Lot's wife's resilience as a figurative lens for critically inspecting the ethical quandaries arising from geopoliti-cal conflict sites. Chapter 6 examines a relatively unknown Victorian novel in the genre of lost world romance fantasy, Alfred Clark's *The Finding of Lot's Wife* (1896). A piece of virtual tourism, the novel assembles an ad hoc gathering—English adventurers, American scholars of biblical antiquity, a local Bedouin tribe, an otherworldly monastic community—and the re-sulting plot engine roams from unintentional comedy to catastrophe. In essence, Clark's narrative bricolage shows how the confluence of the de-veloping disciplines of comparative religion and cultural anthropology, to-gether with the highly visualized aesthetic of nineteenth-century Oriental-ism, contributed to the novel's unusually provocative merger of kitsch and cultural critique. Clark reinvents the legend of Lot's wife by converting the cautionary tale of moral turpitude into a stark lesson on the perilous consequences of intercultural contact in the emerging theater of colonial Palestine. For this innovation alone, the novel warrants interest. Clark's central contribution to the Sodom archive, however, resides in the novel's prescient staging of a world in which we can observe the convergence of insights associated, on the one hand, with Hans Blumenberg's philosophi-cal anthropology of myth and, on the other hand, with the theological residue in Levinas's writings.

A peculiar assemblage, no question. You can hear the gears shift in Clark's design. Nonetheless, the novel achieves a quirky grandeur by con-firming Blumenberg's faith, avant la lettre, in myth's resilience for con-fronting the imminent peril associated with the "absolutism of reality." Blumenberg's phrase refers to the contingent onset of a "pure state of in-definite anticipation" called "anxiety" or "intentionality of consciousness without an object."[25] Because such an event is never entirely behind us (the imagined "point of no return" never arrives), the lability of myth, and its meaning-making function, performs therapeutic cultural service.[26] *The Finding of Lot's Wife* advances this kind of argument too, but ultimately the novel is more interested in examining moments when the therapy breaks down. Such moments expose what Arendt calls the "small track of non-time" opened up by "the activity of thought."[27] What Clark presents, however, is not a narrative image of the resourcefulness of thinking, but rather an advance echo of the harrowing ethical prospect of infinite self-giving, in a Levinasian key.

One of the names Levinas gives to this drama is a theological figure, the self-emptying action of kenosis, which finds paradigmatic expression in the Philippians hymn, Paul's lyrical condensation of the traumatic and exalted events in the Christ story (Philippians 2:6–11).[28] Given the currency of the so-called conflict thesis between science and religion in late-Victorian England, it is perhaps not so surprising that Clark's fantasy expedition to Sodom should incorporate suggestive markers of kenosis. Kenosis was one of the most hotly debated topics in nineteenth-century Christology, in part because of the perennial theological difficulties posed by the easy confluence of self-abandonment and self-transcendence in the language of the Philippians hymn.[29] Clark is no theologian, but his interest in the ethical provocations of kenosis is as keen as Levinas's—and perhaps more viscerally arresting because of its narrative immediacy. This feature powerfully contributes to the innovation *The Finding of Lot's Wife* brings to the Sodom archive. Clark's ingenious intertwining of Blumenbergian and Levinasian treatments of myth effectively refigures the legacy of Lot's wife. Clark shows how the lethal and reparative dimensions of that legacy asymmetrically impinge on each other in an arresting narrative image of dread commingled with hope.

The book's final chapter examines the prospect of unhoped-for discovery that Albert Memmi, one of the inaugural architects of colonial discourse analysis and precursors of postcolonial theory, brought to the figure of Lot's wife in his first novel and first published work, *The Pillar of Salt* (*La statue de sel*, 1953).[30] The novel presents a richly detailed, semi-autobiographical, and scrupulously confessional account of the splendors and miseries of a native son's coming of age in French-occupied Tunisia. During this period, Tunisia witnessed colonial Vichy rule, the spasm of German occupation, and the eventual liberation by Allied forces. The novel is narratively satisfying as a quasi-documentary report on a life wrecked in the colonial endgame in the Maghreb. It achieves its distinctive critical voice, however, from Memmi's careful pacing of the incremental discrepancies between what the youthful protagonist gradually acquires as a traumatic form of cultural and political literacy and what he intermittently intuits as a dimension of ethical responsiveness and responsibility that does not corroborate the knowledge or convictions afforded by such hard-won literacy.

The narrator's dawning self-identification with Lot's wife, as the paradigmatic instance of paralyzing introspection in the face of a double bind, is as predictable as it is poignant. The real interest of the narrative argument, however, turns on Memmi's delicate crafting of the missed rendezvous between the boy's conscious assent to the virulent legacy of the Sodom narrative and the critical rejoinder figured by the boy's intuitive and gradually immersive contact with the other face of Lot's wife. This is the face that testifies, through action, to the ethical awakening born of intimate familiarity with the difficult edge joining home to homelessness.

In a very real sense, *The Pillar of Salt* brings us full circle. For starters, the novel's world proves amenable for thinking how Arendt's critically willed hope in natality's reparative power may speak to the risk and promise of hospitality at the heart of Levinas's ethics of vulnerability. Crucially, the novel places such a colloquy under the canopy of Augustine. This is not only the Augustine of the *City of God*, whose voice echoes in Arendt's notion of the newness (*novitas*) afforded by the memory of natality, but also the Augustine of the *Confessions*—the text that famously worries over the wounding conflict between the narrated and narrating self, and absolves the conflict through an ecstatic embrace of allegory's world-making and world-repairing powers.[31]

There is no redemption for Memmi's protagonist, at least not in the theological sense. The denouement nonetheless remembers the concluding pages of the *Confessions* for the ethical promise they hold, by imagining the generative outcome that may follow from a felt impasse. Through this memory work, *The Pillar of Salt* finds common cause with the texts and artifacts assembled in this book. It too holds in its gaze the filament of mutual regard between the two faces of Lot's wife, and its critical equipoise enlarges understanding of the biblical figure's status as a neglected resource for appreciating the difficult yet bracing span of hospitality's claims.

There is perhaps nothing surprising in emphasizing the framing notions of figure and hospitality, for they are hardwired into the exegetical traditions that have culled scripts for moral pedagogy from the foundational narrative in Genesis. My decision to open each chapter with a visual artifact, however, tacitly nods toward the different angle of approach that has predominated in the critical scholarship on the biblical myth. In the main, the all-too-brief episode of abortive flight has served as a renewable resource for examining the mechanisms of what Martin Harries aptly calls "destructive spectatorship."[32] One of the upshots of the emphasis on fatal gazing has been a sharpened appreciation of how modernity's turn to the psychological and political engines of trauma has replaced the premodern sense of unregulated vision as one of the main routes of sin. Taken as an ensemble, this body of critical literature demonstrates both the range and the abiding familiarity of Lot's wife's provocation as portal to the deep history behind what Martin Jay calls the "denigration of vision" (or "antiocularcentric discourse") in twentieth-century thought.[33]

The correlation of vision with optics and perspectivalism, which rose to prominence in Renaissance theories of painting and architecture, no doubt helped secure the subsequent prestige of vision's affinity with modernity's totalizing regimes of spectacle. The story, however, harbors complications, which derive from vision's supple adaptability as figural shorthand for the capacity to move beyond the closed dialectic of scopic domination and entrapment. Late modern strands of hermeneutic phenomenology have abundantly described and debated this region of encounter, and its main merit lies in its intuition of a relatively open and experimental dialectic of exposure and solicitation. The ensuing attunement fosters a self-critical grasp of the vital, if always partial and sometimes precarious, correlation of vision with transformative understanding. It also supplies the framing presupposition for this book's distinctive emphasis on the ethical provocations that arise from the intertwining of figural expression and the polar imperatives of hospitality.

From the Sin of Sodom to the Flesh of Lot's Wife

Maurice Merleau-Ponty's phenomenology of carnal being offers a touchstone for my inquiry. Famously, Merleau-Ponty translates Edmund Husserl's notion of the "lived body" (*Leib*) as the shared "flesh of the world" (*la chair du monde*).[34] The translation emphasizes the co-implication of the affective registers of touch and sight in an enveloping network of chiastic exchanges between "the sensing and the sensed."[35] Such intertwining expresses the intercorporeal drama that Merleau-Ponty also calls the "topology of being."[36] For Merleau-Ponty, the topological image eschews allegiance to a fixed Archimedean point of sovereign rationality or its attendant scientistic trappings of instrumental objective knowledge. Merleau-Ponty's topology instead endorses an incarnate rationality that replaces data-driven notions of "concept, idea, mind, representation" with "*dimensions*, articulation, level, hinges, pivot, configuration."[37] I will return to this last word in a moment.

If topology, thus described, carries a hint of the machinic, Merleau-Ponty's folding of the term into the more pliable notion of the flesh reminds us that the movement at issue here is not that of an automaton. For Merleau-Ponty, the flesh subsumes individualized or personalized connotations of embodiment, as well as rote behaviors, into a relational field in which the situated (topical) character of experience necessarily includes strands of proximity, exposure, and indebtedness to a host of both creaturely and inanimate life forms. The "flesh of the world" thus imagines human selfhood as a contingently privileged form of reflection on the uncertain calculus of what it means to exist in and with a world where the relation between immanence and transcendence is felt, if not known, to be undecided. This is a world, in other words, of textured immanence and humbled transcendence. In this regard, Merleau-Ponty's *topology* of being is necessarily also a *tropology* and a *typology* of being. It is tropological because it bears witness to experience's inherently rhetorical, and thus expressively tropic, dimensions: *How can I say or show what I mean?* It is typological because it is inherently impressionable, sustaining a deep memory of the striking or imprinting action denoted by the Greek word *typos* (and its Latin translation, *figura*): *How should I respond to what has just taken me by surprise?*

Given that typology is not his word of choice, Merleau-Ponty can hardly be chastised for not dwelling on the significant Pauline legacy of typological perception in shaping the secularizing orientation of the Christic dispensation—its commitment to the world, with an eye to its unfinished and flawed character. Yet it is worth recalling that in the Letter to the Romans Paul uses the word *typos* to emphasize the ecstatically wounded dimension of the lived time of human experience.[38] Certainly, Merleau-Ponty's use of the word *flesh* dispenses with the accumulated doctrinal and theological associations of the equivalent word in the Pauline canon, *sarx* (as in "sinful flesh" [Rom. 8:3]).[39] Phenomenologically, however, Merleau-Ponty's "flesh" carries a discernible Pauline undertow, not because the term preserves the antithetical dynamic of flesh and spirit associated with Paul's theological anthropology, but rather because it recasts antithesis as co-implication and transformative combustion. Merleau-Ponty's neologism stands for the resilient capacity to be surprised by unseen or unthought dimensions of what relational being may come to mean.

For this reason, Merleau-Ponty's sense of the "flesh of the world" as an improvisational mode of "configuration" introduces a presiding spirit for the itineraries I pursue in this book. In the essay "The Intertwining—The Chiasm," Merleau-Ponty's rumination presents a richly suggestive account of how the vital secret to the thought of the flesh—and its value to the art of hospitable perception—hinges on its peripatetic associations:

> The flesh is not matter, in the sense of corpuscles of being which would add up or continue on one another to form beings. . . . In general, it is not a fact or a sum of facts "material" or "spiritual." Nor is it a representation for a mind. . . . The flesh is not matter, is not mind, is not substance. To designate it, we should need the old term "element," in the sense it was used to speak of water, air, earth, and fire, that is, in the sense of a *general thing*, midway between the spatio-temporal individual and the idea, a sort of incarnate principle that brings a style of being wherever there is a fragment of being. The flesh is in this sense an "element" of Being. Not a fact or a sum of facts, and yet adherent to *location* and to the *now*. Much more: the inauguration of the *where* and the *when*, the possibility and exigency for the fact; in a word: facticity, what makes the fact be a fact.[40]

The passage is notable for showing the productive gap between sense perception's intuitive play and categorical knowledge's symbolic and linguistic forms. It is perhaps no surprise that Merleau-Ponty's descriptions of the flesh repeatedly invoke its gestational rhythm. Understood as the "formative medium of the object and the subject," flesh is a kind of ambient "pregnancy," for the precise reason that it mobilizes "a power to break forth, productivity (*praegnans futuri*), fecundity." In this capacity, flesh proves host to "a birth of meaning, or a wild meaning [*un sens sauvage*]," the shapes of which are irreducible to merely anthropological projections of the exotic or inchoately known.[41] Indeed, the "wild" dimension of flesh is not a distinctive attribute of a specific body or collectivity. Rather, it intimately concerns the elemental and anonymous "generality of the Sensible in itself," which includes a ceaseless dynamic of "reciprocal insertion and intertwining" through which "my seeing body subtends this visible body, and all the visibles with it."[42]

It is well known that the religious connotations of the flesh preserve a long history of omnibus condemnatory judgment. (Thus the medieval aphorism against "the world, the flesh, and the devil.") Merleau-Ponty's idiosyncratic handling of the notion is not immune to suspicion of a different stripe: indulging in complacent generalities with a normative bent.[43] The value I draw from Merleau-Ponty's idiom, however, turns on a specific dimension of the generalizing trait, a region where the general and the normative do not coincide. The sheer eclecticism of Merleau-Ponty's descriptive terms conveys his abiding attention to the element of adventure and risk—part of the inferred gestational rhythm—woven into even the most ordinary and familiar manifestations of corporeal and sensory experience.

Time and again, Merleau-Ponty's descriptions of carnal being remind us that the ordinary and familiar are rarely the last word, so to speak. This is so because perceptions of the ordinary and familiar invariably rely on the interplay of the senses, and it is precisely such interplay that "begin[s] the paradox of expression."[44] What Merleau-Ponty means by "the paradox of expression" is a difficult nut to crack, however. One implication, which Bernhard Waldenfels has drawn out, holds particular relevance for the inquiry I pursue in this book. Waldenfels notes the inherently equivocal positioning of the expressive event between the extremes of "pure innovation" and "pure repetition."[45] The achievement of either extreme, he points out, would vitiate the expressive operation entirely, since "purely creative discourse would say *nothing*; purely repetitive discourse would have nothing *to say*."[46]

Waldenfels's qualifying comment enters into the orbit of concerns I pursue in this book, because it calls attention to the inherent restiveness of the condition of in-betweenness. Even as it participates in the launch of stable circuits of meaning, in-betweenness also nourishes meaning's nomadic potential—its figural drift both into and away from the hospitality question. Because it endlessly "differentiates itself from itself," as Waldenfels puts it, the expressive operation "is never entirely meaningful nor does it ever reach its full potential; it is never completely at home and up to a certain point is always alien to itself."[47] Crucially, the factor of alienness does not merely concern the expressive gesture in a solipsistic theater. Alienness also impinges on expression's unforeseen career after its launch into the extended flesh of its host environments. Merleau-Ponty touches on this point in "The Intertwining—The Chiasm," with the telling description of the participating concert of the "touch-vision system" and the "reflexivity of the movements of phonation and of hearing" in realizing the expressive character of the flesh as "the point of insertion of speaking and thinking in the world of silence."[48]

There are, of course, untold continents in the "world of silence" and they are not, as Merleau-Ponty points out, "indivisible glaciers of beings."[49] Like all members of the "*flesh* of things," they are given over to what Merleau-Ponty calls "dehiscence," a striking botanical metaphor for the splitting open of a seed pod, for example, at the moment of ripening.[50] With this metaphor, even the utopian energies sometimes attributed to Merleau-Ponty's argument lean toward the thought that the "point of insertion" of human expression "in the world of silence" is an essentially unruly affair. It includes dead ends, accidental encroachments, and collateral damage—matters carrying ethical import.[51]

The restive and ambivalent concert of welcome and curiosity that subtends the "flesh of things" guarantees that its capacity for "never-finished differentiation" cannot be quarantined.[52] Merleau-Ponty's insight on this score thus supplies a useful, and ethically suggestive, coordinate for mapping the figural scope of Sodomscape and in particular its relation to the queer legacy of Sodom as it pertains to Lot's wife. Now is a good moment to revisit that legacy by imagining the figural resemblance between the essential in-betweenness of Lot's wife in the Sodom story and the volatile and increasingly porous field of inquiry that queer studies currently occupies.

Almost by definition, the field harbors persistent territorial conflicts over the proper methods of inquiry and legible boundaries of queerness. Semantically, the word *queer* now oscillates between its modern sense as mark of sexual identity and contemporary rezonings of the word's earlier, premodern sense as departure from the norm (where it may imply either an aberration of a given entity or the onset of the new in any domain of activity or thought). Grammatically, the word also now oscillates between the adjectival position (whereby anything—objects and events as well as persons and even metaphysical entities—can acquire a queer dimension) and the nominative case (naming a stable if not immutable component of sexual identity).[53]

By no accident, perhaps, recent skirmishes in queer theory have mirrored the semantic volatility of the word *Sodom*.[54] In the main, the triggers concern methodological and quietly political standoffs that have arisen from heightened attention to nonessentialist and historically dynamic codings of personal or group identity. A telling case is early modern scholar Valerie Traub's call for a "queer historicism" that seeks to remain more attentive to the local contexts of events depicted in the historical record— more attentive, that is, than the speculative work represented by scholars such as Madhavi Menon and Carla Freccero in proposing alternative strands of queer affect and practice that do not pretend to map readily onto the available descriptive codings within a given cultural location.[55] From the perspective unfolded in Sodomscape, debates of this kind ultimately seem to participate in what Freud called the "narcissism of small differences," and by this I mean simply that both "queer historicism" and the more speculative expressions of queer theory fall within a spectrum of critical interest in mapping the rich historical variance of connections between sexual behaviors, affects, and identities.[56]

The question of ethics, however, even as it touches on the suggestively queer condition of finding oneself caught between conflicting codes of value or allegiance, remains largely a tacit dimension of such debates. I do not wish to imply here that queer theory (and the internal conflicts it now bears as a defining attribute) has no relation to the question of ethics. Indeed, the animating force of queer theory (as Michel Foucault's *History of Sexuality* made clear) has profound ethical implications, insofar as the critical investigation into the historicity of the meanings of sexual behaviors speaks to a desire to make visible and to solicit respect for aspects of human experience that have been misrecognized or disowned or condemned by dominant (and restrictive) modes of understanding the reach of human behaviors across historical periods and cultures. In essence, the term *Sodomscape* foregrounds the *tacit dimension* of queer theory and, in effect, stands sentinel over the deep history of this feature from biblical antiquity to contemporary cultures. The historical moorings of Sodomscape presented in this book lie adjacent to—but are also irreducible to—the transhistorical reception of Sodom that has repeatedly correlated the condemned city with the sexualized problematic of iniquity. In essence, the guiding animus of Sodomscape is to treat that problematic as symptom of the hospitality crises waged in the foundational biblical account in Genesis 18–22 and reopened, provocatively, in key pages of Derrida, Blanchot, and Levinas— pages that remember the ethical dimension of the Sodom story in ways that queer theory has largely forgotten.

In other words, in envisioning how an ethics of the flesh may be sought from the figural history of Lot's wife, this book offers no sustained engagement with the important work being produced by inquiries into sexual identity or performativity or affect. Instead, one of the chief aims of my project is to issue a reminder that the question of ethics, if it is to remain faithful to the difficult yet bracing insights of Levinas's ethics, does not ascribe special privilege or exceptional status to *any* single attribute that may go into a given person's or group's received sense of self or identity. The conditions of ethical vigilance and ethical attunement to what is urgently at hand (and also only ever partly grasped) necessarily arise from the place where one stands—one's situated position as an ethical subject. But these conditions necessarily also reach out to what is not already assimilated, and remains ultimately unassimilable, from the vantage point of any of the attributes one possesses.

It is for this very reason that my argument finds in Merleau-Ponty's notion of the "flesh" the galvanizing principle from which to reflect on the ethical provocations that Derrida, Blanchot, and Levinas detect in the Sodom story. For *Sodomscapes*, as for Merleau-Ponty, "flesh" is not a synonym for the individuated, sexed, gendered, class-marked, or racialized body. "Flesh" is the name for the unregulated arena into which these attributes—any of them, in unpredictable ways—must venture when they are called to assist in responding to the ethical claim that arises and compels attention. In this regard, "flesh" is closer in spirit to Levinas's notion of the "face" than it is to phenomenally graspable notions of "body." In this specific sense, the argument of *Sodomscapes*, far from "queering" the queer, may be said to track the ethical "face" of queer theory. This element would be the part of the Sodom story and archive that queer theory has not (yet) seen as its own concern and the measure of its own commitment to an ethics of witnessing.

This again is why Merleau-Ponty's phenomenology of the flesh serves as an impetus for the itineraries taken up in this book, even though from here his idiom will float into the background. For me, Merleau-Ponty's legacy comes down to this. Attending to the flesh means patient attunement to the occluded double binds and chance novelties that inform and deform the rhythms of lived experience. Such attunement, over time, discloses counterintuitive ways of understanding what counts as a life in the context of divergent claims of being-with and being-for. To borrow one of Merleau-Ponty's words, these notions of collective being "configure" hospitable spaces for vigilant dwelling between the substantialist dream of resemblance and the mutating dynamism of otherness.

The Genesis text does not give Lot's wife a name. Let's give her one. Her name is "flesh."

Kiefer's painting knows this is true. It also knows that there is no answer to the two questions I posed at the outset: What happened to Lot's wife, and who owns the story of what she saw in Sodom? More precisely, it knows that there is no answer worth remembering without respecting its figural character, in all the senses we have seen. With this in mind, let us look again at the painting.

The blasted landscape draws the eye into the genocidal apparatus of the railway transports administered by the Deutsche Reichsbahn during the Nazi regime. There is no evidence of the human cargo being given over to the machinery of degradation, slaughter, and disposal, and the announced figure of Lot's wife, as already noted, is nowhere to be seen. So what do we see? Train tracks. Signs of environmental as well as political disaster. And a conspicuous performance of the centuries-old technique of linear perspective. The aesthetic and ethical provocation of the work resides in its perspectival detail—the vanishing point does not sustain its mandate as the organizational center of the composition, because it does not subscribe to its traditional rhetorical function. Its solicitation does not welcome the viewer into the represented scene to occupy a sovereign vantage point. Follow the train tracks. The line of the vanishing point dissolves beneath the horizon. Evacuated, or suspended, space. There is no denying the effect of this gesture as an instance of "scopic trauma."[57] But the painting's figural argument resides elsewhere. The recoil from the evacuated center of the painting tells us that the figure of Lot's wife is not in the painting. The figure arrives in the viewing position—wounded but not destroyed—occupied by anyone who looks at the work in the mode of patient attunement well captured by Paul Claudel's aphorism: "the eye listens."[58] Scopic trauma is the beginning, not the end, of the story. Merleau-Ponty's sense of the "flesh," with its chiastic reversibility and synesthetic fluency, is at work.

Here, finally, the essence of figure appears. It is not simply a visual element in the fabricated landscape. It is also an event, which opens onto untapped tributaries of hospitable engagement. This engagement may be found through sustained affective interest in the unseen consequences of imaginary solidarity not so much with the diversity of life forms that participate in the "flesh" of the world as with the undeclared dimensions of their vitality. It is now time to turn from Kiefer's moment to the studio of Maître François in fifteenth-century Paris. Historically, the distance is long; figurally, not so much.

CHAPTER I

Exodus, Interrupted: Lot's Wife and the Allegorical Interval

The eternal duration of the interval in which a statue
is immobilized differs radically from the eternity of a
concept; it is the meanwhile [*entre-temps*], never finished,
still enduring—something inhuman and monstrous.

—EMMANUEL LEVINAS, "Reality and Its Shadow"[1]

Delicately limned veils of crimson flame, descending from the sky, are just beginning to cast a shadow over shimmering pink and ochre buildings, and a verdant, bosky landscape (plate 2). Signs of distress punctuate the cityscapes. Prostrate bodies, as though already struck dead, fill the streets, while other figures look heavenward with hands raised in supplication or alarm. Annihilation is imminent, but not for all. To the left of the condemned cities, angelic emissaries guide Lot and his daughters to safety, following the road's vertical ascent. A ribbon of sacred text, the road's lexical twin, silently proclaims the orthodox path, the *methodos*, of salvation. Lot and his daughters have just survived Lot's forced choice to offer his daughters as surrogates for the angelic visitors, whom Sodom's residents threatened to violate (Gen. 19:1–25). Another trial of hospitality awaits the endangered family. For now, however, they have reason to hope for safety. Anticipating the "ruling metaphor" of Pascal's wager, they are embarked.[2] Between the two scenes of imminent expectation, between hope and dread, stands Lot's wife, fully accomplished, it appears, as the figure of a precipitous eschaton.

The illuminated manuscript miniature before you is the work of Maître François, the leading Parisian illuminator in the fifteenth century's latter half. It appears in Raoul de Presles's (1316–82) vernacular translation of Augustine's *City of God* (ca. 1473).[3] In this chapter, the image serves as a prism for reflecting on the basic figural furniture of the hospitality question. The miniature lends itself to this angle of inquiry because the design's artfully composed elements gather many of the topics Maître François's era associated with Lot's wife and her perceived errors. (All of the errors attributed to her, it turns out, fall into the ambit of hospitality crises.) My aim, then, is heuristic. How do the miniature's compositional details speak to *allegoria* and *figura*'s easy complementarity, which, as expressive gestures in the assembled panorama of disaster and rescue, weave together diverse threads of world-making meaning and value?

A twofold assumption lies behind this question. The miniature's eloquence in part derives from its conformity to prevailing exegetical habits, which treated allegory as a supple mode, or host form, of figural expression. In other words, the miniature (and the text it adorns) knows nothing of the radical split between allegory and figure asserted by Erich Auerbach in the influential 1938 article "Figura." For Auerbach, "allegory involves an abstract sign that leads beyond itself," and its flight into abstraction "devalues the relevance of the historical record."[4] The figural method, on the other hand, "establishes a connection between two events or persons, the first of which signifies not only itself but also the second, while the second encompasses or fulfills the first. The two poles of the figure are separate in time, but both, being real events or figures, are within time, within the stream of historical life."[5] Maître François's illuminated panoramic vista remembers what Auerbach overlooks: the mutual participation of allegorical and figural expression "within the stream of historical life." In the miniature, both terms corroborate Auerbach's vivid description of figural realism's revealing power: "history, with all its concrete force, remains forever a figure, cloaked and needful of interpretation" and, as such, "remains open and questionable," pointing to "something still concealed . . . something other that is promised and not yet present."[6]

The miniature also espouses a view of figural expression that borders on another region of territorial intrigue—the *Institutio oratoria*, from Latin rhetorical tradition. Quintilian formulates what would become a standard definition of allegory as "continued metaphor."[7] Allegory pursues and ramifies the spirit of metaphor as embarking toward communicable meaning. Quintilian also recognizes allegory and irony's shared property as deviations from normal speech, though he is uncertain whether the species of irony called antiphrasis bears any relation to allegory's polysemous energy and generative fecundity. Indeed, antiphrasis "derives its name from negation," and can turn the oppositional cast of irony into an unworlding gesture: unfettered negation.[8]

Over time, the problem Quintilian touches upon became one of Romantic and modernist aesthetics' signature concerns, reaching its starkest expression, perhaps, in Paul de Man's deconstructive poetics. As Gordon Teskey has shown, these latter stages of surveilling the vexed border between allegory and irony bear witness to the bracing yet paralyzing thought that irony names the "abyss of the infinitely possible," which generates "every possibility of figurative language," even as it also disintegrates them.[9] On this account, the suspicion that irony may well be the unthought origin of all expression affords no harbor from the thought that irony also, as Teskey puts it, "devours its host from within."[10]

The trajectory just described makes it difficult to claim that Maître François's illuminated image is innocent of irony's workings. This is so because irony's base of operation is not a documentable set of traits ripe for inspection and classification. Rather, irony informs the encounter between the artwork and its receivers. Put simply, the dynamic of critical distance, understanding, and empathetic engagement necessarily passes through moments of ironic dislocation.[11]

If we accept that Quintilian's perplexity indeed leads to what Teskey describes as allegory and irony's antagonism and tortured interdependence, it speaks a truth that is thinkable but not livable. It consigns allegory to the role of a dogmatic administrator of knowledge, using all of its resources "to impose schematic order on historical process."[12] As for irony, it is a lost cause, and cannot stand for anything. Against its own critical momentum, it vanishes—like the Cheshire cat, all smile and no body.[13]

Maître François's panorama is not suspicious of allegory. Rather, it maintains that allegory's capacity to give form to a "world we can value and a narrative in which we can live" does not disintegrate in the face of the built world's mystifying or maladaptive aspects.[14] This is not to say that the world it represents is an entirely peaceable kingdom. The pictured event, after all, chronicles catastrophe and peril, while the composition itself, with its graceful lines and saturated color palette, cultivates a serene aesthetic ambience. In art-historical terms, the latter trait no doubt helps identify the work as a typical example of Maître François's era. Even so, its serene ambience is more than a trait of the work's painted surface. Rather, it introduces an extended pause into the aesthetic encounter with the work, affording an occasion to dwell with the prospect of a world in which beauty and violence, neither fixed to any single allegorical intention, coexist.

By treating Maître François's image as an *occasion* rather than a closed system, my argument pursues the premise, variously expressed in the long history of philosophical hermeneutics and phenomenological aesthetics, that the artwork's ontological enigma turns on its capacity to transcend the conditions of its making. (Merleau-Ponty's notion of the "flesh of the world," described earlier, includes this premise.) In brief, art gives both material and virtual shape to the event interred in the word *occasion*'s etymology. The "work" of the artwork entails a falling out (*occidere*, from *cadere*) of its perceived boundaries, including the proprietary claims of the work's local historical setting as well as the work's legibility as either allegorical or ironic coding.

Into what does the "work" of the artwork fall? In the epigraph to this chapter, Emmanuel Levinas supplies an answer. What Levinas sees and decries in the artwork is what the statue paradigmatically incarnates: the unending and vagabond interval of the "meanwhile" (*entre-temps*).[15] Levinas's polemical stance is not without relevance to the matters addressed here, and I will take up the question of his specific animus toward art later on. For the moment, I will only stipulate that the meanwhile's lapse from the concept's schematic clarity and already elucidated systems of meaning is precisely what allows space and time to enter into the silent and stilled choreography of the miniature's visual and narrative details.

Inhabiting this interval means consenting to a certain errancy in reading the events and images that make up the illuminated panorama's represented lifeworld. Here errancy means more than error. Errancy stands for exposure to unmapped regions of neighborly proximity and communication between premodern and late modern turns to the Sodom archive. Such exposure turns the risk of error into promise, by disclosing occasions for critical reflection on the fluency of allegory as a means to capture, re-enflesh, and stand guard over the fugitive heart of the meanwhile. In Maître François's depiction of the flight from Sodom, the statue of Lot's wife is the icon of this sense of the meanwhile.

Speaking Other

By happy coincidence, the image you are looking at also belongs to a text by Augustine. Biblicists and historians of sexuality have long recognized the importance of Augustine, and the *City of God* in particular, in estab-

lishing the association of Sodom's catastrophic end with divinely authorized prohibitions of homosexual acts (*stupra in masculos*).[16] Augustine also
recognized Sodom's semiotic indeterminacy. His moralized reading of the
transformation of Lot's wife makes this feature clear:

> For what else does it signify that those who were rescued by the angels
> were forbidden to look back, save that we must not return in spirit to
> the old life [*non est animo redeundum ad veterem vitam*] which he who is
> regenerate by grace casts off, if we expect to escape the last judgment?
> Lastly, Lot's wife stood fixed in the spot where she looked back, and by
> being turned to salt supplied a bit of seasoning for believers, whereby
> they may be salted with wisdom to beware of following her example.[17]

For Augustine, Lot's wife serves as a savory inducement (*condimentum*) for
the pious reader to understand all transgressions, whether sexual or not, as
roving symptoms of moral recidivism, a rooted refusal to participate in the
saving action of grace. There will be more to say later about a secondary
feature: Lot's wife as index of an interminable dialectic between memory
and forgetting. The latter problem, which famously occupies Augustine in
Book 10 of the *Confessions*, admittedly receives scant attention in Augustine's reading of Genesis 19. I mention it in passing because Augustine's
reflection on the biblical episode prompts a glancing but significant recollection of Paul's use of the word *allegory*. This appears in a passage that
became one of Christian exegesis's proof-texts of salvation history: Paul's
description of the covenantal economy in Galatians 4:21–31. For Paul, allegory functions as the crucible through which a decisive distinction between two women (Hagar and Sarah) and two corresponding covenants (of
the flesh, of the promise) presents itself. As we will see, one of Lot's wife's
core provocations concerns the figure's intermittent status as a limit case
of the bond between covenantal and allegorical imaginations in the Pauline
grammar of redemption.

One simple question takes us directly into the arena. What kind of allegorical reading does Augustine produce here? The conventional name in
high medieval exegesis is tropology, part of the so-called fourfold method
of Christic allegoresis. According to the fourfold method, Scripture is
treated as an integrated constellation of spiritually radiant events, mapped
onto the "old"/"new" covenantal dyad.[18] With this hermeneutic, a given
event recorded in the Old Testament (such as the destruction of the Cities
of the Plain) acquires the status of an ontological hybrid. The literal/his-
torical aspect (*littera, historia*) harbors a textual and figural aspect (*figura*).
Since the historical event preserves a trace of the divine hand in history,

its figural aspect carries centrifugal force. The historical domain simultaneously carries a kernel of intimacy with events in the life of Christ and
the Church on earth (the Christocentric sense of allegory), as well as with
stages in the moral progress of the soul (tropology), and the eschatological
consummation of the Church triumphant (anagogy).

Augustine himself worked out a fourfold scheme of allegorical interpretation, with slightly different terms and emphases.[19] I use the later and
better-known scheme in part because the word it enlists to refer to moral
and ethical choice—or conflict—aptly mirrors the gesture that seals the
fate of Lot's wife: a deviating turn or trope, from the Greek *tropos*. As
the Genesis text also suggests, the factor of sudden onset carries a silent
provocation. Indeed, the unsettled significance of the figure of the turning
woman comes primarily from the text's minimalist treatment of the flight
from Sodom. The narrative places two enigmatic details in close proximity
without explaining the nature of their relation: the unnamed promptings
for the turn and the aberrant character of the event that follows. It bears
recalling that bodily metamorphosis, a signature feature of Ovidian poetics, is a *rarissime* element in the Torah's narrative repertoire.[20] Two tropic
enigmas thus converge in Genesis 19:26, and their convergence adds a
note of restiveness to the figure—or rather to the sense to be made of the
figure's place in the Genesis text's mapping of providential history.

Tropic instability is of course not alien to biblical textuality. Midrashic
and exegetical operations depend on it, in different ways.[21] Nevertheless,
the specific association of tropism with abortive rescue in Genesis 19 acquires telling resonance in Maître François's image's textual environment,
the Augustinian corpus. The tropological habit of mind is the paradigmatic
figure of Augustine's linguistically ambivalent view of consciousness itself.
A primordial dream of plenitude—the virtually unbounded and polytropic
potential of language and thought—discovers the countervailing pull of
contingency and finitude. In the domain that Augustine famously calls the
"place of unlikeness" (*regio dissimilitudinis*), things fall apart, communication misfires, and irreparable damage occurs.[22]

Broadly speaking, the interest in proliferating modes of allegory speaks
to the effort to make sense of this fundamental rift, a division borne by the
word *allegory* itself. The compound of *allos* (other) and *agoreuein* (to speak
in public) could mean either "speaking other" or "speaking of the Other."[23]
The latter sense typically harbors a specific communicative imperative, as
well as an eschatologically driven state of conviction or urgency, whereas
the former principally concerns itself with various expressive means, rather
than singularity of purpose or topic.

In essence, "speaking other" conveys symbolic action's cosmopolitan character, even as it also suggests the potentially homogenizing effects of the implied instinct for accommodation. "Speaking other" shelters the teleological consolation of sameness that generally informs *animal symbolicus*'s desire to make sense out of the sheer *thisness* of what presents itself to sense and thought. It domesticates the roving apprehension of the anonymous givenness of the ambient surround—all the stuff from which meaning is made and unmade. "Speaking other" is the medium of exchange though which hospitality's conditional claims, in Derrida's sense, achieve currency. "Speaking of the Other," however, bears witness to hospitality's unconditional claims. These claims issue from a voice altered and scarred by a transformative encounter that resists and challenges, even as it solicits translation into the economies of signification making up the received sense and interests of the historical world.

The Greek term, *kosmopolites*, attributed to Diogenes Laertius, hosts both of these allegorical orientations in their capacity as constituents of a living practice, beyond the more narrowly conceived domains of writing and reading texts. From this expanded vantage point, Diogenes's "citizen of the world" does not simply refer to being at home everywhere. It also means being in touch with the condition of homelessness everywhere.[24] What Paul calls the "scandal" (*scandalon*, "obstacle") of the cross (1 Cor. 1:23) appeared on the stage of history some two centuries before Diogenes. Yet, the Pauline trope refigures the cosmopolitan ethos chronicled by Diogenes, precisely because it issues from a domain irreducible to either signs or concepts, even as it also seeks a means of dwelling in communicable forms. To a large degree, allegory's post-Pauline career takes notice of this domain. Over the *longue durée*, allegory indexes a history of turns or gestures discriminating between "speaking other" and "speaking of the Other," in view of the scandal of the cross and its unpropertied space at the contested margins of schematic meaning and under the shadow of imperial Christianity.[25]

The Maternal Body of Allegory

For Christian allegorists in the proto-orthodox ecclesial culture of the second and third centuries, the question of how to navigate between allegory's two faces (as medium of shared, communicable knowledge and as repository of hermetic intuition) carried specific and urgent stakes. Scripture's privileged character hung in the balance, considered both as ground for meaning's effective historicality, and as trace of meaning's esoteric or mystical reservoirs. To favor one orientation over the other was to risk liquidating either Scripture's historical specificity or transcendent claims, the ultimate risk being, in effect, the eventual dispersal of both Jewish and Christian dispensations in a generalized ("pagan" and cosmopolitan) culture of "speaking other." The essential point of this long and complicated history is that Augustine's reading of Lot's wife confronts this cloven space in a manner that discloses more than he can say or know.

To see how this is so, we need to return to Augustine's glancing memory of the Pauline allegory's *locus classicus* in Galatians.[26] Paul's allegory reclaims a family drama: the Genesis story of the births of Abraham's two sons, Isaac and Ishmael. In Paul's hands, the story's figural suggestiveness adjudicates the opposing claims of two rivals in the first-century Jewish-Christian communities in Galatia: James, whose traditionalist position insists on Mosaic law's continued binding force; and Cephas (Peter), whose more accommodating, yet erratic, position toward Gentile practices Paul seems to view with something like atavistic horror (Gal. 2:1–14). Paul's reading of Ishmael and Isaac's rivalry speaks to the historical depth and resonance of Galatia's troubles, while it also insists on the centrality of the Christ event in the covenantal drama, which now includes Galatia. Paul wants the Galatians to understand that they must choose and openly embrace their true genealogy, which appears in the figural (i.e., typological) relation between Isaac and Christ: "you, my friends, are children of the promise, like Isaac" (Gal. 4:28). The letter's exasperated notes ("You foolish Galatians! Who has bewitched you?"; Gal. 3:1) indicate Paul's vexed awareness of the Galatian communities' difficulties in grasping the choice's transcendent clarity.

Besides exasperation, Paul also spells out his sympathetic participation in the travail. Emphasizing his readiness (discursively, at least) to become "all things to all people" (1 Cor. 9:22), Paul describes his concern in terms of a mother's labor pains: "My little children, for whom I am again in pain of childbirth until Christ is formed in you, I wish I were present with you now" (Gal. 4:19). Here, Paul introduces the word *allegory* into his lexicon, associating the word not with Ishmael and Isaac, but with their mothers, Hagar and Sarah. Allegory is Paul's Hellenistic name for a communicative event or process that transpires over time, according to a gestational rhythm of anticipation, suffering, and deep contingency. Paul's critical gesture here stipulates that allegory gives body, through the uterine imaginary, to a *choice* between covenants—between different ways of "speaking of the Other."

One can gauge the palpable difficulty of the choice by Paul's attribution of the matriarchal names "Hagar" and "Sarah" to the two covenants. The covenant of Hagar, after all, stands not only for the Mosaic law ("Hagar is Mount Sinai," Gal. 4:25). Its semantic field corresponds *grosso modo* to a mix of Jewish and Gentile practices common to parts of the first-century Mediterranean world's social fold. Hagar's covenant is essentially the world of the familiar, the cultural milieu's sheer givenness and accumulated habits of "speaking other." By contrast, Sarah's covenant stands for Paul's mystical experience of the Christ event, which he presents as the prism through which all aspects of the covenantal drama participate in the adventure of "speaking of the Other."

It is a piece of historical irony that Paul's strategic use of the word "allegory" and the childbirth metaphor prefigured the tension over primogeniture between the two religious communities that emerged from the ferment of Hellenized Jewish-Christian communities after the destruction of the Second Temple: rabbinic Judaism and the Christian *ecclesia*. Which was the favored heir? This story has been well told in biblical scholarship, and does not need rehearsal here. What I want to retain is the principal discursive consequence of this tale of sibling rivalry.[27]

One of the signal accomplishments of the emergent Christian orthodoxy in the second and third centuries—the gradual consensus over the canonical bible's core elements, with "old" and "new" testaments—helped transform the nature of the allegorical legacy relayed through Hellenistic culture. Typology, allegory's close cousin, was already a legible instrument of "speaking of the Other" in Jewish exegesis.[28] It provided the narrative syntax linking the separate events of the Jewish scripture's covenantal drama. Reclaimed as an instrument of canon formation in the early Christian church, typology acquired an ambivalent edge unique to the Christian way of "speaking of the Other." Typology became an implicit instrument of theological anti-Judaism, in the sense that it helped promote the perception of Jews as a "living anachronism," surviving remnants of the "old" dispensation, caught in an ambivalent symbolic relation—part kin, part neighbor, part stranger—to Christian orthodoxy's "new" covenant.[29] In this light, it is not difficult to grasp how typology, under ideological critique's scalpel, could present a discursive model of reification as well as supersession. Insofar as it allowed for the conditioned appraisal of an event, person, or group as means toward an end, typological figuration also enabled the perceived entity's corresponding apprehension, outside of its eschatological significance, as no more than a disposable thing.[30]

The figural history of Lot's wife gives witness to this divided legacy, participating in it without submitting entirely to the endgame I have just described. At times, as we will see, the salt pillar testifies to allegorical coding's resilience, both as a world-building resource and as a means to identify and police dangerous zones of habitation. At other times, the figure introduces a disorienting surplus, standing sentinel over uncharted territory in what Auerbach called the "the stream of historical life."[31] If these regions fall outside allegory's domesticating ambit, they do so by remaining in touch with the "never finished" space-time that troubles Levinas: the "meanwhile."[32]

Phantom Figure

Let us recall, then, that in the Genesis type-scene Lot's wife is an interrupted figure, calcified in the forbidden gesture of looking back. In her postbiblical recensions, however, she is a wandering figure, embodying the shifting thresholds of accommodation and refusal that inform the practice of hospitality. She marks transversal borderlines between established traits of kin, neighbor, guest, and stranger in different cultural locations. Anticipatory signs of this movement can be detected in Paul's strategic citation of the Leviticus commandment: "You shall love your neighbor as yourself" (Gal. 4:14). The citation, which occurs moments after the allegory of Hagar and Sarah, recapitulates one of the allegory's central points: to dissuade the Galatians from observing the ritual practice of circumcision (and thereby declaring their allegiance to the Mosaic law: Hagar's covenant).[33] For my purposes, what is striking about Paul's citation is not its transumption of the Leviticus passage into a virtual summing up of Sarah's covenant (i.e., Christic *agape*). Whichever Paul you want to imagine here—the radical Jew or the proto-Christian apologist—the argument essentially concerns an ethical register of action. How you act determines who you are.

Another, more narratively specific way to construe the question of the neighbor in Paul's allegory brings Lot's wife back in our sights. The Abrahamic cycle, as biblical narrative generally, observes what Robert Alter, after Herbert Schneidau, has called the rule of "paratactic metonymies."[34] According to this rule, reported events appear as specific manifestations of thematically contiguous concerns, which recur with different accents, shapes, and degrees of legibility in historical time. This is, in effect, the DNA of typology. Whatever its archaeological origins, the Sodom sequence, Alter argues, "is crucial not only to Genesis but to the moral thematic of the Bible as a whole," because the Sodom sequence is "the biblical version of anti-civilization."[35] More precisely, the sequence's placement, "firmly lodged between the enunciation of the covenantal promise and its fulfillment," establishes Sodom as "the great monitory model, the myth of a terrible collective destiny antithetical to Israel."[36] Sodom is the anti-covenant. The fact that it enjoys a neighborly position, discursively, within the Abrahamic cycle discloses the tenuous border between Sodom and Israel on the ethico-historical plane of the covenantal promise. Sodom figures Israel's imminent fate outside the covenant.[37]

Although Galatians does not mention Sodom, Paul's particular handling of the Hagar and Sarah allegory discloses its spectral presence. Consider the allegory's narrative structure. The first part rehearses the biblical story's elementary elements in Genesis 16 (the escalating tension between Sarah and Hagar in Abraham's household), and it closes with Paul's reminder that Sarah's command in Genesis 21 ("Drive out the slave and her child") holds Christic significance. Paul's maternal-covenantal-allegorical scheme is straightforward. The Galatians must learn to see that the true "children of the promise" (Gal. 4:28) belong to Isaac's typological genealogy, and must come to understand that the "promise" finds transparent expression in Paul's visionary mapping of new covenantal agreement terms. The message's clarity, however, depends on an intertextual omission. In the Genesis source text, the two corresponding type-scenes for Paul's allegory do not constitute a seamless unit. Between them lies the Sodom sequence's narrative "meanwhile" (Gen. 21:18–19).

Paul's elision of the Sodom sequence produces a textual equivalent of recessional space in pictorial design. Rhetorically, the elision introduces an undecidable element into Paul's allegory. Is the forgotten archive of the "meanwhile" simply too evident for words in Paul's biblically literate environment? Is it irrelevant? Unthinkable?[38] These questions remind us that undecidability is *not* nothing. In this context, it is eloquent, for it suggests the unexpressed intimacy of Paul's argument with the deleted memory of Lot's wife. Recall that the heart of Paul's allegory preeminently concerns itself with the problematic choice between maternal figures, Hagar and Sarah. The omitted Sodom text enlarges the scope of the choice by conjuring up the missing maternal figure from Genesis 19. Thus summoned, Lot's wife assumes a neighborly relation not only with the maternal subjects of Paul's allegory, but also with Paul's own allegorizing voice, expressing urgent desire to speak through the figure of labor pains.

This intertextual fold complicates Paul's allegory's easy symmetry. Just as Sarah prefigures Paul's voicing of the Christic covenant, Hagar prefigures alternative sightings of the covenantal economy in Galatia. Her story corresponds to the positions of James and Cephas (as well as any other dissenting factions that historical reconstruction could conceivably produce, including so-called Gnostic rivals to the texts that would become canonical in Christian orthodoxy).[39] The phantom figure of Lot's wife, however, reminds us that the historical domain holds recessional spaces— shifting arenas of conflict and accommodation—which can only be retrospectively voiced or imagined. To recall Paul's own position in the Christic drama: belatedness tells.

It is important to remember that the relation between Hagar and Sarah is not a clear-cut antithesis. Hagar is not quite the anti-covenant (Paul's own argument does not go so far), and neither is Lot's wife; both survive the exile imposed on them. Hagar survives through the transmission of blood: Ishmael's progeny. Lot's wife, too, survives through her children. Her two daughters' incestuous congress with Lot after the destruction of Sodom produces two of Israel's rival nations, the Moabites and Ammonites, each of which biblical narrative principally associates with anti-covenantal (and sodomitic) depredations: idolatry and habitual violations of hospitality. Crucially, however, Lot's wife also survives in a way that has nothing to do with biological kinship or the transmission of cultural tradition. Transformed into a pillar of salt, she survives as catastrophe's remains, the mute witness to an event that exceeds even as it solicits language's cognitive and communicative resources.[40]

In biblical tradition, this limit experience opens onto divinity's transcendent domain. The biblical corpus attests to allegorical transcription's edifying resource in making sense of the event. Wisdom literature enshrines the negative exemplarity of Lot's wife, reading the salt pillar as the enduring monument of an "unbelieving soul" punitively marked by divine judgment.[41] Paul's silence on this point neither confirms nor denies the tradition. Lot's wife thus stands sentinel over a domain unbound either by Paul's supposed pastoral intentions or by the local historical circumstances of the letter's reception. The inscrutable gravitas of the unspoken remnant lays out the prospect of an imaginary covenant, bound by one thing only: assent to, or capture by, an encounter that radically transforms the way one thinks of one's place in and obligations to tradition.

Abrahamic Gazing

The prospect I have just described appears in the miniature gracing Maître François's depiction of the flight from Sodom in Raoul de Presles's text of the *City of God*. This is evident in the compositional trait described earlier: the quietly jarring interface of the cited disaster and the suavity of the pictorial design. The exegetical lens supplied by Augustine's paraphrase in the *City of God* focuses on the orthodox heart of the matter. Sodom, the inverted image of the heavenly Jerusalem, is uniformly wicked. Augustine assents to the proposition foregrounded in the Genesis text regarding the blindness immediately visited upon Sodom's citizens after their attempt to violate Lot's guests. Maître François's prostrate figures with hands raised in alarm corroborate the point. The depicted recognition of imminent disaster in no way troubles the juridical and irreversible logic of the episode: abomination elicits a corresponding measure of law. These people *deserve* to die.

The judgment also has a color: pink. The miniature's invitation to think pink across a range of hues and intensities trains the eye to welcome the affective distinction between the doomed cityscapes and the escape route.[42] The painted panorama thus recognizes the implied rigor of retributive logic, but it also presents more to the eye than edifying code. For one, there is the triad of ochre-colored buildings at the right edge of the image. Ochre is the color that wonders what Lot's wife sees. How should we read this chromatic tropism? The miniature supplies a clue by incorporating *quattrocento* developments in recessional space and perspectival techniques, yet without creating a deterministic visual field. We are a long way from the Albertian regime's geometricized space and implied sovereignty of the optical *mathesis*. Here the eye is free to wander, vagabond, over the narrative cosmos's assembled elements.

The miniature invites us to consider, among other things, how its visual choreography places the viewer in relation to the four principal Sodom gazers in the Genesis proof-text: Lot's wife, Lot, the angels, and Abraham. Lot's wife clearly dominates. Wherever the eye moves—whether following Lot's daughters, moving in stately procession with Lot and the angels toward the biblical inscription, or scanning the rhizomic network of roseate cityscapes—the salt statue stands at the crossroads of the scene's multiple vectors. All roads, so to speak, lead back to Lot's wife. The scene's composition appears to suggest, however, that her viewing position is not to be taken up. Her status as focalizer is an empty citation, lacking narrative consequence.

Consider in this regard the presentation of the escape route. The winding road on which the entire company has embarked dissolves into the pure verticality of the biblical script in the upper left margin. For Lot and his daughters, the pain of exile is resolved by immersion in the Exodus narrative and its anagogical prospect, the heavenly Jerusalem. The road following the direction of the statue's gaze, however, precipitously cuts off behind the animals. No alternative and competing version of the Exodus narrative enters the field of vision. (From the fleeing woman's designated line of sight, the ochre-colored buildings in Sodom are also off-route.)

Literally, there is no going back to the point of origin of Lot's wife's particular exodus. The Sodom presented in the scene is thus not quite the same Sodom that provokes the fatal turn. Nor is it quite the same Sodom that greets Lot's panoramic gaze at an earlier stage of the narrative, where it appears as an avatar of Eden and the fertile Nile Valley (Gen. 13:10–12).[43] The miniature's juicy color palette remembers this nuance, but does not secure its place in the narrative protocol. In other words, two instants of a Sodom that will be lost to history pass before the viewer: the evanescent passage of the Eden-like situation in Genesis 13, and the unseen Sodom held under the gaze of Lot's wife.

Whose gaze, then, does the panorama solicit? If we confine ourselves to the Genesis source text, two candidates come forward: the angels and Abraham. The Hebrew text suggests an affinity between the two perspectives. In Genesis 18, three angels visit Abraham and Sarah to confirm God's promise of Isaac's miraculous birth. Leaving Abraham's tent, they "look down" on Sodom (Gen. 18:16). This scene of angelic observation is the narrative catalyst for the Sodom sequence proper (Gen. 18:17–19:37). The sequence closes with the incest plot of Lot's daughters, but the end of Sodom coincides with a scene of solitary viewing. Abraham "looks down" on the blasted landscape (Gen. 19:27). As Robert Alter points out, the symmetry between the two scenes is reinforced by the use of the same verb to depict the act of looking down (*shaqaph*).[44] The verbal echo suggests the nature of the insight shared by the angels and Abraham. Each embodies the operative force of what Jan Assmann calls the "Mosaic distinction" (the "distinction between true and false in religion") as the enabling frame for symbolic knowledge of the cosmic order.[45]

Arguably, the miniature places the viewer in a position that approximates an Abrahamic panorama. This is what, and how, Abraham would have seen had he looked over Sodom just before the final cataclysm. The edifying point is unmistakable. The Abrahamic scopic regime corrects the error of Lot's wife through a proper, rehabilitative discernment (a point not lost on rabbinic and patristic thought).[46]

Animal Entourage

The lapidary surface of the miniature's panorama carries distinctive traces of the edifying gesture. Consider, for example, the easily overlooked foreground action. Two bovine creatures lick the statue's thigh. Once observed, the animals loom large in the composition, if only because of their suggestive placement behind the boulder and before the break in the road. This formal play of disclosure and concealment stages allegorical signification's capacity as an exegetical tool. Broadly considered, the animals figure the moralizing tradition of associating Sodom's sins with bestiality, the term taken here to indicate any behavior that confounds entrenched hierarchical distinctions between humans and animals. Accordingly, the spectacle of Lot's wife as salt lick offers an occasion to review embedded associations of Lot's wife with debasing motions.

Though Paul has nothing to say about Lot's wife, his older contemporary Philo of Alexandria presents a powerful exegesis of Lot's wife's moral errancy, developed across several treatises. The Alexandrian thinker's characteristically hybrid method—applying Hellenistic exegetical protocols to the Torah—leaves its signature in his various approaches to the figure.[47] In the *Questions and Answers on Genesis and Exodus*, for example, Philo treats the episode's literal (that is, historical) dimensions as evidence of the monitory purpose of God's miraculous intervention in the natural realm. The conversion of Lot's wife into a salt pillar underscores the gravity of the covenantal value attached to trusting obedience.[48] Philo's allegorical register, however, turns the episode into an exemplum of a different commonplace: the hierarchical structure of soul, mind, and senses as rehearsed in Hellenistic philosophical tradition (Middle Platonism in particular).[49]

On Philo's account, Lot's wife figures "the wife of the mind," or "sense perception" with its tacitly gendered inclination "toward sense-perceptible things which are external rather than the things seen internally by reason."[50] In what could also be called a Philonic rendering of primary narcissism, Lot's wife identifies so completely and indiscriminately with the sensory realm that she becomes part of it: an "inanimate thing," separated "from the mind, for the sake of which it was animated." To be sure, diverging from the sacred *telos* of the rational mind carries an ethical charge. Thus, in the treatise on drunkenness (*De ebrietate*) Philo identifies Lot's wife as the figure of routinized custom (*synètheia*), opposed to the truth of *logos*.[51] Elsewhere, moving in for the kill, he presents her as evidence of mental indolence, an irreparable lapse in ascetic discipline, leading to "blindness in understanding."[52] Can bestiality be far behind?

The Statue

As noted earlier in this chapter, the partially hidden animals stage the elementary structural dynamic of allegory—the play of concealment and disclosure. Follow the gaze of the animals. It takes you directly to the more exorbitant staging of the same dynamic. Lot's wife *qua* statue appears in the *Venus pudica* pose, with hands simultaneously concealing and calling attention to breasts and pubis. The configuration attests to a truism in medieval Christian art and spirituality: an ambivalent perception of the body, which promoted, as Michael Camille argues, "the equation of statuary with nudity, and of nudity with shame."[53] The equation also helped cultivate another truism: allegory as a means of having your cake (or salt condiment) and eating it too. On this score, allegory saves appearances by asserting figural imagination's power to disclose and police the unseen. However, the miniature also knows that *figura*'s revealing power includes distortions.

First things first. How did Lot's wife take the form of a statue? In the Hebrew text, Lot's wife turns into a pillar (*netziv*) of salt. The dominant tradition in Christian art and devotional thought remembered Lot's wife as a statue, principally because in the canonical Vulgate translation Jerome used the word *statuam*.[54] Notwithstanding its residual connotation of a standing object (from the Latin root *stare*), the word primarily designates sculpted form. On philological grounds, perhaps, the translation of Lot's wife into a statue is a kind of betrayal, but ideologically it secures the transfigured remains as an object of allegorical and aesthetic fascination.

The fascination stems in part from the kind of negotiation we may observe in the miniature. Together, the gracefulness of the depicted stance and the condemnatory narrative context present the statue as a visual précis of rival scopic regimes in Christian art: iconophilia and iconophobia. There will be more to say about this rivalry later on. It bears mentioning here that both types of religious imagination (iconophilic and iconophobic) encountered a paradox in contemplating the effects of the fabricated image. The paradox turns on the image's capacity to reenact what could be called the primal scene of hospitality in Augustine's theological anthropology: the mixture of welcome and risk attending human perceptions of matter and spirit coupled in the created order.[55]

The miniature does not dissolve the paradox. Indeed, the pictorial details' supple mnemonic register suggest that the miniature enjoys the paradox, even plays with it. Consider its handling of the middle term of Michael Camille's equation. Nudity. Or nakedness. According to Camille, in medieval tradition there is no essential difference between the two words. If you bracket "nudity's" basic semantic register—corporeality as such—two structural elements of allegory remain. Nudity both signifies and embodies disclosure. That disclosure's embodiment redounds to shame has everything to do with the powerful biblical tradition beginning with the story of Adam and Eve's fall and taking influential shape in Augustine's account of the primordial transgression's consequences in the *City of God*.[56]

The loss of Edenic innocence and the pain of exile find bodily expression in Augustine's phenomenology of shame, which is nothing if not efficient (because it neatly correlates two superficially opposed aspects of humanity's fallen condition). The sight of the unclothed body as both source and occasion of shame is symptomatic of the burden of divided consciousness (or conscience): knowledge of self under the (punishing) gaze of the Other.[57] The rebound from such ravaging insight sounds a retreat from the inviting openness (and strangeness) of the created world into the protective sheath of learned habits. In turn, this enclosed habitat fosters a perilous collapse of differences: the mistaking of signs for things. Such confusion amounts to a one-way ticket into the empire of the senses and its neighboring domains of idolatry and carnal concupiscence. Shame and shamelessness thus converge as two interlocking halves of the distorted symbolic register defining the "place of unlikeness" in Augustine's confessional account of human errancy.[58]

Eve, the named genetrix of the biblical and Augustinian repertoire on shame, finds apt iconographic expression in the classical *Venus pudica* pose, with its double signification of modesty and venereal provocation. In *quattrocento* art, one of the most harrowing redactions of the Venus-Eve typology appears in Masaccio's depiction of the expulsion from Eden (fig. 2). Unsurprisingly, Masaccio's Eve does not resemble the nude figure in Maître François's image. It resembles a Masaccio. That is, the composition corroborates known traits of Masaccio's painterly signature.[59] The *Venus pudica* pose tells us we are looking at a recognizable allegory of shame. But Eve's facial expression, her mouth contorted into a soundless cry, transfigures the allegory. Through the opened mouth, which no speech can translate, shame cedes to something else, something not fully recuperated by the story of transgression. Nameless grief, not blame, commands our attention here.

The figure of Lot's wife in Maître François's miniature also resists easy allegorical coding, but not in Masaccio's manner. The statuary element underscores Lot's wife's estrangement from the trappings of her historical lifeworld. The suspended "meanwhile" of the denuded figure visibly differs from the surviving entourage's conventional late-medieval gear and the surrounding cityscapes' architectural signature. The virtual zoom effect is telling. Nothing appears to trouble the statue's congenital link with the *Venus pudica* / Eve typology. (The figure's sinuous shape clearly draws on contemporary conventions in statuary form, but in the immediate narrative

Figure 2. Masaccio (Maso di San Giovanni) (1401–28), *Expulsion from Paradise* (1425–28), Brancacci Chapel, S. Maria del Carmine, Florence, Italy. Courtesy of Scala/Art Re-source, NY.

context this feature functions as code for eschatological timelessness.) Not even the figure's expressionless face carries distracting complications in the way that the face of Masaccio's Eve, by contrast, seems surcharged with unassuaged grief. Indeed, in the miniature's representational idiom, all the faces are blank surfaces. Accordingly, the statue's identity as an exemplary configuration of shame and idolatrous fascination seems secured. Indeed, viewed in isolation, the statue could be simply mistaken for a classicizing avatar of Eve—except for one detail. It is the defining trait of Lot's wife: the backward-turning glance, captured in the nude statue. This merger of details—imagining nudity as the confluence of an unveiled spectacle and a stilled tropism—quietly pauses over the question of whether the statue's allegorical transparency has been fully achieved.

The Augustinian context helps locate this question's moorings. As noted, Augustine reads the turning gesture through a Pauline lens (the Galatians allegory). He does not go so far as to map the allegorical significance of the relations between temporal demarcations (the old/new dyad) and sartorial distinctions (clothed/unclothed bodies). Paul does, however, and most suggestively in the depiction of the relation between "old" and "new" covenants in Ephesians.[60] The discussion begins with a rehearsal of what must be left behind—in particular, the soul-blighting practices imputed to Gentile cultures. Paul places these in the vicinity of sodomitic and Egyptian abominations: "You must no longer live as the Gentiles live, in the futility of their minds. They are darkened in their understanding, alienated from the life of God because of their ignorance and hardened hearts. They have lost all sensitivity and have abandoned themselves to licentiousness, greedy to practice every kind of impurity" (Eph. 4:17–19). Correction takes the form of holy anamnesis. You must recall, Paul says, the Christic *paideia*'s core lesson: "You were taught to put away your former way of life, your old self, corrupt and deluded by its lusts, and to be renewed in the spirit of your minds, and to clothe yourselves [*enduo*] with a new self, created according to the likeness of God in true righteousness and holiness" (Eph. 4:22–24).

The sartorial allusion gives pause, because it begs the question of the imagined body's status, since Paul directs it to shed old habits (garments here figuring practices of the self at home with itself) and don new ones. The body's transient passage through nakedness signifies neither shame nor virtue (in Pauline terms, neither corrupt flesh nor glorified, spiritual body). Nakedness is none other than the hidden hyphen between hospitality's different yet overlapping covenantal claims (its "conditional" and "unconditional" faces).[61] Though literally unmentioned in the Ephesians allegory, nakedness tacitly witnesses Paul's pastoral emphasis on ethical choice over mystical dispossession, which is the pivotal event that turns nakedness into a verb. This, for Paul, is the drama of conversion, through which the unconditional charism of the Christ-event informs the conditional rhythms of everyday communal life.

I hasten to add that Lot's wife does not always assume the form of a nude statue, even in cultural locations where normalizing strains of the allegorical temper are largely intact. Whether clothed or unclothed, and even when separated from recognizable statuary form or human attributes, however, the figure retains the basic trait of signifying not only disclosure of something otherwise hidden, but also *exposure* to the edge of the thinkable. In Paul's Hellenized culture, the name of the action conjured by the implied passage through nakedness in the Ephesians allegory is *phronesis*, or prudence, cautious deliberation and choice in the exercise and adventure of practical wisdom.[62]

The abundant iconographic vocabulary for prudence includes the gesture of turning backward or forward, the represented motility symbolizing memory and foresight's convolutions in the process of reasoned choice.[63] As it happens, the distance between the gestural symbolism of prudential circumspection and the *Venus pudica* pose is not great. The two come together in the sculpted figure thought to have influenced Masaccio's treatment of Eve: Giovanni Pisano's personification of Prudence (1302), which graces the famous pulpit in the Pisa cathedral (fig. 3).[64]

Let us turn again to the statue of Lot's wife in Maître François's miniature. The suave posture of the statue remembers something of the marriage of prudential reflection and the *Venus pudica*. As in Pisano's sculpture, the figure's *contrapposto* (counterpoise) absorbs the two visual codes into a harmonized whole. Conceptually, the merger is not hard to conceive, since *contrapposto* technique entails the organic twisting of a figure on its vertical axis. One accomplishment of the technique, both in classical statuary and in *quattrocento* developments, is to add naturalistic nuance to the compositional syntax of human form—the assemblage of parts into a whole. Notably, the technique also creates the illusion of movement. In the prudential scheme, it figures the contemplative stance roused to action. All of this appears in the miniature.

From the corridors of religious orthodoxy, several ways to regulate understanding of the tilt of the head through allegorical schema impose themselves. As Madeline H. Caviness points out, in medieval illustrations

Figure 3. Giovanni Pisano (1248–ca. 1314), *Temperance and Chastity* (1302–10). Pulpit. Duomo, Pisa, Italy. Courtesy of Scala/Art Resource, NY.

of Prudentius's *Psychomachia* the "disjuncture of backward-turning head and forward-facing body" denotes the figure of Heresy.[65] Similarly, patristic allegorists discerned and safely dispatched the prudential quotient, sometimes with impressive ingenuity. In Origen's *Homilies on Genesis*, for instance, the transformation into salt spells the essence of the moral, rather than the backward look, because "salt represents prudence, which the woman lacked."[66]

The miniature before us remembers these established assumptions, but it also remembers the double mechanism at the heart of allegory. The swarming of visual codes in the exodus landscape stages the permeable border between allegory's fabulistic element (the rudimentary elements of the story or plot), and its discursive tissue (narrative nuances and stylistic details). The interweaving of these elements contributes to the miniature's way of adding a question mark to the biblical story. The result is not wholesale subversion, subversive intent being in any event like irony: a hard thing to measure over time. Instead, the miniature introduces something more lasting. The particular negotiation of discursive flesh and fabulistic scheme in the suavely imagined, stilled gesture of Lot's wife launches a second-order exodus. This exodus pertains not to the depicted story, but rather to the event that the image of the statue incarnates and holds in suspense. The event is a fall into the tropic space between the artisanal craft that produced the artifact and the ongoing work of critical attunement and imagination initiated by the depicted world's graceful distancing from accomplished meaning. In this space, the allegorical intention attributed to the work and the allegorizing equipment of the viewer/reader meet each other, exchanging roles of host and guest.

What, then, would the full ambit of the Abrahamic gaze see in the statue? It would see the petrified form of shame and heresy. It would also see the stilled instant of the coming-to-be and making-legible of shame and heresy. In the scene of arrested deliberation, it would thus see the foreclosure of other, untold impressions. In the scene's aesthetic gracefulness, it would find cause to dwell on the strangeness, the anomaly, of the depicted event. It would encounter, without being able to solve, the enigma of what prompted the backward turn and look. And, in the perceived enigma, it would find the mirror of its own engagement with the miniature.

The Backward Look

Lot's wife's backward look toward her adoptive home uniquely registers the limit of allegorical coding's prophylactic appeal, in the sense that the eyes looking back toward Sodom are dead, beyond the reach of any implied meaning they may be thought to harbor. On this score, the eyes' empty axis of speculation and memory is arguably the biblical story's single most provocative element. In a word, the combined fascination and frustration of the episode fold well into Martin Jay's account of the denigration of vision in modernity. As Jay argues, the anti-ocular turn in twentieth-century philosophical and aesthetic cultures harbors the deep memory of biblical taboos against looking.[67] We have already encountered some of this legacy in Augustine's phenomenology of shame. Benchmark texts in the cultural history of shame like Augustine's do not entirely account, however, for the critical investment in imagining what and how Lot's wife sees in looking back. We need to think of shame not simply as a dispositive element of divided consciousness and the "lust of the eyes," but rather also as an index to the archive of hospitality crises lodged in the Sodom story and its traditions.[68]

From this perspective, the dossier on prohibited looking opens not with Augustine, but with the first-century Jewish historian Flavius Josephus. In *Jewish Antiquities*, Josephus tacitly acknowledges that his chronicle's intended Gentile readership may find the fatal transmutation dubious. He therefore claims to have seen the pillar himself. With this claim, Josephus became the accidental patron saint of pilgrimages and expeditions to the shores of the Dead Sea, journeys typically informed by the desire to see the remains of catastrophe. Josephus's remarks make two contributions to the archive on Lot's wife. First, he justifies the apparent punishment by identifying her disobedience not as a passing impulse, but instead as a symptom of a particularly insidious chronic or habitual errancy: curiosity.[69] Second, he implicitly identifies his own eyewitness account as documentary evidence of a more benign, indeed pious, curiosity: the desire to seek out and welcome confirmatory signs of God's hand in salvation history.

In these two regards, Josephus stands as sentinel before the vast continent of premodern reflection on *curiositas*, which includes a rich vein of biblical commentary, as well as ethico-political and philosophical tributaries of classical thought.[70] Of the canonical voices—Plutarch, Tertullian, and (again) Augustine—none makes explicit, as Josephus does, the figural connection between Lot's wife and curiosity. Yet the collective archive provides suggestive elaboration of what is otherwise implicit in Josephus's judgment: the felt association of curiosity with moral concupiscence, rapacious meddling, and, at its farthest reaches, a habit of morbid introspection. All these traits pool together as expressions of the mind's indiscriminate tropism.[71]

Conceptually as well as historically, Tertullian's view of curiosity stands between the verdicts of Plutarch and Augustine. Perhaps more clearly than Plutarch or Augustine, Tertullian gives voice to the equipoise in late antiquity between curiosity's opposing aspects: "legitimate and necessary" on the one hand, "exorbitant and indolent" on the other.[72] Tertullian's patient examination of curiosity's equivocal character also marks the fault line between hospitality's two faces. "Legitimate" curiosity supplies the affect helping sustain hospitality's economical functioning in its normative aspects; "exorbitant" curiosity spells the risk of open borders. In other words, curiosity's malignant aspects disclose the unregulated proximity of pagan philosophy that the Christian dispensation's emergent orthodoxy refuses to assimilate.

Tertullian's specific innovation lies in introducing a semantic neologism to describe one of the most troubling features of heretical and pagan curiosity alike. Outside the sacred canopy of the Christic *scopus*, the curious suffer from what he calls *scrupulositas*, a chronic fear that contaminates every project or goal, whether directed outward or inward. Curiosity's unbearable scruple breaks the sheath of accommodated knowledge. Migrating outside the domain of delusory ambition or pride, curiosity assumes the gnawing aspect of existential anxiety.[73]

More remains to be said about Tertullian's scruple, but I want to pause here to reflect on specific sodomitic expressions of the problem Tertullian describes. Philo provides detailed examples in his account of the literal sense of Lot's wife's transgression. He finds three reasons for the angels' command not to look back, and each helps flesh out the premodern dossier on the perils of morbid curiosity. First, the interdiction aims at preventing the survivors from rejoicing over the "misfortunes of others."[74] In view of the presumption of Sodom's deserved extinction, giving free rein to *Schadenfreude* at such a juncture "may be just," but "is not humane." Second, the interdiction shows divine care for the survivors by precisely limiting the otherwise intolerable suffering that their "pity and compassion" for lost friends and neighbors would arouse at the cataclysm's sight. Third, the interdiction bans the profanation of sacred places. Sodom, visited by the violent hand of divine justice, now incarnates a secret that belongs to divinity alone: the nature of the victims' agony. Accordingly, "to investigate and examine how they suffered is an act of impudence and shamelessness and not of reverence, with which it is the part of the rational nature to live most carefully, constantly and familiarly."[75]

Philo's handling of the kinship between Sodom and curiosity's perils is characteristically cosmopolitan, in the sense that his literal reading of the flight from Sodom effectively marries covenantal values with a Hellenized program of ascetic training and adherence to prevailing mores of decency. We should pause, however, over Philo's suggestion that the last instants of Sodom belong to the secret of sacred violence.[76] For Philo, the "outcry" [*za'aq*, "clamor"] (Gen. 18:20) of the city meets its counterpoise in the silence that enshrouds the city as it enters, in death, the secret intimacy between sacred and profane.

Philo's caveat deepens the scene's fascination in a specific way. The *frisson* of the untouchable makes a precursory foray into the disciplinary process that would transform habits of self-care into what Michel Foucault called the putting of "sex into discourse," so as to create new regions of secrecy and disclosure, as well as intensifications of pleasure and shame.[77] It is not exactly sex, however, that Philo puts into the allegorical space between Lot's wife and Sodom. What he provides, instead, is a dilated pause in which libidinal curiosity, an ethics of secrecy, and an ethics of hospitable discretion commingle.

Several pages from the literature of talmudic and midrashic haggadot ramify Philo's intuition. In the *Genesis Rabbah*, Rabbi Isaac explains the transformation of Lot's wife thus: "She sinned with salt. The very night the angels came to Lot's door, what did she do? She went out to all of her neighbors, saying 'Give me some salt, because we have guests.' She wanted the Sodomites to know that guests had been received in Lot's home."[78] Unlike Josephus's commentary, which simply points out the habitual unruliness of her curiosity, the midrash identifies Lot's wife as the lethal link between inhospitality—the prominent sodomitic sin in biblical tradition—and curiosity. Salt, one of the biblical signs of covenant as well as tribal hospitality, is here converted into the opposite signification, and the conversion takes the form of a betrayal of a secret.[79] The request for salt becomes the means through which received distinctions between inside and outside, guest and enemy, collapse within Lot's own household. Through salt, Lot's wife discovers a way of "speaking other" that registers ethical, rather than sexual, sodomitry.

The midrashic explications of Sodom's ruinous events elaborate the targumic tradition of pondering over how Lot's wife's curiosity exposes shared lineaments between sexual and social violence.[80] The talmudic literature, however, also ventures sympathetic vantage points, echoing Philo's nuanced grasp of the several engines of curious gazing. The *Targum Neophyti*, for example, presents a mitigating view of the backward turn, by emphasizing the promptings of familial concern: "since Lot's wife was a descendent of the people of Sodom, she looked back to see what ultimately would happen to her father's house."[81] The shadow of an enigma falls over the targumic recognition of transgression's contingent moorings. As Philo's literal reading also suggests, familial or maternal affect as such is not condemned. Instead, the punishment turns on the failure of Lot's wife to observe the specific hierarchy of attachments and welcoming gestures on which the covenantal community's integrity depends. Her error does not replicate the "outcry" of the Sodomites, but it does not have to, since what she accomplishes is apparently just as damaging. Her choice of familial bonds over the covenantal imperative of trusting obedience to the divine author of covenant merely enlarges the compass of anti-covenantal behavior. Or does it?

The question just posed takes on particular iridescence in Jewish mystical literature. The eighth-century *Pirkê de Rabbi Eliezer*, for example, ventures that Lot's wife, looking back (*vatabet . . . me'aharav*, "looking [from] behind him") out of concern for her married daughters, saw the face of the Shekinah, or immanent presence of God.[82] The multiform aspects of the Shekinah in Jewish thought militate against a dogmatic reading of the encounter's nature. Let us honor the spirit of the midrashic corpus, then, by imagining how the mention of the Shekinah may be productively mobilized.

Consider the etymology of the word. The root *sh-k-n* "designates both setting up a tent and dwelling."[83] The indwelling character of the Shekinah manifests itself not only in sacred places (tabernacle or temple), but also in figures of guiding or chastising action, including thingly protagonists, like pillars of fire and cloud, as well as angelic emissaries. The Shekinah, in other words, expresses itself in manifold operations, giving purpose and direction to the inhabited "meanwhile" of the people of the covenant during their exile and wanderings in the desert. Also at the moment of death. Tellingly, the biblical proscription against directly seeing God was modified in rabbinic literature by the stipulation that "the just see the face of the Shekinah before dying."[84] Such considerations do not vitiate the question of Lot's wife's transgression. Instead, they envision branching dimensions of biblical and extra-testamental textuality that prove accommodating hosts to unexpected ways of "speaking of the Other."

Lot's wife's exposure to the Shekinah marks the close of this chapter's itinerary. It is time to consider where we have arrived. First off, what I want to retain from the inscription of the Shekinah in the figural history of Lot's wife is not the antiscopic implication. The corpus of midrashic reflection on Genesis 19 invites us to remember something else, the mystical intrigue of Lot's wife in the limit-experience of dying. From this perspective, the sudden transformation of Lot's wife into a salt pillar (or statue) opens onto a region of allegorical "othering" that the dominant exegetical traditions tend to overlook. The textual production of the pillar/statue registers the intermittent concealment and disclosure of a cadaver. Contact with a cadaver, of course, is one of the principal occasions of ritual defilement in biblical tradition, to which the Levitical and Deuteronomic prescriptions, together with the Mishnah purity codes, supply ample witness.[85] Such massive regimentation signals, among other things, the peculiar status of the cadaver as the crystallization of the porous boundary between being and nonbeing, the boundary where sacred and profane converge.

Technically, these considerations have no bearing on the Genesis text's depiction of the flight from Sodom. There is after all no cadaver on the road to Zoar, the place of rescue. There is only the escaping woman, and then the calcified object. This very elision, however, also occupies the troubling place of the scruple in Tertullian's idiom: the sense of something both missing and intolerably present. In this regard, the surrogate figure of the pillar/statue sustains the uncertain boundary, and the untenable event, which the encounter with the cadaver embodies. Neither a cadaver nor a funeral monument, Lot's wife's transfigured remains nonetheless encroach on both entities' ontological purview.

Maître François's illuminated miniature incarnates this gesture of encroachment. The stilled tropism of the statue gives eloquent though silent witness to what never fully happened in the urgency of exodus: an unfinished and unending death, and abandonment held in the gaze of the Shekinah. Flash forward some five hundred years. Maurice Blanchot's and Emmanuel Levinas's shared turn to the Sodom archive testifies to the enduring provocation of what Maître François saw in the figure of Lot's wife. This is the next station on our itinerary.

CHAPTER 2

The Rise of Prophecy: Figural Neuter, Desert of Allegory

[Literature] is not beyond the world, but neither is it the
world itself: it is the presence of things before the *world*
exists, their perseverance after the world has disappeared, the
stubbornness of what remains when everything vanishes and
the dumbfoundedness of what appears when nothing exists.

—MAURICE BLANCHOT, *The Work of Fire*[1]

There's no getting around it. The route connecting Maître François's illuminated rendering of the flight from Sodom to Blanchot's and Levinas's
guarded turns to the Sodom archive has no historical warranty. Blanchot
and Levinas's mutual interest in the question of art charted a wide-ranging
interrogation of the enigmatic fact of the artwork's existence and the un-
quiet character of art's aesthetic and ethical open-endedness, conducted
across several genres and historical environments.[2] Their expedition, however, did not pause at the late-medieval scene of manuscript illumination.

There are many mansions, of course, in the house of historical inquiry.
The forensic model, with its ascetic protocols for capturing "the way it
really was," is not necessarily the most reliable arbiter of what counts as a
viable vantage point.[3] As Lynn Hunt reminds us, the construction of history is "an ongoing tension between stories that have been told and stories
that might be told."[4] This feature, Hunt argues, makes it "more useful to
think of history as an ethical and political practice than as an epistemology
with a clear ontological status."[5] Hunt's relevant assumption here is that
the ethical and political dimensions of the "practice" of history are bound
up with the narrativity of practice.

In other words, the tellable (and disputable) character of events imparts a figural dimension to any encounter that participates in what Hunt aptly calls the "gesture" of history—the gesture that brings material and meaning together.[6] Gesture, in this sense, remembers Merleau-Ponty's interest in the configurational dynamic at work in the "flesh of the world." Indeed, as we saw in the introduction, Merleau-Ponty's notion of the flesh includes a threefold gesture. The launch toward meaning always takes place somewhere (this is its topological character). It carries marks of exposure to what lies outside itself, both spatially and temporally (this is its typological character). And its expressive power entails deviations of one kind or another as it charts a path between "pure innovation" and "pure repetition" (this is its tropological character).[7]

The Rising Road

To discover the figural route between Maître François's illuminated world and the philosophical conversation between Blanchot and Levinas, we need to look again at the literal escape routes on the image's painted surface. The composition trains the eye to follow the road leading Lot's entourage to safety. The road dissolves into the pure verticality of the sacred text inscribed on the ribbon floating above the angel's hand. The message is clear. The right *methodos* (pathway and reading protocol) leads to immersion in divine *logos* and the orthodox narrative of providential history (the very message proposed by the host text, Augustine's *City of God*). The stilled gesture of Lot's wife, transfigured into a statuary pose, points in a different direction, leading the viewer/reader to discover that Maître François has given the naked statue a kind of body double: the parallel vertical figure of the rising road behind the cities (fig. 4).

The road is empty, and its destination cannot be determined (in either spatial or temporal terms) by reading off the fact of its serene denuded appearance. As such, the empty road invites an imaginative entrance into the curvature of the arrested backward glance, which directs the viewer's gaze toward the unseen horizon, hidden behind the forest at the distant hill's summit. The concert of the statue's *contrapposto* gesture and the serpentine road enlarges the compass of what I have been calling the Abrahamic gaze, by recognizing that the depicted itinerary—the unfinished *methodos* or untaken path behind Sodom—carries traces of an immemorial presence of the past, outside the scope of remembered metaphysical or mystical domains, and outside the rectilinear composition of historical process.

Figure 4. Maître François (fl. 1462–80), Illuminated miniature, detail. Augustine, *La Cité de Dieu*, trans. Raoul de Presles (Paris, 1469–73), Bibliothèque nationale, RC-C-05149, Ms. français 18–19, Manuscrits occidentaux; f. 111. Courtesy of Bibliothèque nationale de France.

In the *mise en scène* that unfolds from where we now stand on the rising road, the Abrahamic gaze discloses a scruple, which derives from being charged with more than the eye (or knowledge) can bear. We can now return to the disturbance that Tertullian calls *scrupulositas*—the outsized burden of a vanishingly small perturbation of the mind—and consider its scope. *Scrupulositas* guarantees the uncanny familiarity of Tertullian's thought in modernity, but not because the word prefigures modernity's rationalist thesis of autonomous self-reflexive consciousness. Rather, *scrupulositas* testifies to the inchoate shape of contingent identifications and raptures that trouble the myth of subjective autonomy.

Scrupulositas is Tertullian's name for the encounter with abyssal, heteronomous regions in consciousness and in its enveloping environment (its "flesh," to recall Merleau-Ponty's term). The long-range legacy of *scrupulositas* looks something like this. Between the Genesis account of the fall into mortality (and the knowledge of finitude that comes with self-awareness), and Martin Heidegger's famous existential analytic of the mortified consciousness that constitutes being-in-the-world, stands the immeasurable and unanswerable quotient that Tertullian finds in curiosity's rapacious aspect and its fixation on scruples. The long-range view, of course, is a synthetic artifice. The artifice nonetheless has the virtue of pointing up the radical irresolution to the problem Tertullian detects. That is, it brings occluded disturbances to the foreground by suggesting that the troubling edge to Tertullian's notion of the ruinous scruple has less to do with its sense of an ever-widening distance between human faculties of desire and their transcendent object, than with the opposite problem. *Scrupulositas* stands for suffocation, the paralyzing sensation of being trapped under a dead weight. Tertullian's scruple resembles the anxiety of insomnia—being caught within the material density of an absolute, nonhuman presence that resists the surrogational and allegorizing motions of thought.

Martin Heidegger's well-known existential analytic of curiosity as a mode of deracinated consciousness takes its cue primarily from Augustine's moral critique of *concupiscientia*. Tertullian's grasp of the traumatic fall-out from curiosity's strange duality (being everywhere and nowhere at the same time) passes through Heidegger's analytic and opens onto Blanchot's and Levinas's mutual turning toward the Sodom archive.[8] The route I have just described derives from two features of Tertullian's thought. First, Tertullian's preoccupation with the scruples of curiosity differs in emphasis from Augustine's analysis of the "snares and dangers" awaiting the soul in curiosity's "immense forest."[9] Second, Tertullian's exegetical case studies of *scrupulositas* include an unusual and suggestive handling of the Sodom story.

Like Augustine, what Tertullian seeks is not authenticity but salvation. For him, as for Augustine, the problem of authenticity belongs to the soul's covenantal and exilic drama. To use the Bonaventurian trope, if the "itinerary of the soul" (*itinerarium mentis*) seeks immersive contact with the Christic Logos, the pathway entails the ascetic regulation of curiosity.[10] Unlike Augustine's project, however, Tertullian's pursuit does not coincide with the emerging ecclesial orthodoxy's apostolic and dogmatic language for the "rule of faith."

For our purposes, the most relevant signs of the parting of ways appear in the *Adversus Marcionem* (*Against Marcion*, ca. 208 CE). Continuing the attack mounted some years earlier by Irenaeus of Lyons in the *Adversus Haereses* (ca. 180 CE), Tertullian's polemical treatise robustly dismantles the radical yet persistently popular views for which Marcion had been excommunicated in the middle of the second century. Notoriously, several of Marcion's views ran afoul of the mainstream *ecclesia*'s canon-building initiatives. Suspect items included Marcion's rejection of the entire Hebrew bible for inclusion in the Christian canon, and Marcion's severely pared down list of admissible Christian documents.[11] Without lingering over the specifics of Tertullian's role in the so-called Marcion Controversy, what matters is the textual evidence in the *Adversus Marcionem* of Tertullian's own ambiguous position in the wars of canonicity. Tertullian's turn to the Sodom archive takes us to the heart of the matter.

In the main, Tertullian's allusions to the Sodom narrative occur during his critique of Marcion's modified version of the Gospel of Luke. (Not coincidentally, of the four gospel texts that would become canonical, Marcion's recension of Luke is the only candidate that Marcion admitted into his canon, and Luke is the only gospel text in which Jesus's ethical instructions make exemplary use of the story of the flight from Sodom.)[12] As J. A. Loader has pointed out, Tertullian's turn to the Sodom material shows more than consternation at Marcion's effort to sever the typological liaison between Hebrew and Christian scriptures.[13] The figural ambit of Sodom extends beyond the anti-Marcionite focus to include a withering commentary on the doctrinaire tendencies of mainstream views of the ecclesial community's proper bounds. Thus, Tertullian's allusion to Lot's wife in the fourth book of the *Adversus Marcionem* includes a veiled indictment of institutional orthodoxy's premature foreclosure of Christic revelation's continuing unfolding in the "meanwhile" between the Christ-event and the eschaton.[14] For Tertullian, in other words, Sodom is not simply the figure for Marcionite error. Sodom is also the figure for the saving remnant's unwarranted assumption that it has the last word on received protocols for mapping providential history.

To make sense of Tertullian's double-edged application of the Sodom story, we need to recall that Tertullian composed the *Adversus Marcionem* at a fairly late stage of his writing career, probably shortly after developing an interest in an alternative expression of Christian community. The particular circumstances of Tertullian's eventual departure from ecclesial orthodoxy remain, to a large degree, a matter of conjecture. What follows is a thumbnail sketch of what appears to have happened. Shortly after his conversion to the Christian church of Carthage, near the end of the second century, Tertullian came to the defense of certain radical ascetic practices associated with a controversial sect, later known as Montanists (after Montanus, the charismatic Phrygian prophet who, together with two female prophets, Maximilla and Priscilla, founded the sect around 170 CE). Recent scholarship suggests that while their discipline was severe—they viewed remarriage after a spouse's death as virtual adultery, doubted whether serious sins could be fully pardoned before death, and worried that ecclesial bureaucratization was diminishing the charismatic spirit of the apostolic age—the Montanist program probably did not violate the early church's emerging doctrinal ethos.

Nevertheless, their advocacy for the continued, postapostolic presence of the Paraclete in contemporary prophetic utterance put them at odds with the gathering consensus, which favored establishing a canonical Christian testament (together with exegetical commentary) as the sanctioned vehicle through which the wisdom of the Paraclete made itself known in the postapostolic era.[15] One of the offending traits warrants a brief pause: the movement advocated ecstatic prophesying as a means of disclosing the continuing inspiration of the Paraclete. Paraclete, it bears noting, is the Greek term for Shekinah. In this instance, however, the encounter with the Shekinah does not produce apophatic rapture, as in Jewish mystical tradition. Instead, it produces new, and unauthorized, ways of "speaking of the Other" in the public fora of the ecclesial community.[16] It is no surprise, then, that the emergent doctrinal edifice viewed the continuation of prophetic discourse as a potentially wayward supplement, even where such discourse, as in the case of the Montanist "New Prophecy," restricted its concerns to matters of pastoral care.

It may seem that none of this directly bears on Tertullian's glancing allusion to Lot's wife in the *Adversus Marcionem*. However, the arc of Tertullian's career traces out what in retrospect becomes legible as the long-range provocation of Lot's wife in the figural history of Sodom. Consider the following elements. For starters, Tertullian's interest in morbid curiosity, with its foretaste of existential anxiety. Next, his radical asceticism, which speaks to an eschatological sense of time running out. Next, his fidelity against all odds to a troubling rival discourse of revelation (Montanist prophecy). Finally, his turn—no more than a glancing departure, perhaps—from the path of orthodoxy.[17] These elements recapitulate Lot's wife's position as the silent placeholder for critical interrogation of the juridico-ethical terms of the covenantal drama encoded in Genesis 19. It is important to recall, in this context, the equivocal dimension to Tertullian's handling of the Lot's wife trope in the *Adversus Marcionem*. The text aligns the stalled figure with the emergent orthodoxy's inflexible scruples. From the ecclesial hierarchy's standpoint, however, the reverse image obtains. The Montanist movement stands in the position of Lot's wife, principally because of its unorthodox fidelity to the apostolic past.

The association of Lot's wife with the disturbance of prophecy makes it possible to see how Tertullian's shadow falls across the rising road in Maître François's miniature. We must train our sights on a figural provocation that resides precisely in what is absent from the rising road. Unlike the redemptive escape route on the left side of the panorama, the rising road holds no textual inscription. Lot's wife's association with prophetic utterance, and with alternative modes of welcoming the voice of the Paraclete, has been quietly forgotten. The visible difference between the inscriptive appearances of the two roads, however, also introduces a countervailing perspective. Perhaps the rising road does not stand only for the work of forgetting. Perhaps it also remembers prophecy's dislocating and denuding dimensions, outside of its pastoral and pedagogical functions. From this perspective, in silent colloquy with Lot's wife's transfigured remains, the rising road harbors the difficult weight of prophecy. This is the scruple that renders prophecy irreducible to propositional content. In this specific regard, Maître François's miniature narrows the distance between Tertullian's Montanist excursions and Maurice Blanchot's powerfully evocative meditation on prophetic discourse's covenantal ethics.

Blanchot and Levinas in Sodomscape

Reviewing biblical tradition's diverse types of prophetic utterance, Ian Balfour helpfully reminds us that "prophecy cannot be reduced to prediction."[18] Prophecy's predictive function shares space with other expressive features, notably intercession and diatribe. The prophetic genre is more than an assemblage of various speech act types, however. It also names an experiential condition of dislocation and uprootedness. As Gerhard von Rad points out, the prophet's "call meant relinquishing normal social life and all the social and economic securities which this offered, and changing over instead to a condition where a man had nothing to depend upon, or, as we may put it, to a condition of dependence upon Yahweh and upon that security alone."[19] Following the thread of these insights leads us to the philosophical threshold where Blanchot's and Levinas's shared interest in the Sodom archive comes into view. The first step opens onto Blanchot's idiosyncratic rumination over prophecy's dislocating power.

In the 1957 essay "Prophetic Speech," Blanchot draws out the peculiar spatial and temporal dispossession brought about by prophetic utterance.[20] Prophecy, he argues, enters biblical narrative as the bearer of an impossible future, or rather of the future-as-impossibility, "a future one would not know how to live and that must upset all the sure givens of existence" (*BtC*, 79). In this regard, prophecy reactivates biblical tradition's deep memory of exodus and wandering in the desert. Something more essential than the anthropological moorings of the biblical nexus of desert and prophecy captures Blanchot's interest, however:

> [W]e wonder if the experience of the desert and the recollection of no-madic days when the land was only promised might not express a more complex, more anguishing, and less determined experience. The desert is still not time, or space, but a space without place and a time without production. . . . [I]t is a time without past, without present, time of a promise that is real only in the emptiness of the sky and the sterility of a bare land where man is never there but always outside. The desert is this outside, where one cannot remain, since to be there is to be always already outside, and prophetic speech is that speech in which the bare relation with the Outside could be expressed, with a desolate force, when there are not yet any *possible* relations. (*BtC*, 80)

Characteristically, the lyric intensity of Blanchot's language carries a rip-tide, in that the "experience" he describes resists paraphrase or transla-tion into more accommodating terms. Indeed, Blanchot's idiom does not so much describe as perform the intimate relation between prophecy and desert.

In essence, prophecy's incantatory yet vertiginous gesture voices the desert. The voicing at issue here is not descriptive, propositional, or pre-dictive, and the desert that it incarnates is clearly not the commonplace, empirical sense of the word. (It is "without place.") Rather, prophecy in Blanchot's sense introduces an event that makes a claim on you and blocks recourse to the escape route of alibi. In this specific capacity, it marks the threshold at which "speaking of the Other"—the revelatory extreme of allegory—expresses the urgency and proximity of a call that exceeds all determinate content or meaning. As Blanchot puts it, prophetic speech "imposes itself from outside, it is the Outside itself, the weight and suffer-ing of the Outside" (*BtC*, 82).

In a perhaps surprising turn of thought, Blanchot insists that the "bare relation" with the "weight and suffering" of the Outside—an encounter that appears to resist conceptual mastery—does not produce paralysis. The affective capture that it installs carries with it "a perpetual taking-to-task of man in the confines of his power" (*BtC*, 83). This "perpetual" accusation sparks a movement of return—not temporally or spatially, but ethically—to the world-building potency of covenantal exchange. Thus, prophecy's "bare relation with the Outside" kindles attention to the encroaching prox-imity of "primal powerlessness, wretchedness of hunger and cold, which is the principle of the Covenant, that is to say, of an exchange of speech from which the surprising justice of reciprocity emerges" (*BtC*, 80). Here again, though in refigured terms, we find the mooring of the hospitality question that Derrida will later examine. The affective range of prophetic speech in Blanchot's essay charts a movement from radical dispossession (a response to hospitality's unconditional claims) to reawakened commitment to the adventure and risk of being in common with others (where hospitality's conditional claims must also be reckoned with).

At this very juncture, Blanchot mentions the Sodom episode. Blanchot focuses not on the legendary enormity of the city's affront to the covenantal promise, but on the burden of God's "anxiety," or scruple. This burden impels God to confide his anxiety to Abraham: "'Am I going to hide from Abraham,' says God, 'what I am going to do?'" (*BtC*, 82).[21] By citing the words that inaugurate Abraham's interrogation of God's justice, Blanchot identifies his own discourse (and not just in this essay, as we will see) as a continuation of the denuding exposure begun, but not finished, in Genesis 18–19.

Neither the Genesis text nor the dominant biblical tradition, nor Blanchot for that matter, gives speech to Lot's wife. On this score, imagining a covenantal "exchange of speech" involving Lot's wife would seem to invent a lacuna. Yet the lacuna is a pregnant reminder that figural history, being a species of "counter-history," presupposes reading against the grain of the archive.[22] As it happens, the depicted silence of Lot's wife in the Sodom narrative suggests her proximity to the very eventfulness Blanchot ascribes to prophecy. From Blanchot's perspective, prophecy's crucial feature is not its articulated content, but rather its dislocating force. One detail in Maître François's miniature indicates such proximity.

Snails

Look again at the escape route (fig. 5). Cattle are not the only animals on the road. Snails form part of the procession. Unlike cattle, snails are unusual flourishes to the iconographic signature of the flight from Sodom, but they easily assimilate into the edifying argument. Late-medieval visual and homiletic cultures displayed broad fluency in parsing the snail's symbolic suggestiveness.[23] The animal's worm-like appearance, apparent sluggishness, and burrowing habit promoted its association with the creature identified in psalmic tradition as the emblem of impiety and indolence.

The intimacy of the snail's body with its shell promoted a rival perception, however. The alternating appearance of interment and reanimation

Figure 5. Maître François (fl. 1462–80), Illuminated miniature, detail. Augustine, *La Cité de Dieu*, trans. Raoul de Presles (Paris, 1469–73), Bibliothèque nationale, RC-C-05149, Ms. français 18–19, Manuscrits occidentaux, f. 111. Courtesy of Bibliothèque nationale de France.

figured the intimate bond of death and resurrection in nature's seasonal rhythms, as well as in Incarnational theology and salvation history. The latter nexus of associations accounts for the snail's appearance in one of the exemplars of the medieval book of hours, the *Très Riches Heures du Duc du Berry*.[24] December's zodiacal Capricorn emerges from a snail in the starry sky, and thus signals the approach of the new year (plate 3). The wreath of snails and blossoming columbines surrounding the depiction of the gospel legend of Christ feeding the multitude underscores the more overtly biblical dimension to the theme of rebirth and life-giving nourishment (fig. 6).[25]

In the manuscript of the *City of God*, the snails' appearance on the road delicately balances both sets of associations—condemnatory and redemptive. Congregating around the pillar of salt, they seem to enforce the received negative judgment against Lot's wife. Yet the congregating pattern at the same time suggests a more complex judgment. The creatures' broad distribution on the road also suggests their figural function as hyphens connecting the stranded and inanimate figure of Lot's wife with the surviving remnant being escorted to safety by the angels. A further, secret correspondence arises from the snails' dispersal. Legendarily deprived of hearing, sight, and articulate sound, the snail icons share in the inscrutable recesses of silence and sensory absence otherwise only found in one other figure in the scene: the transfigured woman. In their study of the snail's rich iconographic tradition, Yves and Françoise Cranga conclude that the creature's figural allure resides in the provocative expressivity of its ontological status as a "being of the in between," journeying along the fine edge

Figure 6. Limbourg Brothers (Herman, Pol, Jean) (fl. 1399–1416). Multiplication of the Loaves and Fish. Illuminated miniature from the *Très Riches Heures du Duc de Berry*. 1416. Ms. 65, f. 168 verso, Musée Condé, Chantilly, France. Photo: René-Gabriel Ojéda. © RMN-Grand Palais/Art Resource, NY.

"between God and the devil, tragedy and comedy."[26] This interstitial aspect suggests the snail's further propensity to incarnate what Blanchot calls
the "bare relation with the Outside," which soundlessly informs the onset
of prophetic utterance with "desolate force" and "primal powerlessness."

Maître François's illuminated page amplifies the profoundly equivocal
bearing of the "bare relation" by imagining the silent concert of snails and
salt statue on the road from Sodom. One last detail emphasizes the peculiar fittingness of the snails' placement on the road and the resulting
companionable relation with the transfigured woman. Consider the imperceptible process of mineralization and the infinitized algorithm of the
spiral that produces the snail's shell's nacreous sheen and elegant shape.
Through these organic tropisms, the snails present congenial associates of
the fleeing woman's calcified figure, with its captivating *contrapposto*. In this
capacity, the barely visible creatures touch upon the salt statue's aesthetic
provocation.

Here again we encounter the fine edge that separates the idol from the
icon, and that testifies to the uncertain divide between immobility and ani-
mation. En route, the collectivity of snails and salt statue discloses a space
of sheer receptivity to the divided legacy of the image in Christian art's
deep history. The specific collusion of iconographic arguments along the
escape route remembers the charisma of the statue in late ancient Christian
speculation—as the manifestation of the holy contemplation's essence and
the "stability of the transcendent world."[27] It also remembers the iconophobic view of the image as an ontological shell game, so to speak, a ruse
that dangerously blurs the hierarchical boundary between spirit and matter. The imagined deception turns on the suspicion that a little—perhaps
no more than a scruple—of the idol's captivating power inheres in the
icon, and that a little is already too much.

Statue as Desert

It is now time to reconsider the long-range provocation of that statuary
figure that graces Maître François's rendering of the flight from Sodom.
As noted earlier, the statue's canceled gaze holds a deep memory of the
biblical prohibition against graven images. In this figural space, the statue
also incarnates the treacherous substrate to the "bare relation with the
Outside" as seen by Emmanuel Levinas, whose influence on Blanchot's
interest in the ethical call of prophecy cannot be overestimated. Levinas's
occasional writings on art never quite resolve a scruple—a resilient trace
of iconophobia—borne of the suspicion that aesthetic attunement carries

a hidden price, distracting from the otherwise astringent lucidity of the ethical claim made by the Other in what Levinas calls the "face-to-face" relation, where the "face of the Other at each moment destroys and overflows the plastic image it leaves me, the idea existing to my own measure . . . the adequate idea."[28]

We can imagine what Levinas would see in the miniature, because one of his most acerbic denunciations of the artwork addresses the very form that gives pause on the road from Sodom. In the 1948 essay "Reality and Its Shadow," Levinas's indictment dwells on the statue's negative exemplarity:

> A statue realizes the paradox of an instant that endures without a
> future. . . . An eternally suspended future floats around the congealed
> position of a statue like a future forever to come. The imminence of
> the future lasts before an instant stripped of the essential characteristic
> of the present, its evanescence. It will never have completed its task as
> a present, as though reality withdrew from its own reality and left it
> powerless. In this situation the present can assume nothing, can take on
> nothing, and thus is an impersonal and anonymous instant.[29]

For Levinas, the statue perfectly expresses the scandal of the image because, in blurring the Platonizing distinction between model and copy, it discloses more than mimetic subterfuge. The statue discloses the parallel reality it shares with "the time of *dying*" (*RIS*, 141). Unlike death, which is not an experience, the time of dying is the singular experience of immersion in the "eternal duration of the interval—the *meanwhile*" (*RIS*, 141). On Levinas's account, the artwork performs a profane subreption of the time of dying, precisely by giving it material form: "Art brings about just this duration in the interval, in that sphere which a being is able to traverse, but in which its shadow is immobilized. The eternal duration of the interval in which a statue is immobilized differs radically from the eternity of a concept; it is the meanwhile, never finished, still enduring—something inhuman and monstrous" (*RIS*, 141). For Levinas, every image devolves into an idol; thus, "every artwork is in the end a statue—a stoppage of time, or rather its delay behind itself" (*RIS*, 137). The corrective alternative is not the icon but rather the "concept" (*RIS*, 141). With a tacit Hegelian flourish, Levinas correlates the concept's schematic clarity with the "quality of the living instant which is open to the salvation of becoming, in which it can end and be surpassed" (*RIS*, 141). On this account, there is no distinction between idol and icon, no play of resemblance and difference. There is also no distinction between "speaking other" and "speaking of the Other" through allegory's tropic resources. Indeed, allegory, Levinas insists, belongs to the "non-truth" of art, whereas "truth is accomplished in cognition" (*RIS*, 136).

As Jill Robbins points out, Levinas's thoughts on art's ethical possibility underwent subtle tempering in the decades following the publication of "Reality and Its Shadow." The scruple's relaxing, however slight, likely owes a good deal to the sustained, friendly reciprocity of thought between Levinas and Blanchot on a topic of abiding mutual interest. Both thinkers are drawn into the gravitational field of fascination exerted by the disturbing materiality of the "fact of the 'there is [*il y a*].'"[30] Calling it a "fact" is somewhat of a misnomer, for the *il y a* is not amenable to clinical analysis. (The "it" in "it rains" cannot be called to account, for example.) In essence, the term *il y a* testifies to the enveloping presence of impersonal existence without being. To borrow Gerald L. Bruns's expression, *il y a* is "existence refractory to any category of being."[31]

If the thought of the *il y a* shuttles between Blanchot and Levinas, this is in part because the term describes the subliminal pulse of radically neutral a priori conditions of being-in-the-world. These are the very conditions that give rise to and impinge upon the artwork and the ethical relation. The delicate give-and-take between Blanchot and Levinas in thinking about the topic owes a good deal to the different tenor of their responses to the *il y a*'s pervasive reach. For Blanchot, admiring and bracing wonder; for Levinas, something closer to atavistic horror.[32]

In "The Poet's Vision" (1956), however, Levinas ventures a revised assessment of the work of art, in cautious homage to Blanchot's polemical assertions of the anonymous expressivity that informs literary space and aesthetic production.[33] This moment is doubly significant. It marks a turning point in the philosophical conversation between Levinas and Blanchot, and opens up a figural landscape for reassessing the strangely captivating event to which Maître François's image gives luminous form.

Now to return to "The Poet's Vision." Levinas's desire to bear witness to what Blanchot sees leads to a telling metamorphosis in Levinas's imagistic repertoire: "In Blanchot, *the work uncovers, in an uncovering that is not truth*, a darkness. . . . As in a desert, one can find no place to reside. From the depths of sedentary existence a nomadic memory arises. Nomadism is not an approach to the sedentary state. It is an irreducible relation to the earth: a sojourn devoid of *place*. Before the darkness to which art recalls us, as before death, the 'I,' mainstay of our powers, dissolves into an anonymous 'one' in a land of peregrination."[34] The desert replaces the statue, though nakedness remains. The veiled allusion to nakedness in the stipulated act of "uncovering" no longer discloses the substratum of idolatry, transgression, and shame that held sway in Levinas's earlier diagnostic. Instead, nakedness aligns the "authenticity of art" with the aptitude of "literature to recall the human essence of nomadism" (137). Levinas goes so far as to allow that such disclosure "must herald an order of justice" (137), though the qualifying, modal verb carries both an ambivalent subnote and a measure of hope.

Levinas above all appreciates Blanchot's *The Space of Literature* (1955) manifestos for their critical rejoinder to Heidegger's pages on the poetics of dwelling and the luminous use of the Greek temple to express the work of art's play of concealment and unconcealment, earth and world. Famously, Levinas has nothing to do with this. Yet he does not raise the questions that would later surface in the notorious *l'affaire Heidegger*, concerning the relation between Heidegger's philosophical enterprise and his Nazi affiliation. Levinas's concerns in "The Poet's Vision" are both narrower and more global, in that the primary problem he detects in Heidegger is the ethical blind spot in the implicit sense of entitlement and privilege informing the "dazzling analyses of dwelling." His critique focuses on the architectural instance: "Heidegger's world is a world of lords who have transcended the condition of needy, wretched human beings, or a world of servants whose only concern is for these lords. Action, there, is heroism; dwelling, the prince's palace and the temple of the gods, which are seen as part of the landscape before being places of shelter" (138). Here Levinas finds common cause with Blanchot's aesthetic vision to the degree that "it has nothing in common with the Heideggerian world that art renders inhabitable" (137).

The crucial difference turns on Blanchot's invocation of the humble and fragile modes of dwelling that the hieratic and monumental gravitas of temple and palace in Heidegger's scenographic imagination tends to elide. "Art, according to Blanchot," concedes Levinas, "far from elucidating the world, exposes the desolate, lightless substratum underlying it, and restores to our sojourn its exotic essence—and, to the wonders of our architecture, their function of makeshift desert shelters" (137). Levinas's language echoes the imagery of interminable, Abrahamic wandering and exile that informs Blanchot's meditations—in a Levinasian vein, one might add— on the writings of Franz Kafka and Saint-John Perse in *The Space of Literature*.[35] It is tempting to consider that "The Poet's Vision" also continues the related imagistic thread spun out in Blanchot's earlier essay "Literature and the Right to Death," which appeared in *The Work of Fire* (1949).[36] That essay draws inspiration in part from Levinas's haunted meditation, in

Existence and Existents, on the "anonymous rustling" of the "there is" (*il y a*)
—the intuition of "existence without existents."[37] The essay also pushes
beyond Levinas's comfort zone in its intrepid rumination over literature's
disturbing affinity with the insomniac's sentence of "blind vigilance" without reprieve, given over to the "stupor of a confrontation in the depths of
obscurity" (*WoF*, 328).[38]

Perhaps inevitably, the interrogation leads Blanchot to the biblical
archive. The resulting assemblage of biblical prototypes for literature's
strangely generative impotence, its "empty power," presents an original,
if incomplete, attempt to extend and revise Sodom's figural and ethical
legacy (*WoF*, 331):

> Literature says, "I no longer represent, I am; I do not signify, I pre-
> sent." But this wish to be a thing, this refusal to mean anything, *a
> refusal immersed in words turned to salt [changés en sel]*; in short, this des-
> tiny which literature becomes as it becomes the language of no one, the
> writing of no writer, the light of a consciousness deprived of self, this
> insane effort to bury itself in itself, to hide itself behind the fact that it
> is visible—all this is what literature now manifests, what literature now
> shows. (*WoF*, 328–29, my emphasis)

Blanchot's allusion to Lot's wife is brief, but pointed. In its immediate context, the allusive gesture conveys something more than the trivial observation of words' changeable meanings. The image of words "turned to
salt" makes for a fitting entry in Blanchot's mythopoetic vocabulary. Not
because of the metamorphic element as such, but because of the resulting
picture of anonymous obduracy. The image speaks to the genetic link in
Blanchot's thought between the notorious "neuter" dimension of literary
space and the disorienting empire of the *il y a*.[39] Here it pays to recall
Blanchot's earliest depiction of the *il y a* as an "interminable" condition of
exile: "This existence is an exile in the fullest sense: we are not there, we
are elsewhere, and we will never stop being there."[40]

Importantly, Blanchot's image of words turned to salt drifts out of the
prevailing moralizing of the exegetical tradition of Sodom lore and mi-
grates into the region of trauma. This is not quite Levinasian trauma. That
is, Blanchot does not draw on the "original trauma" (*le traumatisme originel*)
that for Levinas indicates the primary scene of ethics, founding the subject's condition of radical passivity and responsibility before the face of the
other.[41] The subject of Blanchot's argument is not human, for one thing,
and the event that interests him takes place in a domain—the materiality
of language and literariness—that Levinas largely holds at arm's length

from ethics.[42] Nonetheless, the prosopopaic cast to Blanchot's language (he imagines literature voicing its attributes as if it were a dramatis persona) places the described action in an unsettled zone between thingly and human being. Without necessarily earning Levinas's imprimatur, Blanchot's depiction of literature's escape from the business of representing and signifying—that is, making something that can be processed for consummation—harbors an ethical dimension. This is so because the image of words tuned to salt remains irreducibly equivocal. This feature is bound up with the ceaseless substitution the image performs: it conveys tropic movement but resists capture as an achieved form. The image, such as it is, does not signify a meaning ready for use. Rather, it witnesses a departure that, strangely, keeps coming back to disturb and challenge us. Like prophecy.[43]

Blanchot's mobilization of the coiled tension between signifying and witnessing lays bare the provocative coalescing of aesthetic and ethical concerns that the figure of Lot's wife introduces into Sodomscape. To see how this is so, we must consider the figural environment in which Blanchot places the allusion to the pillar of salt. Blanchot's version of Lot's wife is the last in a sequence of three biblical exempla at the heart of the essay. The first Old Testament allusion, to the Shekinah, retraces the speculative path introduced in rabbinic commentaries on Lot's wife: "Whoever sees God dies. In speech what dies is what gives life to speech; speech is the life of that death, it is 'the life that endures death and maintains itself in it.' What wonderful power. But something was there and is no longer there. Something has disappeared. How can I recover it, how can I turn around and look at what exists *before*, if all my power consists of making it into what exists *after*? The language of literature is a search for this moment which precedes literature (*WoF*, 327). We observed earlier that the *Pirkê de Rabbi Eliezer* explains the fate of Lot's wife by reading it as an instance of the mystical embrace of death that comes with gazing upon the face of the Shekinah. At the outset, it looks as if Blanchot develops a different line of thought. The glancing allusion to the rabbinic archive morphs effortlessly into a linguistic variant of Hegel's assertion of the power of the life of the spirit ("the life that endures death and maintains itself in it").[44] As his commentators have noted, however, Blanchot's Hegelian cast is tempered by qualifications, and this passage presents a telling instance of such demurral.

The retreat from the logic of sublation assumes the figure of a backward turn, a turning to "look at what exists *before*." It would be hard to ignore the Orphic resonance to this phase of the argument. Indeed, the passage recalls Blanchot's well-known use of the myth of Orpheus to describe the aporia of artistic inspiration. For Blanchot, famously, every artist is a latter-day Orpheus, insofar as the artist pursues the ultimacy of the desire to reach the point at which "everything collapses into the certainty of failure where there remains only, as compensation, the work's uncertainty," marked by the all-too-present trace, the stubborn scruple, of "something extinguished."[45]

Blanchot's most celebrated treatment of the myth, "The Gaze of Orpheus," was first published in 1953 and appeared two years later in *The Space of Literature*, the volume that also included Blanchot's other significant consideration of the Orpheus myth ("Rilke and Death's Demand"). The details of publication history should not prevent us from reading the figural gesture in "Literature and the Right to Death" as an early sketch of the more florid Orphic ruminations to follow. The local discursive entourage counts for something, too, providing a rare snapshot of a foray into a specific biblical archive—the Shekinah/Lot's wife nexus—that will be superseded by the choice of Orpheus. The initial choice of Lot's wife, and the subsequent elision of that choice, presents a revealing figural subtext to the mythopoetic evolution of Blanchot's thought.

Is anything lost in translation? The Shekinah/Lot's wife nexus harbors the same equivocal endgame that Blanchot exploits in the Orpheus myth. That is, it also expresses the difficult complicity of the forbidden and the unbearable. The Orpheus myth, however, stands at the headwaters of a massive transcultural investment in pondering the richly intercalated strands of libidinal affect, transgression, sacred violence, and poetic inspiration in the extended drama that Norbert Elias called the "civilizing process."[46] Quite simply, as a cultural artifact, the story of Orpheus enjoys a deeply embedded seductive appeal, as well as an archive of creative appropriation, that has no precise equivalent in the combined legacies of the Shekinah and Lot's wife. This factor alone helps explain Blanchot's turn to Orpheus. On the other hand, the Shekinah/Lot's wife nexus remembers the desert, in Blanchot's sense. It remembers the desert as "a space without place and a time without production," and it remembers this with a visceral purity that is strictly commensurate with its narrative impoverishment.[47] Only Orpheus would be on Emma Bovary's reading list.

The glancing intuition of the link between the Shekinah and Lot's wife thus testifies to Blanchot's fundamental interest in art's witnessing over its signifying properties. The remaining prototype in the sequence gives a clearer picture of the stakes in the turn to the biblical archive. Blanchot's

use of the story of the raising of Lazarus—*Lazare, veni foras*—is more de-
tailed and more complexly organized than the treatment of the two Old
Testament allusions. This is perhaps not surprising, given that the New
Testament proof-text (John 11:1–46) is also the more fully rendered narrative episode. On formal grounds, then, the alternative it presents to the
Orpheus myth is legible in a way that the allusions to the Shekinah and
Lot's wife are not. The Johannine allusion yields a scene very different
from the *folie à deux* of Orpheus and Eurydice. The miracle at Bethany is
the seeming capstone to a story otherwise focused on the resilient bonds
of friendship and communal solidarity in mourning rather than erotic captivation. In Blanchot's retelling, however, these dimensions represent the
road not taken, for his interest lies elsewhere. Initially, he treats the story
as an allegory of sublation. The resurrection of Lazarus figures the passage from the "primordial depths" of "dark, cadaverous reality" to "the
life of the mind" (*WoF*, 326). This is the precise point at which Blanchot
recalls the Shekinah and, as noted, the intervention warps the sublationary
argument. When he picks up the thread of the Lazarus commentary, the
emphasis falls not on edifying recuperation but on what is lost or abandoned in the achievement of negation: "[Literature] wants the cat as it exists, the pebble *taking the side of things*, not man but the pebble, and in this
pebble what man rejects by saying it, what is the foundation of speech and
what speech excludes in speaking, the abyss, Lazarus in the tomb and not
Lazarus brought back into the daylight, the one who already smells bad,
who is Evil, Lazarus lost and not Lazarus saved and brought back to life"
(*WoF*, 327). Blanchot's counter-reading of Lazarus focuses not on the res-
urrected body, as in the Johannine proof-text, nor on the desire for contact
with the spirit of the beloved in the underworld, as in the Orpheus myth.
The sought-after "intimacy of the unrevealed" entails a pause in thought,
a passivity patient enough to dwell on "the side of things" before they are
subsumed into meaning. The ease with which the conjured scene moves
from pebble to the decomposing flesh of Lazarus's corpse (the latter a classic example of an untouchable thing in biblical purity codes) tells us that
the unrevealed side of things includes something other than the fantasy of
primordial harmony unmarked by language and culture. It includes, with a
clearly Levinasian inflection, an attunement to the "infinite disquiet, formless and nameless vigilance" that inheres in the "obscure power" of things,
beyond the dichotomous rule of transgression, with its meticulous prescriptions for distinguishing clean from unclean, natural from unnatural.

   The Levinasian inflection to Blanchot's language in this essay, however,
interrogates rather than endorses the type of iconophobic strain on display

in Levinas's contemporary diatribe in "Reality and Its Shadow." By offering up the prospect of contact with Lazarus's dead flesh as paradigm for what happens in the "language of literature," Blanchot's argument trades on the *frisson* of a still-palpable aura of transgression surrounding the cultural imperative to follow rules for disposing of the dead. However, the argument does not stop there. Insofar as the conjured scene aspires to the condition of a *figure* for the "nameless vigilance" and "infinite disquiet" that transpire in art, the argument also mounts a critique of the taboo that consigns art to the jurisdiction of the idol and the *immonde* (the unclean).

In particular, Blanchot's Lazarus figure, "the one who already smells bad, who is Evil," attributes to the work of art a compelling occasion to interrogate the aesthetic premises underlying what Jan Assmann calls the principle of "normative inversion" (the "construction of cultural otherness") in the outworking of the Mosaic distinction (the "distinction between true and false in religion").[48] In biblical terms, the distinction between the ritually impure cadaver and the imputed sins of Sodom is not insignificant. In Blanchot's argument, however, the neighborly relation between Lazarus and Lot's wife is both logical and necessary. Within the biblical typology he sets up, if the "intimacy of the unrevealed" leads to "the stupor of a confrontation in the depths of obscurity," the journey must end in the desert and in the percussive sounding of prophecy, the "place without place" that Blanchot broods over in the essay "Prophetic Speech." The journey must also push beyond the reflexive assumption of transgressive contact with the cadaver. Between Lazarus and the face of the Shekinah, only one figure presents itself as the exemplary witness to this place in the biblical archive: Lot's wife.

There is no mention of pillar or statue in Blanchot's rendering of what happened in the flight from Sodom; only the amorphous image of "words turned to salt." But that is not all. Consider the passage that segues from the Lazarus episode to the sodomitic allusion.

> [Literature] is not beyond the world, but neither is it the world itself:
> it is the presence of things before the *world* exists, their perseverance
> after the world has disappeared, the stubbornness of what remains
> when everything vanishes and the dumbfoundedness of what appears
> when nothing exists. That is why it cannot be confused with consciousness, which illuminates things and makes decisions; it is *my* consciousness *without me*, the radiant passivity of mineral substances, the lucidity
> of the depths of torpor. . . . By turning itself into an inability to reveal
> anything, literature is attempting to become the revelation of what
> revelation destroys. (*WoF*, 328)

This richly allusive passage deserves to count as one of the most luminous and searching descriptions of the aesthetic provocation of Lot's wife. Blanchot imagines the sudden crystallization of a quasi-image—"the radiant passivity of mineral substances"—achieving here the aesthetic captivation of the image dispossessed of the distinct phenomenal appearance of the image itself. This lapse, or errancy, marks the clandestine onset of a figural community housing three essential aspects of Blanchot's literary-philosophical project. Blanchot's quasi-image of Lot's wife speaks to the "universal anonymity" that materializes in literary space, the impenetrable neutrality of the brute material facticity of things, and, movingly, it suggests creaturely and thingly openness to what prophecy promises, beyond human intention. This is the "revelation of what revelation destroys." Its unnamed aegis, in an unfurled gesture of expression without content, is Lot's wife.

There are many ways to understand what Blanchot had in mind many years after writing this essay when he referred to Levinas as "our clandestine companion."[49] The sodomitic undertow to that philosophical companionship marks the concluding lines of "The Poet's Vision." With caution, Levinas marshals Blanchot's aesthetics to counter what he takes to be the insidious spirit of "calm possession" in Heidegger's poetics of dwelling. He detects in Blanchot a salutary engagement with the poetic implications of the "monotheist revelation," in its capacity to expose a "new dimension of Height and Ideal." Such exposure, he suggests, defeats the "subtle hermeneutics" and also, one supposes, the residual allegorical equipment that go hand in glove with the Heideggerian system's "Hellenic 'truth of being.'" This premise leads to Levinas's eloquent echo of Blanchot's argument in "Literature and the Right to Death": "In the accursed cities where dwelling is stripped of its architectural wonders, not only are the gods absent, but the sky itself. But in monosyllabic hunger, in the wretched poverty in which houses and objects revert to their material function and enjoyment is closed in on all sides, the face of man shines forth" (*WoF*, 139). "Accursed cities" inhabit a wide ambit in the bible, including the city founded by Cain (Gen. 4:17), the urban setting of Babel (Gen. 11:1–9), and Jericho (Josh. 2:6). The most likely reference, however, is to the condemned Cities of the Plain. This is the only locus that corresponds to the sights Blanchot sets upon the bible's desertified landscapes. All the more reason, then, to notice how Levinas's turn to the Sodom archive follows Blanchot's train of thought, pushing beyond the received logic of crime and punishment, and the regime of normative inversion, to a bruising vision of destitution. Gazing over the accursed cities, Levinas shares with Blanchot the search for "the side of the day that day has rejected in order to become light" (*WoF*, 328). Like Blanchot, he sides with Sodom's unthinkable dimension, which Abraham broaches when he interrogates the nature of God's justice in the decision to destroy Sodom.

Levinas's question: "Does Blanchot not attribute to art the function of uprooting the Heideggerian universe? Does not the poet, before the 'eternal streaming of the outside,' hear the voices that call away from the Heideggerian world?" Levinas's answer: a guarded yes. In Sodomscape, the figural backdrop to both question and answer is consequential. As conjured by Levinas, the "accursed cities" are memorable not as paragons of rooted inhospitality, but as sites of exposure to the "primordial obscurity" of existence.[50] This mutating—and denuding—scene does not include the pillar of salt. That specific memory comes to Levinas belatedly, in a commentary on Blanchot's fiction that appeared in print a decade after "The Poet's Vision."[51] Levinas's conjuring of the image of a blasted cityscape instead shows the essential point that Blanchot discovers in the image of words turned to salt. Both images serve as figural testimony to the place occupied by Lot's wife in Sodomscape. In other words, Lot's wife shadows both images as their unspoken matrix. Fittingly, the figure's "primordial obscurity" situates it as the clandestine companion to Levinas's and Blanchot's shared and evolving thoughts on the ethical dimension in literature's "infinite disquiet," as it works "to become the revelation of what revelation destroys."

The Desert of Allegory

The cityscape that comes to the fore at the close of "The Poet's Vision" remembers Blanchot's conviction, voiced in "Literature and the Right to Death," that literature "is a concern for the reality of things, for their unknown, free, and silent existence; literature is their innocence and their forbidden presence" (*WoF*, 330). Maître François's miniature, I am suggesting, presents a premonitory figure of Blanchot's insight, particularly as it bears on the intimacy he detects, in "Prophetic Speech," between art and the denuding force of prophecy. It is now time for a brief backward glance. Recall the equivocal appearance and posture of the statue of Lot's wife. The figure fills the "meanwhile" of the painted image with a host of associations—deserved punishment, apophatic passion, preternatural calm, and ontological ambiguity. The figure does not choose, it does not judge; rather, it issues a space for questioning. In particular, the figure speaks to

Blanchot's sense of nakedness as an essential exposure that touches on, yet remains distinct from, the revelatory power of disclosure.

For Blanchot, nakedness is the factor that best conveys the distance between prophecy and allegorical intention. Blanchot's intuition probably owes something to Paul—the Paul of Ephesians, at least—as well as to Levinas. "Prophetic words," Blanchot writes, "possess neither allegory nor symbol." Instead, "by the concrete force of the words, they lay things bare, in a nudity that is like that of an immense face [*visage*] that one sees and does not see and that, like a face, is light, the absolute quality of light, terrifying and ravishing, familiar and elusive, immediately present and infinitely foreign, always to come, always to be discovered and even provoked, although as readable as the nudity of the human face can be: in this sense alone, figure."[52] For Blanchot, what is "readable" in prophecy exceeds any determinate content, to the degree that prophecy's originary truth derives from the impact of its incarnate dynamism, a point Blanchot illustrates through the triple pun on "figure." In French, the word means both "face" and "symbol." The homonym preserves the Latin sense of *figura* as expression of plastic form and elaborated figural language conducted over time. In turn, *figura* carries a translated memory of its Greek precursor, *typos*, the word for a mark or impression, together with its cognate, *tupto*, a blow or striking force.[53] Through the punning surplus, Blanchot's description remembers what the regularizing exegetical tradition of figural (or "typological") reading forgets. Blanchot's description remembers that prophetic language both informs and deforms exegetical practice, and that there is no algebraic formula for the marks it leaves in history, or on the land and people that it addresses.

Reading Maître François's miniature with Blanchot's essay in mind enlarges the compass of the allegorical crisis figured by the naked statue. The exposure of Lot's wife, concentrated in the arrested turn toward Sodom, introduces a "face" of prophecy that the biblical narrative itself both remembers and forgets by withholding the stranded woman's literal speech. To grasp the impact of such exposed absence, we must suspend the familiar presumption of a punitive strike against Lot's wife. We must learn to detect in the stilled aspect of her gaze and her monumentalized silence a cipher for the restlessness that Blanchot finds in the prophetic utterance. From this prospect, the figure can be said to commemorate prophecy's specific violence, as "that speech always spoken and never heard that doubles [articulate speech] with a pre-echo, rumor of wind and impatient murmur destined to repeat it in advance, at the risk of destroying it by preceding it."[54]

From this prospect, the figure's evident obduracy presents itself as the inverted memory of the nomadic intention specific to prophecy, "a wandering speech that returns to the original demand of movement by opposing all stillness, all settling, any taking root that would be rest."[55] From this prospect, the backward look complicates rather than confirms the covenantal dyad of "old" and "new" by introducing a middle term. Between "old" and "new" lie untold forms of thinking the "new," which are not found on the road Lot takes out of Sodom. Rather than a simple gesture of refusal or misguided attachment, the backward look also testifies to prophecy's preemptive force, what Blanchot describes as "this primal eagerness, this haste, this refusal to be delayed and attached."[56]

Looking again at the miniature, let us imagine Lot's wife as the silent partner in Abrahamic gazing, the one who remembers the desert in a way Abraham perhaps forgets. Let us imagine that what she sees or hears in the desert is the "time of a promise," which punctuates recorded history without essentially belonging to it. Like the title of the book in which Blanchot's essay on prophetic speech appears, the desert holds "the book to come" (*Le livre à venir*). This book's trace appears in the figural history of Lot's wife. Though Blanchot himself has more to say on this topic, we turn now to other encounters with the calcified figure that intervene on the road between the fifteenth-century miniature and Blanchot's universe.

CHAPTER 3

Remembering Lot's Wife: The Structure of Testimony in the *Painted Life* of Mary Ward

[F]aith never shuts itself upon a truth given by God, but, by
its very nature, sees clear through every truth to the infinite
truth-giver himself, and thus is always ready to receive every
possible revelation from God. A faith which made some sort of
reservation about the future, a faith which was only willing
to accept such words of God as it had measured by the
standard of its own reason, would not be Christian faith.

—HANS URS VON BALTHASAR, *A Theology of History*[1]

I am looking at a capital "L" (fig. 7). It belongs to a series of ornamented letters, talking letters (*iniziali parlante*), produced in the studio of the six-teenth-century Florentine typographer Bartolomeo Sermartelli.[2] Sermar-telli's "L" stands for Lot. You can see Sodom in flames, on the horizon to the left of the letter's spine. Filling the space bounded by the spine and foot is the cave near Zoar, where Lot's two daughters, believing them-selves and their father to be the sole survivors of the catastrophe, have hit upon the solution that will ensure the family's survival. Given the incest scene's visual prominence and ethical provocation, it is easy to forget that Sermartelli's letter also depicts the story's most startling instance of divine retribution: the sudden cancellation of Lot's wife from salvation history.[3] Where is Lot's wife in Sermartelli's design? The mutating figure, near the left margin, is barely visible, lost in the background.

The discreet position of the figure makes it easy to miss, but also pro-vocatively indicates an event that falls outside the operative scope of the normative relation between testimonial sign and historical event in re-ceived protocols of biblical literacy. The figure is literally *avant la lettre* and symbolically beyond exegetical capture. Through this single gesture,

Figure 7. Bartolomeo Sermartelli, "L[ot]." Courtesy of Special Collections, Honnold/ Mudd Library of the Claremont Colleges.

Sermartelli's "L" silently witnesses a tectonic shift in the understanding of Lot's wife's negative exemplarity—the figure's identity as type of impenitent error and improvident curiosity—in Reformation and Counter-Reformation biblical cultures. By siting the prospect of illegible elements in the story of the flight from Sodom, Sermartelli's "L" marks an important juncture in Lot's wife's figural history. The letter imagines Lot's wife as the figure of the unthought in the Abrahamic cycle: an impossible yet lived intimacy between the chosen and the cast out.[4] In this chapter, I argue that the essential paradox of such intimacy takes material shape in the career of the early modern missionary adventurer Mary Ward (1585–1645). Known as the "Jesuitress" in both Romanist and reformist circles, Ward pursued with impressive entrepreneurial skill a progressive, and controversial, pastoral program, which ran afoul of the judgment of ecclesiastical authorities on both sides of the confessional divide.[5] The record of Ward's strenuously contested pastoral ambitions and misadventures constitutes a powerfully suggestive witness to the figural range and provocation of Lot's wife in ecclesial history. But that is not all. This witnessing gesture, I propose, is also reciprocal, in the sense that the sodomitic undertow to Ward's career effectively enlarges and reorients understanding of the transhistorical scope and critical legacy of Ward's community-building ethos.

First, however, I need to narrow the parameters of what I intend by figural history. Its semantic field is conspicuously marked by the normative procedures of biblical typology, memorably described in Erich Auerbach's account of the exegetical practice underpinning literary *figura*'s Western tradition, to say nothing of the Hegelian reading of that tradition, whereby *figura*'s proleptic orientation constitutes a premonitory symptom of history's supersessionist drive: from mythos to logos.[6] The continued cultural force of these controversial legacies remains in play in what follows; yet the sense most relevant to this chapter's guiding animus can be found in the revisionist typology, both anti-Hegelian and antidogmatic, that briefly flourished in European Catholic theology between World War II and the Second Vatican Council. I begin there.

The so-called *nouvelle théologie*, associated with the work of Marie-Dominique Chenu, Jean Daniélou, Henri de Lubac, and Hans Urs von Balthasar, among others, mounted a strenuous critique of orthodox Catholicism's prevailing neo-Thomist rubric. That rubric, codified in Leo XIII's encyclical *Aeterni Patris* (1879), responded to the modernity's perceived secularism by effectively declaring that the essential meaning and purpose of salvation history had been authoritatively parsed in the scholastic principles inherited from Counter-Reformation era recensions of Thomist theology.[7] Proponents of the *nouvelle théologie* confronted the ecclesiastical hierarchy's apparent refusal to face up to unprecedented pastoral and ethical challenges posed to the church in the postwar era. They contested the privilege neo-Thomism gave to an ossified system of dogmatic rationality and to an intransigently legalistic approach to moral questions, neither of which bore more than a superficial resemblance to the deeply assimilative and dialectical character of the Angelic Doctor's intellectualism. *Ressourcement* theologians (the name preferred by the movement's leading voices) sought to reengage the spiritual passion and wide-ranging intellectual curiosity that had informed Thomas's effort to bring the wealth of contemporary human knowledge, as received from Hellenistic, Arab, patristic, and mystical traditions, into contact with the biblical and Pauline proof-texts of orthodox Christianity. The guiding intuition of *ressourcement* theologians was that the church's essential vitality resided in its capacity to respect and to deepen the transhistorical mutuality of pastoral and theological expressions of Christic revelation.[8]

Henri de Lubac's contributions to the *ressourcement* movement provided unflinching descriptions of the at times bruising yet generative intimacy between Incarnational, Trinitarian, and Eucharistic paradoxes in theological history, and the analogous *complexio oppositorum* through which diverse historical embodiments of the church could be said to remain in communion with each other, without being reducible to dogmatic expression.[9] In essence, de Lubac's enterprise, like many of his peers', inhabited a figural understanding of the paradox and mystery informing the varied manifestations of the body of Christ. Although wholly conversant with the wide range of figural invention found in the canon (scriptural patterns, patristic and medieval elaborations), de Lubac's sense of figure was not primarily exegetical.[10] It did not assume the unitary legibility of providential history as mapped in the scriptural canon. Neither did it prescribe a devotional regimen of imitative models designed to gauge the progress of the soul (e.g., through type scenes from biblical narrative and saints' lives). Rather, it gave witness to the profoundly *sacramental* character of the figural. Figure, in this sense, was not so much a conveyance of meaning or a mnemonic aid as an intuitive flashpoint, generating intimacy of contact and communication between natural and supernatural orders and between pastoral and theological orders of truth.[11] For de Lubac and *ressourcement* theologians in general, advocacy of the figural life of the church was not meant to jettison the rationality of the neo-Thomist language favored by the Vatican, but rather to restore it to a condition of genuine and productive dialogue— intimate contact—with the mystical symbolism of biblical language on the one hand, and the exigencies of the contemporary world on the other. In short, figure stood for the risk of exposure to forgotten, suppressed, or unthought dimensions of the sacramentality of the church.[12]

Ressourcement theology significantly influenced the ecumenically progressive agenda of the Second Vatican Council (1963–65), but it would have been hard to predict such an outcome in the preceding decade. Pius XII's encyclical *Humani Generis* (1950) issued an emphatic castigation of the movement, reasserting the neo-Thomist ethos of the papal magisterium and stigmatizing the *nouvelle théologie* with the twin charges of "false irenicism" and "dogmatic relativity."[13] To return to the place where we began, *ressourcement* theologians found themselves cast into the figural space Sermartelli assigns to Lot's wife, a space suspended between excommunication from the ecclesial community (narratively rendered as the sudden extinction of the Sodomites in the Genesis text) and full membership (the survival of Lot and his daughters).[14]

Humani Generis does not mention the Sodom narrative. This is no surprise, given the entrenched association of Sodom with a perceived moral disorder (stigmatized sexual practices) not directly at issue in the present circumstance. The encyclical nonetheless enters Sodom's figural orbit by invoking the fundamental aberration of the Sodomites in the Genesis narrative: rooted inhospitality, of which the scenes of anticipated sexual violence are but a symptom. To borrow Robert Alter's words, the Ur-sin of Sodom, inhospitality, includes a "nexus" of associations designating an ethos of anti-covenant: the spectral manifestation of all that threatens the Israelite community's place in the covenantal economy.[15] The encyclical remembers that threat through a strategic volley of images, designed to raise precisely the kind of free-floating contamination anxiety conjured up in scriptural tradition and in Sodom's long cultural history. Thus, the "dogmatic relativity" of the *nouvelle théologie* is called both a "disease" and a "deadly fruit." Such language is generic enough to convey the perceived enormity of the threat. Yet, through its invocation of the biblical proof-texts linking disease, sin, and death, it is also specific enough to define the *nouvelle théologie* as modernity's latest iteration of the catastrophic anti-covenantal gesture: the reversion to Sodom.[16]

What was most irksome about the *ressourcement* ethos in the magisterium's view was the fact that the movement's prospective decoupling of the covenantal economy and the dogmatic utterance's timeless authority was disseminated from theological and educational strongholds within the *ecclesia*. *Ressourcement* theology spoke to the erosion of the magisterium's declared distinction between Catholic teaching and modernity—a border crisis, that is, between *veritas* and *historia*, the framing categories of the covenantal drama to which, in Auerbach's reading, the typological imagination, *figura*, served as middle term. The paradigm of that crisis and its mutating character is Lot's wife.

The Hidden (Catholic) Face of Lot's Wife

Let's take a second look at Sermartelli's letter. Consider again the design's suggested visual encryption. Similarly gauged depictions of Lot's wife abound in early modern visual media, testifying to the era's fluency in using perspectival composition and recessional space to pictorially indicate Lot's wife's radical homelessness. The backward turn's catastrophic consequence, which the exegetical tradition gives indisputable prominence, is here italicized by the visual calculus of negative magnitude. The enormity of Lot's wife's errancy finds its proper gauge in the sheer difficulty of locating the distant figure in the blasted landscape.

This oblique element retrieves the etymological suggestiveness of the Hebrew word for pillar (*netziv*), the thing into which Lot's wife is transformed in Genesis 19:26—*netziv* refers to a lookout, garrison, or boundary marker.[17] I take Sermartelli's "L"—more precisely, the graphic trace positioned outside and before the "L"—as sentinel to a network of kinships. These kinships are dispersed across different cultural locations, between the Sodom story and variously documented experiences of early modern Christian subjects, who find themselves not simply cast as erring soul or prodigal daughter, but also called to witness events suspended between *historia* and *veritas*. This place is the vanishing point where *figura*—Auerbach's middle term between *historia* and *veritas*—discovers its proximity to disaster.

Christology has always recognized the peculiar radiance of this place. It is the crux of the Passion narrative, the cry of the abandoned Son on the Cross: "*Eli, Eli, lema sabachthani*"/ "My God, my God, why did you abandon me?" (Matt. 27:46). One of the *ressourcement* theologians' signal ambitions was to reemphasize this moment of abjection's centrality in the incarnational mystery and, by extension, in the church's historical being. In *ressourcement* thought, for example, Christic time's "valid meaning" does not issue, in the manner of the neo-Thomist tradition, from "some timeless philosophical or mystical 'eternity.'" Rather, it sustains a condition of vigilance, of readiness "to say yes to everything, to be available for everything, always open to the infinite."[18] From this vantage point, *Humani Generis*'s position ran counter to a genuine theology of time, such that it tried to inoculate the very possibility of revelation from exposure to the contemporary *ecclesia*'s historical horizons. In contrast, *ressourcement* theology sought to reopen communication in Christian thought between the decisive figure of dispossession (the cry of abandonment on the Cross) and the particular challenges of modernity, without insisting on a preestablished doctrinal standard of recuperative truth.

To the extent that it sought to remain open, in von Balthasar's words, to "every *possible* revelation from God," *ressourcement* theology entered into a relation of what could be called patient proximity to one of the most trenchant postwar atheologies of time, Maurice Blanchot's *The Writing of the Disaster*: "The disaster: break with the star, break with every form of totality, never denying, however, the dialectical necessity of a fulfillment; the disaster: prophecy which announces nothing but the refusal of the prophetic as simply an event to come, but which nonetheless opens, nonetheless discovers the patience of vigilant language. The disaster, touch of the powerless infinite: it does not come to pass under a sidereal sky, but here—a here in excess of all presence. Here: where, then?"[19] Blanchot's language throughout *The Writing of the Disaster* carries resonances from several tributaries of biblical and ethical thought, not least Emmanuel Levinas's provocative associations of passivity, responsibility, and vigilance.[20] I am not concerned here with that particular history, and still less do I propose to conflate Blanchot's project with that of the *nouvelle théologie*.[21] What interests me is the point of friction between the two contemporaneous projects, the mutual, though not identical, access each gives to the rupture and consummation of meaning disaster brings about. That encounter illumines a way into the corridor between *veritas* and *historia*, the domain that belongs not to *chronos*, with its consolation of manageable time, but to *figura*, understood not as the finished image of experience or thought, but as the passion (or "infinite passivity," as Blanchot would say) of the image unmoored from either knowing subject or timeless model.[22] Lot's wife stands here, at the crisis point, the *punctum*, where disaster lodges, where home and homelessness collapse into each other, and where Sermartelli's design and Blanchot's question—"Here: where, then?"—converge.

It is no accident that in the twentieth century Lot's wife should be reclaimed in art and literature of the Shoah as a sign of the paralysis of memory and the limits of historical comprehension in the wake of catastrophe, or that the figure should surface in the burgeoning critical literature on childhood sexual abuse as an emblem of the "contemporary drama over recovered memory."[23] In such instances, to take up the position of Lot's wife is to be caught in the vortex of Blanchot's "break with the star," made witness to the "excess of all presence" that marks the traumatic history's peculiar consistency, outside collective memory's economic circulation and cultural patrimony's prudential disbursement. There are ways to parse the question, however, that open up otherwise undetected tributaries in Lot's wife's figural history. In these zones of contact with the Sodom narrative's legacy, the paradoxes of witnessing become the means through which the arrested gesture of looking back—the Genesis text's figure for stalled mourning—yields a revisionist typology. This revisionist typology envisions disaster and survival as converging terms of an ethics of action, undertaken for the sake of what may be grasped from the past's wreckage and vigilantly postured toward a categorically unknown future.

The career of the English Catholic "Jesuitress" Mary Ward illustrates the gesture just described, as can be discerned in the series of paintings commissioned by the religious community that Ward founded in the first decade of the seventeenth century. Composed somewhere between the 1630s and 1670s, the so-called *Gemaltes Leben* (*Painted Life*) both commemorates and, against all odds, argues for the legitimacy of Ward's religious community under the proselytizing mandate of the Counter-Reformation. Nowhere, however, in the documentation of Ward's career, is the figure of Lot's wife explicitly mentioned. Traversing different grounds—different crises, different losses—from those precipitating the figure's resurgence in late modernity, Ward's career parses the subtextual domain of the Sodom narrative in a manner exquisitely tuned to her anomalous and precarious place in both Counter-Reformation and Stuart theopolitical worlds. Translating the career, the *Painted Life* solicits a hermeneutic attuned to the figural afterlife of the Sodom story's estranged woman. We are not looking for pillars.

The task, then, is to follow the curve traced by the figure's dispersal. The movement has a double origin, beginning with two foundational voices in ecclesial history, each of which represents a decisive turn in orthodoxy's patristic and Reformation eras: Irenaeus of Lyons and Martin Luther. Together, their respective readings of Lot's wife identify the contradictory terms of the domain inhabited by Mary Ward. In the *Adversus haereses* Irenaeus decides, against the preponderance of biblical tradition, that Lot's wife does not signify abjection, sin, or depravity. Instead, she is the *ecclesia*'s biblical type, the sanctified community: suffering, patient, stranded in history, and holding onto the promise of the bridegroom's return.[24] She is the paradigmatic martyr-witness; her arrested gesture of looking back anamorphically renders her steady gaze on history's providential design, particularly its deepest recesses: the pillar figuring the empathic witness to all that was annihilated in Sodom's destruction. Irenaeus's reasons for this astonishing (it is tempting to call it proto-Benjaminian) counter-reading of the Sodom text can be ascribed to his thought's typological features, for which he is remembered in church history: his insistence, contra Marcionite and Gnosticizing views, that the integrity of the bond between "old" and "new" testaments is profound and inviolable (even Lot's wife can be recuperated) and his intuition that the eschatological promise of Christ's resurrection is premised on an ecological and recursive experience of time.[25]

In 1526, Erasmus established the *editio princeps* of the *Adversus haereses*. But Irenaeus's revisionist reading of the Sodom text was largely lost on the sixteenth century's humanist-reformist exegetical cultures. Luther's commentary on the Sodom text, in the 1539 lectures on Genesis, offered a judgment that spoke more powerfully to the reformists' controversialist sensibility. Lot's wife, he argued, is the typological emblem of the papists' refusal to let go of the past's bankrupt authority—that is, the Catholic past. Like Lot's wife, they "are looking back and thus disregard the word they have before them."[26] Their gaze is faulty precisely because it is not historical enough: it fails to recognize the continued unfolding of God's providential design through the reformists' enterprise.

The Romanist response appears to have been that of silence. Irenaeus's idiosyncratic insight did not make its way, to my knowledge, into Counter-Reformation assertions of apostolic fidelity. Not until *ressourcement* theologians undertook a careful rereading of the patristic antecedents of Thomist thought did Lot's wife's ecclesial significance resurface, notably in de Lubac's survey of female figures in biblical narrative and patristic exegesis.[27] Luther's reading, on the other hand, catalyzed a subgenre of controversialist and homiletic literature in England, in which Lot's wife encapsulated the perils of papist survivalism in the reformist world. No surprise that the figure of Lot's wife should surface in both juridical and pastoral responses to the Gunpowder Plot. The mythography of the narrowly averted disaster seemed to corroborate reformists' suspicions of the papist enclave's alternately intransigent and volatile character. The Gunpowder Plot also indicated the alarming relevance of the specific problem foregrounded in the Genesis story: how to measure Sodom.[28] After the onset of the Jesuit mission to England in the 1580s, the papist remnant in England, the new sodomitic diaspora, had become a diversified community constituted by known or suspected recusants, church papists (of uncertain allegiance), and, most troublingly, multiple apostates, all of whom could be thought of—and were so conjured in homilies—as monstrous recurrences of the recidivist gesture exemplified by Lot's wife.[29]

Framing Lot's Wife

Perhaps more than any other episode in early modern political history, Gunpowder Plot confirms the underlying logic of Karl Marx's witticism that "all great world-historic facts and personages" appear twice, first as tragedy and then as farce.[30] The farcical part has many faces, the most jauntily memorable being the jingle "Remember, remember the fifth of November." The species of tragedy put in motion by the conspirators, however, remains difficult to gauge. While the machinery of the plot in some respects had the makings of a terrorist strike, recent historiographical opinion tends toward less spectacular assessments, partly as a corrective to the Grand Guignol caricature.[31] Apart from the sheer messiness of the tangle of partial knowledge, mixed motives, and tactical gestures on the part of the main players (including agents of the Jacobean government), the most significant feature of the plot is that it was abortive. This circumstance lent a spectral aura to its reentry into history as a broadly disseminated species of borrowed traumatic memory. More than any other element, the quality of *unfinishedness* helped mold the conspiracy's post hoc career to the malleable contours of sodomitic figuration. The point Robert Alter makes about the Sodom trope's structural purposiveness in biblical narrative also holds for the Gunpowder Plot in Jacobean England's theopolitical climate. Both instances occupy the uncertain threshold between memory and history, and in this capacity each stands not as a discrete entity or sequence of events, but as a floating nexus of projected and felt dangers.

Consider the opening phase of the plot's reentry, which took shape as an anniversary with trappings that over time proved an adaptive hybrid of various genres. November 5, the day of the discovery of the gunpowder barrels in the cellars of Parliament, was quickly converted by an Act of Parliament into an official day of thanksgiving for providential deliverance. The new holiday—one of "those peculiarly Jacobean holy days," as Peter E. McCullough puts it—supplied the occasion for ritualized exercises in nation-building, which were correlated, not coincidentally, with the intensification in many quarters of reflexive antipapist sentiment.[32] Commemorative festivities included a mix of secular and religious elements— including, famously, bonfires, liturgical services, anthems, and a subgenre of homiletic exhortation, the so-called Gunpowder Plot sermons. The latter were delivered in several venues—at court as well as from church pulpits and public pulpits (preeminently Paul's Cross)—and they displayed a remarkable heterogeneity of rhetorical and exegetical tactics.[33] The bravura effects were achieved through adroit combinations of familiar homiletic genres—jeremiad, thanksgiving, and confutational disputation—placed in counterpoint to acts of textual fidelity, or pious recidivism, which returned auditors and readers to the biblical proof-text used in the inaugural Gunpowder Plot sermon by William Barlow, the Book of Psalms (Psalms 18:2, "The Lord is my rock, and my fortress, and my deliverer").[34]

Psalmic material became the standard proof-text in the corpus of Gunpowder Plot sermons, most likely because the deliverance trope promoted a collective cathartic reflex to what might have been—a tremor of phantasmic solidarity.[35] One of the era's most engrossing Paul's Cross sermons, however, demonstrates the Sodom story's galvanizing appeal in the homiletic rhetoric of providential vigilance. In 1607, Robert Wilkinson, a favorite preacher of Henry, Prince of Wales, gave a fiery sermon at Paul's Cross on the Lukan text "Remember Lot's wife" (Luke 17:32).[36] The theme of deliverance only nominally governs the sermon. What captures Wilkinson's imagination is the precarious distance between the asserted doctrinal (and governmentally supported) clarity of confessional difference, and the social and moral experience of ambiguity in navigating the sometimes illegible borderlines between papist and reformist worlds.[37]

At the sermon's climax, Wilkinson issues a list of twelve "memoranda," designed to serve critical instructions for his auditors. While it does not stint on pastoral bromides (for example, associating Lot's wife with the spiritual perils of the "perverse and crooked of heart"), the list also discloses a fairly thorough diagnostic of the equivocal texture of social experience in an ideologically complex world, where the relation between religious, confessional, and political inclinations was in fact unsettled.[38] For a case in point, consider the sermon's denunciation of apostates. The text superficially assigns blame for such errancy to individual moral corruption.

> No man that begins a good course, and then quailes in it . . . shall ever have part in God . . . such a raging lust there is in nature to do forbidden things. . . . And there is a breed of such singular spirits that turne their backes upon us, and go to Sodom, only for that cause, because we go to Zoar, Fugitives & runagates of the Romish Church, that have renounced not their country only, but their faith too, and there by barking like dogs in a den, to pronounce for heresie whatsoever we say . . . sworne enemies to Church and Common-wealth, to Prince, Priest, people, and to all men.[39]

Recourse to the fallen state of human "nature" is a pastorally convenient gesture, but Wilkinson's language also gives witness to a more contingent provocation. The insidiously diplomatic terms of the recently promulgated Oath of Allegiance (1606) had already exacerbated confusion over the "nature" and degree of the relation between political allegiance and religious "loyalty with doctrinal protestantism."[40] As Michael Questier argues, the Oath was "a diabolically effective political cocktail," precisely because its seeming agnosticism in doctrinal matters tended "to confuse catholic attempts to keep apart religious and political loyalties so that they could no longer distinguish between their allegiance to the king and allegiance to the Church of England."[41] Wilkinson's florid description of metonymic contagion—"sworne enemies to Church and Common-wealth, to Prince, Priest, people, and to all men"—thus presents a telling homiletic variation

of Jan Assmann's principle of "normative inversion," the ideological tactic that mobilizes selective forgetting and repression in order to produce
captivating images and stories of "cultural abomination."[42] In this instance,
Lot's wife stands both for the perceived threat of English Romanist subversion (the apostate-traitor), as well as the unacknowledged but socially consequential dilemma of the double bind produced by the oath's presumption
of a univocal and global allegiance to the Jacobean church-state.

In a related key, the separate memoranda addressed to the men and
women in the assembled congregation indicate the sermon's understanding of how the domestic household had become a liminal site on post-
Reformation England's confessional map. Patriarchal norms in protestant England may have assigned to husbands and fathers the privilege of
religious as well as legal stewardship over the household. As Frances E.
Dolan points out, however, "Catholicism in a country without monasteries or churches empowered women as custodians of household religion"
as well as key collaborators in the development of clandestine networks of
devotional practices and sacramental observances.[43] The "memorandum"
that the salt pillar issues to "you women"—"Not to straggle or decline too
much from the good steppes and admonitions of your husbands, for as a
souldier flying from his captaine, or a sheep wandring from the shepheard,
so is a wife forsaking him whom God hath ordained to be her guide"—
tacitly acknowledges one of the hidden folds in the fabric of religious and
political conformity: the household with a recusant wife and nominally
protestant husband.[44]

The memorandum, perhaps unavoidably, falls into circular reasoning
in the sense that the persons tacitly addressed—recusant women—would
by definition not be in attendance at St. Paul's churchyard. Their husbands might be, however, though church attendance in this circumstance
provided no guarantee of full or authentic conformity. One of the much-
debated tactics of papist survivalism was the temporizing practice of outward conformity and inner demurral associated with so-called church papists. It is perhaps no surprise that Wilkinson declares this species of prag-
matic navigation between the polar energies of confessional controversy to
be one of the most insidious avatars of Lot's wife:

> Luke-warm men . . . you that are neither hot nor cold; you whose feete
> are to Zoar, but your face to Sodom; you that go one way and looke
> another, that move forward & looke backward; Professors in mouth,
> Atheists in life; Protestants in appearance, Papists in heart; zealous in
> shew, nothing in deede; heere is for you. Elias speaks to you: Why

halt ye betweene two opinions? I would ye were either hot or cold: Be
something, or be nothing: Lots wife was not in Sodom, nor in Zoar,
but betweene Sodom & Zoar, in the mid-way betweene both, and yet
destroyed; and if you be neither hot nor cold, God shall spew you out
of his mouth. Remember that.[45]

Here and elsewhere in the sermon, Wilkinson obsesses over the problem
of in-betweenness as paradigmatically rendered by Lot's wife: "there is no
analogie, proportion, or way unto it," he declares.[46] His own descriptive ter-
minology vacillates not between "pillar" and "statue" (the standard translations of the Hebrew word *netziv*), but between "pillar" and "lumpe."[47] To
be somewhere between pillar and lumpe is to be nowhere—a bewildering
vacancy—on Wilkinson's moral and signifying compass. "Be something,
or be nothing," he advises.

In what he calls the "mid-way" between these two "things" there lies
a further, encrypted instruction. Wilkinson's dogged insistence on the
clarifying property of decisive choice harbors a gathering call to imagine
ways of remembering Lot's wife and her proposed exemplarity that are
not reducible to the prudential calculus of the solitary thinking subject,
the social category of wife, the naturalized estate of woman, or the logic
of dichotomous difference underwriting early modernity's controversialist
narratives of confessional identity. Wilkinson's declarative fiat thus sounds
a quick retreat from what the sermon's intensive gaze repeatedly touches
upon: the pastorally rebarbative intuition of the ambient groundlessness of
ethical choice. This is the enigmatic terrain over which Lot's wife stands
sentinel, ambiguously poised between the blind hand of chance, the contingencies of human will, and the mysterious workings of grace.

Typology and Testimony

I take the topical event that haunts Wilkinson's sermon—Gunpowder
Plot—as my point of entry into the career of Mary Ward. Biographically,
she was separated by only one degree from the scandal. Her father, Marma-
duke Ward, was among the suspects rounded up in the early stages of the
inquiries into the plot.[48] Ideologically, Ward's career was separated from
the scandal by degrees difficult to measure. Unlike the Gunpowder Plot
conspirators, Ward was no terrorist, but the fact that her principal ambition—to establish a worldwide teaching and missionary religious order for
women based on the Jesuit protocol—observed the Counter-Reformation
mandate to reclaim lands lost to reformist heresy was no consolation to

the Protestant church-state. Moreover, in the Romanist enclave, Ward's career also reactivated the sodomitic problem of counting, in the sense that Ward's personal sense of mission, by taking up the apostle Paul's call to be "all things to all men" (1 Cor. 9:22), repeatedly challenged the Romanist hierarchy's sense of how far a woman should go in embodying the apostolic and militant ethos of the *ecclesia*.[49] In effect, Ward's movements across Europe and in England placed her at the intersection of two orthodox vantage points, reformist and Romanist, and the target she represented was a virtual antitype—a repetition with difference—of Lot's wife, the errant woman and witness to a community found to be irregular and in some respects scandalous.

As already noted, Lot's wife is not explicitly mentioned in the archive on Ward. The figure functions rather as the narrative infrastructure and embedded testimony of Ward's unorthodox social practice and combustible relations with ecclesiastical authorities on both sides of the confessional divide. Consider, in this light, the arc of her career. In recent decades, Ward has been celebrated as a pioneering figure, advancing female ministry within the Catholic Church and promoting public education for girls. Superficially, Ward's career is legible as an instance of the post-Tridentine mandate of educational expansion and reform directed toward the faith's global propagation (and reterritorialization).[50] Despite Ward's declared good intentions, however, the church hierarchy possessed neither the language nor the pastoral incentive to make sense of, and still less to endorse, Ward's radical program for a female apostolate governed neither by traditional rules of claustration or conventual garb, nor submission to episcopal authority. Full recognition would not come until after the progressive mission of *ressourcement* theology (its so-called deadly fruit) had found expression in the widespread pastoral reforms of Vatican II.

The one thing Ward most wanted and needed was the intervention of the papal magisterium on behalf of her enterprise. But Ward's repeated petitions to three successive pontiffs failed to win unmitigated support. In 1631, contretemps turned into catastrophe, with the publication of Urban VIII's papal bull (*Pastoralis Romani Pontificis*) extinguishing Ward's institute (known as the School of the Blessed Mary). Less than a month after Urban VIII signed the bull, Ward, then residing in Munich, was arrested and imprisoned on charges of heresy. One year later the charges were dropped. But the central terms of the bull remained in force.

Certain women or virgins, having taken the title of Jesuitresses . . . [and] on the pretext of living a customary religious life . . . wander

about at will and . . . employ themselves at many . . . works which are
most unsuited to maidenly reserve. . . . [These] poisonous growths in
the Church must be torn up from the roots lest they spread themselves
further. And, therefore . . . we totally and completely suppress and
extinguish them, subject them to perpetual abolition . . . and we wish
and command all the Christian faithful to regard and repute them as
suppressed, extinct, rooted out, destroyed and abolished.[51]

Without naming the extinguished city, the text implicitly places Ward's
community in the shadow of Sodom, and its language (like that of *Humani
Generis* in 1950) is rigorously faithful to the dominant rhetorical function
of sodomitic allusion within the intertextual fabric of biblical prototypes.
Sodom is the intimate enemy, the image of broken covenant, and the hallucinatory reminder of the fine edge separating the chosen community from
disaster.

As it turned out, the impact of the bull was not total. The lapses are
telling, in the sense that the document's uneven reach over time and space
shaped what may be called the intermittent history of Mary Ward's enterprise. After 1631, scattered remnants of the community survived, notably
in Bavaria, under the quiet ad hoc protection of sympathetic bishops. In
1703, partial approbation of the diaspora community was allowed, but it
was not until 1877 that the Congregation of Propaganda granted full confirmation of Ward's institute. In the event, formal recognition of Mary
Ward as founder of the institute was the act of a twentieth-century pope,
Pius X, in 1909, and, as suggested, the full measure of Ward's intentions
for the institute (the incorporation of the Ignatian Constitutions into the
protocol of the order) was not realized until 1978, not until the revitalized
ecumenical ethos of Vatican II had left its imprint—*tupos, figura*—on the
church.[52]

Ward's place in the annals of Counter-Reformation history is assured, in
part because of the archival labors of Jesuit historians going back as far as
Tobias Lohner in the late seventeenth century. The contributions of historians belonging to Ward's institute have been no less significant, and the
list is long. All have been keen to minimize the gap between hagiography
and critical biography, although it must be said that none is entirely successful in this regard. Only recently (2008) has a critical edition in English
of Ward's several writings appeared in print.[53]

The *Painted Life* has not received comparable attention. Despite the
clear cultural and art historical interest of the ensemble, to date no critical

edition of the visual narrative exists, and most accounts of the paintings in recent scholarship tend to treat the works as ancillary proofs of Ward's aspirations and achievements.[54] The basic facts regarding provenance can be told in a few words. The paintings are housed in the convent of the congregation in Augsburg. The range of dates of execution is uncertain, although it has been conjectured that the founder of the Augsburg house installed the paintings there in 1662.[55] Lohner's biography (1689) seems to have been the first to use the paintings to corroborate incidents described in written archives, but it is by no means the last to do so. The words written by Mary Chambers in her 1882 biography of Ward have evidently acquired the status of a mantra. The paintings, she wrote, constitute a "rather singular kind of testimony to numerous facts in Mary Ward's life."[56] Virtually all modern biographies replicate Chambers's assessment, tacitly ascribing a numinous (quasi-photographic) authority to the representational medium of painted, visual narrative.

Although it is surely high time for a more critically aware, historicized account of the *Painted Life*, my approach does not entail treating Chambers's remark as a precritical artifact. I think Chambers's words are absolutely right. The *Painted Life* indeed constitutes "a singular kind of testimony to numerous facts" relating to Ward's legacy. To see how this is so, however, it is necessary to recognize the semantic volatility of words such as *singular* and *testimony* as they bear on "facts." To put the matter in terms of Ward's complicated excursions into the figural afterlife of Sodom, I suggest that the *Painted Life*'s testimonial power reclaims Irenaeus's counter-reading of Lot's wife. In both cases—and this is the decisive factor—the pillar does not stand for paralysis. It stands for survival and, more, for unanticipated means of survival. That single change of orientation invites us to consider how the paintings' mimetic apparatus may not be entirely governed by established or dogmatic iconographic conventions of pictorial argument. Again, we are not looking for literal pillars. In other words, in the *Painted Life* mimetic craft discovers, inhabits, and is marked by the testimonial provocation of the mutating figure in the Sodom narrative. By entertaining the fictive consanguinity of Irenaeus's intuition and the visual grammar of the *Painted Life*, we can better grasp the scope of the paintings' commemoration of the at-once radiant and abjected figure of Ward's idea of ecclesial community, together with its doubled orientation, looking backward and forward at the same time.

Neither art historical connoisseurship nor the early modern florilegia of ecclesiastical commentary will be of much help in decoding the Irenaean subtext to the *Painted Life*'s visual argument. Instead, I turn to what could be called a late modern footnote to Irenaeus's habit of mind, one of Jacques Derrida's last and most beautiful ruminations on the "structure of testimony."[57] The essay, *Demeure*, takes the form of a commentary on Maurice Blanchot's postwar testimonial fiction titled "The Instant of My Death." Both texts emphasize the profound equivocality of testimony. This trait turns on two seeming contradictions, which constitute what Derrida calls the "testimonial condition."[58] Testimony would not be testimony were it not singular, "unique and irreplaceable."[59] But its singularity must also be exemplary—that is, replaceable by substitutes or cognates. Otherwise, testimony would be mere idiosyncrasy. The first condition of testimony, then, is that in the instant of its articulation, the singular becomes universalizable.[60] The second condition turns on the relation of this at-once singular and universal event to time. The one who gives testimony—the witness—is necessarily a survivor. Whether the event in question is banal or extraordinary, "one testifies only when one has lived longer than what has come to pass."[61] Yet a kind of temporal vertigo disrupts the "commonsense ordering of time" that would otherwise guarantee testimony's belated status, as well as juridical value. Because of the first condition of testimony (as point of articulation between the singular and the universal), the matter of testimony—the event to which testimony gives witness— is, at the same time, interred and reactivated in discourse. As Blanchot insists, what is caught in the sights of testimony is "the imminence of what has always already taken place."[62] And, as Derrida points out, "this is an *unbelievable* tense."[63] "This is why," he adds, "reflection on testimony has always historically privileged the example of miracles." This is also why "testimoniality belongs *a priori* to the order of the miraculous"—because when one testifies, "even on the subject of the most ordinary and the most 'normal' event, one asks the other to believe one at one's word as if it were a matter of a miracle."[64]

It is perhaps not surprising that Derrida's meditation repeatedly gestures toward the paradigmatic place of Christian martyrs in church history, and thereby aligns itself with Irenaeus's counterreading of Lot's wife. The testimonial acts of the martyrs are apt figures of a discourse that closes the distance between singularity and universality, while also defining the flash point at which historical, chronological time bursts into an eschatological time zone punctuated by a messianic urgency. The instance of martyrological testimony also marks the juncture at which Derrida's meditation broaches concerns registered in the Augsburg paintings. The case I want to make here is that the *Painted Life* of Mary Ward sustains the "testimonial condition" of which Derrida writes, and that it does so with a figural discretion that captures the peculiar historicity of the surviving remnant of Ward's community, for whom the series was presumably composed in the last decades of the seventeenth century.

We need to recall that the first viewers of the *Painted Life* were very much aware that Ward's aspirations had been deleted from the rubrics of ecclesiastical history, and that the community's prospects for rehabilitation were slim. The *Painted Life* responds to these facts by mobilizing the visionary component to Ward's apostolate. Although no tableau directly depicts the events of 1631, the historical reality and binding political force of the papal bull are neither disowned nor ignored. Instead, they are recalibrated according to the testimonial force and scope of Ward's visionary experience.

Panel 38 in the series is especially suggestive (fig. 8). The devotional scene, depicting Ward's orthodox commitment to Marian devotion together with the practice of the rosary, provides the setting for a polemical divine communication and consolation. "God," the text reads, makes "known to her that [the] prosperity, progress and security [of her institute] did not depend upon wealth . . . and the favour of princes, but [only] . . . on 'Him from whom proceed all strength . . . and protection.'" Anyone acquainted

Figure 8. *Painted Life*, panel 38. Published by permission of Congregatio Jesu Augsburg, Germany. Photo: Studio Tanner, Nesselwang.

with the course of Ward's career would have known that princes (at least Continental ones) were not her problem. In sum, the painting should be taken as a tactful reminiscence of where the real problem lay. The text indicates that the vision occurred on the "feast of Saint-Peter-in-Chains 1625."[65] This is not the date of Urban's bull, of course, but it does mark the beginning of the apparent end of Ward's project. The schools that Ward founded in Rome were shut down in 1625. The notation of the feast day is a pretty clear marker of the papal authority that would ultimately globally suppress the institute. So too is the object that figures prominently in the pile that signifies "junk" in the foreground (fig. 9). The florid headgear looks like a papal tiara to me. With such a visual cue virtually italicized, it would not be surprising to discover a papal bull in the vicinity as well.

If testimony conveys the "imminence of what has always already taken place," panel 38 in the *Painted Life* corroborates the point. The stark black bar dividing Ward's devotional scene from the pile of discarded emblems of ecclesial and political authority discloses the hidden burden and promise of this condition, which is to recollect a past that "has never been present."[66] This single compositional detail discloses the central testimonial act in the *Painted Life* at large, which is to present the historical erasure of the community as phantasmatic symptom of its imminent justification.

A further element from the visual grammar of the argument underscores the point. I am looking at red chairs. Red chairs in the *Painted Life* testify to the vexing asymmetry between two competing claims of discursive au-

Figure 9. *Painted Life*, panel 38, detail. Published by permission of Congregatio Jesu Augsburg, Germany. Photo: Studio Tanner, Nesselwang.

thority in the matter of the institute: Ward's word and the papacy's word. I say "asymmetry" because Ward's ambition was clearly more problematic than that of the pontiffs she dealt with. Ultimately, Urban VIII had simply to say yes or no. There was no fundamental discrepancy between spiritual and apostolic or political domains in the pope's judgment. Ward, on the other hand, had to say both yes and no, at the same time, positioned as she was between her visionary convictions and her steadfast allegiance to the Apostolic See. After 1631, her community had no option but to take up residence in the discrepancy between yes and no, and between historical and eschatological time: the time of *figura*.

Part of this story is conveyed in the first painting in the series, which depicts the first word Ward was said to have uttered as a child, the messianic name of "Jesus" (plate 4). The toddler stands next to a red chair, with the word *Jesus* filling the space in between. It's a charming domestic miracle: baby's first word—in this case the transition from *infans* to Jesuitress-to-be. The presence of the chair reinforces the ordinariness of the event. The child is gaining entrance into the symbolic domain of language, but still needs the support of a chair to move about. Considered in context, however, as the inaugural event in the *Painted Life*, the visual nexus of speaking child, numinous divine name, chair, and the chair's vivid red color—the color of cardinals and the blood of martyr-witnesses—carries a more pointed argument. We are invited to dwell on a virtual nonevent and on the complicated stakes to be considered in giving testimony to the *eventfulness* of a nonevent.

What is not happening in the painting can be thought of as the reverberation of a visual pun: Ward is not speaking "from the chair," ex cathedra. The phrase, of course, had not yet assumed its place in the dogmatic description of the pontiff's discretionary power to speak with supreme and infallible apostolic authority. This would not be formalized until the First Vatican Council, in 1870. But the phrase was already being used instrumentally in Counter-Reformation discussions of the scope of papal prerogatives.[67] In any event, neither Ward nor her community needed the dogmatic formulation to appreciate the binding force of the pontiff's apostolic authority as expressed through the actions of the *Propaganda Fide* or the promulgation of papal bulls. The argument in the painting, however, is not unilateral. The visual nexus represents both Ward's prescient deference to ecclesiastical authority, and the charisma of her voice as unmediated channel of messianic truth. More precisely, the tableau represents the noncoincidence of ecclesial and messianic truth, and the divergence is no more than a filament between chair and hand.[68]

Other paintings more squarely address the practical effects and visionary prompting of Ward's discursive agency. The second panel depicts Ward's refusal of a marriage proposal, one of several arranged by her parents. Seated decorously in a red chair, she is *in cathedra*, so to speak, just saying no (plate 5). Panel 22 depicts the informal constitution of Ward's first community in 1609. Several young English "ladies of noble birth," all seated in red chairs, are "won over," the marginal text reads, by "Mary's edifying life and persuasive words" and cross over "with her to Saint-Omer, to serve God in the religious state under Mary's direction." The depicted society of red chairs testifies to the foundational impact of Ward's "persuasive words" (plate 6). Panel 34, on the other hand, presents the conspicuous absence of the red chair. Commemorating one of Ward's several mystical experiences, the painting shows the usual furniture of Ward's intimate space: private devotional altar, four-poster bed, walls cast in shadow, geometrically patterned floor. Instead of the chair, typically situated between altar and bed, we see Ward's luminous vision of Christ (fig. 10). We also see the effect of the substitution. In a sacred autopsy Ward's heart is exposed, revealing the incised figure—*tupos*—of Christ in miniature.

Figure 10. *Painted Life*, panel 34. Published by permission of Congregatio Jesu Augsburg, Germany. Photo: Studio Tanner, Nesselwang.

Other panels confirm the code promoted by these samples. When Ward is seated in the red chair, she is making things happen, moving proactively toward the fulfillment of her apostolic vision. Conversely, when the chair is empty (or occupied by someone else), Mary's submissive or passive position is emphasized. When the chair is displaced, as in panel 34, we witness the theoretical and theological ground of Ward's apostolic program, its investment in the Christic paradoxes of the Incarnation and the Passion, to the point of dissolving logical distinctions between passive and active. The radiant focal point of the tableau—the replica of Christ's image incised in Ward's heart—envisions a space for legitimate ecclesial enterprise unseen by the papal magisterium.[69]

The most provocative instance of the red chair occurs in panel 24 (plate 7). The painting depicts the second of three mystical visions that Ward's writings define as decisive stages in her understanding of the course her apostolic mission should take. The second vision (in 1611) arguably posed the greatest testimonial challenge, for it touched on the pivotal question of which exemplar Ward would follow in devising the rule for her institute. In two letters, written nearly a decade after the vision, Ward recalled the terms of the divine instruction "without adding or altering one syllable": A voice not heard "but intellectually understood" said, "Take the same of the Society [of Jesus]."[70] The challenge Ward's descendants faced was to hold in mind several equally compelling truths about the instruction: that the terms were divinely inspired, unambiguous, preposterous, and also principally responsible for Ward's eventual collision course with the Apostolic See.

Panel 24 renders the required negotiation. The caption makes no mention of the Jesuit order, noting simply that Ward "received quite plainly by an interior voice in what way she was to organize her Institute." But the red chairs are eloquent. On the right-hand side we see Ward recovering from an illness and taking instruction from a confessor or spiritual adviser, who is seated in a red chair.[71] The caption says nothing about this conversation, but from what is known about the dismay with which Ward's "Jesuitical" intentions were generally met by her Jesuit advisers, the priest is likely not saying, "Follow your interior voice."[72] More likely, the authority of the red chair is invoked to recall the opposition of the ecclesiastical hierarchy to Ward's Jesuitical program. In any case, the tableau's most arresting detail is not the occupied chair, but the empty one. This chair takes up the space typically occupied by a window in the *Painted Life*. Like many of the windows in the series, the chair lies on a devotional axis between Ward and sacred image, italicizing the visionary component to

Ward's devotional practice. It also adds something that a window, in this painting, could not.

The empty red chair is the figure of the double truth that would remain in force for centuries. Empty, the chair figures the absence of the papal seal of approval, which kept the community outside the canonical history of religious orders—stranded between Sodom and Zoar, in Lot's wife's place. Empty, the chair figures the lingering presence of another body of knowledge, the memory of Ward's visionary conviction and the "divine Truth" that authorized it. Here, again, is Lot's wife's place, as remembered by Irenaeus, but largely forgotten by the orthodoxy he helped found. In sum, the red chair is not so much an iconographic surrogate for the salt pillar as a witness to the intuition lodged in the figure's recesses: the mutating character of the distinction between the ecclesial community's perceived and real borders.

No wonder that by the end of the seventeenth century the legend of Ward's particular interest in this painting had taken its place in the community's collective memory. One of the community's first archivists, Mary Cramlington, recorded word of Ward's having commissioned this very painting (date unknown); shortly after the publication of the papal bull, she gave specific orders that the painting be placed in keeping, urging her companions to remember that current "times are different from what they have been and will be."[73] Even if apocryphal, the story is as true as the red chair's double truth.

In view of the institute's twentieth-century rehabilitation, Mary Ward seems to have had the last word. Or has she? Here it pays to recall the uneven career of a nurturing condition for the modern advancement of Ward's vision: the legislated reforms of Vatican II have enjoyed only mitigated success in orienting the direction of global Catholicism in the late twentieth and early twenty-first centuries. Consider in this context the status of Ward's case for beatification. In 1983 John Paul II declared his intention to "beatify her in his pontificate," and, given his documented efficiency in advancing candidates, interested parties would have had every reason to expect breaking news before the turn of the millennium.[74] With an irony that surely would not have been lost on Ward, the case is still pending in the Congregation of Rites.[75]

It cannot be said that the secular world should be waiting breathlessly for signs of progress on this score, especially when the more legibly consequential goal of securing Ward's place in the canon of English women's writings is now virtually assured. But the conjecture is not idle, because it holds in reserve another speculation that warrants attention. We need only pause to consider how the political impact of the pontiff's views of the marriage between theology and ecumenism, between *veritas* and *historia*, extends far beyond parochial or denominational demarcations of the contemporary *ecclesia* in the global community. Although Benedict XVI was known to have been a former advocate of *ressourcement* theology, in part because of its declared investment in mining patristic reservoirs of thought, it is far from clear whether the current magisterium will be susceptible to the radical intuition housed in Irenaeus's writings and reclaimed in Ward's apostolic career. Such a prospect, if realized, would impose recognition of the intimacy between the *ecclesia*'s living face and the turning, mutating figure of Lot's wife, the figure that both embodies and interrogates the limits of hospitality toward the outsider.

Mary Ward surely belongs in the canon of early modern women's writing. Just as surely, the testimonial condition advanced by the reversals and contretemps of her career opens a productive breach in canonicity and periodization's territorial instincts—the engines of cultural tradition and apostolic authority alike. Through this breach, the archived data of Ward's enterprise may be said to enter into the continuing ethical and theological provocation of what Irenaeus saw in the Sodom story, and this, I have been arguing, deserves critical recognition. The silent, patient witnesses to Ward's legacy are the anonymous hands that invented a pictorial lexicon and grammar for expressing the strange but vital figural kinship between pillar of salt and red chair in the *Painted Life*.

CHAPTER 4

Avant-Garde Lot's Wife: Natalia Goncharova's *Salt Pillars* and the Rebirth of Hospitality

Every end in history necessarily contains a new beginning; this beginning is the promise, the only "message" which the end can ever produce. Beginning, before it becomes a historical event, is the supreme capacity of man; politically, it is identical with man's freedom. Initium ut esset homo creatus est—"that a beginning be made, man was created," said Augustine. This beginning is guaranteed by each new birth; it is indeed every man.

—HANNAH ARENDT, *The Origins of Totalitarianism*[1]

Out of the crush of sculptural masses and planar angles, bruised thunderheads enshroud the sky. Shards of flame plummet toward the bleached walls of the distant city and the arid expanse of desert, their diagonal chute jarring against the vertical thrust of pale, monumental figures (plate 8). The allusive title—*Salt Pillars* (*Solianye stolpe*)—gives the painting passport into the Sodom archive, even as it also introduces a counting error into the representational scheme with not one, but four pillars (and five subjects: observe the two conjoined figures in the first pillar). The aberration, far from violating an essential feature of the biblical *fabula*, declares the painting's investment in exploring the limits of what counts as a Sodom text.

The supernumerary element makes palpable the implicit link in the biblical narrative between the sudden mutation of Lot's wife (Gen. 19:26), and the earlier bargaining scene between Abraham and God (Gen. 18:17–33). Remember the sorites paradox in ancient Greek logic: if you remove grains of corn from a heap, one by one, when does the heap cease to be a heap?[2] In the Genesis text, the shifting numerical quotient is charged with ethical and political significance. How many exceptions to Sodom's scandalous ethos must be found in order to recognize the mixed and uncountable character of the community, and to suspend the established criterion for deciding Sodom's place in the ultimate taxonomy (life/death)? As we have seen, the Sodom narrative's discursive orchestration nuances the question, suggesting the secret affinity between two turns: the fatal eleventh-hour turn of Lot's wife, and the discursive turn whereby Abraham stalls the momentum of God's juridical fiat by interrogating the fatal logic undergirding it. As we have also seen, this element resurfaces in the developing archive of tactics for remarking the place of Lot's wife in Sodomscape. Natalia Goncharova's *Salt Pillars* significantly expands the range of the biblical figure's provocation by imagining Lot's wife as the fault line in a modernist interrogation of art's ethical possibility and eventual political aptitude.

June 17, 1914; Galerie Paul Guillaume

In Paris, the inaugural exhibition at the Galerie Paul Guillaume features the first European retrospective of two rising stars from Russia, Natalia Goncharova (1881–1962) and her mentor and companion Mikhail Larionov (1881–1964). *Salt Pillars*, composed by Goncharova in 1908 or 1909, is not included, but the work's constellation of aesthetic tactics, amply represented elsewhere in the exhibition, draws attention in the contemporary notices published by Guillaume Apollinaire, indefatigable champion of modern art and the exhibition's informal sponsor.[3] Three weeks before the opening, Apollinaire gives advance notice in *Paris-Journal* of the spectrum of innovative art movements on display. Identifying Goncharova as "the leader of the Russian futurist school" and Larionov as "the leader and inventor of the rayonnist school," he calls attention to the eclectic ensemble of Goncharova's works: "According to those who have seen them, these works are a mélange of Matisse, Picasso, Picabia, Gleizes, Metzinger, Kandinsky, fauves of every kind, cubists of every tendency, and futurists of every nationality."[4] Shortly before the exhibition closes, Apollinaire provides readers of *Les Soirées de Paris* with an appreciative and telling aperçu of Goncharova's eclecticism:

> Natalia Goncharova has boldly accepted the influence of the great
> French painters, or those painting in France, who, for the last twenty
> years, have alone maintained the noblest tradition of art. This sublime
> contact with the true Occidental tradition inspired the great Russian
> artist to seek out the secrets of the rich Oriental tradition that appeared
> to have found definitive form in the folk art of the Russian Empire.

The very sizable *oeuvre* of this prolific artist thus stands as a glorification of the infinitely subtle and infinitely true artistic objectives that succeeded impressionism in France, thanks to Cézanne. Her work is also a revelation of the marvelous decorative freedom that has never ceased to guide Oriental painters amid their sumptuous treasure of forms and colors.

Natalia Goncharova, then, commands an aesthetic in which the great and intellectually satisfying truths of today's scientific art are combined with the appealing subtleties of Oriental art. To this, Mme. Goncharova has added, first the modern harshness contributed by Marinetti's metallic futurism and, second, the refined light of rayonnism, which is the purest and newest expression of contemporary Russian culture. . . . This art is in accord with the newest and most daring experiments undertaken by French artists. . . .

These experiments show that a universal art is being created, an art in which painting, sculpture, poetry, music, and even science in all its manifold aspects will be combined. . . . The names of the various schools have no importance other than to designate this or that group of painters and poets. But they all share a desire to transform our vision of the world and to arrive, at last, at an understanding of the universe.[5]

By 1914, the creative ferment of modernist and avant-garde artistic practice had yielded a heterogeneous constellation of experimental techniques and material resources. This is what Apollinaire's mention of "today's scientific art" embraces. The seeming ascendancy of a supersessionist ethos is also evident—thus Apollinaire's promotion of the "infinitely true artistic objectives" enabled by Cézanne's break with impressionism. But a more suggestive instinct shapes his endorsement of what the proliferating schools have in common. The ensemble exhibits the "desire to transform our vision of the world." At stake are the means through which the mimetic faculty and mission of art are to be interrogated and reconfigured, rather than left behind. The abstraction and geometrization of space found in Cézanne and variously pursued in the schools Apollinaire names—from fauvism to cubism, rayonnism, and futurism—accomplish their conceptual and aesthetic ends not by annulling but by defamiliarizing and rethinking the relation between painted image and reality, figure and ground. Elsewhere Apollinaire describes cubism, for example, as "the art of painting new structures out of elements borrowed not from the reality of sight, but from the reality of insight."[6] As Mark C. Taylor puts it, "[t]he movement from Cézanne to Braque to Picasso marks the transition from a phenomenology of perception to a phenomenology of conception."[7]

A passage from an album Goncharova kept (ca. 1911) indicates the affinity of her aesthetic enterprise with Apollinaire's capsule statement on cubism:

> Do drawings of things, the landscape, people just as they appear at a given moment in your imagination; fear nothing, no deformity of any kind, no fabrication, no fantasy. Try out various styles and methods, emphasizing first one part, then another, now movement, now the very position of the object itself in space and its relationship to others. Change them according to your imagination and instinct, urge yourself to do it precisely that way or in accordance with the idea that you have worked out consciously in your own mind.[8]

While it was clear by 1914 that Goncharova's enterprise, as indicated by the "various styles and methods" on display in the Paris retrospective, followed a radically different trajectory from that of Pablo Picasso or Georges Braque, there is no mistaking the shared drive toward the emancipatory rezoning of what may be said to count as figural realism. Goncharova's specific debt to Picasso's cubist innovation, however, is less clear. The difficulty arises from a tangle of contributing factors: the uneven scope of contact between modernist movements in Moscow and Paris; the nonlinear character of her creative activity, which complicates assessment of her works' chronological sequence; and her written equivocations about the nature of her relation to Picasso and cubist innovations.[9]

Her equivocal stance is worth pausing over, because the terms guiding her divergent narratives of influence convey her desire to sustain a negotiated position between two worlds, a position that Apollinaire's text recognizes but also coarsens in the mention of her work's "sublime contact" between the "true Occidental" and "rich Oriental" traditions. Apollinaire's assessment is partly accurate, to the degree that it registers the complicated calculus of margin and center informing prerevolutionary Russia's self-identity as a cultural crossroads with its own colonizing ambitions. But the pitch of the narrative, as it rises toward the visionary invocation of an impending "universal art," sounds a discordant note. The heralded universality oscillates between two conflicting poles of attraction: a genuinely cosmopolitan eclecticism on the one hand, and on the other a sublation of difference to be achieved precisely through "sublime contact" with French modernism.

In the short run, the discordance was tempered by events that neither Apollinaire nor Goncharova could have predicted. Apollinaire's advance notice acknowledges the principal reason for Goncharova's presence in Paris in 1914: "[T]he Russians have made a real success of Mme. Goncharova; they have not been niggardly in their commissions. She was, in fact, asked to do the scenery for Rimsky-Korsakov's *Le Coq d'Or*, which will be given by the Ballets Russes this season. Russian futurism will thus be given all the honors at the Opera House."[10] The sensation caused by Goncharova's sets and costumes for *Le Coq d'Or* led to a long and successful professional relationship with impresario Sergei Diaghilev.[11] The cachet earned by *Le Coq d'Or*, however, did not seal her reputation as the exemplar of Russian futurism, with its blend of mechanistic and neoprimitivist forms.[12] As Jane Sharp points out, Goncharova's designs for *Le Coq d'Or* and the productions that followed cultivated European viewers' taste for the exotic by presenting "spectacular displays of color and simplified form" that drew on Russia's Byzantine and folk heritage—the success of which "forever marked Goncharova as a Russian artist rather than a transnational avant-garde artist of the time"[13] (plate 9).

Other, more dramatic lines of force on the geopolitical map—World War I and the cascade of revolutions in 1917—further impeded both Goncharova's range of movement and public perception of the eclecticism she brought to Russian modernism's vanguard. By 1919, Goncharova and Larionov had become permanent expatriates in Paris, and for Goncharova the move to the nominal center of avant-garde experimentalism proved a contributing factor in the developing misrecognition and marginalization of her place on Apollinaire's map of "universal art." Her reputation as a set designer for Diaghilev became something of a screen memory, effectively muting the nuanced and unsettling character of Goncharova's aesthetic hybridity.

The muting is already underway in Apollinaire's paratactic distribution of the Occidental and Oriental traits on display in the Paris retrospective. Jane Sharp's groundbreaking monograph on Goncharova's prerevolutionary ambitions and achievements indicates that the artist's reception in contemporary Russia tended toward the obverse—notoriety pitted with controversy and scandal.[14] One source of her notoriety lay in the uncertain apprehension of her work's "pattern of assimilation and disavowal," which variously expressed "her dual status as cultural emissary (mastering various contemporary Western styles) and as colonial subject whose primary goal is to oppose the cultural hegemony of the West."[15]

Perhaps not surprisingly, Goncharova's notoriety, both as an avant-garde artist and a woman artist, generated acclaim as well as controversy. The "anti-artist" and "suffragist of Russian painting" was also an unmitigated "overnight sensation."[16] Between 1913 and 1914, the writer Ilia Zdanevich harnessed the apparent unruliness of Goncharova's aesthetic signature by nominating her oeuvre as a prime exponent of the avant-garde drive toward what he called *vsechestvo* ("everythingism").[17] On Sharp's account, the theory of *vsechestvo* historicized Goncharova's art practice in a novel way: "Just as in Goncharova's art various transpositions of style and technique relax the boundaries that have fixed culture, ethnicity, class, and gender, so too history is created through interactions and judgments made here and now. History, like art, should be appreciated for its contingency upon real events, which, Zdanevich explains, are experienced as chaotic sequence . . . not as a story with a predetermined outcome" (258). Tellingly, Zdanevich's view of modernist historicity, as embodied in Goncharova's work and career, emphasized a "peripatetic homelessness that captured the real conditions of avant-garde practice"—conditions that would include Goncharova's own emigration to Paris and the phosphorescence of *vsechestvo* in Russian modernism.[18]

With its hybrid syntax of neoprimitivist and avant-garde elements, *Salt Pillars* presents early evidence of the heterogeneity and bracing aesthetics of homelessness that would later fall into the orbit of *vsechestvo*. However, if *Salt Pillars* announces the disorienting ethos of *vsechestvo*, the painting also harbors a certain singularity. According to Sharp, "the dramatic landscape in *Salt Pillars* makes this work unique in Goncharova's oeuvre: it is a narrative composition."[19] Sharp is right, though the piece's specific choreography invites a slightly altered gauge. The "dramatic landscape" more than incarnates "narrative composition," because the painted world presents as an unresolved encounter between narrative and non-narrative form.

To be more precise, the composition stages a scenographic mutation through which the foregrounded mass of volumetric planes seems at once to emerge from and withdraw into the representational code for cataclysm. There are, then, two interrelated but not identical dramas in the painting: the citational turn to the foundational Sodom narrative housed in Genesis 19, and the torsion produced by the contrasting vectors of movement between different symbolic registers and aesthetic techniques. This assemblage of dramatic energies constitutes what I want to call the painting's sodomitic kernel—its way of reactivating the figural provocation of Lot's wife in order to reflect critically on the limits and mutable potential of the Sodom narrative's signifying scope and force.

Goncharova's Turn to the East

In chapter 1, I discussed how the illuminated page from Augustine's *City of God* marshals the resources of sculptural *contrapposto* to configure Lot's wife as the amenable site of prudential deliberation (*phronesis*). With the entourage of the hybrid aesthetic called *vsechestvo*, the cantilevered torque to Goncharova's *Salt Pillars* reinvents *contrapposto* and enlarges its field of ethical reflection and disturbance. To see how this is so, we must consider the peculiar fittingness of Goncharova's turn to the archive of Scythian artifacts in *Salt Pillars*. In 1912, Goncharova made the case for the *kamennye baby* as a source of inspiration for Russia's developing modernist aesthetic. Their utility was both distinct from and parallel to that of the African masks that had inspired Picasso: "Cubism is a good thing, although it is not entirely new, especially in Russia. The Scythians, in blessed remembrance, made their stone statuettes [*kamennye baby*] in this style. . . . These are sculptural works, but in France, too, Gothic and Negro sculptural representations served as a point of departure for cubism in painting. In the past decade, in France, Picasso is the foremost talented artist working in a cubist manner. In Russia, it is your humble servant."[20] By 1913, Goncharova's turn to the East (*vostokofil'stvo*) acquired a more polemical cast. The desire to differentiate European influences from those associated with territories annexed by Imperial Russia (including regions associated with ancient Scythia, e.g., Ukraine and Crimea) lent the stone statuettes a particular atavistic potency as decayed signs of an archaic origin from which both "Occidental" and "Oriental" cultures devolved, but to which the Eastern inflection, as incarnated in Russia, remained closer in spirit.

Contemporary ethnographic and archaeological opinion was in fact divided over the *kamennye baby*'s historical and ethnic provenance. The artifacts were variously attributed to prehistoric Scythian votive or funerary practices, the Mongol empire's medieval westward expansion, or early modern Central Europe's eastward extensions of female oracle or goddess of the dead *Zlata baba*'s ritual veneration. Not even the represented gender was assured, since the word *baba* (woman) was thought to derive from the Turkic *balbal*, the gender-neutral word for "statue." Goncharova's interest in the statuettes was likely enhanced by the unfathomed, and possibly unfathomable, mystery of their origin and ritual function.[21]

Decades after the composition of *Salt Pillars*, Goncharova returned to the topic of the *kamennye baby* in an interview: "Russian art is unlike any other. Archaeologists have been doing excavations. They found statues buried in the steppes, next to skeletons, dating from a remote time, very remote. These tiny creatures were placed there to stand guard over the dead."[22] By dwelling on the figures' apparent funerary function, Goncharova points up the value of ritual practices and sacralized objects in securing collective memory's resilience over time.

To flesh out the tactical significance of Goncharova's fascination with the muted, hieratic scene unearthed in the steppes, we need to recall Maurice Halbwachs's description of the contingencies informing collective memory's seeming resilience. Halbwachs argued that "[t]he rite may be the most stable element of religion, since it is largely based on material operations which are constantly reproduced and which are assured uniformity in time and in space by rituals and the priestly body."[23] Halbwachs also recognized that such stability was founded on an illusion, to the degree that the perception of stability derived from a multipronged "self-conscious effort on the part of memorialists to stay or at least to disguise the processes by which traditions slowly evolve."[24]

The processual and dialectical cadence of collective memory, as Halbwachs describes it, also includes an anticipatory parsing of the paradox Derrida ascribes to testimony—the double helix of singularity and exemplarity. "Any testimony," Halbwachs argues, "would seem to require the contradictory requisites that the witness leave the group to observe the facts as they happen, and that he reenter the group to report these same facts. In succession (and almost at the same moment), he must undo and then reaffirm his identity as member of the community."[25] By replacing succession with near simultaneity, this description of the testimonial drama—the event that, for Halbwachs, constitutes one of collective memory's founding gestures—broaches witnessing's uncanny temporality. Let us recall Derrida's insistence on the temporal vertigo conveyed by Blanchot's rendering of what testimony holds in its sights: "the imminence of what has always already taken place." As Derrida puts it, "this is an *unbelievable* tense."[26]

Here is how Sharp, without identifying it as such, apprehends the testimonial gesture in *Salt Pillars*. The painter's facture, "inflecting the surface of the canvas with shardlike facets," recreates the rugosity of the blasted landscape out of which rise the totemic figures.[27] The inscrutable collectivity that takes shape in the painting, however, complicates Sharp's astute observation of the communicative potency of Goncharova's painterly technique. Undoubtedly, the "affirmation of painted surface as material suggests that for Goncharova pictorial representation is coextensive with, and thus can shape, lived experience."[28] That being so, the specific nature of the hybrid figures, composites of salt pillar and stone woman, testifies to the constitutive role of collective remembrances in the tissue of "lived experience"—and of the susceptibility of both to anamnesiac vertigo. The painting, in other words, not only stages an encounter between a modernist aesthetic (precubist forms) and conventional traits of representational mimesis (the fusion of landscape and decodable narrative), it also presents the encounter as a drama of hospitable accommodation, in which divergent tributaries of collective remembrance converge, without coalescing into a unified or coherent story.

The sign of this unfinished and restive event is Lot's wife, refigured in Goncharova's landscape as a virtual necropolis of memory places—mnemonic aids whose relation to their respective contents has been disfigured, subjected to interference by competing reservoirs of information. The "monument to an unbelieving soul," as dogmatically rendered in the apocryphal book of Wisdom (10:6–7), is here. But it is not alone. It shares company with vestigial monuments whose provenance, precise commemorative function, and testimonial purpose are shrouded in mystery, runic rather than propositional.

The Genesis text itself, let us recall, introduces a grain of speculative ambiguity into the sense to be made of the fatal metamorphosis of Lot's wife. The structural link to Abraham's concern for Sodom's inhabitants complicates the contravening suggestion of the complicity of the backward glance in Sodom's anti-covenantal ethos, its pandemic of inhospitality. Goncharova's conception enlarges the tacit import of the Genesis text's narrative design by imagining Lot's wife as figure of *radical hospitality*, host to the paradox inherent to the "testimonial condition"—the intertwining of the singular and the exemplary—and host, as well, to the related aporias, the "interminable, uncrossable thresholds," as Derrida calls them, that constitute the lineaments of hospitality.[29]

Sodom Transit through the Philosophical Archive

My wager here is that the play of abstracted and representational forms in Goncharova's compositional design produces a stalling effect that gives material, if nonverbal, substance to the unsaid intimacy between Lot's wife and the question of hospitality, as it finds expression in late modern philosophical reflection on the Sodom archive. What I ask you to keep in mind in what follows is the critical suggestiveness of the discursive rhythm of encroachment and withdrawal that stands in for the explicit mention of the biblical figure. It is precisely because of this feature, I argue, that the figure of Lot's wife—no longer a figure, strictly speaking, but rather the figure's suspenseful proximity—harbors an intimacy with both hospitality's promise and risk, at the edge of propositional meaning. It is this very edge, I am arguing, that Goncharova's experimental design incarnates in *Salt Pillars*.

For Derrida, hospitality names an impossible hybrid of two mandates: "*the* law of absolute, unconditional, hyperbolical hospitality" and "all the laws (in the plural) of hospitality, namely, the conditions, the norms, the rights and the duties that are imposed on hosts and hostesses, on the men or women who give a welcome as well as the men or women who receive it."[30] The ethical problem arises from an "obsidional situation," a state of siege or capture in which hospitality's hybridity cannot be neutralized or disowned: "We will always be threatened by this dilemma between, on the one hand, unconditional hospitality that dispenses with the law, duty, or even politics, and, on the other, hospitality circumscribed by law and duty. One of them can always corrupt the other, and this capacity for perversion remains irreducible. It *must* remain so."[31] Derrida is well aware of the biblical archive of juridical and narrative reflection on this problem, so it is perhaps no coincidence that his principal proof text in *Of Hospitality* comes from the Sodom story. He focuses on the episode in which Lot tries to avert the Sodomites' rape of the two guests in his home by offering to substitute his two virgin daughters (Gen. 19:1–11). The scene echoes the encounter that introduces the Sodom narrative proper: Abraham's hospitality toward the visitors, God and his messengers, who approach his tent at the oaks of Mamre (Gen. 18:1–16). This, Derrida points out, is "the great founding scene of Abrahamesque hospitality."[32] All the more reason for us to recall the dissymmetry between the symbolic economies informing the hospitality that transpires in the two dwellings, Mamre and Sodom.

Abraham's gifts of food, drink, and shelter at Mamre appear to confirm the intimacy between the covenantal relation and the ethics of *Sittlichkeit*, though the compliant nexus established at Mamre later subverts in the *akedah*, the binding of Isaac (Gen. 22:1–24). The *akedah* famously prompts Søren Kierkegaard's critique of *Sittlichkeit* ethics together with the nesting of counterarguments that follow in its wake—notably, Levinas's contestation of the apparent "teleological suspension of the ethical" that issues from Abraham's double bind, as well as Derrida's parsings of the discord between Kierkegaard and Levinas. A crucial nuance for our purposes is

Derrida's eventual focus on the concord between the two thinkers, which occurs over the course of his inspection of hospitality as the organizing figure of Levinas's writings on ethics, politics, and religion.

The relevant text in this regard—Derrida's commemorative homage to Levinas, *Adieu to Emmanuel Levinas*—mentions neither the *akedah* nor the Sodom narrative. Yet its way of voicing Levinas's intuition of the antimony at the heart of hospitality indirectly gestures toward Levinas's own tactical interest in the Sodom narrative. In *Adieu*, Derrida observes how Levinas's thought falls under the "general structure" of hospitality. "[D]iscourse, justice, ethical uprightness have to do first of all with *welcoming*," and as such observe the ambiguous "*shibboleth* of the threshold [*seuil*]" afforded Levinas by the chance circumstance of the French tongue's particular choreography of homonyms, through which the "language of the *hôte*, of the host, and language as *hôte*, as guest" converge and also touch upon the "extremely significant play between *recollection* [*recueillement*] and *welcome* [*accueil*]."[33] In this domain, the welcoming gesture is harnessed to the risk of the Abrahamic double bind. In Derrida's suggestive formulation, "possible hospitality to the worst is necessary so that good hospitality can have a chance, the chance of letting the other come, the *yes* of the other no less than the *yes* to the other."[34]

It is worth noting the uneven reach of Derrida's argument here. The just cited passage both honors the harrowing implication of Levinasian "welcoming" and remembers something of what Kierkegaard calls the "ordeal" and "temptation" to which Abraham's silence in the *akedah* gives witness, but Derrida's interrogation of the "tenable threshold separating pervertibility from perversion" also passes over the full import of Levinas's specific recollections of the disparate Abrahamic narratives.[35] Notably, as he attempts to redraw the boundary of ethics in Kierkegaard's reading of the *akedah*, Levinas remembers the intercessory Abraham:

> [W]hy does Kierkegaard never speak of the dialogue in which Abraham
> intercedes for Sodom and Gomorrah on behalf of the just who may
> be present there [*à cause de justes qui peut-être s'y trouvent*]? Here, in
> Abraham, the precondition of any possible triumph of life over death
> is formulated. Death is powerless over the finite life that receives a
> meaning from an infinite responsibility for the other, from a diacony
> [*diaconie*—servitude] constituting the subjectivity of the subject, which
> is totally a tension toward the other. It is here, in ethics, that there is
> an appeal to the uniqueness of the subject, and a bestowal [*donation*] of
> meaning to life, despite death.[36]

Levinas's turn to the Sodom narrative is doubly provocative. First, it demonstrates the extent to which Abraham's career confirms that ethical subjectivity entails "an infinite responsibility for the other" (as opposed to
the "exhibitionistic, immodest subjectivity" Levinas detects in the sublime
isolation of Kierkegaard's knight of faith).[37] Second, it marks a threshold in
Levinas's own response to Kierkegaard, insofar as it serves as preamble to
Levinas's guarded appreciation of Kierkegaard's "philosophical novelty":
"the idea that the transcendence of the transcendent truth resides in its extreme humility," which "allows us to glimpse a truth that is not a disclosure
[*dé-voilement*]" but instead "an ever-recurring inner rending of doubt" that
"puts an end to the game of disclosure, in which immanence always wins
out over transcendence."[38] As Levinas puts it, "given that transcendental
truth can manifest itself authentically only as persecuted . . . one may wonder whether the *incognito* should not be the very mode of revelation—and
whether the truth that has been said should not also appear as something
about which nothing has been said."[39]

The factor of the *incognito* trains the eye toward the unthought element, the dark matter, in Levinas's handling of Abraham's suspenseful
dialog with God. Here *Sodom itself* becomes the site of what Levinas later
calls the "new situation" driven home by the "permanent rending" of persecuted truth. Levinas's text recasts Sodom as something other than the
place destined for the "annihilating flame." The name *Sodom* morphs into
the exemplary ethical conundrum to which both Kierkegaard and Levinas
attest with different accents, and which Derrida resumes in the expression,
at once tautology and "radical heterology": *Tout autre est tout autre* ("Every
other [one] is every [bit] other").[40] If Abraham's words and actions may be
said to introduce this vertiginous thought, Lot's wife's sudden capture in
the middle distance voicelessly and arrestingly *embodies* it, even though the
latter disclosure is kept at arm's length in the otherwise close inspections
by Kierkegaard, Levinas, and Derrida.

This collective indifference regarding Lot's wife can partly be explained
by using Ockham's razor: keep it simple. Under this rule, the provocation
of Lot's wife's sudden bolt from the preserve of the happy few, unsurprisingly, does not and cannot rival Abraham's heart-stopping adventure. While
it might seem frivolous, a more nuanced explanation comes from applying
the Goldilocks porridge principle. The Sodom story supplies just the right
amount of discursive detail to establish not only Abraham but also Lot
and Lot's daughters as protagonists or narrative actants exemplifying the
intimacy between ethical deliberation and the aporias of hospitality in the

covenantal drama. With Lot's wife, there is at once too much and too little to digest. On the one hand, she meets a spectacular and exorbitant fate that is hard to fold into the presiding representational codes for catastrophe in the Genesis text. On the other hand, she is a cipher, bereft of the kind of narrative exposition, however rudimentary, that would guarantee her legibility as a protagonist, like her kin, caught in the coils of ethical conflict. The single biblical verse that marks her emergence as a site of thought or decision or agency shows no more than the performance of the forbidden act followed by the sudden mutation—that is, by the narrative's launch into an alien register for depicting historical events and consequences.

In other words, the verse harbors a discrepancy between the *memorable* visibility of Lot's wife's place in the Sodom narrative, and the abortive condition imposed on the *tellability* of her story by the pivotal event's extreme narrative compression. It is thus both peculiar and fitting that the place of Lot's wife, the mute witness, in the postbiblical philosophical archive on Sodom should appear mainly under refraction: captured, but not named in the perfectly congealed, yet bottomlessly referential redundancy that supplies Derrida's mantra for thinking on the Abrahamic crisis—*tout autre est tout autre*.

The Time of the Threshold

Our detour through the philosophical archive on hospitality has taken us some distance from Goncharova's encounter with Lot's wife. The distance traveled, however, also takes us back to our point of departure. We are now in a better position to appreciate how Goncharova's unusual depiction of Lot's wife constitutes an incognito, yet vital member of that kinship among modernity's revisionist and visionary thinkers of the "obsidional situation" in which the question of hospitality repeatedly returns to the "*shibboleth* of the threshold."

Goncharova uses novel means to italicize this vertiginous feature. She introduces the cloning fantasy of multiplying pillars. This device, a clear distortion of the biblical proof-text, produces a tonal ambiguity with the slightly comic tease of unstoppable replication. The consequent staging of a bewildering confusion of model and copy foregrounds the experimental nature of the assembled elements in Goncharova's design: the Scythian allusion, the precubist vocabulary, the tensed play of abstraction and storied representation, and the ambiguous orientalizing turn (*vostokofil'stvo*).[41] Among these elements, Goncharova's recessive yet legible handling of retributive justice—the exegetical tradition's explanatory scheme for the mutation—is worth pausing over. In *Salt Pillars*, this feature presents a type of conceptual rather than purely visual anamorphosis, marking an important watershed in what could be called the second-order mutation of Lot's wife. The painting presents itself as host to the proliferation of modernity's diverse reappraisals of Lot's wife's provocative power.

One particular feature of Goncharova's painting predicts the conceptual rift, related to the operative force of time, that will be put to various use in subsequent renderings of Lot's wife's aborted flight from Sodom. The biblical fabula's retributive scheme exploits an economic order of time—events occur in a chronological sequence of units (segments or points). Such a schema views time as the neutral horizon on which relations between cause and effect, potentiality and actuality, and promise and fulfillment are normalized and given predictive force. However, a different conception of time also informs the fabula, as well as the Abraham cycle at large, and it takes unusual shape in *Salt Pillars*. This feature is not the opposite of chronological time—it is not the apocalyptic *eschaton* or the notion of atemporal eternity. Rather, it is saturated time: *kairos*, the time of opportunity.

Kairotic time is not simply subjective time either, but rather time put at the subject's disposal. To borrow Giorgio Agamben's captivating phrase, "*kairos* is nothing more than seized *chronos*."[42] The précis summarizes the word's instrumental appearances in the therapeutic vocabulary of Hippocratic medical discourse and, more famously, in the Pauline archive of terms for redemptive, messianic time—typological prefiguration, recapitulation, fulfillment (*plērōma*), and presence (*Parousia*). All of these terms feed into the inflection kairos adds to *chronos*, as suggested by Agamben's explication of the critical difference: "Whereas our representation of chronological time, as the time *in which* we are, separates us from ourselves and transforms us into impotent spectators of ourselves—spectators who look at the time that flies without any time left, continually missing themselves—messianic time, an operational time in which we take hold of and achieve our representations of time, is the time *that* we ourselves are, and for this very reason, is the only real time, the only time we have."[43] The operational endowment of kairos is precisely not "supplementary time," but rather a way of dwelling with time, of interrupting and accomplishing it. In this regard, as Agamben points out, kairos informs the "small-scale model for messianic time" found in the symbolic charisma of Sabbath, as understood in rabbinic and patristic traditions: "Saturday—messianic time—is not another day, homogeneous to others; rather, it is that innermost disjointedness within time through which one may—by a hairsbreadth—grasp time and accomplish it."[44] Sabbath observance, in other words, ritually localizes what kairos makes available, potentially, at any moment, which is the literal sense of *Parousia* ("to be next to") as the capture of the very disjointedness of the "now."[45]

Kairos is the time of decision through which the aporias of hospitality issue their claims. To extend Derrida's terms, kairos is what navigates and gives operative force to the paradoxical mutuality of waiting and surprise, which enables hospitality's peculiar condition of vigilance: "to let oneself be swept by the coming of the wholly other, the absolutely unforeseeable [*inanticipable*] stranger, the uninvited visitor, the unexpected visitation beyond welcoming apparatuses.[46] In the Sodom narrative, this very condition materializes in the unannounced conversion of Lot's wife into the pillar of salt, the figural concretion of hospitality's restive vigilance. In the dominant exegetical treatment of the flight from Sodom, of course, vigilance is primarily apotropaic, narrowed to mean warning of an anticipated threat, but not issued from a stance of confusing proximity to the condition of the exiled woman. The early modern sermon literature mentioned earlier drives home the point. Vigilance is for us, not for her; and vigilance is all that keeps us from becoming her.

Goncharova's *Salt Pillars* reopens access to the kairotic thrust and aporias of hospitality through its playful errancy from the biblical fabula. Quite simply, the painting shows too many pillars. Multiple outcomes, multiplying senses of the past. But there is more. The column on the far left—the inaugural pillar in the series—introduces a temporal torque not replicated elsewhere in the painting (fig. 11). Here, the hybridity that arranges the painting's elements on an East/West axis—and that also imposes a certain distance from the dogmatic topicality of the biblical referent—takes a further turn by producing an image combining traits of maternity, parurition, and eventfulness in the company of mourning. It would not be out of court to observe the rudimentary traits of a Pietà in this figure.

Crucially, the pillar's unusual composite form serves as a memory place of one of the highly charged terms of the covenantal promise: offspring. Moreover, to judge from the Abrahamic cycle's recurring cues, the offspring directly correlate with the aporias of hospitality. Recall, for example, Sarah's laughter at word of the impossible conception; or Abraham's silence as he climbs Mount Moriah with Isaac in tow; or Lot's daughters' anxious reflections on the means of survival in the face of extinction. These elements, so many figures of the "absolutely unforeseeable stranger," sound the passage of kairos in the indicated times of gestation and parurition. The ensemble produces the *ostinato* of messianic time, subliminal

Figure 11. Natalia Goncharova, *Salt Pillars*, detail. Image © 2015 Artists Rights Society (ARS), New York/ADAGP, Paris.

and pervasive, in the Sodom narrative. Of all the innovative features that *Salt Pillars* brings to the Sodom archive, perhaps the most surprising is the gesture that begins the multiple iterations of Lot's wife with a composite maternal-parturitional figure and monumentalized memory of embodied messianic time. This is the time of onset.

Goncharova's unprecedented addition to the iconography of Lot's wife exemplifies the eclecticism of her aesthetic practice, though this detail does not appear to have generated much interest in her critical reception. Nevertheless, it indicates her work's kairotic and messianic undertow, both generally and in the specific painterly environment of *Salt Pillars*. Following a period of vociferous disparagement, contemporary artist Alexandre Benois voiced his newfound appreciation of Goncharova's enterprise by endorsing what he saw as her work's "messianic preview of the impending battle with 'philistinism' and 'American deviltry' associated with developed capitalism in Russia."[47] Benois appears to have domesticated the eccentricity of Goncharova's vocabulary by aligning it with the standard avant-gardist promotion of art's transformative capacity. The nationalistic utopianism animating Benois's judgment, however, may not have squared with Goncharova's critical attitude toward the homogenizing instinct she found in Russian Academicism's prevailing protocols and Russian identity's statist canons.

Benois's likely misprision of what was at stake in Goncharova's disorienting "everythingism" speaks to messianic thought's tendency to settle into a "determinate characterization and specific configuration"—a dogmatic Messianism—whose truth is won by sacrificing messianic thought's genuinely critical-utopian character. John D. Caputo's assertion of the essential distinction between Messianism and the messianic is relevant here. Unlike the punctual temporality of Messianism (where the integrity of the decisive event, or its anticipated return, depends ultimately on indefinite deferral), the messianic is founded on the "absolute structure of the promise."[48] The "structural future" held open by the messianic marks what Caputo calls "the absolutely undeconstructible" exemption to the tangible claims made on the present by memory and anticipation. Such an exemption shears off from "stable horizons of expectation, transgressing the possible and conceivable" precisely by exposing the present (or, more exactly, the substantialist mythos of historical time) to the stranger dwelling in its midst—that is, to the unforeseeable opening, here and now, to hospitality's regime.[49] In essence, the messianic is what prevents kairos, the time of decision, from congealing into dogmatic or routinized knowledge.

Plate 1. *Lot's Wife*, 1989. Anselm Kiefer (German, 1945–). Oil paint, ash, stucco, chalk, linseed oil, polymer emulsion, salt and applied elements (e.g., copper heating coil), on canvas, attached to lead foil, on plywood panels; framed: 350.00 × 410.00 cm (137 ¾ × 161 ⅜ inches). The Cleveland Museum of Art, Leonard C. Hanna, Jr. Fund 1990.8. Image © Anselm Kiefer.

Plate 2. Flight from Sodom. Detail of Illuminated miniature. Maître François (fl. 1462–80). Augustine, *La Cité de Dieu*. Bibliothèque nationale, RC–C–05149, Ms. français 18–19, Manuscrits occidentaux, f. 111. Courtesy of Bibliothèque nationale de France.

Plate 3. December. Calendar miniature from the *Très Riches Heures du Duc de Berry*. Limbourg Brothers (fl. 1399–1416). Ms. 65, f. 12v., Musée Condé, Chantilly, France. Photo: René-Gabriel Ojéda. © RMN–Grand Palais / Art Resource, NY.

Plate 4. *Painted Life*, panel 1. Published by permission of Congregatio Jesu Augsburg, Germany. Photo: Studio Tanner, Nesselwang.

Plate 5. *Painted Life*, panel 2. Published by permission of Congregatio Jesu Augsburg, Germany. Photo: Studio Tanner, Nesselwang.

Plate 6. *Painted Life*, panel 22. Published by permission of Congregatio Jesu Augsburg, Germany. Photo: Studio Tanner, Nesselwang.

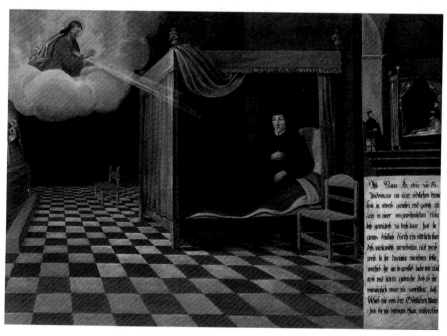

Plate 7. *Painted Life*, panel 24. Published by permission of Congregatio Jesu Augsburg, Germany. Photo: Studio Tanner, Nesselwang.

Plate 8. *Solianye stolpe* (Salt Pillars), 1909. Natalia Goncharova (1881–1962). State Tretiakov Gallery, Moscow, A. K. Larionova–Tomilina Bequest. Image © 2015 Artists Rights Society (ARS), New York / ADAGP, Paris.

Plate 9. *Le Coq d'Or*. Scene design for a city square, 1937. Natalia Goncharova (1881–1962). Natalia Sergeevna Goncharova Designs for *Le Coq d'Or* (MS Thr 422). Harvard Theatre College, Houghton Library. Image © 2015 Artists Rights Society (ARS), New York / ADAGP, Paris.

Plate 10. Dead Sea Works Ltd., Israel, 2007. Detail of murals. Photo courtesy of Jay H. Geller.

Goncharova's contemporary fascination with the rich tradition of Orthodox religious iconography (in the years 1909–11) helps illumine the unusual nature of the messianic argument in *Salt Pillars*.[50] This tradition's appeal was widespread in the avant-garde community. As John E. Bowlt suggests, it is no accident that Kazimir Malevich's famous *Black Square on a White Background* (1913), one of the exemplars of geometric abstraction produced in the first generation of Russian modernism, was described by the artist as "the true, real conception of eternity."[51] The claim had visceral impact in the exhibition "0.10" in Petrograd (1915–16), for the painting literally reoccupied the area reserved for the icon in the Orthodox liturgy, the upper corner of the room (*krasnyi ugol*).[52]

The secular and avant-garde community's mining of the aesthetic and devotional canons for Byzantine Orthodox art sparked controversy, however, and Goncharova's involvement was found particularly offensive. For starters, it was unprecedented for a woman artist to undertake and exhibit major works treating religious subjects. The further aggravation of the seeming irreverence of her approach provoked the ire of critics and censors.[53] Shortly after her 1914 retrospective exhibition opened in St. Petersburg, the religious-themed works on display were declared blasphemous by the Spiritual-Censorship Committee of the Holy Synod and removed by the police.

Goncharova's supporters argued that the assertions of "premeditated deformation of holy persons" in the banned paintings were based on a misunderstanding of the artist's secular intentions.[54] Such a distinction, however, did not address the heart of the problem. For one thing, the institutional hierarchies of both church and Academy had already established that the conventions of nineteenth-century academic realism were to be maintained as the canonical means of translating Byzantine iconography into national and popular art forms. Goncharova's modernist vocabulary flew in the face of this directive. The noted hybridity of her aesthetic practice proved especially challenging. Consider, for example, the compositional tactics at work in one of Goncharova's most accomplished Marian works, *Coronation of the Virgin*, which was composed shortly after *Salt Pillars* (fig. 12).

The painting stages the subject of the Coronation as a virtual crossroads of diverse traditions: painterly elements drawn from El Greco and Velázquez blend with techniques of copying found in Russian broadsheets and icons. The painting perfectly illustrates how Goncharova's "mixing of traditions denied the viewer the reassurance of any single art historical

Figure 12. Natalia Goncharova, *Religious Composition: Coronation of the Virgin*, 1910, detail. Oil on canvas. State Tretiakov Gallery, Moscow, A. K. Larionova-Tomilina Bequest. Image © 2015 Artists Rights Society (ARS), New York/ADAGP, Paris.

context."[55] As Sharp suggests, the resulting mongrelization of art-historical lineage appeared to contaminate analogous notions of unified national identity and destiny by exposing them to a dialogic ethos, in which the relation between originality and derivation, prototype and copy, could be seen as "mutually defining."[56] The disorienting character of Goncharova's avant-garde experimentalism also secured the artwork as a vocative act that solicited the viewer into the role of "responsive cocreator," not simply of aesthetic experience as such, but also of the transformative potency that such experience could impart to other spheres of human activity.[57]

Indeed, it is precisely this intuition of world-constituting possibility that was at issue in the diverse expressions of messianic expectation found in avant-garde manifestos and contemporary art criticism, as attested by Apollinaire's expansive rhetoric and Benois's more overtly nationalistic instinct. To judge from remarks she made ca.1913/14, Goncharova appears to have grasped a discriminating nuance that contemporary voicings of messianic expectation did not always express: "My way is with the Victorians [*viktoriiantsy*] who yearn to create new life, but without expecting a messiah—since I myself bring forth a new form of art and life—in painting this is Rayism, the pure doctrine of painting, and in life it is my bright, unpretentious reception of all that surrounds me, and a specific attitude to all things. That is, having studied the views circulating in society and winnowed through upbringing, I am free."[58] Goncharova's "way" navigates between the particular appeal of messianism, of whatever dogmatic stripe, and the generative ferment associated with the messianic, which is lodged in the unnamed "specific attitude to all things." Goncharova's Marian works could hardly be called exemplars of the "pure doctrine" of the rayonist aesthetic, but they did not need to be. By no accident, the accusations of blasphemy, which were provoked by the paintings' unorthodox admixture of old and new, as well as canonical and popular forms, emphasized the formal property of the offense. The works' evident *bezobraznost*— formlessness, disfigurement—constituted an aesthetic aberration that betrayed a perilous aptitude to induce ontological panic.[59]

Salt Pillars did not attract the lexicon of abuse and scandal to which most of Goncharova's religious-themed works were subjected, perhaps because the particular components of the painting's hybrid aesthetic did not directly touch on the sensitive points of the institutional directives for producing religious art. Notably, the Sodom story was not a canonical topic.[60] Though the charge of "formlessness" may not have been specifically directed at *Salt Pillars*, there is some warranty for applying the notion to this work. We need only remember that forms of historical comprehension, though responsive to the locality of experience, are not reducible to the stuff of the local, if only because the very sense made of the local depends on a constitutive deformation, a passage through figural and virtual dimensions of the real. The trait of "formlessness," as it pertains to *Salt Pillars*, supplies a transit between the local documented controversies in which the charge of *bezobraznost* turned up, and the deep history of critical engagement with the sodomitic exemplar of disfiguration. As we have seen, the sheer range of adaptive response to the legend of Lot's wife cumulatively suggests an extended theater of mutational transference, ranging from Robert Wilkinson's homiletic *horror fusionis* at the moral and political contagion radiating from the "lumpe of salt" to Irenaeus's counternarrative, which deliberately warps the dominant testamental sense of the stranded salt pillar as negative exemplar and refigures it as the testimonial incarnation of the corporate body of Christ, the *ecclesia*.[61]

There is reason to tarry with Irenaeus in particular. Irenaeus's attention to the flight from Sodom passed into virtual oblivion, but his commentary on another biblical scene, Luke's account of the Annunciation, supplied a patristic touchstone for what would become a quasi-canonical voicing of Mary's participatory role in the Incarnational drama. It also supplied a conceptual urtext for the iconographic resources that Goncharova drew upon for her overtly Marian works.[62] Two narrative details in the Annunciation scene captured Irenaeus's interest: the quality of Mary's assent to the disclosure made to her and the nonnormative, indeed unnatural, means through which her body—its virginal state in particular—assumes a posture of welcome to the future, or, more precisely, to the adventful character of kairotic time, the coming-to-be of the messianic. The first detail occasioned Irenaeus's influential account of the typological scheme through which Mary's trusting fidelity to the word she receives serves as redemptive recapitulation of Eve's decisive role in the fall from Eden. The second detail suggested to Irenaeus the mutual implication of regenerative and counterintuitive dimensions of embodiment—the complex tissue of lived lives—to be found in the "new generation" issuing from the Christ-event.[63]

The lush foliage of subsequent thought on these details (from patristic and medieval commentary to important twentieth-century documents like *Lumen Gentium*, the dogmatic constitution of the Catholic Church issued by the Second Vatican Council) cumulatively established Mary's figural significance as type of the Church. Apart from the devotional and pastoral appeal of Mary's fidelity to a divine call, the resilience of the "Virgin Mother

Church" locution depended to a large degree on the charismatic paradox of the simultaneously virginal and generative body. This figure not only lent rhetorical heft to Mary's intercessory role as privileged go-between (*conciliatrix*) between Christ and the Church.[64] It also promoted adherence to the ecclesiological structures and theological principles upheld by the Church (with different accents in Roman and Orthodox dispensations) as unadulterated—that is, virginal—vessels of inspired truth.[65]

The experimentalism on view in Goncharova's Marian works provoked ambivalent critical reception for a host of reasons. Most of these were related, as Sharp's analysis shows, to the low threshold of tolerance in contemporary Russia for Goncharova's way of staging "mutually defining secular and religious cultural experiences."[66] Subsisting within these cultural lines of force, however, is the specifically *figural* provocation issued by Goncharova's inclusion of the Marian topic in her religiously themed oeuvre. The stylistic assemblage in the *Coronation of the Virgin*, for example, both recognizes the ideologically prescriptive encodings of procreative virginity in Marian veneration and converts these into facets of a dynamic gesture of aesthetic ecumenism. Through this double gesture, Goncharova's Marian idiolect reclaims the adventurous spirit, if not the canonical outworking, of Irenaeus's intuition of the Virgin Mother trope as an exemplary figure of hospitality to the advent of the new.[67]

It is *Salt Pillars*, however, that provides the terrain in which to consider the Marian legacy's overlooked sodomitic quotient. Irenaeus's counter-reading of Lot's wife, as we have seen, emphasizes the regenerative and sustaining potency of the "foundation of the faith" suggested by the strange confluence of stability and transitivity in the thing she becomes. The thing in this case is a specific type of event. The standing figure gathers the exemplary co-implication of the gravitas of the memorial monument, the provocative liminality of the threshold marker, the existential trauma of dereliction and persecution, and the symbolic lability of salt.[68] Irenaeus's account of the scene of metamorphosis in Genesis 19 does not introduce explicit Marian allusions into the testimonial function of the pillar of salt. But *Salt Pillars* does. Goncharova's inclusion of the enigmatic scene of parturition unearths a deep memory of the figural potency of Lot's wife as the virtual connective tissue in the Eve/Mary typology.

Just as Goncharova's precubist vocabulary disfigures conventional protocols for representational form, the anonymous figure of parturition invents a way to apprehend the figure of procreative virginity—the Marian body—against the grain of Mariological tradition. Both Roman and Orthodox strands of that tradition mainly tended to press the figure into service as sign of the unadulterated transmission of doctrinal norms or ecclesial orthodoxy, thus issuing the promise of viable passport from the "eschatological tension" of Christological time into institutionally sanctioned prescriptions for the realized ideality of the body of the Church or grace-filled community.[69] *Salt Pillars* remembers the anarchic intimacy of the virginal body and the ascetic aura of the desert.[70] The painting's fractured planes present the confluence of these two imaginary topographies, together as both sentinel and host to an irreducibly kenotic or self-emptying anonymity at the heart of experience.

In its own way, Goncharova's painting initiates the kind of encounter Blanchot describes in the essay on "Prophetic Speech" as the "bare relation with the Outside"—Blanchot's a-theological desert.[71] The painting's glancing gesture of parturition also announces the generative potency that such "bare relation" holds in reserve, just as for Blanchot the desert, even though unmoored from its traditional exegetical appeal as a space of ascetic discipline, remains "that place without place where alone the Covenant can be concluded and to which one must always return as to that moment of nakedness and separation that is at the origin of true existence" (*BtC*, 80).

It is important to remember in this regard that for Blanchot the desert— which is coextensive with the essence of prophetic speech—is neither allegorical nor symbolic. Rather, it consummates the sense of the literal by pushing it beyond its currency in normal usage as designator of empirical information, and emphasizing instead the capacity of the literal to convey the urgency of an irremissible call. Like the unconditional face of hospitality itself in Derrida's account, the nexus of desert and prophetic speech reminds us of an existential ultimacy: "we are always given over to the absolute of a meaning, just as we are given over to the absolute of hunger, of physical suffering, and of our body of need; that there is no refuge against this meaning that everywhere pursues us, precedes us, always there before we are, always present in absence, always speaking in silence" (*BtC*, 85). Perhaps surprisingly, for Blanchot the event of being "given over to the absolute of a meaning" constitutes a primordial and fundamental form of sociality. "Prophetic speech," he writes, "is originally dialogue"—not because it facilitates the exchange and circulation of information, but because it strips away alibis, opening up a space of mutual exposure (*BtC*, 82).

The biblical touchstone that Blanchot selects to illustrate the point comes from the Sodom narrative (Gen. 18:17–33): the "spectacular" moment when God confesses to Abraham his anxiety over the decision to destroy Sodom (*BtC*, 82). What interests Blanchot here is the manner in which the scene of decision, whereby God brings Abraham into his confidence, captures an "essential" trait of dialog by disclosing the shared and porous border between dialogic endings and beginnings (*BtC*, 82). On Blanchot's account, "God, when he speaks, needs to hear his own speech— thus become response—repeated in the man in whom it can only assert itself and who becomes responsible for it" (*BtC*, 83). Indeed, the fraught nature of the ensuing dialog in Genesis 18 indicates Abraham's attunement to the enveloping and restive call to responsibility.

As we observed earlier, however, the settlement that closes Genesis 18 —the mutually agreed upon minimal condition for rescinding the lethal judgment—does not answer once and for all the questions regarding the nature and limits of justice and the bounds of what counts as a righteous act. The extended narrative context reactivates these very questions, notably in the repeated scenes of viewing the catastrophe in Genesis 19: the forbidden gaze of Lot's wife, followed by the sanctioned gaze of Abraham. The latter coupling, in particular, elucidates the full import of Blanchot's reopening of the Sodom archive in order to reflect on how dialog, prophetic speech, and desert converge as sentinels over a shared provocation: "As if all speech that begins began by answering, an answer in which is heard, in order to be led back to silence, the speech of the Outside that does not cease" (*BtC*, 83).

In "Prophetic Speech" Blanchot makes no mention of the paired scenes of silent gazing upon the destroyed community. Yet it is precisely these scenes that give narrative heft to Blanchot's intuition of the dialogic character of "all speech," the very trait that ultimately leads back to the incessant and silent "speech of the Outside." Moreover, the evident dissonance between the two gazing postures, Lot's wife's and Abraham's, reinforces Blanchot's claim that prophetic speech does not issue measurable propositions or dogmatic truths, because the essential force of its agency is dispossessive: "When speech becomes prophetic, it is not the future that is given, it is the present that is taken away, and with it any possibility of a firm, stable, lasting presence" (*BtC*, 80). The jarring and improbable intimacy between the two scenes of silent witness over the doomed cities' smoking ruins in Genesis 19 thus corroborates Blanchot's point that prophetic speech's *interruptive* character provides its power to disclose the disorienting co-implication of beginnings and endings. As he puts it, prophetic speech "is essentially linked to a momentary interruption of history, to history become an instant of impossibility of history, a voice where catastrophe hesitates to turn into salvation, where in the fall already ascension and return begin" (*BtC*, 81).

The messianic undertow to Blanchot's remarks may be traced in part to the text that prompted their occasion. "Prophetic Speech," first published in 1957, is nominally a review of André Neher's *L'essence du prophétisme*. More broadly, however, the essay testifies to Blanchot's developing engagement with Levinas's parsing of the question of ethics in relation to messianic thought.[72] Contextual mappings of the type just described are unquestionably informative, but it is equally important to remember that the core methodological premise governing the sense of what counts as context in such mappings derives from a specific model of forensic history. The forensic model takes as its backdrop the sequential rhythms and topological partitions of chronological time and canons of documented influence and tradition. From such a vantage point, the task of discerning the relation between Goncharova's and Blanchot's respective visions of the messianic folds in Sodomscape must depend on the trick of distant analogy.

If we adopt the inverse stance, however, and treat the messianic question not as an *object* of investigation like any other, but instead as a *tidal orientation* within a roving frame of inquiry—in other words, if we actually inhabit the messianic question—a different picture emerges. It becomes possible to see the messianic aesthetic in Goncharova's *Salt Pillars* as a proleptic seizure, in a painterly medium, of the very intuition that informs Blanchot's characteristically lyrical yet unnerving descriptions of prophetic speech. *Salt Pillars*, in other words, is the painterly incarnation of "a wandering speech that returns to the original demand of movement by opposing all stillness, all settling, any taking root that would be rest," a wandering that "tells of the impossible future" even as it "also tells of the 'nonetheless' that breaks the impossible and restores time" (*BtC*, 81).

From this perspective, the telling difference between Goncharova's and Blanchot's arguments has less to do with the anchorage of their respective historical and cultural locations per se than with the fact that Goncharova's contribution to the Sodom archive enhances and completes Blanchot's perspective avant la lettre. *Salt Pillars* remembers what Blanchot's argument forgets. The painting remembers that it is Lot's wife's recidivist turn to Sodom, together with Abraham's, that makes it possible to see how the essence of messianic kairos, the capture of what Agamben calls the "innermost disjointedness with time through which one may—by a hairsbreadth—grasp time and accomplish it," inheres in the Sodom archive.[73]

Messianic Natality

The inaugural monument in Goncharova's painted necropolis—the Pietà-like configuration of mourning and maternity—carries an additional provocation. It invites us to imagine how the folds of messianic inquiry bring Blanchot's ruminations into close proximity with those of a contemporary thinker not commonly associated with Blanchot's philosophical and literary enterprise: Hannah Arendt. The epigraph to this chapter identifies one of the touchstones of Arendt's political ontology: the link between natality ("the new beginning inherent in birth") and action ("the capacity of beginning something anew") as the twin engines of human freedom.[74] This touchstone, famously indebted to Augustine's theological anthropology of the human's endowment with the "supreme capacity" to create beginnings, is also famously vexed, in part because of the ambiguity of the concept of natality as it appears over the course of Arendt's writing career, from the dissertation on Augustine to the final, unfinished tome, *The Life of the Mind*.[75]

On the one hand, natality, considered as "the fact of birth," appears strangely mortgaged to a kind of biological determinism (i.e., you never forget completely where you come from and the debt is never paid in full).[76] On the other, the concept also appears to stand for the material embodiment of the radical newness indicated by the etymological root of action (from the Greek *archein*) and associated, on Arendt's account, with political engagement's ferment: "beginning something new on our own initiative."[77] It is no surprise that there is a robust tradition in Arendt scholarship of puzzling over the seeming post hoc character of the link between the two faces of natality. The notion seems to beg the question of when the mental faculties of thinking and willing—the preconditions for what Arendt calls the "second birth" of "word and deed" through which "we insert ourselves into the human world"—become species-specific and endowed with ethical and political significance (and risk).[78]

I will return to the ambiguous character of natality in chapter 7. For the moment, I want to note that natality is perhaps best thought of as a *figure* rather than a concept.[79] Here it pays to recall figura's buried association with *typos*, the word that signifies the onset of a wound or blow. Figura is a synapse, at once gap and means of transit and communication. The figural cast to Arendt's shifting matrix of thought on natality appears most clearly in Arendt's turn to an allegorical parable by Franz Kafka, in the introduction to *Between Past and Future* (1961). The parable reads like a limit case of a tellable story. A man on a road finds himself caught in battle between two antagonists, one who "presses him from behind" and another who "blocks the road ahead."[80] Instead of leading to a clear outcome, the conflict produces a suspended moment of reflection in which the unnamed protagonist ("he") imagines himself being taken out of the fray and afforded the occasion to survey and judge the respective claims of the forces in conflict. For Arendt, it is precisely the "utter simplicity and brevity" of the story that conveys the iridescence of the "activity of thinking, of settling down in the gap between past and future" (*BPF*, 10, 13).

Without putting it in so many words, Arendt's allegoresis of Kafka's "thought-landscape" presents the activity of thinking as a *figural drama* unfolding between two divergent sightings of the habitat of thought. On the one hand, the parable rehearses "the old dream which Western metaphysics has dreamed from Parmenides to Hegel of a timeless, spaceless, suprasensuous realm as the proper region of thought," while, on the other, it detects the tacit affinity between the imagined "region of the spirit" and the essential eccentricity of "the path paved by thinking" (*BPF*, 13). The eccentric character of the "path" turns on the paradoxical fact that it is at once always and never the same. As Arendt puts it, the itinerary opened up by thinking is a "small track of non-time" that subsists "in the very heart of time," and "unlike the world and the culture into which we are born," it "can only be indicated, but cannot be inherited and handed down from the past; each new generation, indeed every new human being as he inserts himself between an infinite past and an infinite future, must discover and ploddingly pave it anew" (*BPF*, 13). The eccentricity of thinking, on Arendt's reading of Kafka's parable, thus turns on its repeated negotiation of the interval between remembrance and anticipation. Indeed, it is this very feature— thinking's affinity with in-betweenness (rather than with knowledge or information or rule-driven cognition)—that brings into focus, for Arendt, the otherwise improbable link between Kafka's modernist text and Augustine's foundational intuition of natality as the nexus of human being and what Arendt calls the "abyss of freedom":[81] "Only because man is inserted into time and only to the extent that he stands his ground does the flow of indifferent time break up into tenses; it is this insertion—the beginning of a beginning, to put it into Augustinian terms—which splits up the time continuum into forces which then, because they are focused on the particle or body that gives them their direction, begin fighting with each other and acting upon man in the way Kafka describes" (*BPF*, 10). Arendt's thought experiment performs what it describes, by interrupting the canon of historical periods and inventing a meaningful connection between the disparate cultural locations and writing scenes of Kafka and Augustine.

What is meaningful here is the disclosed symmetry between the formal inconclusiveness of Kafka's parable and the conceptual ambiguity that inheres in natality, with its tangled associations of indebtedness, gratitude, immemorial rootedness, radical contingency, and the sense of redemptive possibility that comes with the fracture and risk wrought by new beginnings. What Arendt sees in the "bare, 'abstract'" character of Kafka's parable could be said as easily of Arendt's unfinished and at times contradictory treatment of the various attunements of natality (*BPF*, 9).[82] Kafka's fiction and Arendt's mode of philosophical argument are analogously imbued with a figural cast that discloses their shared trait as fissured artifacts of thought—not closed systems, in other words, but renewable invitations to enter into the event they give witness to. Arendt calls this event the "most vital and the liveliest part of reality"—the adventure of thinking itself.

Arendt herself, it must be said, would not likely turn to a painting—even an avant-garde work like *Salt Pillars*—to examine how the legacy of natality informs aesthetic contributions (like Kafka's story) to the "experience in thinking" (*BPF*, 13). To judge from her reflections on the relation between art, ethical bearing, and political action in *The Human Condition*, Arendt's conception of the typology of art form observes in the main the Aristotelian hierarchy of mimetic production. On this account, all of the basic art forms—painting, sculpture, music, poetry, drama—may be understood as reifications of thought, or "thought things."[83] The mixed character of such artifacts expresses the highest achievement of *homo faber*: the fabrication of material illusions of permanence, artifacts testifying to the "sheer durability of the world of things" and thus issuing a "premonition of immortality." Not the "immortality of the soul or of life," however, but "something immortal achieved by human hands." That is, to the degree that it is recognized as an artwork, the artifact expresses the transcendence achieved by the activity of thought, making it "tangibly present, to shine and to be seen, to sound and to be heard, to speak and to be read."[84] Following Aristotle's argument in the *Poetics*, Arendt maintains that such revealing power is not equally distributed, however, across the spectrum of aesthetic forms. The "specific revelatory quality of action and speech"—core constituents of ethical choice and political decision—is most fully realized in the species of *mimēsis* found in the drama of theatrical performance, which alone is equipped to render with compelling transparency "the living flux of acting and speaking."[85]

Yet Arendt's description of her own practice in writing the essays gathered in the volume *Between Past and Future* presents a suppler and less prescriptive methodological perspective on the question of how aesthetic artifacts outside the scene of drama may both represent and participate in what Arendt calls a "thought-event."[86] Following the cue found in Kafka's fiction, Arendt intends the pieces to be read as "exercises" governed by one aim only: "to gain experience in *how* to think." As such, they are nonprescriptive; or, as Arendt puts it, "the problem of truth is kept in abeyance; the concern is solely with how to move in this gap [between past and future]—the only region perhaps where truth eventually will appear." Crucially, "truth" here falls outside the orbit of doctrinal terms or utopian projections. Instead, it is correlated with thinking's fidelity to the interplay and conflict between "remembrance and anticipation" and its dual allegiance to "criticism as well as experiment." On this score, the formal and material properties of specific genres of human expression matter less for the ways in which they may be resolved into a hierarchical typology than for what they hold in common despite their different modalities of fabrication. They share the capacity to induce force fields in which thought's world-making and world-questioning activity begins.

Here it pays to observe a neighboring drift of thought in *The Human Condition*. Notwithstanding the formalist and Aristotelian inflection to her aesthetic premises, Arendt cedes space to an eschatologically tinged Pauline idiom in addressing the peculiar, quasi-animate character of the reification that pertains to artworks:

> In the case of art works, reification is more than mere transformation; it is transfiguration, a veritable metamorphosis in which it is as though the course of nature which wills that all fire burns to ashes is reverted and even dust can burst into flames. . . . [T]his reification and materialization, without which no thought can become a tangible thing, is always paid for . . . the price is life itself: it is always the 'dead letter' in which the 'living spirit' must survive, a deadness from which it can be rescued only when the dead letter comes again into contact with a life willing to resurrect it, although this resurrection of the dead shares with all living things that it, too, will die again.[87]

The Pauline source text mobilizes the figural drama of letter and spirit in the service of a theological hermeneutic, which aims at enlarging and reorienting the scriptural legacy of covenantal commitment to include the advent of Christic revelation.[88] Arendt's post-theological appropriation of the Pauline figure brackets the Christic argument, while retaining Paul's intuition of the urgent contingency of messianic now-time, and assigning its interruptive force to the agentive space that develops from the contact between the artwork and its readers, auditors, or spectators.[89]

Arendt's interest in the transfigurative potency that inheres in the "contact" between the artwork and its receivers opens a portal to the aesthetic experimentalism built into Goncharova's creation of a sodomitic "thought-landscape" in *Salt Pillars*. Let us recall the impression of plasticity that informs the work's three-dimensional appearance. We have already noted Jane Sharp's astute account of how Goncharova's technique, by "inflecting the surface of the canvas with shardlike facets," collapses the distance between the finished, inert character of the work and its genesis as a thought-event.[90] As Sharp points out, the textured materiality of the painting "suggests that for Goncharova pictorial representation is coextensive with, and thus can shape, lived experience."[91] Attending to the full scope of the materials brought to bear in the composition—plasticity coupled with the plurality of allusions and representational gestures—allows us to venture a more detailed parsing of what goes into the shape of "lived experience" as conjured in the painting.

Salt Pillars invites its viewers to grasp the sodomitic kernel to lived experience. There is more at stake here than a rehearsed and regulated memory of catastrophe. The painting's provocation resides in the hidden intimacy it discloses between the ostensibly seamless rhythms and habitual behaviors that typically count as the principal mooring of lived experience and the interruptive interval—what Arendt calls the "small non-time-space in the very heart of time"—through which the activity, or, more precisely, the drama of thinking, rediscovers its affinity with the figural suggestiveness of the desert as a "space without place" (*BtC*, 80). Observing Blanchot's intuition, Goncharova's painted desert takes away "any possibility of a firm, stable, lasting presence" (*BtC*, 79). *Salt Pillars* also knows that what Blanchot calls the "experience" of the desert, though it is "without place," is not empty. The painting's austere landscape is populated, quite literally, by testimonials to the twin, quasi-transcendental riddles to thought: the ambiguities of natality and the aporias of hospitality. The testimonials are, of course, the multiple pillars, runic reminders that the interval between "dead letter" and "living spirit" is not the province of the solipsistic thinker, but the task faced by those who recognize the precariousness as well as redemptive possibility found in the condition of being together alone.

CHAPTER 5

Soundings in Sodomscape: Biblical Purity Codes, Spa Clinics, and the Ends of Immunity

When you travel through Judea . . . space unfolds before you
without end . . . and you feel a secret terror, which, far from
crushing your spirits, gives courage and summons creative
insight [*le génie*]. Extraordinary scenes everywhere reveal a land
worked over by miracles. . . . Each name encloses a mystery;
each grotto announces the future; each summit echoes the voice
of a prophet. God himself spoke on its shores: the desiccated
torrents, the fissured rocks, the half-opened graves testify to the
wonder; the desert seems to remain mute with terror, as if it dared
not break its silence since hearing the voice of the Eternal.

—FRANÇOIS-RENÉ DE CHATEAUBRIAND, *Itinéraire de Paris à Jérusalem*[1]

September 12, 2000, Ein Bokek, Israel. I stand defeated at the shores of the Dead Sea.

It is still possible to recapture something of François-René de Chateaubriand's suavely austere reverie overlooking the Dead Sea in the early 1800s, but to do so you have to climb the heights of Masada at dawn (fig. 13).[2] There is a piece of irony in the detour. Not because the sublimity effect so readily encountered in the nineteenth-century archive of Dead Sea expeditions must be deliberately sought out, away from the sprawling industrial and consumerist complex that now dominates the profile of the region, but because discovering the optimal perspective depends, quite literally, on occupying one of the most carefully tended yet controversial *lieux de mémoire* in contemporary Israel.

Famously, Masada is what remains of the catastrophic encounter between occupying Roman forces and the last Jewish stronghold at the end of the first Jewish-Roman War (66–73 CE). More precisely, what remains are three remnants: the archaeological site, which was added to the UNESCO World Heritage List in 2001; Josephus's account of the fall of Masada in *The Jewish War* (78 CE), the sole contemporary written record of the siege;

Figure 13. View of the Dead Sea and Jordanian Hills from Masada. Photo courtesy of Jay H. Geller.

and a second-order historical archive testifying to the broad spectrum of commemorative narratives concerning the mass deaths at Masada.[3] The latter body denotes a species of mnemonic inscription that came into currency in colonial-era Palestine, extending into and including the modern Zionist revival and the emergence of the nation-state of Israel.

As Yael Zerubavel's study of this record suggests, Masada's conversion into a galvanizing symbol of Jewish-Israeli identity is not a straightforward story. The sensitive element is the felt need to stabilize the meaning of the deaths—whether as shameful suicides, tragic martyrdoms, exemplary acts of heroic resistance, or evidence of persecution lifted out of its premodern context and introjected as a " 'Masada complex' that distorts Israelis' perception of their own situation" in the crucible of Jewish-Arab conflict in the Middle East.[4] On Zerubavel's account, "both the activist and the tragic commemorative narratives of Masada coexist in contemporary Israeli culture and are called upon by different groups or in different situations," which is to say that Masada remains a potent yet divisive site of mnemohistorical recuperation in Israeli social and political life.[5] If Masada stands for "the creativity of collective memory within the constraints of available records of the past," not many degrees of separation stand between it and the accumulating reminders of collective memory's explosive plasticity.

None of this was more than a transient impression in mid-September, when I took in the panorama of the Dead Sea from the South Gate of Masada. The circumstance would nonetheless seize up in memory shortly after my return home. I had left the region just days before the Second Intifada and the ensuing spasm of violent response and counterresponse to then Likud leader Ariel Sharon's controversial visit to the Temple Mount in Jerusalem. While Masada had no direct bearing on the events, the association is not desultory. The site prominently figures in the region's generalized atmosphere of vigilance toward the chronic precarity of boundary-drawing measures. The site's alleged proximity to Sodom is also not a trivial geographical detail. To be sure, the case of Masada—in particular, the site's emotive power and provocative specificity—has no precise equivalent in the figural history of Sodom and Lot's wife. There is, after all, no nationalized cathexis to Sodom, nor for that matter is there a supranational equivalent of the kind associated with confessionally bound devotional attachment (and pilgrimage, real or imagined) to sacred sites like Mecca or the Church of the Holy Sepulchre in Jerusalem's Old City. But the very distinction proves a clarifying agent.

Many LGBTIQ communities, even those for whom biblical literacy is patchy at best, recognize that the persistent stigma of queerness in the broader culture finds one of its most potent and historically malleable symbols in the name and evocative sound of Sodom. To my knowledge, however, the modern phenomenon of gay tourism—one of the more robust instances of queer marketing—does not include organized expeditions to the Dead Sea. The region is not among the destinations globally marketed as gay "homelands" or "meccas," such as San Francisco, Sydney, Berlin, Amsterdam, and Tel Aviv.[6] There are pilgrimages to Oscar Wilde's house in Chelsea and his tomb in the Parisian cemetery of Père Lachaise, and to the Stonewall Inn at 53 Christopher Street in New York City; but to Sodom, no. This is so in part because the physical site of Sodom—the material occasion and prop for the operation and furbishing of collective memory, at least as Maurice Halbwachs's thesis would have it—remains a matter of archaeological conjecture. Consider this: both Israel and Jordan lay claim to territory thought to have been occupied by the ancient Cities of the Plain, either on the southwestern or southeastern edge of the Dead Sea. Modern-day tourists to Jordan are invited to view the pillar of salt near the sanctuary of Agios Lot at Deir Ain Abata (another UNESCO World Heritage site), while tourists on the Israeli side of the Dead Sea are

– Salt Lake City

directed to the rival pillar near Ein Bokek, where I stand, some fifteen kilometers from the sanctuary of Agios Lot (see fig. 1 in the preface).[7]

But would archaeological consensus make a difference? Cultural histories of the lived idea of Sodom, as manifested in recorded social practice from antiquity to the present day, remind us why it would not. Put simply, the imagined genealogy of Sodom in the arts and human sciences is a testament not so much to Sodom's aptitude as a site of collective memory as to its mute eloquence as vagabond witness to a missed rendezvous.[8] Communities apt to invest in the idea of Sodom—or, more accurately, to whom the idea of Sodom is given as mythic origin—do not as a rule find in the story of Sodom what biblical scholars and historians of sexuality have long known about the Genesis text's depiction of the city. The unexamined, or discounted, element turns on the *tactical* function of Sodom in the narrative nexus that gives body to the Abrahamic cycle.[9] In this capacity, the transgressive sexuation of Sodom (notably the conflation of homosexual activity and violence) is not so much a prima facie negative exemplar as a narrative symptom of surplus—of unaccommodated meaning and uncharted possibility—in the Abrahamic cycle's wide-ranging interrogation of the scope, and price, of the intertwined community-building values of covenant and hospitality.

Paying attention to the correlation of surplus with the unsaid, the unheralded, and the unthought does not simply add further folds to the legacy of Sodom as an effective paradigm of what Jan Assmann calls "normative inversion."[10] Instead, it reorients and enlarges the sense of what the figural tropism of Sodom might yield, not in opposition to, but within, the normative's expressive lineaments. What if Sodom's enunciated sexual traits were sustained in memory and deposited in history not as quarry to be policed or protected—and in either case construed as a determinate part of individual or group identity—but instead as a contingent provocation for diverse inspections of the minimal—or, better, *sustainable*—conditions for sociality? This is, after all, the basic question lodged in the Sodom narrative. Notably, the question obtains in the disjunctive region between the two faces of Sodom. Names congeal easily into simple semaphores, so let us recall what the Genesis text shows. Sodom is the site that Abraham gazes upon from Mamre, "the great founding scene of Abrahamesque hospitality" as Derrida puts it.[11] Sodom is also the site that meets the backward-turning gaze of Lot's wife in the middle distance between disaster and rescue.

The question I have just posed falls in the middle distance between the two episodes, and this topological detail makes all the difference, because it appreciates the integral role of Lot's wife in the Sodom story. Where the commemorative resources of LGBTIQ communities are concerned, however, the critical force of the question is muted, to the degree that the briefly riveting passage of Lot's wife through the biblical story counts as little more than white noise. Much the same could be said of the figure's place in critical histories of sexuality addressing the queer legacy of Sodom, where emphasis typically falls on the implied scene of homosexual rape (Gen. 19:4–11) and the incest between Lot and his daughters after the catastrophe (Gen. 19:30–38). Yet it is Lot's wife's very inarticulacy in a narrative otherwise busy with urgent calls for decision and action that disrupts the narrative's momentum and draws the neighboring episodes into the "bare relation with the Outside"—Maurice Blanchot's desert.[12] For Blanchot, let us recall, the desert is not an empirical place that you can visit and leave at will. It is an event that overtakes you in the moment of your unguarded attunement to what encroaches upon you, and blocks access to the alibis that would otherwise dilute its force. It is "that place without place where alone the Covenant can be concluded and to which one must always return as to that moment of nakedness and separation that is at the origin of true existence."[13] Silent witness to the foundational yet dislocating principle of covenant, the desert holds in reserve the stirrings of an "exchange of speech from which the surprising justice of reciprocity emerges."[14]

The ruined fortress at Masada makes for a peculiarly fitting place from which to consider the asymptotic drift I have just described. Here I stand, at the *omphalos* of a still-vital mythos, however disputed, of an epochal event in the history of an *ethnos*, a people and a religious tradition, a commemorative site imbued with passionately felt claims staked on a national destiny. Masada shares a question with the biblical profile of Sodom. What are you willing to do, or give up, and how far are you willing to go for the sake of the dwelling—which is both a habitation and a form of living—you feel called to stand for and protect?[15] At Masada, it is hard to escape the question's visceral immediacy. The sovereign perspective Masada affords over the imagined topography of Sodom makes it equally clear that the question does not sound with the same accent where the Sodom story's diffused legacies are concerned. The essence of Sodom, and in particular the enigmatic face given to Sodom by Lot's wife, must be sought *elsewhere*, in the sense that localized determinations of commemorative practice capture neither the conjectural nor material grounding of the conjured place.

As suggested in the preface, the *elsewhere* that adheres to Lot's wife belongs to the mutating syntax and unruly historicity of Sodomscape. Approaching the shores of the Dead Sea from Masada, one discovers what the archive of expeditions to the region rehearses time and again. The sole remnant of the catastrophe, emphatically attested by Josephus in the *Judean Antiquities*, is in fact hard to locate. Sometimes the legendary pillar was believed hidden by the fluctuating level of the sea. This is the explanation recorded in the fourth-century account of the Roman pilgrim Egeria.[16] Sometimes the remnant was found on the northern or eastern shores. For the fifteenth-century German pilgrim Felix Fabri, the pillar's empirical absence provided the occasion for pious viewing—not of the salt pillar but of a more refined spiritual *condimentum*, a Vulgate-inspired "statue" of "white marble" seen "with the eye of steadfast faith."[17] By the nineteenth century, it was regularly identified as one of a number of exposed rocksalt columns with vaguely anthropomorphic features on the eastern escarpment of the prehistoric diapir, or domed rock formation, called Mount Sedom. Near the end of the century (1898), German geologist Max Blanckenhorn merrily conveyed the embarrassment of riches that met the eye trained on finding evidence of the fatal metamorphosis: Mount Sedom offered a "harem of wives."[18] What Blanckenhorn's *bon mot* did not need to spell out is that the anthropomorphic element, then as now, must be taken with a grain of salt, so to speak, since the prevailing candidate at Mount Sedom is around sixty-five feet high. Eye of faith indeed.

Let us recall the lesson of the photographic testimony to the vaguely anthropomorphic object that contemporary tourists are directed to find at Mount Sedom. The more provocative remnant of Lot's wife in the region resides not in the designated salt outcrop, but instead in the region's scattered expressions of the figure's narrative conundrum—the porous interface of motion and stasis. This piecemeal rendering of the legendary topography of Sodom is not locatable on a map. Instead, it is hidden, and on the move, in plain view.

For starters, there is the highway on which I stand. Its progenitor dates from the 1920s, with the establishment of the British Mandate of Palestine and the ensuing decades-long project of building a network of roads and railways throughout the region.[19] The modernized transportation grid is the material hyphen through which the figural legacy of biblical and premodern Sodom—the conceptual tangle of topics concerning hospitality, exile, and the commemorative work of pilgrimage—reappears, transfigured, in the contemporary crush of everyday life in the region. The carefully tended nature reserves and broad spectrum of hotel complexes punctuating the shoreline represent the most thoroughly assimilated avatars of the ur-trope of Sodom and Lot's wife: the precarious guest-host relation.

The sprawl also harbors what may be called the sodomitic calculus involved in the Dead Sea area's appeal as a site of ecotourism. The very notion of ecotourism negotiates, for better or worse, the aporias of hospitality factored as an ecological concern. Friction on this issue arises whenever ecotourism's commercial apparatus offends or bypasses the espoused virtues of respect for biodiversity, equilibrium of local ecosystems, and mitigation of conventional tourism's carbon imprint. Consider, then, the strange concert of the two most aggressively pursued and advertised enterprises in the Dead Sea region, on both Jordanian and Israeli shores: the health spa culture and the mammoth chemical production industry. To different ends, both advance a program of benevolent parasitism of a natural host, exploiting the Dead Sea's mineral resources. In practice, both represent limit cases of that program—de facto interrogations of the calculus for deciding the viable compass of a benevolent guest-host relation.

Just Relax

The spas at Ein Bokek and Ein Gedi issue such an interrogation in a way so obvious as to be imperceptible. They reclaim something of the premodern sense of leisure (*otium*) as the purpose of work and the highest expression of human culture.[20] They do so by regulating time and space for access to that *rarissime* item in modernity's prevailing ethos of instrumentalized consciousness, documented labor hours, and price-indexed work product: the specifically restorative and therapeutic virtue of leisure. As the Italian saying goes, *dolce far niente*.[21] For Aristotle, as for Augustine and Thomist tradition, the virtue was allied to what Heraclitus called "listening to the essence of things," and what medieval thought generally held to be the province of *intellectus*, unmediated and undistracted intuition (as opposed to the sifting operation of *ratio*, logical deliberation).[22] In this capacity, leisure functioned as host to a threshold event by facilitating exposure to the numinous element penetrating and animating the material, mundane envelope of creaturely existence. Indeed, to be human—to be capable of the *vita contemplativa*—was to be intimately involved in that numinous element. The intuitive faculty borne of leisure was, for Aquinas, "non proprie humana, sed superhumana"—an intrinsic eccentricity.[23] The eccentric character of leisure, however, was not entirely on the side of the angels, since the salutary aspect of inactivity or respite was situated in ambiguous proximity to the opposing, and more widespread, sense of *otium*, in both classical and Christian traditions, as the morally and spiritually enervating condition of lethargy. Christian homilists knew this to be the root of the one of the seven deadly sins: sloth or pernicious idleness (*acedia*).[24]

In this story, the anti-covenantal shade of Sodom makes more than one telling appearance. In the Vulgate translation of Ezekiel, Jerome uses the word *otium* in the litany of sodomitic abominations to which Jerusalem has fallen prey (Ezek. 16:49): "Behold, this was the iniquity of thy sister Sodom, pride, fullness of bread, and abundance of idleness was in her and in her daughters, neither did she strengthen the hand of the poor and the needy."[25] In the postbiblical career of Sodom, as we have seen, the ambiguous face of *otium* returns in the divergent treatments of Lot's wife— whether as cautionary tale of the spiritual ambush awaiting both idle and meddling curiosity or as mystical figure of the dilation of eschatological patience through which the ecclesial community remembers its moorings in the desert.

The spa cultures at Ein Bokek and Ein Gedi do not force a choice between the two faces of *otium* because the choice—indeed, the very idea of the need to choose—does not present itself. Simply put, orchestrated leisure in spa mode is designedly secular. Not in the macro-historical sense supposed by secularization arguments, but in the more modest sense of time spent taking care of what is at hand in the immanence, the *thisness*, of a given life-world. This particular mode of sustenance is a multilateral conversion project, through which visitors to the region are placed in an interactive relation with natural elements from the local environment. The spas and clinics are, quite literally, vital zones in the *skin* of the Dead Sea— the material membrane of resources, activities, and transactions that constitute the life of the region and reexpress the region's genotype as Sodomscape, parsing the question of what hospitality can bear.[26]

Sodomscape with Lesions

To grasp the underlying rationale for the extended compass I am attributing to the sense of skin in Sodomscape, we should notice first that the cultivated *otium* found here hosts an array of treatments for psoriasis and other skin disorders. Clinical services include climatotherapy (regulated exposure to sunlight, including narrow-band UVB radiation, combined with bathing in the Dead Sea's mineral-rich waters), pelotherapy (mud pack therapy), and balneotherapy (thermo-mineral baths).[27] On the face of it, the relation between psoriasis and Sodom does not appear very compelling. The disorder bears few if any of the properties likely to trigger recognition of the hallucinatory logic of contagion that lent cachet to HIV disease, for example, as the modern epidemiological incarnation of the stigma of Sodom. Psoriasis has no venereal associations and it is rarely fatal. It is disfiguring, however. This feature, in particular the unpredictable character of the onset, provides passport into the heart of the medico-cultural archive of Sodomscape. In this archive, the biblical "outcry" (*za'aqat*) against virulent inhospitality recedes into the background. In its place, ritualized protocols for regulating the physical appearance of communal integrity become the determining factor.

In biblical antiquity, psoriasis was one of several conditions, designated by the term *ṣāra'at* (צרעת), that presented as irruptions in the normal ecology of the skin, giving the appearance of contaminated or decomposing flesh. The irregular pattern of recurrence and abatement helped identify such instances of skin morbidity as manifestations of a disturbing liminality, the onset of a living death, and therefore ritual uncleanness treated by observing Levitical protocols of ritual purification, including a prescribed sequestration period.[28] The narrative just described constitutes one of the sedimented memories of boundary negotiation harbored by the Dead Sea spa cultures.

To appreciate the drama in the mnemonic background, however, we need to think of what happened to the word *ṣāra'at*, the first lexical witness in the biblical archive to the symptoms of psoriasis. What happened was a deceptively innocuous event, a small matter of translation with decisive consequences. When the Septuagint version of the Torah was compiled in the third century BCE, the koine Greek word *lepra* took the place of the Hebrew *ṣāra'at*. A reasonable translation, for both words generically marked a battery of symptoms, rather than named specific diseases. Two collateral effects issued from this. On the one hand, the target word *lepra* acquired the aura of symbolic defilement associated with the Levitical source word *ṣāra'at*; on the other hand, the principally medical and cutaneous reference of *lepra* helped occlude the suppler application of *ṣāra'at* as a mediating term in the negotiation of two conversant, but not identical, symbolic values in the Levitical purity codes: bodily boundary protection and social boundary protection. Tellingly, the linguistic root of the word *ṣāra'at* signifies, broadly, a sudden striking action, and in the catalogue of Levitical proscriptions *ṣāra'at* applies equally to breaches in human skin, animal hide, clothes, and house walls. The specifically biomedical significance of *ṣāra'at* was thus nested within a much larger, culturally cohesive symbolic correlation of social (and covenantal) risk with unregulated orifices and discharges of several kinds. *Lepra* denotes, more narrowly, scaling skin. In the Hippocratic archive, *lepra* sometimes indicated symptoms correlated with medical contagion, but not reliably with a symbolic expression of moral or religious defilement.[29]

The passage of the word *lepra* into the biblical archive thus gave *lepra* a new career as both agent and recipient of a transculturally labile semantic reach. In this cast, it became the common term for "ritually unclean skin disease" in the Christian New Testament, and so it remained through the various conciliar decisions that produced the biblical canon in the fourth century.[30] *Lepra* gained further currency after Jerome transliterated the word as the equivalent of *ṣāra'at* in the Latin Vulgate. The equivalency was virtually sealed in the vernacular when the word *leprosie* replaced *lepra* in the first translations of the Hebrew Bible and the Christian Testament in the fourteenth and sixteenth centuries. By this time, however, the specifically ritualized character and symbolic grammar of the perceived contagion had already evolved into the permuting ensemble of responses associated with the wide range of "leprous" diseases and disorders in the medieval period. As the expanding field of interdisciplinary work on disease clusters associated with medieval *lepra* has shown, the responses were protean—charitable action, therapeutic regimens, institutionalized segregation, and persecutory tactics—and the responses constellated unevenly across Western Europe.[31]

The consensus among medical and biblical historians, however, is that the mildly infectious disease still commonly known today as leprosy (mycobacterial leprosy, or Hansen's disease) most likely was not a referent of either *ṣāra'at* or *lepra* in the texts that established kinship between the two words. The ancient name for mycobacterial leprosy—*elephas* or *elephantiasis*, later called *elephantiasis graecorum*—was coined by Greek physicians in the third and second centuries BCE, describing the disfiguring lesions associated with the most severe, lepromatous type of leprosy. The word *lepra*, however, was an accommodating host. Its welcoming canopy may well have been used to include what modern diagnostic protocols would recognize as symptoms of the milder, tuberculoid type of leprosy in the broad spectrum of disorders also covered by the word *lepra*—including psoriasis, which fell under the rubric of *psora* (itch) as well as *lepra* in ancient Greek medical writings.[32]

Both Pliny and Galen, among other purveyors of Hellenistic medical knowledge, observed morphological distinctions between *elephantiasis* and *lepra*, but their observations were not systematically aligned with the respective terms. By favoring the accommodating lexical tent of *lepra*, both authorities furthered the word's generic branding, but not the full force of the stigma—that came later, as an ironic consequence of the word's ecumenical adaptability. Not coincidentally, the Hellenistic medical archive also helped open semiotic pathways that eventually led to the exclusive assignment of the word *elephantiasis* to a disease unrelated to leprosy, but presenting symptoms superficially similar to those found in its advanced stages: the parasitic infection lymphatic filariasis, the disease that came to be known, with a subnote of exoticism, as "Barbados leg" in the eighteenth century.[33]

It probably goes without saying that the rhizomic habit of attribution just described represents an obsolete perceptual horizon, superseded by the one that underlies an elementary fact from the modern biomedical perspective. Lymphatic filariasis, Hansen's disease, and psoriasis have nothing in common. From the standpoint of biomedical rationality, our itinerary seems to have led to an outpost both conceptually and historically remote from contemporary Dead Sea spa cultures. But, if one takes into account the shifting and sometimes imperceptible concatenations of language and event that continue to haunt or at least complicate the biomedical perspective, we have actually remained in place, merely pausing to observe subcutaneous layers of what I am calling the *skin* of the Dead Sea. Dispensing with the need for an Archimedean vantage point, this viewing angle considers the multidirectional network of sodomitic memory schemes and *topoi*—transmission routes that both carry and redirect the senses and imagined perimeters of Sodom and the costs to health, social cohesion, and communal identity associated with the name.

Here it pays to recall the semantically silent or neutral suffix to the word *Sodomscape*. The transposed Teutonic marker for the act of shaping or instituting (*-scape*) reminds us of a perhaps obvious but relevant observation. Words, like the cellular mitosis of skin, have variegated life cycles, follow migration routes, and observe tacit protocols of hospitality and segregation through which shifting conjugations of sense and feeling are made and unmade.[34] This shaping element also contributes to the critical potency of the contact, the ambient touch, between the biomedical rationale for the psoriasis management regimens at the Dead Sea spa clinics and the sedimented memory of contagion or dangerous hospitality that inheres in the observed vicinities of Sodom.

Seeing through Otium

By Galen's era, the Dead Sea's mineral resources and the nearby thermal springs were legendary for their therapeutic effects on open wounds and skin lesions.[35] Psoriasis, under cover of the term *lepra* and its cognates, had already begun a liaison with *otium*, but its modern expression at the Dead Sea is to a large degree the product of the gradual decoupling of psoriasis from leprosy. Clinical differentiation of the pathophysiology of psoriasis from that of leprosy was not established until the 1840s. Accordingly, it was not until the mid-nineteenth century that the conjoined cultural histories of psoriasis and leprosy began to drift apart, having been marked for centuries by the shared stigma of spontaneous bodily disfigurement and venereal contamination, as well as the resulting common prospect of segregation into lazar houses and quarantined colonies.[36] Gerhard Armauer Hansen's discovery of the infectious agent of leprosy, *Mycobacterium leprae*, in 1873 introduced a new era in the understanding and treatment of the disease, to the effect that it is now possible to envision effective containment of leprosy if not outright global elimination.[37] Psoriasis, however, remains an altogether more unruly phenomenon. Inarguably, the nineteenth century saw significant advances in the disorder's clinical picture of histopathological features. Twentieth-century developments in molecular and genetic study have led to the current widely held identification of psoriasis as an autoimmune malfunction. Abnormalities in T-cell activity or primary alterations in the lifespan of keratinocytes (the most common type of skin cells) appear to be a trigger, but the exact nature of the underlying mechanism remains elusive.[38] I will return to this point shortly.

The fork in the road here—the splitting of diagnostic genealogies— gives cause to observe how the particular installation of supervised *otium* at the Dead Sea introduces a zone of interference into the figural drama of Sodomscape. This is not to say that the spa clinics present an accomplished design for neutralizing or forgetting the negative stigmas associated with Sodom. Any tourist will likely report that the physical profile of the region pays scant attention to Sodom's scandalous history. There are no *aide-mémoires* prompting such recognition, except for the brief and dutiful mentions of the biblical story found in guide books. Or the isolated road sign. But the term *recognition* is perhaps a misnomer for the type of encounter solicited in Sodomscape. Insofar as recognition presupposes a symmetrical relation between mutually reflecting subjects (and a stable hierarchy of designated subjects and objects), something other than recognition is warranted by the particular assemblage of therapeutic and sybaritic facilities at the Dead Sea. We need to bracket the cognitive machinery of recognition.

Judith Butler persuasively argues for the need to respect the distinction between recognition and apprehension. This is a pertinent nuance.

"'Apprehension' is less precise," Butler claims, "since it can imply marking, registering, acknowledging without full cognition. If it is a form of knowing, it is bound up with sensing and perceiving, but in ways that are not always—or not yet—conceptual forms of knowledge."[39] While "not always" and "not yet" may sound like admissions of a deficit, it is precisely the unsettled reach of apprehension that gives it value. As Butler suggests, apprehension "can become the basis for a critique of norms of recognition" and, more broadly, of prevailing horizons of intelligibility.[40] The critical potency of apprehension is allied to the mutable thresholds of receptivity, curiosity, and the intuitive motility of *intellectus*, all of which find an enabling condition in the very phenomenon harnessed by the spa cultures to a variety of ends: the mode of dwelling called leisure.

Apprehended through the ambient sensorium of leisure, the spa cultures present a way of suspending the stigmas of Sodom not by banishing or ignoring them, but rather by retaining the schema of expulsion on which they depend and redirecting the schema's boundary-protective instinct to the issues at hand: the localized medico-therapeutic regimens for skin disorders. In essence, the problematic anti-covenantal legacy of Sodom persists, but in an altered and virtually unrecognizable form, a *figural* conversion, through the multilateral regimen for restoring the protective sheath of the skin to optimal functionality. This particular mimesis of a virulent legacy seems both innocuous and auratically charged—quick with critical possibility.

If the operation just proposed also seems dependent on a forced analogy—between the mythic depiction of life and death in biblical Sodom and the routines on offer to contemporary visitors to the Dead Sea spa clinics—it pays to remember the long tradition in political thought of understanding the human not as a settled given but as an experiment. To borrow Giorgio Agamben's term, the human is the "anthropological machine" where two kinds of life—*zoe* (biological, creaturely life common to all living beings) and *bios* (the province of political community and action specific to humans)—intermingle and acquire distinct, but negotiable, purviews.[41] The distinction between *zoe* and *bios* is less a line in the sand than a threshold. It is, more precisely, the *interested* (*inter-esse*) and roving expression of the vitality of "the being of the between," to borrow Henk Oosterling's apt phrase.[42] The *cordon sanitaire* implied by such articulation is thus a gesture, not a destiny. And, like Sodom story's pillar of salt, the gesture rises out of a surrounding movement of "dis-position."[43] If Sodom, as I have suggested, is the essence of landscape, then Lot's wife is the dispositive essence of figure—figure's genetic compact with the in-between. The Dead Sea spa clinics are the vital expression of this intuition.

With this in mind, I want to spell out some of the phenomenological implications of *otium*, because it is at this level that we can appreciate the currency of Sodom and its most enigmatic avatar, Lot's wife. *Otium* exposes its transient residents to the prospect of falling outside the conventional rubric of time as unfolding succession of events. The outside of this scheme is not in fact a place so much as an apprehension, in Butler's sense, of the intimacy of being enmeshed in "pure immanence."[44] The phrase "pure immanence" is Gilles Deleuze's way of indicating that the seemingly empty time offered by indefinite life is an *absolute* designation without, however, naming a void.[45] Indeed, Deleuze instead emphasizes the word *absolute* to figure the expansive matrix of "immediate" and depersonalized consciousness, which subsists in the passage from empirical time to the transcendental constitution of time.

This passage entails the very movement ascribed to Lot's wife in the biblical Sodom narrative. The salt pillar memorializes an ephemeral yet decisive act, a looking back that suspends the common-sense disposition of time as a passing of instants in succession and, in its place, encounters what is transcendental about time: its ontological dimension. In the Genesis text, this dimension is suggested by the imperceptible conversion of the woman's backward look, a punctual event, into the indefinite temporality, the *entre-temps* or "meanwhile," of the pillar-statue. The "looking" implied in the conversive action is not an intentional gaze, and neither is it an optical phenomenon per se. Rather, it is a glancing encounter with the fundamental condition from which arises the common-sense notion of time as movement and succession.

It is not hard to see how such intuition might be disorienting when you consider the array of seeming paradoxes that attend the encounter. As Levi R. Bryant puts it, "the past is that which *was never* present, the present is that which *is only ever present*, and the future is that *which will never* arrive."[46] If time here seems devoid of motion and communicative possibility, it is precisely because it lies "behind" recognition, so to speak, as the blind spot that enables the empirical sense of time to function as the default mechanism, the untroubled given, for maintaining the consistency of perceived relations between various categories of identity: subject and object, proximity and distance, figure and ground.

To look into time's ontological dimensions is to apprehend it not as a moving vehicle, taking things from instant to instant, but as the vehicle—in the sense of *medium* or *suspension*—in which movement happens.[47] From this it follows that all three dimensions of time co-insist within the empirical experience of the present, even as they retain their absolute

difference. Their concert means that the work of the present—the empirical construction of passing events and varied intensities of recollection and anticipation—is inherently fissured, which is to say, inherently
in relation—or, better, *ripe for relation*—like the shifting site of a graft.
Because of this virtual dynamic of wounding and ramification, time's lived
experience is exposed, incessantly, to unthought dimensions of the present's purchase, with its passing immediacy, over the past and future.[48]

The dedicated field of *otium* in the Dead Sea spa cultures presents a living image of this type of immersive *entre-temps*. The immersion is not permanent, of course. There is no more than a virtual going through the looking glass, but that is enough to introduce torsion into the empirical sense,
or recognizable shape, of what is at hand. And it is enough to announce the
enfolding rhythm of an unregulated encounter with what is essential to Sodom's figural persistence, which is not the property of any of its empirical
designations. The essential is Sodom's status as a figural architectonics of
hospitality capable of undergoing extreme topological variation.

What the Skin Sees

For a case in point, consider the principal objective of the medico-
therapeutic regimens on offer in the Dead Sea region. The spa clinics attend to the skin's ecology, and specifically to the vital zones of connection
and negotiation between inside and outside elements. Crucially, the skin
treatment protocols focus attention on the aleatory interface between immune and autoimmune responses. In recent years, medico-cultural literature has questioned the solvency of the immunity metaphor from a number
of vantage points, some of which I will summarize shortly.[49] The language
of immunity, however, is not likely to be interred any time soon, since the
reflexive assumptions it harbors—the allure of the privilege of exemption,
the desire for security or sanctuary—occupy critical stations in Sodomscape, not least in the entourage that includes the spa cultures on the edge
of the Dead Sea.

As a new sounding point, then, let us review the rudimentary significance of the immune/autoimmune dyad in standard medical discourse.
While the first term encompasses the mechanisms contributing to the
functional integrity of the organism and its protective perimeters, the second subverts the organism's integrity through a threefold miscalculation in
"immuno-competence" at the biosemiotic level: (1) hypervigilant policing
of the border between "self" and "not self"; (2) precipitous engagement
of defense mechanisms (production of antibodies to destroy perceived an-

tigens); and (3) selective short-circuiting of the rich variance of immune responses to different types of antigens and allergens (the host's misrecognition of benign or compatible or self-generated substances as invasive).[50] Among the various dermatological and rheumatic diseases treated at the Dead Sea clinics, psoriasis presents Sodomscape's essential phylogenetic profile. Consider the disorder's clinical picture: the palette of symptoms, the uncertain pathogenesis, the diversified treatment regimens, which include diplomatic negotiations between hopeful prognosis and anticipation of relapse. Together, these elements identify the disorder as an unstable threshold event in the clinical and therapeutic resources of the still-regnant medical doxa on autoimmune disease.

The threshold includes the "being of the between" that transpires in the quietly defamiliarizing encounter between the psoriasis protocol and its host, the geographic region that harbors the stilled memory of Sodom—Sodom stigmatized as the dangerous neighbor, the enemy within, the apocalyptic incarnation of anti-community. Emancipated, in principle, from this zone by modern medical knowledge, psoriasis nonetheless carries a *white stigma*, a nameless, roving provocation.[51] From the medical standpoint, the provocation is partly associated with the sheer unpredictability of the clinical outcomes of the treatment protocols. The disease progression narratives, in other words, are unruly.

Tellingly, they are unruly in ways that have only transient connections with the progression narratives of HIV disease, where the onslaught of opportunistic infections is more spectacularly associated with Sodom's genocidal subtexts.[52] The subtexts, though invidious, are nonetheless legible, if only because HIV is an infectious disease. As such, it testifies to the solvency of preexisting networks of community and (in theory) it refers to mappable transmission routes. Not so with psoriasis. Its community begins with the disorder's onset. If this event shares features with some types of cancer, for example, psoriasis does not carry equivalent associations of radical danger or terminality. Even so, the uncertain duration and varied severity of psoriatic symptoms—from "nuisance" to disfigurement and disability—pose recurrent psychosocial challenges that may be as disruptive or debilitating as the morphological features of the disorder itself.[53] For the psoriatic subject, the clinical expression of the chronic disorder may prove traumatic precisely because it withholds resolution—whether through cure or decisive prognosis. In this regard, psoriasis is the paradigmatic threshold disorder.

Consider the scaling lesions typical of certain types of psoriasis and commonly identified in clinical studies as an instigator of the dysfunctional affects associated with the disorder. The expression of these internalized stigmas ranges from anxiety, shame, and depression to suicide ideation.[54] Like the tuberculosis sanatoria that became popular in Europe in the late nineteenth century, as well as some of the lazar houses in earlier eras, the psoriasis spas present the prospect of temporary abatement of both psychological and somatic stigmas, and they do so in part by creating an inverted world in which the various presentations of the disorder pass for *ordinary* rather than exceptional bodily states. Considered empirically, this type of mimetic inversion does not escape the self-limiting scope of the promise it affords. What the spas promise, after all, is remission of symptoms and respite from the disease stigma, rather than an altered—and culturally transmissible—orientation toward the condition. A different gauge subsists in the ambient culture of leisure, to which the spa regimens serve as circumstantial host. Because it is unregulated by established protocols of memory and anticipation, the portal afforded by the immersive plane of leisure to the silent operation of the guest-host relation better captures what I mean by the critical provocation, the white stigma, of the psoriasis event.

Imagine what the skin sees. Imagine, in other words, the progression of the disorder as it occurs in the given habitat of skin, which is no other than the "being of the between" silently expressed in the morphology of the skin's surface. The epidermis functions as a complexly partitioned threshold of five interactive layers, ranging from the innermost, the stratum basale, to the outermost, the stratum corneum. As keratinocytes (the basic structural cells of the epidermis) mature and migrate from one layer to another, they become key players in an intercellular drama of hospitality, serving as host to negotiations among the proteins and lipids that enable the skin's resilience and hydration.

For our purposes, two phases of this drama are noteworthy. The first phase is actually unnoticeable, since it concerns nothing other than the equilibrium that produces the appearance of healthy, normal skin.[55] What's worth noting, microscopically, is how the equilibrium is achieved. The stratum corneum is composed of dead cells that shed imperceptibly about every three weeks. In this microecology, the dead are active, cohabiting participants in the life of the skin, because the regular replenishment of this cellular necropolis is what maintains the integrity of the skin and the organism's viability. Psoriasis names what happens when the so-called immune system misrecognizes the cadence just described and compensates for perceived irregularities in the maturation rate by accelerating the cell cycle beyond the sustainable capacity of the stratum corneum.[56] Pursuing a misdirected healing protocol, psoriatic skin erroneously deploys a second growth pattern—regenerative maturation—in emergency response to a phantom wound. Put simply, in psoriasis, the future comes too soon, confounding the ecological balance and communication between living and dead cells. The proliferation of immature keratinocytes at the skin's surface clogs the shedding process, and the *untimely* dead congregate, visibly, in colonies of white scaling cells—plaque lesions.

The drama I have just described is an exemplary instance of the in-between character of Sodomscape. The events are part of a conjugating and differentiating system that resembles only in partial and contingent ways the semiotic regimes that have sought to parse and master its operation. The system falls between the deep memory of symbolic contagion (the Sodom reflex and ancillary matrix of ritual purity codes) and the modern biomedical discourse of immunity, which is governed by the host-invader metaphor, a distant and scientifically naturalized cousin of the cognitive code underwriting the Levitical prescriptions.

To appreciate the scenario's taxonomic peculiarity, consider the status of the dead in the sequence of events. In death, skin cells are neither uncanny interlopers, nor sacred ("set apart") entities. They are vital actants in the organism's ongoing life. The watershed triggering psoriatic response is not the ontological distinction between life and death, but something else—a sequence of timing and counting errors that disrupts the hospitable mutuality of living and dead cells in the epidermal collectivity. Even though it remains incompletely understood from the biomedical standpoint, the disorder's onset may be described as a cellular variant of the sorites paradox housed in the Sodom narrative (Gen. 18). By this I mean that the epidermal crisis is apparently reached through a continuous series of biosemiotic and metabolic miscalculations in detecting the advent of minor but significant changes in the cell cycle's borderline phases (e.g., between functional and nonfunctional aspects of dead cells).[57] In other words, the psoriatic process's foreshortened time scheme misapplies the "fuzzy logic" that is attuned, in healthy circumstances, to subtle changes in the skin's complex system dynamics.[58] As a result, what the surface of psoriatic skin presents is a balkanized area, occupied by conflicting expressions of normality, each following the same bodily doxa at the cellular level but at different, mutually maladaptive speeds.

Another way of putting this is to say that in active phases of psoriasis, the surface of the skin is in a dream state, conjuring divergent incarnations and perimeters of the normal. John Updike, one of the most famous confessional voices in the literature of psoriasis, gets at this point in the essay

"At War with Myself," published in the *New Yorker* in 1985. Near the end of the sometimes bruising rumination, Updike appears to reach an epiphany: "To my body in its eccentric chemistry psoriasis is normal, and its suppression abnormal. Psoriasis is my health. Its suppression constitutes a poisoning of the system, of my personal ecology."[59] Partly because of its rueful ambivalence, Updike's observation suggests how psoriatic lesions function as intermittent sentinels of the critical "being of the between" that the disorder and the evolving treatment regimens together bring to the normative attributions of the body/self relation and correlative self/ not-self dyad. The shape of the normative, of course, depends on where you point the compass, as Updike's essay shows. The essay also suggests how the very idea of the normative, wherever applied, presupposes a two-fold process of sedimentation and filtration, a fabricated regularity that allows for improvisation even as it tends to misrecognize the improvisatory aptitude that sustains it.

The notion of immunity in biomedical discourse is one of modernity's most potent engines of such misrecognition, precisely because the medicalization of the term effectively naturalized what had originally been a tactical solution to a political problem: territorial challenges posed by ancient Rome's imperial expansion. As Ed Cohen reminds us, Roman *municipia* were urban spaces typically situated at the periphery of the empire and designated as sites of a kind of political grafting. Through this process, rights and privileges and obligations (*munera*) of citizenship (together with contingent exemptions or conditions of "immunity") were conferred on non-Roman persons—without dissolving, however, the designated citizen-subjects' preexisting lineaments of attachment to local political authorities.[60] In its juridico-political domicile, immunity proved an adaptive mechanism, and an enduring one. Its modern descendant, the concept of diplomatic immunity, is enshrined in international law.

If the kinship between diplomatic immunity and its biomedical cognate is difficult to recognize, this is so because of the notion's particular migratory fluency. Medieval and early modern formulations of legal rights extended the Roman sense of immunity to property, and from this lodging the notion came to undergird one of the signal features of early modern liberal humanist political thought—the discourse of possessive individualism, with its attendant understanding of the self as defensible and autonomous property. The use of immunity as a descriptor of the self, and of the body it could be said to own, was already thinkable by the time it entered medical writing in the late nineteenth century. In its medical habitat, the notion benefited from the very action it described, swiftly acquiring virtually unassailable stature as the impartial marker of an essential, given property of bodily constitution. The success of immune discourse in the twentieth-century, as Cohen points out, thus entailed a certain "forgetting" of immunity's juridico-political genealogy.[61]

The telling datum, however, is not the fact of the forgotten juridico-political archive as such, but rather the underlying truth of immunity's status as a metaphor with a variegated history. This is a truth worth remembering, principally because it helps us recall that metaphor itself, together with the symbolic currencies it issues, has a long and richly documented association with the improper and the nomadic.[62] In this regard, the truth of metaphor is essentially duplicitous, for metaphor is not simply opposed to regimes of facts or concepts. Apart from any of its specific instances, metaphor also stands for the animating principle behind the expanded field in which facts and concepts congeal into instrumental form and undergo mutation as they drift into new conjugations.[63] To state the matter in terms of Sodomscape's presiding scheme, metaphor is one name for the *hospitable property of language*, through which the diverse incarnations and functions of language—expressive, gestural, cognitive, communicative, and creative—enter into interdependent, sometimes fractious, and evolving relations. In this regard, metaphor is part of the DNA, the generative mechanism, of *figura*, the figural sheath of knowledge and experience poised between memory and anticipation.

Cohen's argument suggests this very property by conducting a thought experiment, imagining "what might have happened if 'community' had achieved the same biological status that immunity did."[64]

> How differently might we live in the world imagining that our "commune systems" mediated our relations with and in the world? How might we experience ourselves as organisms if we imagined that coexistence rather than self-defense provides the basis for our well-being? How might we have organized our care and our systems of healing, or indeed our entire political and economic relations, if we imagined that our ability to respond to corporeal challenge engages our ability *to commune* with others? Might biological *community* enable us to appreciate healing not just as a biomedical phenomenon but also as a political, ethical, and material value?[65]

The somewhat utopian vistas conjured by these questions depend on the proposition that community, immunity's "etymological opposite," necessarily "foregrounds the co-constitutive dynamics of living."[66] In practice, though, the notion of community is not quite the opposite of immunity.

As Cohen's survey of the early history of the terms suggests, the found-ing scenes of Roman *municipia* may be thought of as experimental sites that tested varying degrees of contact and complicity between community and immunity. By the time of the late Roman Empire under Constantine, the ethos of Christian community presupposed an enabling condition of limited immunity from secular obligations expected of Roman citizen-subjects—hence the various exemptions or benefits accorded to the cleri-cal estate (e.g., the legal designation of benefit of clergy). As the developing Christian *ecclesia* further emulated the Roman *imperium*'s architectonics, it was precisely community's immunological reflex that helped gener-ate the ensuing friction between ecclesial and secular claims to political sovereignty.[67]

To be sure, not all histories of community-building follow the same arc. Yet the instance just described plots an instructive trajectory, for its out-working testifies to the complications and internal contradictions lodged in community's etymological reservoir. Depending on how you parse the root *communis*, "community" denotes either "with oneness or unity" (*unus*) or "with gifts or service" (*munus*).[68] What the historical archive suggests, time and again, is the adventure—and deeply contingent outcomes—of negotiating the interface between these potentially conflicting ground rules for viable community: shared values, goals, or heritage on the one hand, and the expectation of mutual service and reciprocity on the other. What the historical archive does not supply—at least not in a one-size-fits-all model—is a critical apparatus for recognizing what counts as the minimal condition(s) for viable interface.

These conditions are culture's perhaps unquantifiable, yet nonethe-less indispensable scruples. Scruples, let us recall, connote the burden of a difficult choice, but they also hold the germs of sustainable community through shared exposure to forgotten resources, tendrils of immemorial belonging that may be therapeutically grafted onto emerging problems. If, as Jean-Luc Nancy has argued, the search for the minimal condition(s) of community entails exposure to the thought that "being-with" precedes "being," the Dead Sea spa clinics remind us that the scope and force of the preposition "with" is inherently *figural*—at once breach and synapse.[69] In other words, the clinics present an occasion for apprehending, in Butler's sense, the suppleness of the attentive "with" as a gesture, a connective tis-sue conducted across both space and time, and released (at least in part) from legislated forms of memory and predetermined consequences.

By attending to the dynamic microecology of skin within the ambient surround of ecotourism, kibbutzim, and neighboring chemical extraction industry, the theater of the Dead Sea spa cultures invites us to consider, further, how community's negotiatory adventure binds to the phantasmic contours of the sorites paradox subsisting in the deep memory, and skin, of Sodom. As already noted, the sorites is primarily associated with arabesques of Stoic logic on the definitional bounds of identity, the conjectured quantity that determines *haecceity* or "thisness." Perhaps its most notorious appearance in the modern era turned up in Justice Scalia's recourse to a sorites variant—the "slippery slope" argument—in the dissenting opinion he appended to the Supreme Court's decision in *Lawrence v. Texas* (2003), the ruling that struck down the sodomy law in Texas, on the grounds that the ruling would trigger an unstoppable habit of juridical permissiveness.[70] The biblical prototype, as we have seen, appears in Abraham's fraught dialog with God in Genesis 18 as the deliberation over Sodom's fate nears its lethal conclusion. Abraham's motive travels in the opposite direction of Scalia's—Abraham seeks to enlarge the scope of protected life—but the underlying question lodged in sorites-logic is the same. How many exceptions to the perceived transgressive ethos of the community must be found in order to revise the calculus and recalibrate the received sense of viable community? The subtext: how much unity or likeness can community sustain, and how far may exemptions to service and reciprocity extend before they expose a given mythos of community to the interruptive and potentially disintegrative forces—the centrifugal potency of metaphor—which it must presuppose and forget as its condition of being?

What might have happened, in other words, if immunity and community had remained legible as co-constitutive *threshold metaphors*—discursive outcroppings that mark frontiers as malleable sites of exchange and encounter, across which entities, organisms, and collectivities of all sorts negotiate and refigure means of survival? This type of question recognizes that there is no genuine choice between immunity and community, because there is no lasting or impermeable border between the two notions. There are only traversals of the figural thresholds these sibling notions together establish in the landscape of hospitality.

One way to maintain the critical resilience of such intuition is to treat expressions of *community* and *immunity* as outcroppings of an ever-shifting and conjugating matrix of part-whole relations—the "arena in which stuff happens," as Jane Bennett nicely puts it.[71] *Assemblage*, the word proposed by Deleuze and Guattari and taken up by Bennett in her recent imagining of a "political ecology of things," is a good word for such a matrix, particularly because of the depth charge it detonates under uncritical or casual assumptions about who and what participates in a community's making. The word's resistance to capture by anthropocentric bias helps foster attention to the "material agency or effectivity of nonhuman or not-quite-human things," and cultivates "more attentive encounters between people-materialities and thing-materialities."[72] Bennett's memory of the Deleuzian archive emphasizes the following dynamic:

> Assemblages are ad hoc groupings of diverse elements, of vibrant materials of all sorts . . . living, throbbing confederations that are able to function despite the persistent presence of energies that confound them from within. They have uneven topographies, because some of the points at which the various affects and bodies cross paths are more heavily trafficked than others, and so power is not distributed equally across its surface. Assemblages are not governed by any central head: no one materiality or type of material has sufficient competence to determine consistently the trajectory or impact of the group.[73]

Bennett's description repays scrutiny not for its celebration of the assemblage's polymorphous diversity and acephalous gathering but for its acknowledgement of the "persistent presence of energies" that keep the assemblage's ad hoc confederations from converting into an inert and fully manipulable object or fact.

With this in mind, it is useful to think of Sodomscape as a specific type of assemblage—an auratically and ethically charged tropism of one of hospitality's urtexts, the Sodom archive, whose mutating configurations participate in the choreography of what Merleau-Ponty called the "flesh of things."[74] What the Dead Sea spa clinics bring to Sodomscape is the floating apprehension that the variegated life cycles of skin are more than a clinical property of a specific body or life form; they also speak to Merleau-Ponty's extended and inherently dramatic sense of what it means to inhabit the flesh. Accordingly, beyond the specific protocols they implement, the therapeutic skin care regimens quietly rehearse a more global lesson—that the tropic persistence of the past is neither an anachronistic obstacle nor a traumatic irruption nor a sacred piece of cultural patrimony. Persistence in therapeutic spa time stands for subsistence of "the most general form of an already-there," a form of fleshly hospitality that belongs to no one in particular.[75] Precisely for this reason, it constitutes a receptive host for beginning again to imagine and conjugate the usable legacies of community and immunity through the fundamental threshold metaphor of skin.

CHAPTER 6

The Face of the Contemporary: Lost World Fantasies of Finding Lot's Wife

> Contemporariness is, then, a singular relationship with one's own
> time, which adheres to it and, at the same time, keeps a distance
> from it. More precisely, it is *that relationship with time that adheres*
> *to it through a disjunction and an anachronism.* Those who coincide
> too well with the epoch, those who are perfectly tied to it in every
> respect, are not contemporaries, precisely because they do not
> manage to see it; they are not able to firmly hold their gaze on it.
>
> —GIORGIO AGAMBEN, "What Is the Contemporary?"[1]

The digital photographs before you belong to Sodomscape in more ways than one (fig. 14, plate 10). Most obviously, they conform to the genre of tourist photography commonly found in the postcards and guidebooks designed to satisfy interest in well-known landmarks of the Dead Sea region. To this end, the photographs also display a characteristic negotiation of the documentary impulse and the taste for the picturesque's "accidental beauty."[2] No more than the illuminated image from Maître François's studio do the photographs pretend to supply historically accurate information about the destroyed city of Sodom, though the reasons for the photographs' agnosticism on this point come from a different set of assumptions about the historical past's legibility. The photographs are casual witnesses to the fact that something more than mere innovation in representational technologies occurred during the five-hundred-odd years between the late-medieval illuminator's craft and the photographs.

The time of innovation included the ascendancy of modern historical consciousness and the corresponding development of the geological and archaeological sciences—the very groundwork that has led to the common understanding of the existence of *two* mythic cities called Sodom.

Figure 14. Dead Sea Works, Ltd., Israel. Photo courtesy of Jay H. Geller.

On the one hand, there is the moralizing myth of the accursed city in the Genesis text, which remains caught up in the speculative machinery for rationalizing (and theologizing) the monotheistic system's retributive logic of violence. On the other hand, there is the etiological myth, purporting to account for the Genesis text's recorded memory of a natural disaster, which may have occurred in the Early Bronze Age. The archaeological evidence of the disaster remains highly conjectural, though the topic remains a regularly discussed item in the religious blogosphere.[3] The photographs reward a different brand of curiosity. What is there to see *now* in the fabled landscape?

The images are thus contemporary artifacts in the ordinary sense of the word. They conform to a familiar and conventional technology of mimetic representation. As Giorgio Agamben reminds us, however, there is another, less complacent way to conceive of contemporariness. The alternative perspective takes critical stock of the conventional gestures toward belonging through which the appearance of the typical may express itself. Ingrained in habit, such gestures preemptively elevate the part-whole relation, the empire of synecdoche, as the sine qua non of what it means to be contemporary. For Agamben, contemporariness refers to something other than the sum of traits that speak to the synchronicity of gathered localities. It relays the metabolism of the local—its flesh (in Merleau-Ponty's sense). This kinetic trait identifies the contemporary as a sense of heightened attunement to the plurality of tactics for *living with* one's time; assuming a specific, malleable, and hospitable relation to varied dimensions of the now, rather than being simply folded into it. My aim in this chapter is to tease out the sodomitic kernel of Agamben's insight by tracking its premonitory design in a little-known yet compelling fictional excursion into Sodomscape, the Victorian lost world adventure romance written by Alfred Clark titled *The Finding of Lot's Wife* (1896).

To return first to the figural cast of Agamben's argument. Agamben's readers will recognize the perhaps characteristic Pauline undertow to his argument. Indeed, Agamben singles out Paul's famous voicing of messianic time—the "'time of the now' (*ho nyn kairos*) [Rom. 11:5]"—as the expression of "contemporariness par excellence."[4] For the matter at hand, the messianic aspect of kairotic urgency is of less import than the textured temporality and untimeliness of the now to which Agamben's Paul calls attention. In this light, it is worth recalling Agamben's baseline definition of the contemporary as "*that relationship with time that adheres to it through a disjunction and an anachronism*."[5] Crucially, the coupling of disjunction and anachronism discloses a "secret affinity between the archaic and the modern," and does so by remembering that the word *archaic* preserves an ambiguous proximity to the origin (*arkhē*).

The archaic does not simply designate a punctual moment in time; rather, it designates a speculative relation with an ungraspable scene of onset. Because of this feature, the thought of the archaic carries a loopback effect. Even as the archaic conjures a backward turning motion toward a foundational moment in the chronological past, the very same motion also "returns to that part within the present that we are absolutely incapable of living."[6] Agamben seems to mean here that the utopian idea of full immersion in the present carries a blind spot. As it must, because the imagined immersive condition blocks access to the vantage point that would afford the desired panoramic understanding of one's passage through the present. The secret of the archaic, then, is that its imaginary compass touches upon the ungrasped "part" of the present, the intimately held but inchoate "mass of what for some reason (its traumatic character, its excessive nearness) we have been unable to live." On Agamben's account, giving "attention to this 'unlived' is the life of the contemporary." Taking Agamben at his word on this point, as I propose to do, means appreciating how the "life" of the contemporary and the "attention" it solicits meet through a shared reliance on the unruliness of figural expression. The moment of disclosive contact does not therefore arrive through a single unified perspective. It arrives without predictive planning, through figural byways of belatedness, dislocation, and anamorphic perception.

Together, the two photographs before us reclaim the imaginary contours of Sodomscape—a figural space poised to convert the appearance of anamorphic disjunction and anachronism, the twin coils of the "unlived," into hermeneutic equipment for "reading history in unforeseen ways."[7] The stilled moment of photographic capture holds open a space for interrogating the nature of the relation between two modes of hospitable dwelling, city and desert. This space, of course, has a history. The basic terms of the question in Maître François's era, for example, rehearsed the associative index inherited from the desert fathers and Augustininan tradition, whereby the condemned Cities of the Plain stand for the profane region of secularity and the desert for sacred asceticism. As we saw in the previous chapter, the material expression of the question in the modern profile of Sodomscape does not so much abandon the theological furniture of the desert/city dyad, as focus attention on a neighboring preoccupation: the ethical and political ramifications of the malleable guest-host relation.

The essence of Sodomscape survives in the assemblage of interrelated and in some regards conflicting activities along the southern edges of the Dead Sea. For starters, let us recall the region's basic topographical features. The delicate ecosystem of nature reserves, including Einot Tsukim and Ein Gedi, lies adjacent to the crush of hotel complexes and spa clinics. A few miles south of the resort district of Ein Bokek, a sprawling ersatz cityscape rises above the coastline. This is the mammoth chemical extraction plant known as Dead Sea Works Ltd., which is mirrored along the southeastern shore of the Dead Sea by its Jordanian rival, the Ghor El-Safi plant owned by the Arab Potash Company.

The Dead Sea Works, captured in the photographs before you, presents Sodom's fully industrialized avatar. The link derives only in part from the physical proximity of the site to one of the conjectured areas in which the ruins of the biblical city were once believed to have been buried, the vicinity of Mount Sedom. The decisive association is *figural*, in a specific way. The plant's operation gives contemporary expression to the heart of the hospitality crisis that Derrida fleshes out by turning to the biblical dossier on Sodom. The crisis expresses the difficult relation between the routine operation of the rules of the game and the sudden upsurge of a double bind. The Dead Sea Works, together with its Jordanian rival, stages the silent erosion of the distinction between these claims.

The metaphor of erosion follows by direct inference from the accelerated development of geological aberrations in the region, to which the Dead Sea Works has contributed in evident ways, though the evidence of geological and environmental hazard is at odds, for the most part, with the dream of the land as benevolent host and catalyst for economic growth. Now largely sustained by international corporate business interests, the dream also retains symbolic resonance for some investors as the contemporary realization of the founder of modern Zionism Theodore Herzl's visionary project.[8] There is no need to ascribe prophetic powers to Herzl to see at least the partial fulfillment of his vision in the Dead Sea Works. The present-day operation enjoys the cachet of being the world's largest supplier of magnesium chloride derivatives and bromine compounds, and the fourth largest global supplier of potash products, which are principally used in fertilizers and livestock feed supplements.

Without question, the Dead Sea Works is a driving engine of the Israeli economy in the global market. It easily follows that the conglomerate's official websites should describe the relation of the enterprise with its physical environs as an act of benevolent and lucrative symbiosis, in tacit absolution of the tortured memory of the violence written into the guest-host relation in the Sodom archive.[9] Notwithstanding the Dead Sea Works' publicized commitment to implementing environmentally responsible policies, and its evident support of the region's substantial tourist industry, a troubling fact remains. The operation is partly responsible for an ongoing ecological disaster. The problem is water. The water level of the Dead Sea, which is the terminal lake of the Jordan Rift Valley, has been falling steadily since the 1930s, and since the 1970s the rate of decline has been measured at one meter per year. The systematic diversion of water from the Jordan River by Syria, Israel, and Jordan for drinking water and agricultural use partly accounts for the Dead Sea's depletion, but it is the particular intervention of the chemical extraction plants, on the Israeli and Jordanian shores of the Dead Sea, that recode the sodomitic text.

How so? Consider the Dead Sea's changing topography. The combination of years of drought and diversionary policies led to the virtual extinction of the southern basin in the late 1970s. After assessing the opportunity afforded by the emerging crisis, the Dead Sea Works built a ten-mile canal to pump water from the northern basin into the nearly depleted southern end, creating a linked system of industrial solar evaporation ponds designed to optimize the chemical extraction process. So far so good, for the chemical industry. But the decades-long water diversion has led to a perverse quid pro quo. The artificially created evaporation ponds in the south basin are estimated to be responsible for as much as forty percent of the steady water loss in the larger north basin of the Dead Sea, and the intervention is also causally implicated in the corresponding rise in the number of sink holes and erosional gullies in the coastal plain. The supposed benefits to the tourist industry come at a paradoxical price. The hotels along the receding waters of the north shore are fast losing the cachet of being seaside resorts, whereas the south shore is threatened by the opposite problem. The evaporation ponds in the southern basin are rising at the rate of eight inches per year because of the steady increase in accumulated sodium chloride from industrial extraction of potash, bromine, caustic soda, and magnesium. The industrially induced rising water level threatens to engulf the southwestern shoreline, where a substantial number of luxury hotels and skin therapy clinics are located.

Several solutions have been promoted in recent years. Perhaps the most spectacularly controversial panacea is the proposed Red Sea-Dead Sea Conveyance Project (the so-called Red-Dead canal), which was formally agreed upon by representatives of Jordan, Israel, and the Palestinian Authority in December 2013.[10] At the official signing ceremony, Israel's Minister for Regional Cooperation Silvan Shalom opined that the agreement was of "the highest diplomatic, economic, environmental, and strategic importance."[11] Notwithstanding Shalom's remark, what the Red-Dead canal project symbolizes is the resilience of the logic of the zero-sum game. Thus far, the interested parties have tended to assume the position of competitor for dominant jurisdiction over precarious resources. Despite the fact that a holistic assemblage ethos is the key to durable solutions, the multiple competing interests in the region, which are entangled with the region's long history as a theater of embattled political contestation, have amply demonstrated the difficulty of moving from territorialized plurality and unproductive dissensus to reparative consensus over land and water use.[12]

We can now see more precisely how the photographs at hand indicate the contemporariness of the Dead Sea Works as a figural extrapolation of Sodom. Even as they document what is there to be seen on the shores of the Dead Sea, the images also present what could be called a techno-allegory of a hospitality crisis. That is, the captured scenes of the industrialized desert cityscape speak to the commercial operation's tacit disavowal of environmental ethical claims in gauging the distinctions between benefit and harm. The second photograph foregrounds the unspoken dimension of the site's contemporariness—its disjunctive aspect—through one eloquent detail (plate 10). The power plant's facades offer a disarming rejoinder to the typical complaint reported by one of the operation's administrative officers: "We have the image of a bully, someone raping nature, destroying the landscape . . . [but] we put huge sums of money to try to minimize the changes to the surrounding areas."[13] The murals painted on the two adjacent buildings convert semaphores of the picturesque (blue sky, cloudscape, saturated desert colors) into an aesthetics of camouflage-as-disavowal.

The painted mirage indicates precisely what is unlived in the contemporary pulse of life and work in the region. What is unlived is a sustainable compromise between the dayglow fantasy of virgin land and ruthless exploitation of the land's resources. In essence, the murals present a vertiginous view of the "now" of the region as the collapse of all legible distinction between aesthetic and instrumental gauges. If you stop at the scenic outlook on Highway 90 directly across from the power plant, this is what murals, in concert, give to be seen. They give the land as it may have been in the immemorial past, before settlement of any kind took root, and as it will have been in a postcatastrophe moment, after its capacity to harbor human dwelling has been exhausted. Here, too, the Dead Sea Works remains faithful to the essential provocation of Lot's wife, the paradigmatic figure of the in-between in the Sodom story, caught between innocence and guilt and equivocally at odds with both positions.

Sodom as Lost World Fantasy

I know of no contemporary work of fiction that enters into the figural drama of Sodomscape as it is currently being waged in the Dead Sea region. The Sodom archive, however, contains one literary document that effectively takes the pulse of a significant moment between the two eras represented by Maître François's illuminated image of the flight from Sodom and the photographic testimony of ecological risk in the environs of the Dead Sea Works. The moment is the 1890s. The text I have in mind was published very near the time that Theodore Herzl's dream of converting the Dead Sea region into an industrialized gold mine was taking shape. The text shows no interest in the then recent development of Jewish settlements in Palestine, but it does exhibit an unusually prescient species of critical attention to the geopolitical sensitivity of the Dead Sea region.[14] This feature supplies the work's credentials as a novelistic outworking of Sodomscape.

A largely forgotten figure today, Alfred Clark was an indefatigable purveyor of popular fantasy and historical romance fiction at the end of the
Victorian era. His novels in the 1890s include *A Dark Place of the Earth*
(1891), a tale of shipwreck that pitches the protagonist into the midst of
embattled conflict between the surviving descendants of Dutch and Portuguese explorers on a volcanic island near Ceylon; *Woe to the Conquered*
(1893), a panoramic account of the Roman Republic at the time of the
revolt of Spartacus; and *In a State of Nature* (1899), an adventure story
detailing the improbable discovery of a lost colony of Elizabethans in the
Arctic. In 1896 he added a uniquely speculative document to the Sodom
archive with *The Finding of Lot's Wife*.[15] Here is a skeletal reduction of the
plot: *Holiday expedition to fabled biblical land runs into conflict with indigenous
tribe. Hostage situation ensues, with cascade of catastrophes. Safe return home is
brought about by miraculous intervention, after near-fatal contact with lethal
remnant of Sodom.*

What one contemporary critic wrote of *Woe to the Conquered* could be
applied to nearly all of Clark's novels, including his contribution to the
figural history of Lot's wife: "considerable historical research is blended
with a high order of descriptive power, and the dead facts of a past age
are vivified into living realities capable of appealing to and arousing the
modern mind."[16] To judge from the divided critical reception of *Lot's Wife*,
however, Clark's attempt to reanimate the "dead facts" of the biblical story
was not entirely successful. The column "Good Reading for Summer" in
the August 1896 issue of the *Book Buyer* praised Clark's imaginative prowess: in his "most extraordinary story," the "influence of [the] pillar on those
so unfortunate as to behold it is weird and astonishing, and has enabled
the writer to construct a situation unparalleled in romantic literature."[17]
The September issue held a different impression: "Mr. Clark's story is the
kind of book that makes History blush and Science wring her hands in
shame."[18] The tenor if not the specific animus of the withering judgment
proved prescient. Out of print for over a century, *The Finding of Lot's Wife*,
together with the author and the body of his work, has fallen into virtual oblivion. In 2010, Altus Press, the enterprising recycler of early pulp
fiction, reprinted the 1896 edition. Featured in the Altus "Lost Race Library," the novel is advertised on the press's website as "quite possibly the
best lost race story ever published."[19]

Quite possibly the ministrations of Altus Press may generate belated
interest in Clark's novel, if only as an object of cultic curiosity. For it must
be said that *The Finding of Lot's Wife* is a monster. A jerry-rigged generic
hybrid, the narrative is concocted of charged gestures at historical and re

ligious sublimity interlarded with caricatures of the Orientalizing strain to ethnographic fantasy. This is not to say the complaint registered in the *Book Buyer*—tarring it as the bringer of scandal to the house of History and Science—correctly identifies the novel's achievement. Rather, to recall Hans Blumenberg's conceit, the specific dissension in the press throws into relief the disorienting effect of the manner in which the novel's "work on myth" disfigures and contemporizes the Sodom story. Before proceeding to the novel, I want to assemble a map of different approaches to myth that appear refracted in Clark's reactivation of the Sodom legend's enchantment.

A Short Guide to Works on Myth

By no coincidence, the voice of the dour critic in the *Book Buyer* echoes the rhetorical call to arms sounded in Andrew Dickson White's monumental *History of the Warfare of Science with Theology in Christendom*.[20] Published in the same year as Clark's novel, White's treatise was one of the century's more florid expressions of the so-called conflict thesis, a quasi-apocalyptic secularism that posited the relation between science and religion as a virulent zero-sum game in which myth was reductively associated with the presumed atavistic, and thus inauthentic, trappings of religious (in particular, Catholic) beliefs and practices. The eighteenth chapter, "From the Dead Sea Legends to Comparative Mythology," makes for instructive reading in this regard. It provides an encyclopedia of Sodom lore, giving particular attention to the divergent and often contradictory construals of the pillar of salt from antiquity to the modern era. Like Sir James Frazer's *Golden Bough* (1890) and other instances of nineteenth-century studies in comparative mythology, White's treatise observes a supersessionist ethos, in which scientific rationality autopsies the magical and superstitious elements of religious thought and inters them as "dead facts" worthy only of historical interest as outmoded expressions of etiological intuition. One suspects Clark's novel would not have stayed long on White's summer reading list.

White reserves special contempt for the rendering of the Sodom legend in the official report of Lieutenant William Lynch's 1848 expedition to the Dead Sea region.[21] Lynch's expedition, which was sponsored by the United States Navy, had gained recognition for the scope and detail of its geological findings, as well as for being the first recorded circumnavigation of the Dead Sea.[22] Like many of his predecessors, Lynch claimed to have found the pillar of salt. Despite the fact that Lynch's text treats the legend

as "a superstition," the note of skepticism pales before the outsized significance of a tiny detail:[23] "One little circumstance added enormously to the
influence of this book, for, as a frontispiece, he inserted a picture of the salt
column. It was delineated in rather a poetic manner: light streamed upon it,
heavy clouds hung above it, and, as a background, were ranged buttresses
of salt rock furrowed and channeled out by the winter rains; this salt statue
picture was spread far and wide, and in thousands of country pulpits and
Sunday-schools it was shown as a tribute of science to Scripture."[24] White's
exasperation as he considers the atavistic peril of Lynch's "picture of the
salt column" (fig. 15) is not fueled by exactly the same motives prompting
Levinas's famous hostility toward artwork. That is, White's complaint does
not stem primarily from the desire to segregate the world of aesthetic reflection from that of conceptual engagement. Rather, White worries about
the mediatization of inadvertently mixed messages in an era where the indiscriminate serviceability of print culture may prove to be the purveyor of
the biblical myth's rearguard action.

"Lynch," he points out, "had innocently set a trap into which several
eminent European theologians stumbled."[25] Recorded evidence of the perverse seduction lodged in Lynch's publication, however, does not diminish
White's allegiance to an evolutionary model of human history, for which
his exhaustive chronicle purports to supply a transcendental optics. Virtually every chapter includes a précis of the kind found in the book's closing
pages: "If, then, modern science in general has acted powerfully to dissolve
away the theories and dogmas of the older theologic [sic] interpretation, it
has also been active in a reconstruction and recrystallization of truth; and
very powerful in this reconstruction have been the evolution doctrines
which have grown out of the thought and work of men like Darwin and
Spencer."[26] White's debt to the Herbert Spencer and Charles Darwin's
evolutionary theories is not systematic and not even very precise, though
the free-floating deism and teleological sense of historical process and enveloping moral literacy found in the *History* are perhaps symptomatic of a
broad cultural disposition to consider the amenability of "evolution doctrines," loosely conceived, to the ascendant historical-critical method in
biblical studies.[27] White's own brand of truth, however, being a fairly blunt
instrument hewn from positivist and rationalist precepts, proved an indifferent measure of the rhizomic habit of truth procedures that was developing in contemporary biblical scholarship.

A watershed was reached a decade after White's *History*, with the publication of Albert Schweitzer's monumental *Quest of the Historical Jesus*

Figure 15. Pillar of Salt at Usdum. Intaglio. William Lynch, *Narrative of the United States Expedition to the River Jordan and the Dead Sea*, New and corr. Ed. (Philadelphia: Lea and Blanchard, 1849). Eran Laor Cartographic Collection, The National Library of Israel, Jerusalem. Image courtesy of The National Library of Israel.

(1906). Schweitzer's arguments, which were subsequently radicalized by the kerygmatic "demythology" of Rudolf Bultmann, laid the groundwork in twentieth-century theological and biblical studies for the decisive partitioning of the Jesus of history and the Christ of faith. From Schweitzer's perspective, the truth of the testamental corpus was not a cognitive quotient derived from winnowing out the mythic residue in the historical archive. It was an interminable task of translation.[28] The horizons broached by Schweitzer's critical gaze afford an intuition of the bottomless character of historicity itself, not only as it pertains to the designated subject of study (e.g., the "place" of Jesus's thought in late-antique Jewish apocalypticism), but also as it inflects the very act of grasping, or receiving, and giving "complete expression" to, the sense(s) of the subject.

For White, the biblical texts are more like a fossil record than a palimpsest, in that they disclose "the most striking evolution in morals and religion" precisely by giving evidence of the processes whereby "vast masses of myth, legend, marvel, and dogmatic assertion . . . have been dissolved and are now dissolving quietly away like icebergs drifted into the Gulf Stream."[29] Bultmann's demythologizing procedure, too, entails the stripping away of the mythic trappings of the kerygma or proclamation that the believing community discovers in the biblical text. But Bultmann's demythology is not a unilateral excision. Nor is the quarry—the grasped sense of the essential meaning (kerygma) of the text—reducible to dogmatic statement or rationalist precept. These distinctions obtain in part because for Bultmann the work of demythology is not a pristine exegesis or archaeology of the text, but rather a hybrid hermeneutic. As Paul Ricoeur explains, Bultmann's demythologization proceeds through the mutual participation and counterclaims of three angles of vision in a "great circle:" the knowledge base of scientific and technological modernity, the purviews of philosophical and existential reflection, and the engaged posture of faith.[30]

On Ricoeur's account, demythologization does not liquidate myth's symbolic aptitude or its status as "the extension of a symbolic structure."[31] Rather, the mission of demythologizing is to work as a solvent on the "hardening" of myth's "symbolic structures into dogmatic or reified ideologies."[32] From this line of reasoning, to demythologize is not to demystify *tout court*, but to maintain an emancipated curiosity toward myth's scope and continued effects. In other words, if myth claims a certain durability, this is not because of its explanatory power or allure as material index of unchanging archetypes of meaning, but rather because of its expressivity as a reservoir of attachments and provocations, and as a catalyst for critical reflection.

Ricoeur's reevaluation of Bultmann's legacy opens onto a region hospitable to Blumenberg's account of myth's constitutive adaptability. On Blumenberg's account, myth concerns itself not principally with explanatory intentions, but rather with establishing horizons of significance (*Bedeutsamkeit*) out of the perceived contingencies of existence. As opposed to mere meaning, particularly in its routinized circulation, significance for Blumenberg provides a defensive and interrogative posture, an "orienting edge of intentionality," toward the sense of indifference in space and time and, more pointedly, toward "the *inhuman* limit of reality's indifference."[33] In consequence, when myths survive their local use, they do so because they continue to strike home as viable resources for addressing problems at hand.

Blumenberg's account of work on myth, in other words, describes a significant means of furnishing the figural dimensions of thought and expression. This is so because both the originary work of myth and its successive reconfigurations serve as responsive reactions to what Blumenberg calls the "absolutism of reality."[34] On the one hand, the absolutism of reality denotes a foundational stage of anthropogenesis, marked by the human deficit of biologically adaptive instincts and the corresponding surplus intuition of unspecified risk or peril—the onset of the "pure state of indefinite anticipation" called "anxiety" or "intentionality of consciousness without an object."[35] The decisive response to this radical contingency is the emergence of the human as the *animal symbolicum*.[36] On the other hand, the absolutism of reality cannot be definitively assigned to an archaic event in history. Its unbounded and nomadic character stems from what Blumenberg calls the essential "eccentricity" of the human in relation to its environment.[37]

In other words, the absolutism of reality subsists, either unsaid or unthought, in the essentially prosthetic nature of cultural formations and in the fundamental ambiguity of the generative and apotropaic orientation they mobilize. It follows, then, that Blumenberg's limit concept is resiliently *contemporary*: "Man is always already on this side of the absolutism of reality, but he never entirely attains the certainty that he has reached the turning point in his history at which the relative predominance of reality over his consciousness and his fate has turned into the supremacy of the subject. There is no criterion for this turning, for this 'point of no return.'"[38]

Romancing the Pillar of Salt

If Clark's reoccupation of the Sodom legend produces a monstrous birth, this is so in large part because the novel both recognizes and disowns the insight distilled in Blumenberg's famous aphorism: "Work on myth knows no Sabbath ['seventh day'] on which it would confirm, retrospectively, that the god of the myths is dead."[39] The manner in which the "finding" proposed in the title (*The Finding of Lot's Wife*) oscillates between interment and resuscitation of the Sodom legend is not an entirely *sui generis* gesture, however, since the narrative's figured ambivalence reflects the characteristic discursive hybridity of the nineteenth-century historical novel.

Haydn White supplies the relevant metric by calling attention to the genre's cultivation of a pleasurable "interference between an imaginary tale of romance and a set of real historical events."[40] As White points out, the tactic's readerly appeal derives in large part from the genre's canny reliance on readers' "presumed capacity to distinguish between real and imaginary events" (as well as historic beginnings and mythic origins) so as to enjoy the chiastic reversal of "affect in which the familiar (the reader's own reveries) was rendered exotic, while the exotic (the historical past or the lives of the great) was rendered familiar."[41] Clark's novel observes this "discursive contract" even as it also gives wide berth to vertigo effects produced by the mutually encroaching horizons of fact and fiction in its fabricated world.[42] To this end, its pages encode a functionalist anthropology of myth consistent with Blumenberg's conceits as well as a demythologizing instinct given ballast by the production of "effects of the real" drawn from archaeological and ethnographic lore. Notwithstanding the negotiated settlement between these two perspectives, the novel's rhetorical posture of suspense also entertains the idea of a contemporary revelation—the upsurge of a kerygmatic encounter with the divine intention encrypted in the lost Cities of the Plain.

The decisive turn occurs at the outset, though it is an unobtrusive move. The novel's primary setting is not a remote historical time and place. Things begin on familiar ground—at home, so to speak—with a conventional discursive engine for producing encounters with the exotic under the generic canopy of romance: the expedition narrative. The title's archaeological tease conjures the era's substantial archive of exploratory ventures and excavations in various "cradles of civilization"—biblical lands, to be sure, including dynastic Egypt and the Fertile Crescent (a coinage introduced in 1906), as well as Mediterranean regions associated with Greco-Roman antiquity. The Sodomscape *mentalité* in Clark's novel carries an allusive register drawn from several of this archive's stations. Not least among these is the developing subgenre of "lost world" fiction made famous by Henry Rider Haggard's popular novel of African adventure, *King Solomon's Mines* (1885), together with the quasi-fictional, romance elements that had become genetically linked to the travel writing genre by the nineteenth century, perhaps most spectacularly so in the career of the American explorer and diplomat John Lloyd Stephens (1805–52).[43] Between 1837 and 1843, Stephens produced several vividly detailed accounts of his travels to Eastern Europe, Central America and the Yucatán, and the region conventionally known today as the Middle East. These works quickly attained international prestige and popularity as vehicles of virtual tourism. In effect, Stephens's narrative aesthetic trades on travel writing's penchant for presenting the chronicle of visited sights as a referred *Kunstkammer* or curiosity cabinet, in which a potentially endless variety of artifacts and wonders gather together into a suspended moment of descriptive capture.[44]

The Finding of Lot's Wife responds to the very same taste. Clark devises a narrative machine composed of four communities that converge in the Dead Sea region: two English travelers, two American explorers, an indigenous Bedouin tribe, and a resident monastic community of Greek Orthodox provenance. Character development, it must be said, is not Clark's strong suit. For the most part, the principal characters' names serve as semaphores of culturally freighted commonplaces.

With almost comic bluntness, the names of the two American travelers designate their bearers as walking personifications of biblical types that encode both the promise and the hazard of covenantal hospitality. They are a father-and-daughter team. The father is a historian-cum-archaeologist named Abraham Payne, whose scholarly quest for the lost origins of desert eremite communities has led him to the region. His amanuensis daughter, who has taken up the disguise of a boy to facilitate the pair's access to the monasteries, is named Isha. The name, as she reports it, "means simply 'woman'" in Hebrew, and "was Eve's first name."[45] In light of the namesake, the girl's transvestite garb presents more than a pastiche of multicultural exotica. It also reads like a whimsical sartorial riff on Eve's universal maternity. Isha is "picturesquely attired" in "loose Turkish trousers" with "a red silk blouse under an embroidered Albanian jacket," a "small fez cap," and "a pair of daintly little Parisian boots" (*FLW*, 103). It is little wonder that her transvestite name should be that of the iconic figurehead of covenantal community in native British lore: Arthur.

It is also therefore altogether fitting that Isha should develop an erotic attachment to the more proprietary specimen of English masculinity at hand, Hal Aylward. Here, too, the name defines the character. The patronymic Aylward, an old Anglo-Saxon name, carries an echo of the writ of ayle, the common-law mechanism for reclaiming ancestral land.[46] The given name conjures up the swagger, charisma, and imperializing ambition of the Lancastrian namesake, Prince Hal, the future Henry V. Lacking the circumstances for international warmongering, Clark's Hal is merely an insouciant prig with a supercilious curiosity toward the sights and adventures that make up the tourists' itinerary. As for his traveling companion, Noel Yorke, the narrator provides no substantive reason to think of him as any less English than Aylward, except for the suggestion, borne by his name, of a divided history of Englishness. The patronymic "Yorke" harbors the deep memory of the geographical dimension of confessional conflict in post-Reformation England, where northern regions like Lancashire, Cumbria, and Yorkshire were commonly identified as Catholic recusant strongholds. Nonconformity remained a legible attribute of the population of York in the nineteenth century.[47]

In sum, the device of tactical nomenclature, though fairly rudimentary, carries the proleptic suggestion of how the interactions of the mixed population variously express the sodomitic mytheme of hospitality and the precarious guest-host relation. Clark develops the narrative point by showing how a shared if patently generic taste for adventure in "the East" brings the two friends to Palestine (*FLW*, 6). Their movements are largely improvisational. After leaving England, "the two men drifted over to Palestine," and at the outset of the novel they appear to have been en route to Jerusalem after a circuit tour of the Dead Sea region. While at Mar Saba, they hear word of a miraculous remnant of the Sodom legend hidden in the mountainous region to the southeast of the Dead Sea, an "extraordinary community of achorites, whose monastery was perched on an inaccessible pinnacle of rock in a lonely valley" (*FLW*, 8). The site, the fabled Monastery of St. Lot, is said to have preserved the memory of Lot and his daughters' miraculous survival through the ritual practice of "pious austerities" that have made the residents "more than human"; the monks are reported to have "attained immunity from death or disease" (*FLW*, 8).[48]

The Englishmen's response to the report underscores the essential difference between them. The legend proves irresistible to Yorke. He is susceptible to the lure of the "sacred," understood in the root sense of the word as that which is set apart (*sacrare*), rare, and endowed with the prospect of danger that the encounter with beings "more than human" might hold. It is worth noting that the narrator equates the young man's avid curiosity with his artistic sensibility. The trait most probably draws on the legacy of David Roberts, whose popular lithographs and paintings of picturesque scenes of Egypt and the Near East helped define the pictorial look of aesthetic Orientalism in Clark's era.[49] Yorke, we learn, "had already made a name for himself as a painter of Eastern scenes and life" (*FLW*, 7). Yorke's sense of vocation to his art, like Roberts', also includes a measure of cosmopolitan engagement: "For a number of years he had spent every winter in Egypt, where he had learned to speak Arabic fluently, and had made himself thoroughly competent with the home-life and modes of thought of the natives" (*FLW*, 7). Such immersive practices would be unthinkable to Aylward, who is already immunized, one could say, by his cultural complacency, which declares itself in his disinclination to show more than passing interest in any of the sights on offer. It is no surprise that he should be completely indifferent to the "weird legend" that fires the "vivid imagination of the artist" (*FLW*, 9). Instead, the bond of friendship, together with the prospect of new hunting grounds for "some sport among the unfrequented mountains" (*FLW*, 10), leads Aylward to acquiesce to Yorke's desire to head back to the Dead Sea in search of the hidden "monastic eyrie" (*FLW*, 9).

For the most part, Clark's depiction of the Beni Azaleh, the Bedouin tribe that serves as the travelers' host and impromptu guide into the Dead Sea region, does not wander far from the expected Orientalized admixture of meticulous ethnographic interest and racialized repulsion. Thus, the description of the sheikh's companion, who occupies a legible station of local privilege, passes easily into the circuit of commodified information. The old man's dress "showed him to be a mûllah or Mohammedan priest. His green robe and turban indicated that he was a hadji, one who had made the pilgrimage to Mecca" (*FLW*, 22). The note of cool appraisal underpinning such journalistic reportage turns several degrees hotter when the aperture on the scene widens: "A number of tribesmen stood around, also several negroes. One of the latter was a huge, Caliban-like creature whose hideous black features, pitted by small-pox, were more like an exaggerated mask representing the brute passions than a human face" (*FLW*, 22). Later on, the narrator discloses the focalized character's name (El Wahsh), but the relevant functions of naming are already accomplished in this passage. The "Caliban-like" aspect anchors the figure to the Shakespearean touchstone for ambivalent and racialized fascination with the prospect of intercultural contact and exchange.

But the "hideous" creature attached to the Beni Azaleh exhibits none of Caliban's critical reflexes or poetic sensibility. His access to the realm of *bios*, human culture and species identity, is mediated through the concert of two expressions of compromised mimesis. His credentials as human are proven by the baseline factor of susceptibility to the ravagement of a disease that famously straddles the human/animal divide. Smallpox is a uniquely human disease, though by Clark's era it was an established piece of medico-cultural knowledge that exposure to closely related animal pathogens (zoonoses)—inoculation with cowpox or its close relative, vaccinia virus—would produce immunity to smallpox. Interspecies commingling, via the transmission route of vaccination, preserves the host species' imagined integrity.

The first appearance of El Wahsh recalibrates the import of such exposure. The pockmarked skin unambiguously declares the figure's human identity, but such understanding of the scarring gains purchase only from the biomedical standpoint. The narrator's interest, in presumed concert with the travelers' gaze, gravitates toward a different and ambivalently held order of cultural legibility. The human trait of El Wahsh (the pitted face) registers as the residue of a precarious mingling of Eurocentric curiosity and panic before the prospect of exposure to—and colonial penetration of—Africa.

Africa is not named in the text, but the mention of the figure's resemblance to "an exaggerated mask" conjures up the notorious "scramble for Africa" that was well underway by the 1890s, the spoils of which included the influx of African art objects into France and Belgium, the centers of the massive colonial project in West and Central Africa. Famously, the French art world's cachet of African masks inspired Picasso's turn (a decade after Clark's novel) to the neoprimitivist aesthetic associated with African artifacts as a key element in his developing avant-garde, proto-Cubist vocabulary. (As discussed in chapter 4, Natalia Goncharova's innovative treatment of the Sodom story may have taken a grain of inspiration from this vocabulary.) Though perhaps unavoidably marked by Eurocentric bias, Picasso's fascination with "primitive" African art was part of a complex tactic of aesthetic and political critique directed with equal force at the sterile canons of academicism in European art and the liberal humanist political tradition's complicity with the predatory operation of the colonial machine.[50]

Picasso's interest in the correlation of African masks and "brute passions" was designedly polemical. Clark's verbal portrait of El Wahsh is more complacent, in that the very prospect of proximity or mutual impingement of any kind between the travelers and the world that El Wahsh represents is disavowed through a doubly dehumanizing mimetic passage-work. The scarred face metaphorically morphs into an aesthetic artifact, one that pointedly does not represent a "human face," but instead presents itself as a decayed avatar of an animist faith in the power of vital energies to take up residence in nonhuman entities—natural phenomena and crafted objects—as well as humans. I say "decayed" because the culture of inter-species respect that inheres, at least implicitly, in the animist ethos appears in Clark's hands as a vanishing line of sight.

The appearance of the scarred face denotes an impassable boundary between host and guest—that is, between the tribal culture in the Dead Sea environs and the Western travelers who traverse the region in pursuit of different but compatible pleasures. It comes as no surprise later on that El Wahsh, although a minor character, should be employed as the instrument of the novel's most violent assertion of cultural purity codes. The episode, which appears near the novel's midpoint, depicts the public murder of Selim, the sole surviving son and heir of Abd'allah Abou Mansûr, the sheikh of the Beni Azaleh, in retaliation for the boy's secret conversion to Christianity.[51] It is also entirely characteristic of Clark's ambivalent and nervous perception of examples of unregulated translation between worlds that a threshold figure like Selim should meet a violent end. So, too, once Selim's sister, Ayéda, becomes susceptible to conversion (hers is erotic rather than religious in nature), the career she follows marks her out for death.

The principal contribution of Clark's novel to the figural history of Lot's wife comes from Clark's subtle mapping of the clandestine, mythic consanguinity of the Bedouin girl and the pillar of salt. The innovative twist that Clark introduces into the Sodom story's episode of fatal metamorphosis is the most carefully guarded secret in the novel—the full measure of the design unfolds in the last three of the novel's nineteen chapters—but the essential lineaments are in place near the outset. In the third chapter, well before the prospect of finding the remains of Sodom becomes a topic of conversation or debate, the two Englishmen's divergent attitudes toward the East effectively splinter the first extended description of Ayéda. Their banter's edginess announces Ayéda's figural position as the precarious threshold where the aesthetic and ethical provocations of the *inter-esse*, the being of the between, are both conjured into view and held in abeyance.

Once settled in the camp of the Beni Azaleh, Yorke catches sight of the girl as she performs a mundane task: milking a camel. The girl observes Yorke as he makes a rapid sketch of her. The episode develops into an object lesson in the ambivalence of the Orientalizing gaze. Yorke invites the girl to look at the image he has drawn—the shared viewing is the first step toward their eventual erotic attachment—but Ayéda does not recognize herself in the portrait's idealized traits. In her view, Yorke has drawn "a most beautiful peri" (one of the fabled *jinni* in Persian mythology) instead of the "Bedawi [Bedouin] girl" she knows herself to be (*FLW*, 35). When Yorke shows the portrait to his traveling companion, Aylward notices a rather different filter. The sketch shows "an English girl dressed in Arab female costume, milking a she-camel" (*FLW*, 36). With characteristic impatience, Aylward accuses his friend of an ethnocentric bias that warps his capacity to accurately document cultural differences. Aylward's own perspective, however, is hardly impartial, and Yorke quickly points out the xenophobic prejudice masquerading as objective precision: "If a girl is dark-skinned, you think she must necessarily be hideous" (*FLW*, 37). The standoff between Aylward and Yorke approaches a condition of descriptive paralysis. This is the price paid for the gathering awareness of the sublationary violence that informs and haunts the power of naming. Aylward's desultory retort—"Who is she?"—lowers the ante by pitching the question toward more objective data, her social station and marriage status. But the narrative satisfaction attached to such information—which in any event Yorke does not yet possess—merely disavows the problem posed by the two friends' disagreement.

The problem is not simply that the world of appearances harbors a plurality of perspectives, but that plurality is not innocent. Not here, not in the camp of the Beni Azaleh, where the dissenting aesthetic judgments of the two Englishmen, far from expressing negotiable opinions, disclose already congealed ideological contradictions in the encounter between East and West, to the point of rendering Ayéda, the purported "paragon of Oriental beauty," virtually invisible (*FLW*, 37). Put somewhat differently, if Ayéda expresses a "face," in the Levinasian sense, its passage must be deduced from the unnerving discrepancy between the career of the picturesque yet enigmatic beauty of the image in Yorke's sketch and the fatal adventure of Ayéda herself, who sacrifices herself under brutal circumstances in order to rescue Yorke from certain death after open conflict breaks out between the Beni Azaleh and the anchorite community.[52]

All of this is to say that the outworking of Clark's narrative design is both purveyor and symptom of the contradictions lodged in the Bedouin girl's unsettled appearance. That said, the way in which Clark fails to solve the problem of Ayéda's virtual invisibility is instructive. In effect, he splits the difference between Yorke's and Aylward's points of view. It takes little prodding for Yorke to confuse the roles of the casual ethnographer and potential suitor as he draws her out in conversation, seeking the kind of collectible data implied in Aylward's question ("Who is she?"). The tactic allows Ayéda to secure her position as amiable host-cum-informant. She willingly provides the chronicle of the Beni Azaleh's political travails while also indicating her revulsion toward the man to whom she is betrothed according to endogamous tribal custom, her cousin El Jezzar. The latter detail sets up the zone of intrigue in which Yorke will eventually assume the role of rival for erotic possession of Ayéda. Though hardly an original plot device, the rivalry between "inside" and "outside" agents for the common object of desire produces the necessary narrative catalyst—the travelers' expulsion from the Beni Azaleh's makeshift shelter.

El Jezzar's assertion of familial and territorial rights over Ayéda prompts his decision to create a makeshift ghetto of intruders in the desert landscape. He deposits the Englishmen at the very place they are seeking, the otherwise inaccessible Monastery of St. Lot, which is enshrouded on a "great isolated pinnacle of rock, some two hundred feet high, with perpendicular sides" (60). The remote monastery provides the setting for the encounter between the Englishmen and the Payne expedition, whose scholarly *randonnée* has already led Abraham and Isha to the site. The American travelers' interaction with the Englishmen advances a highly specific type of knowledge capital that will become indispensable in understanding Clark's narrative tactics for imagining the figural intimacy between Ayéda and Lot's wife.

Quite simply, Abraham Payne views the anchorite community as a curate's egg. He treats their inherited beliefs and traditional practices as superfluous distractions from their purely instrumental value as safekeepers of the proper objects of interest, the material remnants of the community's ancient origins. He laughingly takes up Aylward's mocking request to see some of the "queer relics" venerated by the monks, though it turns out that Payne's professionalized rationality, unlike that of Andrew Dickson White, his real-life prototype, loses some of its resilience upon contact with the monks' archive of relics of Sodom. More than any other item in the collection, the charter of the monastery at once piques and defeats Payne's acquisitive curiosity about the purported sodomitic origins of the monastery itself, as Payne's narration makes clear:

> It is written in archaic Hebrew; and from internal evidence that it contains, I am convinced that the hand that guided the reed that wrote it, became dust at least three thousand years ago. Only about half the writing is legible. I have tried every means that long experience in deciphering ancient manuscripts has taught me, to make out the faded

portions, but with little success; but, by piecing together detached sentences and scattered words, I have been able to gather the general sense of the document.

It begins with the solemn invocation of Jehovah, followed by a prayer for the sins of mankind. A remarkable declaration is then made. It states that, when God cursed Lot's wife and turned her into a pillar of salt, He left it standing at the southern end of the Salt Sea that covered the site of the accursed cities He had destroyed, as a warning to all men against disobedience. But, says the parchment, so many men went mad at the sight of the awful Woman of Salt, that God, in His mercy, removed it to the Valley of Madness, among the mountains, the only road to which lies along the Pass of Many Voices—a narrow way, dark and dangerous. Then follows another strange statement. It says that God further ordained that a House of Mercy should be built in the mountains, the duty of the inmates of which should be to restore to his senses any unfortunate man who might enter the Valley of Madness and look on Lot's wife. That portion of the parchment which apparently specifies how this is to be done is very illegible. All I have been able to make out are several unintelligible references to the Staff of Lot, which, as I told you, is believed by the monks to possess miraculous powers. The mention of it in this exceedingly ancient document goes to show what a unique relic is possessed by the monastery. (*FLW*, 97–98)

The partial information that Payne is able to decode from the ruined parchment installs the composite figure of Lot's wife/Medusa as the novel's ur-secret. As we will see, the subsequent disclosure of the figure in the "Valley of Madness" sets up the novel's culminating expression of the contemporary mythic significance—and unspeakability—of Lot's wife.

Hans Blumenberg's treatment of the Medusa myth in *Work on Myth* provides an entrée to the stakes of Clark's narrative design at this juncture. Unlike the classic psychoanalytical interpretations of Medusa, Blumenberg's rendering eschews a specific explanatory story (i.e., the etiology of the castration complex).[53] In Blumenberg's philosophical anthropology, the Medusa myth holds interest for its metanarrative suggestibility, in that it functions as a portable memory place of the equivocal power of naming. For Blumenberg, naming is the germinating condition of storying in its double capacity of reducing and warding off the anxiety (the "pure state of indefinite anticipation") that Blumenberg correlates with "intentionality of consciousness without an object"—the hallmark of the "absolutism of reality."[54]

In a word, stories "are told in order to 'kill' [*vertreiben*] something"—notably, "to kill time" and "to kill fear," in particular the fear of "unfamiliarity," which marks the dissolving edge of intentional consciousness.[55] On this account, the Medusa's head is not so much a symptom of an archaic anxiety (either on the register of psychogenesis or cultural development) as a testimonial to the achievable and ongoing task of consciousness, which is concretized in the artwork. (The transmutation paradigmatically expresses itself in the legendary aegis of Athena, with its ceremonial display of the Medusa's head.) What is accomplished is the survival of terror. Survival, even if scarred, holds open the possibility of "getting along with" the unnamed quotient that lies outside the grasp of consciousness, by ascribing to this nebulous zone the "capacity to be addressed."[56] There are no guarantees of a happy outcome, however.

The underlying precarity in the negotiation that Blumenberg describes surfaces in Andrew Dickson White's encyclopedia of the supposed "warfare" between science and religion—most emphatically so in the obsessional character of White's assertion that the myth of Lot's wife cannot too many times be relegated to the camp of primitive superstition. For all that, Clark's handling of the Sodom myth makes for the more provocative contemporary voicing (in Agamben's sense) of Blumenberg's argument. Clark mobilizes the undead character of the figural event—the medusan-sodomitic *combinatoire*—hidden in the desert landscape, and the resulting plot device produces the narrative fracture—the bizarre and disastrous consequence of "finding" Lot's wife—through which the element of the fantastic enters the otherwise realist plot and exposes the traumatic fallout from the converging worlds at the edge of the Dead Sea.

The pivotal dimensions of the "finding" emerge as repercussions of El Jezzar's territorial machinations. Having discovered that Ayéda's brother Selim, the sole surviving obstacle to his ambition to claim leadership of the Beni Azaleh, has sought refuge with the monks, El Jezzar leads his men in an attack on the monastery. During the course of the campaign, Selim and the Western travelers are taken prisoner, with Yorke grievously wounded. At this point, El Jezzar's stratagem turns into a murderous spiral. A hospitality crisis ensues. As we have already observed, the revelation of Selim's secret conversion to Christianity convicts the boy of the twin charges of apostasy and treason—pretext enough for El Jezzar to order the boy's public execution. Surmising that word of the Beni Azaleh's inhospitality toward strangers ("news of the attack on the monastery and the capture of the Frank travelers") will provoke retaliatory action on the part of the "Pasha" of the "Holy City," El Jezzar next decides to bury the evidence through a twofold tactic of dispersal (*FLW*, 219). The prisoners are to be escorted to the edge of the tribe's roaming territory and left to survive on their own devices in the forbidding landscape, and the Beni Azaleh will break camp and retreat into the anonymous reaches of "the Great Desert" (*FLW*, 220).

At this point, the narrative splinters in two directions, each of which follows on the fact that the forced exodus takes the company not within marching distance of Mar Saba, but instead into the preternaturally arid region of the Pass of Many Voices—Clark's fictionalized rendering of the famed gorge (the *Siq*) that opens onto Petra's eastern entrance. By the second day of the de facto death march, the entire party begins to show dangerous symptoms of exposure. The scholarly patriarch is the first to succumb. Payne develops heat stroke and goes missing, having fallen into a delirium and wandered away alone, deep into the salt plain, during the night. Desperate, Isha and Aylward set out in search of Payne, leaving the wounded and unconscious Yorke in the makeshift shelter of a cavern.

The group's splitting affords Clark the occasion to produce a novel variant of the biblical flight from Sodom when Ayéda accomplishes her penultimate role as the exemplar of hospitality in both its life-giving and violent aspects. The occasion turns on the exotically colored and interculturally precarious budding romance between Yorke and Ayéda. Ayéda is already situated as the virtually unseizable object of Aylward's and Yorke's contradictory perspectives, as well as the gracious host and transmitter of crucial information to the travelers. Having at once chosen self-exile and been abandoned by the Beni Azaleh for her devotion to Yorke, Ayéda discovers the secluded cavern just in the nick of time. With barely enough water remaining for one person, she leads Yorke on her camel across the salt plain, in hopes of finding the gorge that opens up the way back to the monastery. The several pages detailing the arduous desert crossing, including significant attention to the harrowing emotional and physical extremity of the girl as she copes with the diminishing chances of their joint survival, suggest Clark's interest in mining melodrama's resources in order to enlarge the mythic provocation and pertinence of the sodomitic topos of abortive exodus.

Consider the exquisitely morbid tableau of Ayéda's slow agony. She dies with her gaze fixed on the masterless camel and its unconscious burden, within view of the mouth of the gorge and certain rescue for Yorke but not for her. On the register of narrative realism, it is not implausible to imagine the betrothed couple of Yorke and Ayéda achieving a minimal approximation of the happy end that awaits the Anglo-American couple of

Aylward and Isha: the return to London. For all the ethnographic nuances built into Clark's treatment of the local monastic and tribal cultures, however, the story of immigration patterns from the Levant to England in the late nineteenth century is not a story that fits into the inter-worlding romance scheme of Clark's novel.[57] Instead, Clark foregrounds the ideological impossibility of Ayéda's safe passport into the imagined cultural home into which Aylward and Isha will seamlessly float as members of the normative count.

The sodomitic cast to the episode, however, turns not on the fact that Ayéda dies, but on how she dies. Her manner of death secures her position as a contradictory amalgam of traits caught in the semantic orbit of hospitality. She is at once a paragon of female submission and nurture pitched in the key of heroic and kenotic self-sacrifice, and a typical instance of the outcast whose death goes unanswered for and carries no price. (By contrast, Selim's murder, for all its horror, is the outcome of a juridical procedure.) The trick of the amalgam in Ayéda's case is that all of these traits occupy a zone of indistinction, where sublime necessity takes on an unaccountably contingent, yet nonetheless riveting, configuration of circumstantial forces. Clark's handling of Ayéda's unsettled position between defection and collaboration does raise the question of how the ethically provocative and ideologically troubling circumstances of Ayéda's death and posthumous survival (more on the latter in a moment) may be intimately related to the titular project of "finding" Lot's wife. Could Ayéda and Lot's wife be somehow related? The novel suggests yes. Indeed, the filament of figural intimacy between archaic and modern protagonists (pillar of salt and Bedouin girl) is the core "finding" of the novel and its signature of contemporariness.

Consider, in this light, the form Ayéda's posthumous survival assumes. The closing episode of the novel presents "the Private View at the Royal Academy" in London, at which a small crowd has assembled before a painting that has attracted attention for its promise "to be the picture of the year" (*FLW*, 313). The painting is Yorke's portrait of Ayéda. In a few lines, the rendering of the ceremonial event conveys with ironic detachment a plurality of gazes that conspicuously fails to reach anything resembling aesthetic consensus. The crowd's impression, with the narrator's tacit endorsement, produces the dominant focalization:

> It represented a beautiful Arab girl milking a she-camel in a Bedawîn camp in the early morning. It was exquisitely painted, the graceful

figure of the girl contrasting with the ungainly camel and its still more
ungainly foal standing by, all legs and eyes. Behind the black tents rose
the arid mountains tinged rose-pink by the rising sun. The girl was the
only figure in the canvas. She was looking over her shoulder, smiling
at somebody or something not appearing in the composition. It was a
picture that caught and charmed the eye at once, and exclamations of
admiration and pleasure rose from the crowd before it. (*FLW*, 313)

The portrait appears to be less a commemorative image of Ayéda than a
sanitized translation of her story into the stylized trappings of Bedouin life,
cut to the popular measure of David Roberts' Orientalized picturesque
aesthetic. If this is the future memory of Ayéda, it is indistinguishable from
an act of forgetting.

The final lines of the novel focus on the painting's more complicated
reception by a small group of the expedition's survivors:

Presently a tall young man, with sunburnt face, and drooping mous-
taches, accompanied by a pretty grey-eyed young lady, and followed
by a slight-built, learned-looking old man in spectacles, came into the
room. A fat, dark-faced man in semi-Asiatic costume was in attendance
on them. The party made its way through the crowd to the picture
which was attracting so much notice. It was evident that they had seen
it before.

"It seems to me more beautiful every time I see it!" remarked the
young lady, after they had stood in silence before it for a few moments.

"Poor girl!" said the young man, gazing at the lovely figure in the
picture.

"And poor Noel—he will never forget her," added the young lady.

"What for Mister Yok painting t'is fool-picture—common Arab girl
milking one camel?" muttered their Asiatic attendant, contemptuously.
(*FLW*, 314)

Given what we know of Aylward's peremptory habits, the response the
painting draws from him—"Poor girl!"—may pass for stock pity prompted
by the painting's picturesque semaphores of subaltern life on the edges of
the Arabian Desert. But the contrast with the "admiration and pleasure"
of the crowd also suggests an ethically poignant undertow of regretful understanding of the full range of circumstances that led to Yorke's choice
of subject for the painting. At the very least, Aylward's compassionate response suggests a newfound capacity to see beneath appearances—to see,
in a broadly Levinasian sense—the *face* of things, and to do so through,
not despite, the medium of the artwork. He apprehends, in other words,

the *unfinished* character of Ayéda's story. Similarly, Isha's observation of the intensifying beauty of the portrait says less about the refinement of her aesthetic appreciation than it does about her continued and deepening wonder at being given over, through the medium of the painted image, into the provocation and problem of Ayéda's life and death.

None of this is to say that Aylward and Isha stand for a discernible stripe of progressive Victorian liberalism. Clark's novelistic reach does not extend so far. The episode presents something less expository and more indicative of Clark's searching inquiry into the recesses of the Sodom archive, with its tortured paradigms of the ethico-political conundrums of hospitality. The clearest sign of the gambit appears in the discrepancy between the couple's shared moment of discreet reflection before the portrait and their subordinate companion's appraisal. The contrast openly panders to the element of xenophobic exceptionalism among Clark's readers. Aylward may have lost some of his swagger, but the swagger is communicable and it returns, with a cruelly comic touch, in Clark's scalpel-like rendering of the contempt of the "Asiatic attendant" for Yorke's choice of painterly subject matter. In a word, Clark has the servant give unwitting confirmation of his own subaltern status as the unwitting mimic of the totemic hierarchy of social and ethnic difference that guarantees his station below the English and above the Arab.

The detail makes for a strange ending to the novel. It is as if Clark had decided to wrap things up by resorting to a flat-footed reprise of the romance convention of homecoming, where home means triumphal adherence to unchanging custom. But not so fast. Now is the moment to observe the note of edginess Clark builds into the episode. The closing flourish underscores the precarity of the gaze occupied by Aylward and Isha, situated as it is between two forms of *not seeing*: the crowd's seduction by the conventions of the picturesque and the servant's territorial anxiety. Precisely because of its perfunctory and dismissive tone, the servant's précis of the portrait invites us to look again at the painting's compositional details.

Close attention to the portrait discloses a detail that speaks to an unclaimed viewing position, one that no one in the episode, not even the narrator, comments on: "The girl was the only figure in the canvas. She was looking over her shoulder, smiling at somebody or something not appearing in the composition" (*FLW*, 313). The nexus composed of the backward gesture, the indeterminate predicate of the smile, and the unmeasurable horizon of the girl's gaze incarnates the view from nowhere, an uncharted declension from the world represented on the surface of the canvas. The painting's tracing of the figure's allusive, retrospective encounter with an anonymous gaze adds a new fold to Clark's layered suggestion of the figural kinship between Ayéda and Lot's wife as an unread—and perhaps *unreadable*—image.[58]

To grasp the specific provocation built into Ayéda's portrait, we need to turn back to the episode that presents Clark's unusual treatment of the "finding" of Ayéda's biblical prototype. As we have seen, Payne's decoding of the ruined charter of the monastery tells us what to expect. Clark is going to pursue the inter-worlding instinct of the romance genre by treating the archaic document's account of the medusan property of the Woman of Salt as a literal and continuing disaster. The search for Payne, who has gone missing, leads Isha and Aylward into the "death-like stillness" of the cave where the pillar has been interred (*FLW*, 276). In the darkness, all that Isha sees is the figure of her father, "standing motionless with his back towards her" (*FLW*, 277). The prospect of happy reunion, however, is stalled by a flash of "electrical light" that discloses the titular figure of the novel, set in the midst of the salt cavern's otherwise benign mineral collectivity of "stalactites of great beauty and exquisite purity" (*FLW*, 277).

> Isha's horror-struck eyes had seen in that momentary gleam something that struck her motionless and speechless with fear.
>
> Standing in the centre of the cave, on a block of marble-like salt, was a dazzling white statue so life-like in attitude and expression that it seemed to be moving. Of such blinding brilliancy was it that no human eye could gaze long on it without risk of loss of sight. It was the figure of a very beautiful, though not very young woman, tall, and of graceful form. She was leaning slightly forward, as if in the act of turning. . . . Her bare right arm was extended in an attitude of fear, and she was looking backwards over her shoulder.
>
> There was an expression in the marble-white face, a look of immeasurable, unutterable horror, which seemed to freeze the blood in Isha's veins as she gazed on it. Every feature of the awful face, its terror-drawn muscles, fixed staring eyes and convulsed mouth, was imprinted on her mind forever. The appalling sight so terrified her, that for several seconds after the light had passed she stood as if rooted to the spot. Then, forgetful of everything else in her fear, she turned, and fled shrieking out of the cave. (*FLW*, 277–78)

Succumbing to the flight instinct—in reflexive emulation of the very action that the statue expresses in congealed form—is what saves Isha from the fate that her father and Aylward, more resistant than Isha to the promptings of fear, have been unable to escape. After dragging the two men out of the cave, she discovers that they are equally unresponsive. Both have been reduced to a "fixed stare of frozen horror" (*FLW*, 280). The sign of cognitive vacancy, in tandem with further evidence of the environment's aberrant character, to which I will turn in a moment, leads Isha to the discovery of what "finding" seems to mean in the novel: "She realized at once what had happened. The awful white figure in the icy-cold salt cave was Lot's Wife! The sight of the dreadful face had deprived the two men of their reason" (*FLW*, 281).

Having hit upon the mythic affinity between the biblical story of Lot's wife and the Medusa legend, Clark must solve a narrative problem: how to restore Payne and Aylward to health and get them back en route to England with Isha. The aptly titled chapter ("A Miracle") delivers exactly what was promised in Payne's earlier translation of the charter. The mere touch of the relic instantly cures both men's dementia. Clark nests the miracle in a lushly described account of a Greek Orthodox liturgical service, though the perfumed exoticism of the moment does not negate the fact that the scene is a creaky contrivance. Under cover of the inter-worlding intrigue of the lost world fantasy genre, the episode gives a sop to the credulous and a facile nod to popular Catholicism's adherence to belief in the persistence of miracles in the post-apostolic age. Moreover, the device clearly serves a domesticating purpose.[59] The miracle overtly precipitates the plot-driven advance toward *nostos*, homecoming, and it carries the promise that homecoming will entail a pleasing as well as generically mandated forgetfulness of the traumatic spectacle surveyed by the vacant yet lethal gaze of the salt statue. All the more reason to consider more closely how Clark distributes the shock effect of the medusan-sodomitic hybrid in order to complicate the stakes of the landscape of disclosure attached to the Woman of Salt.

Clark amplifies the scope of the *inter-esse*, the in-between, by introducing a further fold, an extended image of abortive anagnorisis, failed recognition, into the narrative disclosure of the hidden dwelling of the Woman of Salt, which occurs during Isha's and Aylward's desperate search for Payne.

> Lying on the rock-floor all round the mouth of the inner cave were a number of dark motionless objects. When, with hesitating steps and beating hearts, they ventured to approach these objects, they found them to be dead bodies. The light was sufficiently strong to enable them to see that they were those of men dressed in strange garments such as no human beings had worn for hundreds of years past.

Near them lay a crusader in splendid armor, whose golden-crested helmet an embossed cuirass and greaves glinted brightly. . . . All round lay strangely clad corpses, citizens of ancient Rome and Greece, in their plain dark robes; legionnaires with shields on their arms, and Greek archers bow in hand; turbaned Saracens grasping curves scimitars; Assyrians in tasseled garments, long curled hair and beards in cases; shaven-haired Egyptian in semi-transparent linen clothes and thin sandals with turned-up toes; Persians in baggy breeches, long coats and pointed hats; Christian devotees, long-haired and long-bearded, some with self-mutilated hands and feet, and all clasping crosses to their sunken breasts; Arabs, negroes, and men of many other nations, some of which had long been extinct. Scores of bodies lay around, all sleeping the sleep which in the case of most had already lasted centuries. Not a garment was displaced, not a particle of dust rested on any of the motionless figures, not a speck of rust dimmed the polished armor or the arms lying on the rock. Each hollow mummy face had the same expression on it—one of overwhelming horror such as would remain on the faces of men who had died mad with terror. It was a dreadful sight, and Aylward and his trembling companion stood for some moments looking on with horror in their faces and fear in their hearts. (*FLW*, 274–75)

The "horror" of the spectacle proves more than a sensationalist gesture, for it supplies Isha with the image of a historical basis for the otherwise inexplicable fate suffered by Payne and Aylward: "All the dead men around her had, doubtless, centuries before, looked on the Woman of Salt, and had died mad in consequence" (*FLW*, 281). The symmetry between the necropolis of "dead faces turned to her" and the "fixed stare of frozen horror" that has taken possession of her father and Aylward is precisely what enables her to infer the longitudinal persistence of the logic of direct causality. The "doubtless" character of the judgment, however, does not alter the equivocal character of the forensic premises in the immediate narrative environment. The "consequence" Isha infers occupies a space of indecision between belief in supernatural intervention and an implied association of traumatic petrification with mimetic contagion.

Indeed, the neutral, quasi-objective description of the necropolis, which shows what there is to see but not how to see it, suggestively presents the punitive hand of divine judgment as an allegorical cover for a more provocative species of lethal contact. The taxonomic precision of the necropolis bears an uncanny resemblance to the collector's habit, which expressed itself with ludic verve in the early modern cabinets of curiosity before acquiring a more systematic character with the rise of the public art museum in the eighteenth and nineteenth centuries.[60] Clark's necropolis gives pause by suggesting how the emergent ethos of scientific rationality that gave momentum to the collector's habit also contributed to the ascendancy of a culture of reification and a correspondingly flattened and petrified—*ahistorical*—image of history geared to the cult of data collection and "information transfer."[61] More provocatively still, the necropolis intimates the tacit co-implication of the "curatorial aspect" of imagination and the accretive rhythm mobilizing the history of imperial conquest and its colonial extensions.[62] These considerations sharpen the optics of the scene by suggesting how the assembled grid of peoples in the hidden cave may appear encyclopedic but is not innocent. For the most part, the names constitute a digest of groups associated with territorial incursions into the region through which Clark's travelers have also wandered, with no declared understanding of the region's vexed memoryscape.

The stilled dynamic that meets the finally uncomprehending gaze of Isha conveys the heart of Clark's interest in the salt pillar's quiet but perduring association with the disorienting and unnameable character of the *inter-esse*, which resists the captivations of naming. What the episode leaves unsaid (neither the narrator nor any of the characters claim it) but makes available to thought is Clark's intuition that the *face* of Lot's wife resides here, in the anamorphic distortion of what Isha sees. From this uninhabited perspective, the Woman of Salt is neither the source nor the transmitter of devastation from a metaphysical outside. Rather, the statue incarnates a specific type of ideological endgame. Without spirit and without choice, the "marble-white" artifact plays out the dialectical reversal of the predatory habits of adventure and acquisition that have led to the reflexive, and costly, association of *finding* with *owning*.

This is the most daring moment in the novel. It discloses the specific unreadability of the *contemporariness* folded into Clark's narrative venture. For Agamben, let us recall, the contemporary does not refer to the typical instance of a cultural moment or the operative fluency of part-whole relationships. The contemporary expresses a *"relationship with time that adheres to it through a disjunction and an anachronism."*[63] Clark's ingenious emendation of the received sense of the backward turn in the Sodom archive presents the petrified gesture of the statue as the true measure of participation in the disjunctive cast to the contemporary. The true measure is the dangerous scruple that "returns to that part within the present that we are absolutely incapable of living."[64] What the necropolis also shows— though no one in the novel is on hand to apprehend the point—is that the unlivable quotient includes an unabsolved memory of political acquisitiveness in the extended field of interest in the territory that Clark serves up as the landscape of lost world romance.

Clark's necropolis, in other words, invites his readers to contemplate the view from nowhere and to consider the cost of ignoring what the view affords. What the view from nowhere affords is the chance to begin understanding the full scope of intercultural interference in the wake of the coiled legacies of pilgrimage, predatory expedition, and adventure tourism to the so-called holy land. Is this an anachronistic reading of the novel? Perhaps, but Clark's staging of the discovery of the necropolis tells us that this is perhaps the wrong question. At the very least, it is not the most interesting question. The most interesting question resides in the figural connection between the necropolis, with its museum-like character, and the Private View at the Royal Academy. The connection appears through the assembled onlookers' variously uncomprehending observations of the sole detail in the portrait of Ayéda that testifies to the painted subject's proximity to the Woman of Salt. The portrait silently presides over an extended tableau of disjunction and anachronism that both complements and adds point to the contemporariness of the secret necropolis.

The pivot of the narrative tableau (the composite figure of the painting and the visitors to the Private View) resides in the stilled gaze of Ayéda. The direction of her gaze evokes the function of the vanishing point in perspectival painting. Unlike the vanishing point, however, which organizes a spatialized economy of vision into which the viewer is welcomed as the virtual subjective center of the represented world, Ayéda's gaze finds harbor in the spacings between the divided perceptions of the gathered assembly. Her gaze is the icon of a missed rendezvous, and the element that has gone missing is precisely what guarantees the provocative contemporariness of Clark's version of the Sodom legend.[65]

There are two lessons here. The first carries a tacit commentary on the ideological service of the picturesque. To dwell in Ayéda's gaze is to sense, however obliquely, that the "admiration and pleasure" aroused in the crowd by the painting's aesthetic cues is a form of complacent misrecognition. The crowd's rapt attention performs a way of not seeing the complicity of the picturesque in the structural engines of political predation in the landscape that the painting presents as a luminous confection. The first lesson has a tellable story, one that belongs to the history of Orientalism. The second lesson, while not alien to this story, is irreducible to it. How is this so? Follow the direction of Ayéda's gaze. Who, or what, is she looking back at? The mournful ruminations of Aylward and Isha suggest the obvious answer according to the naturalistic protocol of the narrative. Ayéda is looking at the painter, Noel Yorke, the person who has ensured her post-humous survival in the artwork. But the disjunction between the onlook-ers' commemorative inference and the narrator's dispassionate abstention from judgment (the figure is "smiling at somebody or something not ap-pearing in the composition") reminds us that the painted gaze also incar-nates the Levinasian specter of the "eternal duration of the interval . . . the meanwhile."[66] Here, however, Ayéda's gaze does not simply confirm Levinas's negative judgment of aesthetic captivation. Instead, it presents a double anachronism with reparative import.

Looking back over her shoulder, Ayéda smiles eternally at what cannot be seen from any other place but hers. The smile distills a past moment of intimacy that the onlookers will never recoup or fully understand. But the asymptotic drift is more than a sign of ironic dislocation or quietly trium-phant inoculation to the alien world now cosmetically rendered through the mode of the picturesque. The scene of failed recognition harbors the germ of possibility for a way of being-in-common that is not mortgaged to the ruinous logic of dichotomous difference. To follow the narrator's suggestion—not choosing posthaste between "somebody" and "some-thing" in imagining whatever it is that solicits the smile—is to grasp the otherwise inconceivable thought that Ayéda is smiling at an unseen and unanticipated future, a future that has not perhaps forgotten but has for-given and redeemed itself from the violence of the past. If the Woman of Salt remembers and recalibrates the traumatic undertow to the legacy of Lot's wife, Ayéda's smile remembers the other face of the turning figure—the face as gesture of hospitality toward the future in its radical unknowability.

CHAPTER 7

Out of Africa: Albert Memmi's Desert of Allegory in *The Pillar of Salt*

The world *is*, not because it perseveres in being, not because *being*
is its own *raison d'être*, but because, through the human enterprise,
it can be justified in its being. The human is the possibility of
a being-for-the-other. That possibility is the justification for
all existing. The world is justified in its being by human dis-
interestment. . . . More important than God's omnipotence is
the subordination of that power to man's ethical consent. And
that, too, is one of the primordial meanings of kenosis.

—EMMANUEL LEVINAS, "Judaism and Kenosis"[1]

In 1891, the French Jewish philanthropist Baron Maurice de Hirsch
founded the Jewish Colonization Association, for facilitating the emigration of Ashkenazic Jews to agricultural colonies in the Americas. One of
the initiative's most prosperous outgrowths was the Jewish settlement in
Argentina's Entre Rios province, some 250 miles north of Buenos Aires.
The founding residents designed Carmel colony to resemble a Russian
village, reincarnating the image of a lost home. Today, only the cemetery
and the synagogue survive (fig. 16). Following substantial migrations from
the colony, the synagogue ceased to operate in the early 1950s. As a recent
tourist publication notes, the colony itself "is no longer in maps."[2]

The gradual evacuation of the Carmel synagogue and colony has no historical connection with the roughly contemporary fantasy of a redemptive
flight to Argentina that germinates in the final pages of Albert Memmi's
signature autobiographical novel, *The Pillar of Salt* (1953). Yet there is an
eloquent figural connection. It has to do with the specter of homelessness that haunts Sodomscape. For all that, the titular allusion to Lot's wife
seems oddly judged. In the body of the novel proper, the narrator's account of his mounting sense of personal anomie and political disillusion-

Figure 16. Carmel Synagogue, Entre Rios Province, Argentina. Photo courtesy of Jay H. Geller.

ment in colonial Tunisia proceeds without further mention of the Sodom legend until, a few paragraphs from the end of the book, the moment of recognition finally occurs. The narrator's choice of Lot's wife to signpost the psychic paralysis from which he suffers and seeks relief is undoubtedly poignant, but the attentive reader may be excused for wondering whether the payoff from the venture into the biblical archive is worth the wait. The gesture sits oddly with the narrator's hard-won secularism. More importantly, the diagnosis—"I am dying through having turned back to look at myself"—conveys what is at best a myopic capture of the crisis.[3] Traumatic introspection is the symptom, not the explanatory cause, of the felt impasse. Moreover, the pain of this moment quickly and perhaps prematurely resolves itself in the improbable dream of westward flight to Argentina. What could possibly be the relation between Lot's wife and Argentina?

It would be a mistake to gauge the Sodom reflex in the novel solely by the narrator's uncertain emotional navigation. The unusual double cathexis I have just described is but one moment in the Sodom trope's complexly choreographed outworking found in the novel's discursive texture as it incorporates the narrator's affective and cognitive travails into the acutely observed chronicle of life in colonial Tunis. The narrative's dense weave includes the precariously blended communities of Berbers, Arabs, Jews, and French nationals, with the aggregate unevenly distributed across the spectrum of social stations and economic means, from the upper echelons of the settler class to the working poor and destitute. Together, the two imbricated registers of experience (the personal and the socio-political) comprise material ground for the novel's speculative engagement with a theo-philosophically tinged meeting between self-dispossession and self-forgetting. My specific claim is that the novel's place in Sodomscape warrants interest for its unique fleshing out of the myth of Sodom and Lot's wife as an extended drama of kenosis.

Here it pays to revisit one of the exemplary intuitions of kenotic hospitality, held in the deep memory of theo-aesthetic reflection on the transformative potency of figural expression. The scene unfolds in a region of Sodomscape that we have already visited: Irenaeus's counter-reading of the salt pillar as a polytropic figure of the ecclesial community's resilience over tracts of time. Instead of petrification, what Irenaeus sees at work in the figure is the silent operation of Pauline kairos (the contingency of time) and kenosis (dispossessive personhood). These are the two linchpins of the drama of messianic *eventfulness* in time, between "no more" and "not yet."[4] Crucially, Irenaeus's refusal to condemn the fabled shifting appearance of the pillar carries an anticipatory suggestion of Levinas's understanding of the kenotic drama of ethical dispossession. For Levinas, let us recall, the onset of ethical attunement turns on the "strange defeat or defection of identity" that opens a difference between "the ego and itself."[5] This difference, the "*non-coincidence* of the identical, is a fundamental *non-indifference* with regard to men."[6]

In Memmi's treatment, kenosis is not a named topic. The notion's Christological significance therefore remains on the far shore of the novel's biblical memory. Instead, the notion subsists in the narrative as the mutating crucible of chance and choice through which the narrator's horizon of experience comes to accommodate hospitality's polar energies, both promise and risk, in ways unpredicted by the narrative chain of events and misrecognized by the narrator himself. To anticipate this chapter's main argument, Memmi's choreography of unseen and seen reclaimings of Lot's wife captures the figure's launch into unexpected dimensions of what thought can welcome and assimilate. *The Pillar of Salt* thus speaks to the (Levinasian) *face* of the biblical figure. Through this gesture, Memmi's narrative orients the drama of kenosis not simply toward the death of the knowing subject (the psychological cognate of the a-theological "death of God" thesis). The drama passes through that death into the astringent lucidity of the desert.

This is not the physical desert surrounding Tunis. This is the desert understood as the thought-archive where Maurice Blanchot and Emmanuel Levinas find common ground. Here the word *desert* is a holding place for Blanchot's and Levinas's shared interrogations of the uncertain merger of aesthetic and ethical dimensions of the artwork in its "workless-ness" and "empty power."[7] In short, the desert's thought-archive expresses the artwork's silent proximity to two events: the call of prophetic speech in its "primal powerlessness," and the suspension of proprietary and self-regarding thought in the ethical attunement to what is urgently at hand, though unseen.[8]

The essential claim I want to make about Memmi's novel is that its access to the place held at the edge of memory by Lot's wife yields an imaginative horizon that narrows the distance between desert and allegory. As we have seen, this is the very distance that Blanchot tries to maintain in the almost contemporary essay (from 1957) on prophetic speech.[9] Memmi's novel narrows the distance by inhabiting the uneasy interval between "speaking other" and "speaking of the Other"—that is, between the habit of negotiating familiar currencies of cultural belonging and the disorienting exposure to a perspective that registers as alien and incomprehensible. One of the signal merits of *The Pillar of Salt* is that its narrative arc does not cheat on this score; it withholds an unambiguously happy end. Instead, it holds its gaze on the difficult yet bracing proximity between the felt time of dying ("I am dying through having turned back") and the tentative onset of a new beginning.

The critical framework I propose for the novel is avowedly unconventional. The rich topicality of *The Pillar of Salt* easily warrants Francophone postcolonial studies' attention to the novel as a groundbreaking literary testimony of the colonial regime's corrosive effects in the Maghreb. As Judith Roumani argues, *The Pillar of Salt* bears broad comparison with *Le passé simple* (1954) by Moroccan novelist Driss Chraibi in being one of the first indigenous "témoignages to emerge from North Africa" giving vivid expression to the experience of "cultural *déchirement*."[10] The "anguished" autobiographical element in particular "inaugurated a new tradition of existential realism" with a discernible, if implicit, investment in advancing a guarded sense of nationalist self-consciousness and cultural community.[11] Memmi's acknowledged international stature as a key figure in the formative years of postwar theoretical reflection on colonialism—notably in *The Colonizer and the Colonized* (1957)—gives further warranty to the socio-political optic through which Memmi's works are typically read.

There is a ghost in the machine, however. It may be inferred from the relative eclipse in the canon of theoretical critiques of colonialism of *The Colonizer and the Colonized*'s argumentative tactics by the ascendency of Frantz Fanon's and Homi Bhabha's work. Superficially, all three thinkers share a *lingua franca* drawn from Marxist and psychoanalytical theories of subject formation and social organization. There is a strong prescriptive, and even utopian, element to Fanon's and Bhabha's writings that partially accounts for their prestige and influence.[12] This element is not absent from Memmi's nonfictional writings, starting with *The Colonizer and the Colonized* and continuing through his memoir, *Le nomade immobile* (2000); and it undoubtedly issues from the same imperative that may be heard in Fanon's and Bhabha's voices—the call for justice. Yet Memmi's procedure more closely resembles that of the bricoleur, or, to use Edouard Glissant's provocative formula, a "*créolisation*" or "*métissage* without limits" produced by "an encounter and a synthesis of two *différents* . . . whose results are unforeseeable."[13]

For Memmi, the prospect of "*métissage* without limits" pertains not solely to the psychic and social dramas produced by the colonial situation; it also encompasses the heuristic and critical methodologies used to address the problem of oppression in its manifold forms and guises.[14] Thus, *The Colonizer and the Colonized* inveighs against doctrinaire regimens of thought: "Psychoanalysis or Marxism must not, under the pretext of having discovered the source or one of the main sources of human conduct, preempt all lived experience, all feeling, all suffering, all the byways of human behaviour, and call them profit motive or Oedipus complex."[15] In the same text, Memmi acknowledges that the "economic aspect of colonialism"— and in particular the economic underpinning of the "notion of *privilege* . . . at the heart of the colonial relationship"—is "fundamental."[16] But he also refuses to hold up the diagnosis and critique of economic and, more broadly, sociopolitical factors as a magic bullet. In Memmi's oeuvre, therefore, the sociopolitical optic is crucial, but not the sole determinant or gauge of "lived experience" (*le vécu*).

The same may be said for Memmi's relation to cultural (symbolic and mythopoetic) registers of thought and action.[17] Memmi's emphasis on the refractive character of "lived experience," for example, draws on the psychoanalytical notion of the unconscious. It does so, however, not to suppose, as Fanon does, a "reservoir for the authentic subjectivity and freedom of the colonized," but to argue instead for the confluence of cultural and sociopolitical factors in the production of contradictory and even self-destructive behaviors in the colonizer/colonized relationship.[18]

An equally potent vigilance toward the *à-venir* balances Memmi's critical utopian instincts, where what is "to come" correlates not with the infinity of God or conceptual thought, but with the measureless interval of kenotic and kairotic time, the time in which the subject's equivocal bearings— "being outside, and yet belonging"—are put in play.[19] As the agnostic that he is, Memmi eschews such religiously inflected language, except to disparage it. Nonetheless, the Pauline confluence of kenosis and kairos—the double helix of letting go and beginning again—aptly captures Memmi's adherence to a specific kind of double truth. Albert Camus's glancing remark in the preface to the first edition of *The Pillar of Salt* perhaps sees more than it says in observing the Pauline undertow to Memmi's authorial voice: "in any case, writing has been the Damascus road for this nonbelieving Paul."[20] Once again, *The Colonizer and the Colonized* provides the template. As Suzanne Gearhart points out, Memmi emphasizes "the importance of keeping before us the universal significance of the colonial condition" in late modernity, which entails appreciating its internal logic's *inapparent* outworking. Yet Memmi also "demands that we keep before us the particularity of each instance of oppression, which can only be grasped in terms of a process of interiorization, whose reality lies as much in its cultural and individual specificity as in its generality or universality."[21]

For Memmi, the dialectical tension holding universality and particularity in precarious balance is more than a philosophical pirouette. It inheres in the syncopation of "lived experience" (*le vécu*). Where *The Colonizer and the Colonized* presents an aerial view of the paradox of this type of double truth, *The Pillar of Salt* takes readers into the thick of it. The choice of genre—or rather the genre's indeterminacy—is telling. To recall Roumani's point, the novel's autobiographical piquancy proved historically significant, precisely because this feature expressed an "existential realism" that marked an important but also disorienting juncture in the development of a critical voice in Jewish-Tunisian writing.[22] André Wurmser's review in *Les lettres françaises*, which appeared shortly before the publication of the novel, described the provocation in formal terms: "*The Pillar of Salt* is at once a novel, an autobiography, a documentary text, and a sociological study, and many other things as well."[23] More than any other remark in the contemporary press, Wurmser's inclusion of the blanket category of "many other things" captures the broadly felt sense that the novel's disorienting impact related to the fact that it was not so much a hybrid of distinct genres as a tacit dismantling of the very notion of pure or consistent perceptual schemes through which fact might be sifted out of fiction. This feature's emblematic instance is the narrator's decision at the end of the book to immigrate to Argentina. The novel's early reception was virtually unanimous in voicing dismay at the turn to South America to mark the drama's nominal dénouement. Why Argentina? The Jewish press saw this feature as a repudiation of Zionist aspiration; the Arab press saw it as an implicit refusal to endorse the mounting spirit of nationalist solidarity in Tunisia.[24]

There is indeed something provocative about the turn to Argentina. As Judith (Colette) Touitou-Benitah points out, for North African Jews living at the indicated time of Memmi's novel, "feasible destinations were decided by linguistic and cultural criteria," and in this context Argentina was "a real option for Jews of northern Morocco, Tangiers or Larache, but not in Tunis."[25] The turn to Argentina quite literally decenters the novel's realist narrative grounds. It also bears noting that the prospect of going to Argentina appears twice.

After the Liberation and the retreat of the German occupation forces, a preternatural sense of calm briefly descends over the Jewish ghetto. The narrator, however, true to his deeply rooted habit of tormented introspection, develops insomnia instead—in stark contrast to his friend Henry. An enthusiastic and habitual daydreamer, Henry concocts a plan for the two young men to join Henry's newfound uncle in Argentina, "a new country full of untapped resources."[26] The narrator finds the plan typically absurd —"I did not take him seriously, any more than when he had planned a fishing business on the desert coasts of the South. Did the uncle really exist?"—yet he indulges his friend in the fantasy, mostly because it takes the edge off the narrator's own worries about the future. Henry's dream of "wealth in Argentina and the wonderful life out in the open, on horseback, in boots and sombreros" then drops out of view. When it suddenly reappears, as the last chapter's main topic, the dream belongs to the narrator as well, but now in the guise of a forced choice. The improbable ocean crossing is no more than the decision not to die, "to give what is left of my life its last chance" (*PoS*, 335).

One of the novel's cruxes transpires between the two Argentinas—that is, between the first mention of Henry's fantasy and the narrator's ambivalent embrace of the borrowed daydream. The scene is the examination hall in the university library at Algiers to which the narrator has come, after the lifting of the Vichy laws, to take the admission entrance exams. Though the narrator's career at the *lycée* has shown remarkable academic promise (more on this shortly), in the examination hall he experiences the crushing defeat of his fantasy that his intellectual gifts will provide safe harbor in the form of a career path and professional identity. He loses heart—moreover, he realizes the degree to which he has already lost faith in the educational system's liberal pretensions—and he gives up. What is telling about the incident is that it has already occurred in the novel. The novel begins in the same examination hall, and the opening scene treats the same crisis. In the French, the symmetry is inescapable, for the two respective chapters have the same title: "L'épreuve," a word that aptly signifies both the academic exam's institutional format and a personal ordeal.[27] But the symmetry is not perfect, and the swerve out of alignment is crucial to understanding the antirealist, and kenotic, component to the novel's aesthetic design.

Both chapters call attention to the complex intimacy of writing and living. The narrator discovers that simply being a spectacular student will not enable him to write himself out of his condition as Jewish-Berber Tunisian enduring the long sunset of the French colonial presence. Though the sobering insight remains the same, the depiction of the writing that takes place in the examination hall radically changes. In the first *épreuve*, the narrator recovers from his initial paralysis by reverting to the habit of the good student, though there is room to wonder what exactly fills the pages he writes. Determined to avoid the shame of calling attention to his struggle, he lowers his head and pretends to take up the assigned question: "I write anything that comes into my head." He manages to continue writing through the exam period:

> To give myself countenance, to escape, I continued writing for seven hours, like all the others. I even made the most of the extra fifteen minutes of grace granted to the stragglers. That is because my whole life was rising up in my throat again, because I was writing without thinking, straight from the heart to the pen.
>
> At the close of this exhausting session, I had some fifty pages to carry away with me. Perhaps, as I now straighten out this narrative [*en ordonnant ce récit*], I can manage to see more clearly into my own darkness and to find a way out. (*PoS*, x)

It seems at first that the "anything" that comes to mind derives from his classroom training in economics, psychology, and political philosophy. By the end of the *épreuve*, it seems more likely that the "fifty pages" are the unvarnished testimony, *pris sur le vif*, as it were, of the young man's disappointments and frustrations. Instead of writing the exam, he produces a rough draft of the semi-autobiographical novel that will be titled *The Pillar of Salt*.

From this point on, the aura of a Proustian *mise en abyme* floats over most of the novel, such that the ensuing chronicle of family life at the

outskirts of the Jewish ghetto, through the reported splendors and miseries
of school years and the trauma of the German occupation and *Judenrat* in
Tunisia, may be taken to present the narrative coherence of the remembered—or, as the narrator puts it, straightened out—aspects of *le vécu*.[28]
Until we reach the second *épreuve*. In principle, the symmetrical pairing of
the two *épreuves* creates a formal closure through the loopback or *uroburos*
effect of coming full circle. The narrator calls attention to the circularity
of the device at the opening of the chapter: "I have now come to the point
where I began my narrative. Here I am in the examination hall, in the huge
university library. All around me, as far as the distant shelves on the walls,
my comrades are feverishly at work" (*PoS*, 323). The signal for imminent
narrative closure could not be clearer. But the end is rather different from
the one described at the outset of the novel:

> *Soon silence reigned. Not a breath in the vast hall with its hundreds of*
> *students. Each has identified himself with his work, each is alone for the next*
> *seven hours. It is then that it dawns on me, with the white paper in front of*
> *me, that all this no longer concerns me at all.*
>
> This time the spring within me is quite broken; my strength and my
> will power fail me now. I might have stopped before leaving Tunis, or
> at the customs, or in a railroad station on my way, or at the entrance to
> the college. But I stopped in the examination room. It really is the end:
> I shall never be a professor. (*PoS*, 332–33)

Like the snake in the *uroburos* myth, the text swallows up the instrumental
premise of its origin. The fifty pages of life writing that figured in the first
épreuve as the enabling hyphen between the lived, remembered, and written dimensions of *le vécu* dissolve into "white sheets of paper" (*PoS*, 323).
As the narrator points out at the close of the chapter, this "really is the
end" (*PoS*, 333). It is not only the end of the narrator's professional aspirations, but also the end of the novel's assumed reliance on the fact/fiction
dichotomy and the consoling illusion of referential solvency attached to
the reported writing practice that held the germinating seeds of *The Pillar*
of Salt in the first *épreuve*.

The positioning of the two *épreuves*—to be clear: these occur not at
the beginning and end of the novel, but at the beginning and *just before*
the end—gives the novel an eccentric and virtually herniated form. The
final chapter, aptly titled "The Departure," formally introduces a surplus
and unmoored narrative phase. The realist purchase of the narrator's voice
continues, but it issues from a space no longer authorized by the reporto-
rial strategy that silently informs most of the novel. This breach marks

the difference between the two Argentinas. Henry's fantasy is contained within the flashback. Conceivably, it could be found in the fifty pages of urtext mentioned in the opening *épreuve*. Not so with the narrator's subsequent assent to the fantasy, which takes place in a represented "now" that belongs to a strangely posthumous afterlife, not of the narrator, but of the text he is purported to have written. The narrator's choice of Argentina coincides with the novel's drift into an oneiric free fall. As we will see, this strangely diasporic movement at the edges of verisimilitude does not so much repudiate the novel's alleged "existential realism" as push its boundaries toward the desert of allegory and its prophetic implication.

There are several ways to explain the novel's unmooring from its alleged realist grounds. Contemporary readers may have found the flight to Argentina both historically improbable and politically exasperating. Coming as it does in the wake of the paired scenes of writing and unwriting, however, this post hoc torsion corroborates Memmi's amply documented Pyrrhonist reflexes. Notably, the divided dream of Argentina speaks to the author's refusal to swallow autobiographical fallacy's lure. In an interview with Victor Malka, Memmi insists on the genre's fabricated nature: "You must understand that autobiography is a false genre: there's a big difference between living and recounting a life. You dream it, you reinvent it through the very recounting, you never stop seeing it from different perspectives."[29]

The stakes of the gesture may be appreciated by reflecting on the novel's complex and shifting depictions of the sense of being at home. The narrator's developing sense of himself and his place in the converging worlds he inhabits presents an object lesson in the risks that must be assumed to see past the at times deceptive borders of what it means to be at home. As we will see, *The Pillar of Salt* does more than put on exhibit the poisonous hybrid of a colonial machine and a multicultural environment. It also displays the tension between individual and systemic or structural modes of envisioning home as the place where the claims of ethics and justice may be answered to or go unheard.

An eloquent index of this feature is the specific urban situation of the narrator's home. The family dwelling in Tunis is a "shapeless old building" at the bottom of the "Impasse Tarfoune" (*PoS*, 4). Literally a blind alley, the domicile is also a threshold, for the alley lies "at the frontier of the Jewish quarter" (*PoS*, 24).[30] The location comes to symbolize the narrator's divided orientation as he experiences shifting stances of ambivalence toward the several communities that make up his ancestry, social condition, and future prospects. Not least among these is the patrimonial legacy of Jewishness. As Isaac Yetiv points out, Memmi has often remarked that the memory of his childhood in and around the Jewish ghetto of Tunis (La Hara) has been the "matrix" of his work. However, like the several salt diapirs from which the modern tourist may select the legendary pillar of salt at Ein Bokek, the matrix of Memmi's Jewish identity (and that of his narrator in *The Pillar of Salt*) is a tectonic environment composed of varied and sometimes contradictory responses to the different facets of Judaism—religious, cultural, social, and national.[31]

Some of the most luminous pages in the novel occur in the early chapter describing the rituals, foods, and leisure time of the Sabbath weekends, all handled with great delicacy of feeling and innocent nostalgia. The depiction of the bar mitzvah celebration a few chapters later is a more complicated affair, and not only because the narrator is beginning to show signs of adolescent rebelliousness. His chafing observation of the "pettiness" of the "tribal community" (*la tribu*) during the ritual signals the onset of an uneasy confluence of ethnic self-identification and withering critique (*PoS*, 62). The moment of ambivalent attunement forecasts the pattern of territorial friction that will mark, with supple variations, virtually all the ensuing events in the novel. In sum, the bar mitzvah chapter potently expresses the _unmooring_ that the narrative tactic of split perspectives repeatedly introduces into the novel's formal design. The unmooring produces two complementary effects. It calls into question the solvency of the varied incarnations of "home" and "away" that convey the rich topicality of the narrator's adventures: the family enclave, the Jewish ghetto, the predominantly Arab city, the French school system and, by extension, the French colonial apparatus, and, finally, the borrowed dream of Argentina. The sheer repetitiveness of the unmooring, however, also suggests that the narrator's mounting crisis comes not simply from the material attributes of the inhabited environments, but also, and more profoundly, from the irremissible in-betweenness at the heart of sentient experience.

The percussive rhythm of unmooring secures *The Pillar of Salt*'s status as a site of transit and communication—that is, an allegorical machine—mediating colonialism's lived traumas with hospitality's figural aporias. The embedded allegorical element—with its double-voiced aptitude for "speaking other" and "speaking of the Other"—decisively enables the novel's inspection of the linkage between empirical and speculative dimensions of belonging. *The Pillar of Salt* amply supports Memmi's claim that his Jewishness—or rather the tangle of cultural and religious legacies and sociopolitical contingencies that make up what he calls "the Jewish condition"—is a matrix of his oeuvre.[32] The potency of the novel's argument, however, derives no less from a second, formal matrix, which goes unmentioned by the narrator. This is the Augustinian legacy, particularly as exhibited by the narrative design and allegorical denouement of the *Confessions*.

Imagining Augustine and Arendt in Colonial Tunis

In one distinctly mappable sense, Augustine's self-portrait in the *Confessions* is a late-antique *type*, or model, of Memmi's coming-of-age story in *The Pillar of Salt*. Carthage is the memorable scene of the young Augustine's formative years as a student and later rhetoric teacher. This is not, of course, the Phoenician Carthage destroyed by Rome in the Third Punic War, but the city Augustus Caesar rebuilt as a Roman colony and a flourishing provincial metropolis by the time Augustine took up residence there in the Roman empire's waning years. A smaller town neighboring Carthage in antiquity, Tunis rose to prominence after Carthage fell to the Umayyad Caliphate at the end of the seventh century. Memmi's Tunis is largely the cultural invention of the occupying Arab Muslims from the seventh century onwards, and the administrative product of the French protectorate established in the last decades of the nineteenth century. The same era saw Carthage's reinvention as a site of archaeological excavation and, to judge by Gustave Flaubert's perfumed historical concoction *Salammbô* (1862), an imaginary object of Orientalizing fantasy. All of this is to say that the novel's Tunis is at once the modern descendant and the contemporary of Augustine's Roman Carthage. Like its fabled late-antique predecessor, it too heads toward another crushing episode of territorial conflict in the North African theater of imperial and colonial expansion.

The typological kinship between Tunis and Carthage supplies the necessary optic for appreciating the textural richness of the novel's semi-autobiographical depiction of a continuously unfolding encounter between the narrating self, in the "now" of writing, and the narrated self, in the second-order "now" of remembered living. The *Confessions* famously uses the divided optic to convey the propulsive and kenotic dynamism through which the text's composite structure—the topical/speculative conversion narrative—unfolds. Moreover, it unfolds in a way that solves the problem of narrative closure, as the narrating self proceeds through the life-writing phase into the phenomenological reflections on memory and time, and the concluding allegorical exegesis of the Genesis account of creation— Augustine's final speculative "home."

The resulting narrative arc of the *Confessions* also illustrates the iridescent signification of the notion of natality that Arendt found in Augustine's provocative association of human being with the "faculty of beginning" in the *City of God*: "That this beginning, therefore, might be, the first man was created."[33] The cumulative import of Arendt's reflections on the notion, though not spelled out in a specific manifesto, suggests the interpenetrating character of the three faces of natality. Thus, the commonplace event of having been born—factual natality—may be understood as the ongoing basis and mnemonic prompt for other beginnings: "political natality—birth into the realm of action; and theoretical natality—birth into the timelessness of thought."[34] Aside from giving narrative flesh to the notion of natality and its implied experience of unmooring, one of the *Confessions*'s formal novelties is that its divided optic exhibits natality's richly allegorical texture. If natality for Arendt, as Miguel Vatter argues, "names the primordial 'nomadic' condition of human life," the *Confessions* formally locates that condition in the narrator's identity as the space of tensile negotiation between historicity's empirical claims ("speaking other") and the testimonial condition's ethical urgency ("speaking of the Other").[35]

Here it pays to recall Derrida's point that "testimoniality belongs *a priori* to the order of the miraculous," because, when one testifies, "even on the subject of the most ordinary and the most 'normal' event, one asks the other to believe one at one's word as if it were a matter of a miracle."[36] In the *Confessions*, of course, Augustine identifies the order of the miraculous with the divinely authored gift of creation and the mysterious workings of grace, which together insert human beings into the drama of salvific mimesis, the play of image and likeness. While supernatural events per se fall outside her argument's province, Arendt's reflections on the broad spectrum of transformative encounters described in Augustine's foundational text, the New Testament, lead her to set aside dogmatic or crude secularism in favor of a suppler and more precise assessment of what may be said to count as a miracle. The New Testament itself, she points out, includes "passages where miracles are clearly not supernatural events but only what all miracles, those performed by men no less than those performed by a divine agent, always must be, namely, interruptions of some natural series of events, of some automatic process, in whose context they constitute the wholly unexpected."[37] We are not far from the founding scene of ethics, from Levinas's standpoint, as the encroaching intuition of the "gestation of the other in the same."[38]

I dwell on Arendt's Augustinianism because it helps clarify the nature of the typological intimacy between *The Pillar of Salt* and its formal matrix, the *Confessions*. Returning to the novel with both Arendt and Augustine in mind discloses the specific tincture of ethical disturbance, which would otherwise be easy to overlook, in Memmi's handling of the question of natality as it impinges on the paradoxes of hospitality and opens onto Blanchot's "bare relation with the Outside," the desert of allegory, the place where allegory becomes undecipherable.[39] Like Arendt, Memmi eschews the theological and mystical orientation of Augustine's understanding of the event of natality. Again like Arendt, Memmi maintains what could be called a strictly grammatical sense of the miraculous as the incubating and unrecognized germ of the "infinitely improbable" in the commonplace.[40]

For Augustine, natality's doubleness is grounded in a pointedly theological understanding of the interplay of memory and anticipation. Memory of the immemorial gift of creation is salvifically bound to anticipation of creation's eschatological fulfillment in the divine order of human society (the titular "city of God"). Because of the importance he attaches to the Sabbath memories, Memmi's grasp of this interplay retains Augustine's auratic charge. Memmi's sensibility is nonetheless closer in spirit to Arendt's critical distillation, which aims to capture the essential morphology of natality without specifying doctrinal content or endorsing a religious outlook.[41] In *The Origins of Totalitarianism*, as Peg Birmingham points out, Arendt insists on the natality's doubleness: "it is both the event of *initium* with its capacity to begin something new and the event of the *given* with its imperative of gratitude."[42] The premise here is that natality prompts recognition of the elasticity of the given. This trait touches on an immemorial memory of primordial indebtedness to the "miracle of accident and infinite improbability" held in common. The point of contact, though beyond phenomenal capture, is the precondition for the capacity to begin again, precisely because it supports an ambient ethos of unpayable gratitude, grounded in the intuition of the possible.

Like natality, memory may be a source of gratitude, but this trait does not cancel out its capacity as a breeding ground of resentments, both real and imagined. Even without going so far, it may serve as an inducement to perpetuate the shape and rhythm of the familiar. Memory possesses no native immunity to what Arendt calls the tendency of all historical processes to move toward "automatism" and "petrification."[43] Gratitude—of the very stripe that Arendt would recognize as a mark of incipient *novitas*, the human capacity to begin again, against all odds, which natality prompts—suffuses Memmi's memory of the Sabbath rituals in the ghetto, but the memory does not disable the traumatic reflex that appears in the depictions of the hardships and degradations that were also part of ghetto life. In other words, Memmi's artful handling of natality's doubleness recognizes the ease with which double knowledge may mutate into disabling ambivalence.

The chapter titled "The Dance" offers one of the most exorbitant depictions of the narrator's unsought exposure to a world he cannot square with
the "peacefully holy" Sabbath respite (*PoS*, 10). As we will see, such exposure leads the boy unknowingly into the heart (or, to recall, Merleau-
Ponty's figure, the "flesh") of Sodomscape though the coiled tension between welcome and risk at the felt borders of the community. "The Dance"
details the exorcism ritual the women of the family have decided to perform in order to cure the boy's Aunt Maissa of a mysterious ailment. The
physical symptoms, which include "collapsing on the ground and foam-
ing at the mouth," suggest epilepsy; but the women's holistic perspective
places the symptoms in the context of Maissa's chronic social disabilities
(*PoS*, 153).[44] Widowed after a brokered marriage with ruinously unhappy
results, Maissa is now "a pauper with two sick children" (*PoS*, 153). Thus
bereft of her already slim stock in the marriage market, she has become a
deficit to the family. Her condition's encroaching precariousness calls for a
radical diagnosis: demonic possession.

The boy's report of the "somber folklore" behind the ritual—the malignant antics attributed to the *Djnoun* (evil spirits)—shows an uncertain apportionment of distanced ethnographic appraisal and unnerving
proximity.[45]

> The *Djnoun*, those divinities from beneath the earth's surface, are by
> no means charming creatures of man's poetic imagination, capable of
> puckish malice but also of justifiable anger and of love, too. Poor beings
> exiled in perpetual darkness, they are all vicious and cruel, envious of
> man's happiness. . . . That is why they like to pierce eyes, to afflict with
> madness, to twist bones, to paralyze limbs, even to kill. Of course, all
> this has no meaning at all, except in the minds of crazy old women, but
> I always avoided returning, if even as a joke, to this world of human
> miseries and fears. Could I, besides, forget that I too, not so long ago,
> had been careful to cry out, after spilling water on the floor, to evil
> spirits: "Excuse me, please excuse me!" and that I had then felt a cold
> shiver run along my spine? (*PoS*, 156)

With an aplomb apparently driven by paternalistic self-regard, the narrator
behaves as if he were observing a material instance of Lucien Lévy-Bruhl's
theory of the "law of participation," through which "primitive mentality"
experiences a fluid commingling of sensible and supersensible orders of
being.[46] On the other hand, his ruminating response also betrays his susceptibility to the habit of belief that he describes. The disjunction between
verbal and bodily expression conveys the awkward threshold. Expulsive

words designed to mark the impassable boundary between his attitude and the "minds of crazy old women" founder on the visceral evidence of felt complicity that surfaces in the "cold shiver."

The climax of the ritual, which falls at the midpoint of the novel, presents one of the main crises in the narrator's developmental trajectory. The moment gives stark relief to his mounting sense of irreversible alienation from the idyllic perception of homeliness and, importantly, also suggests his attendant failure to see the ethical opening in the very event that registers as an assault on his self-identity. The penetrating irritant is the suggestion put to him by what he sees and hears that if there is indeed a "law of participation," to recall Lévy-Bruhl, it is an ambient resource as much as a danger, secretly capable of both making and unmaking the boundaries between self and stranger, with improvisational fluidity.[47]

The boy scans the scene for signs of the group's *knowing* simulation of the indigenous ritual, without success:

> [T]he terrifying Negro musicians were playing . . . possessed by ancestral rhythms, they were repeating gestures and ritual that, in their childhood or in their distant homeland, had left deep marks upon them. . . . That the musicians should be possessed in this manner was far from surprising: they were from some tribe of the deep South, a strange offshoot of Negro Africa sent out toward the Mediterranean. But the [dancing] woman was a sensible housewife, with children who went to school. . . . The tom-tom seemed to go insane, beating ever faster, struggling against time; the flock of women was seized by nervous spasms, and the dancer was again overcome by her seizures that seemed to tear her apart . . . suddenly the crazy dancer turned toward me—my mother, she was my own mother! To myself, I kept on saying: 'She's my mother, my mother,' as if these mere words could re-establish the lost contact and express all the affection that they should contain. But the words refused to adapt themselves to the barbaric apparition in its strange costume. . . . In the books that I had read, the mother was always somebody more soft and human than all others, a symbol of devotion and of intuitive intelligence. . . . As for my own mother, here she was: this wretched moron, with a spell cast on her by the dreadful music, by these savage musicians, themselves under the spell of their dark and obscure beliefs. . . . But why am I seized by this obscure emotion that is so closely allied to panic? My God, my God, I'm afraid even of my own mother, even my mother has ceased to seem familiar and understandable to me! . . . She was a stranger to me now, my mother, a part of myself become alien to me and thrust into the heart of a

primitive continent. Still, it was she who had given birth to me. What
somber ties still bound me to this ghost, and how shall I manage to return from the abyss into which she is now dragging me? (*PoS*, 160–62)

The scene measures the boy's responses with the metric of racialized and
misogynist fears of contamination. As unaccommodating as it is unchal-
lenged, the metric produces the conviction, as if by fiat, that the shelter
of the home has been violated by avatars of a "primitive continent." As a
result, the boy senses that the impossible has happened. His mother, the
intimate symbol of nurturing domesticity, has inexplicably mutated into a
"barbaric apparition" that threatens the integrity of his own nascent dream
of breaking free of his native city and exchanging the "unworthy worries"
of "family difficulties" for the project—opened up for him by his academic
success at the *lycée*—of a "whole world to conquer" (*PoS*, 82).[48]
   The genealogical turn to his thought both opens and forecloses the implied question of natality by fusing an imaginary legacy of promiscuous
maternity with the interminable logic of the master-slave dialectic: "And
I, well, I am my city's illegitimate son, the child of a whore of a city whose
heart has been divided among all those to whom she has been a slave"
(*PoS*, 96). The place for the question, however, keeps coming up, most
suggestively so in the context of the alternative home he makes for himself
in the school environment. The narrator's name, otherwise given runic
stature as the title of the book's middle section, enters the narrative for the
first time at the opening of that section's inaugural chapter ("The City"),
and it appears there specifically as a problem posed by the bruising self-
image imposed on him at the *lycée*. "In our alley, and at the Alliance School
[run by the Alliance Israélite Universelle], I hadn't known how ridiculous,
how revealing, my name could be. But at the French lycée," he reports,
"I became aware of this at once" (*PoS*, 93). What he discovers is the mutually rebarbative charge of the three names he bears, as though the ensemble were symptomatic of an autoimmune disorder.
   The "brassy" and "glorious" name of "Alexandre," given by his parents
"in recognition of the wonderful West," proves an occasion for mockery
among his classmates. His middle name, "Mordekhai," signifies his "share
in the Jewish tradition" and more particularly the story of deliverance associated with his namesake, the "glorious Maccabee" in the book of Esther. In the *lycée* environment, the name means something other than
deliverance. It marks an intolerable transit point from received narrative
identity to social stigma: "'My home is in the ghetto,' 'my legal status is
native African,' 'I come from an Oriental background,' 'I'm poor.'" "Benil-

louche," with its clear Berber-Arabic origins, carries associations that are both ominous and dubious in equal measure. In the local dialect, the name stands for "son of the lamb," with a subnote of sacrificial violence. In the context of his social experience, it reinforces his outlier status: "Could I be descended from a Berber tribe when the Berbers themselves failed to recognize me as one of their own? I was Jewish, not Moslem; a townsman, not a highlander" (*PoS*, 95).

When the narrator subsequently proclaims "My native city is after my own image," the declaration discloses an understanding of factual natality that remains in thrall to a mythos of promiscuous maternity and paternity, whose coupling produces a monstrous body of nested, carceral identities. Such understanding, it should be said, does not come *tout court* from the optic of the colonial *lycée* system. As the descriptions of boy's *lycée* experience in the middle chapters of the book make clear, however, the seductiveness of the academic regimen assumes the perception of fallenness—a secular outworking of the Augustinian notion of original sin—as its enabling condition.

The climactic chapter in this sequence ("The Choice") spells out the assumption by presenting the narrator's grasp of the pedagogic mission as a proffered promise of conversion: "I did not want to be Alexandre Mordekhai Benillouche, I wanted to escape from myself and go out toward the others. I was not going to remain a Jew, an Oriental, a pauper; I belonged neither to my family nor to my religious community; I was a new being, utterly transparent, ready to be completely remade into a philosophy instructor" (*PoS*, 230). The narrator's resolution is in part the outcome of a conflicted cathexis. His fascination with Marrou, his French instructor, who happens to be "Berber by birth and family background" comports uneasily with his admiration for Poinsot, his philosophy instructor, who comes from the French colonial cadre. While he sees both as "midwives" in his project of rebirthing, he also marks a preferential difference between the two (*PoS*, 219). Marrou's arc of upward mobility and willed Frenchification cuts too close to home, whereas Poinsot seems to incarnate an ideal of seamless apatheia that Marrou himself, the boy notes, cannot help but envy. Poinsot's social performance—including his "careless appearance," so unlike Marrou's "perfect elegance"—conveys the ability "to live at ease under any sky, to hate nothing and to bear everything with ease" (*PoS*, 226). In effect, to the enraptured student, Poinsot's persona represents the apotheosis of Montaignesque skepticism and disembodied Cartesianism: "[b]ecause he viewed the world with an open mind, everything seemed clear and translucent to him. Mysteries, complexes, and difficulties all resolved themselves, in his presence, into clear notions that one could grasp and analyze with wondrous facility" (*PoS*, 225).

Only much later, with the onset of the terrors of the German occupation, does Alexandre discover the moral deficit of the suave persona on display in the *lycée* culture. Poinsot's embarrassed refusal to hide the boy from the Germans and collaborating Vichy police who are rounding up Jews and dissidents disabuses him of the idealized and naïve impression of Frenchness (and its colonial avatars) as the endowment of a limpid mathematical theorem.[49] His eventual reassessment of Poinsot's character, however, is by itself not enough to induce critical understanding of his limited grasp of natality's promise. In essence, the challenge he repeatedly faces outside the Sabbath respite is almost impossibly clear. He must learn to dwell long enough in the "meanwhile"—the *entre-temps* that Levinasian ethics both repels and depends on—to apprehend the more capacious and bracing face of *novitas*, the opening onto unforeseen possibilities for beginning again. The blinkered optic on display in "The Choice," then, marks an important station in the narrator's itinerary, precisely because it puts in such clear relief the shape of the transformative occasion that at several turns *nearly* befalls the narrator. To recall Arendt, this is the prospect of assenting to the "infinitely improbable" thought that even a Damascene sense of *novitas* does not entail forgetting bodily history or disavowing the experiential routes leading to the "here" and "now," where a newfound sense of what it means to be at home may take root.

We are now ready to consider again what is present but unseen in the exorcism ritual. Two registers of the unseen are in play, the first of which returns us to the margin of thought where Arendt and Levinas find common ground. One of the key points of correspondence between Arendt's political notion of natality and Levinas's ethical sense of the face-to-face encounter is the intuition of an event that compels attention and responsive engagement precisely because it exceeds, even as it inhabits, the phenomenal order of experience. This uncountable surplus issues a transimmanent (simultaneously transcendent and immanent) way of "speaking of the Other." In this context, speaking means more than verbal utterance. Speaking is a figure for the full range of expressive gestures that may be used to testify to the felt pulse of the Other's coming to presence and to respect its abiding distinction from prefabricated perceptual schemes. Further, in their respective descriptions of natality and the face-to-face encounter, both Arendt and Levinas conjure the gestating, maternal body as a graphic instance of the limit case of pure relation—the confluence of the intimate and the alien. While neither thinker entirely dispatches the essentialist baggage that may be inferred from the rhetorical turn to the maternal body, the overarching direction of their compatible arguments makes it clear that what is essential for each is not the recycled legacy of proprietary and reductive conceptions of femaleness and female nurture, but rather the gestating body's specifically *figural* provocation as an annunciative event.

Ann W. Astell's coinage—"mater-natality"—approaches this point by expressing Arendt's and Levinas's shared intuition of the intimate linkage between alterity's prophetic and memorial dimensions:

> [T]he alterity within the self—an alterity conditioned by the relation to the Other—always already includes not just the Other that one goes out to meet face-to-face, but also the Other from whom one comes. The latter exists as a passivity at a deeper depth, supporting the still-faceless one in the *Il y a*, even as a mother contributes to the gradual formation of a child into an ethical subject that can assumes its own maternal form, a maternity that is always already there, in men as well as women, by virtue of their being borne by and born of an Other, a mother.[50]

To specify Astell's point further, the "still-faceless" aspect of the gestating embryo has both ethical and political significance; and not because it carries the promise of continuation of the already known—for example, received cultural associations of maternity—but because it expresses the intimate proximity of the unexpected and unforeseen within the horizon of the known. Such felt apprehension also lies at the heart of Sara Ahmed's claim that the generosity at work in any encounter that warrants being called hospitable will solicit a posture of attention to the prospect that *"the one who is already assimilated can still surprise,* can still move beyond the encounter which names her, and holds her in place."[51]

Memmi's depiction of the exorcism ritual captures the tensile energy animating the occasion of mater-natality, though it presents only a glancing allusion to the figure of gestation. The allusive gesture is confined to the boy's observation of the crowd's response to the instructions given by his mother, who is now transfixed in an oracular seizure, to produce the required instruments for the ritual's next stage—red scarves and a white cock. The "compact crowd," he notes, "gave birth to sudden movements" ("Des mouvements naissent dans la foule compacte"), as the women rush off to collect the items.[52] The boy cannot bear to witness the remainder of the ritual and so forecloses the occasion to apprehend the full nature of what is being incarnated in the proceedings. Once all the prescribed items are assembled, he runs out of the house in a cold sweat, alarmed by his susceptibility to the crowd's enthusiasm, and seeks refuge in his friend Henry's house—the very domicile that will eventually shelter the shared dream of flight to Argentina.

The Proximity of Natality, Trauma, and Hope

Argentina, however, is not yet on the horizon, and the hasty retreat to Henry's house provides the boy with no more than a parenthetical and illusory respite. Approaching the house, Alexandre hears Henry practicing a Bach piece on his violin. He knows full well that the enveloping soundscape, patterned with notes following an "exact scheme" with "mathematical" precision, is the musical "expression of a civilization of men who had become masters of the world" (*PoS*, 165, 157). The music issues a rebuke, for it reminds the boy of his more intimate bodily attunement to the different "sounds and rhythms" of Africa (*PoS*, 165). The knowledge that these "ancient and monotonous melodies" move him "far more deeply than all the great music of Europe" proves to him that he is "an incurable barbarian" (*PoS*, 165).

The boy's wry assertion affords the occasion to reflect on the scope of the endgame he believes he has reached in facing up to his "barbarian" character. The semantic harmonics of the word *barbare* are obvious enough, but they also harbor a deeper provocation than Alexandre intends. The word's two dominant associations, drawn from the combined legacies of Greek, Latin, and Arab forms of linguistic and geographic territorialism, are no mystery to him. He perfectly understands that the social and political circumstances of his birth identify him as an uncivilized outsider. He also understands, without spelling it out, that the etymological kinship of the words *barbarian*, *Barbary*, and *Berber* is deeply written into the life scripts available to those born in the Maghreb's geopolitical theater. The *lycée*'s pedagogical culture further refines the lesson by making clear to him how the stigma of his outsiderness expresses itself through his speech. He responds to the francophone mandate by inventing an idiosyncratic speech genre, "a dreadful mixture" (*un infâme mélange*) of the Judeo-Arabic dialect of the streets, the literary *préciosité* learned in the classroom, "schoolboy slang," and his own attempts at linguistic bricolage.[53] The exercise goes nowhere, of course, and not simply because his instructors efficiently police the borders of acceptable speech. Rather, the chastisements and humiliations the boy suffers in the *lycée* setting give institutional sanction to the ambient lessons he has already begun to assimilate in colonial Tunis. In essence, linguistic maternity—the mother tongue—is of a piece with the at-once misogynist and racialized "barbaric apparition" of his mother in the exorcism ritual, together with the boy's gathering sense that the place of his birth is a "whore of a city" (*PoS*, 161, 96).[54]

There is no escaping Alexandre's learned predilection to identify the maternal body—and his congenital association with it—as a perverted *hortus conclusus*, an interminable double bind concocted of utopian longing and atavistic horror. But the novel's narrative design recurrently troubles the narrator's (and readers') expectations that the onset of revelation, of whatever stripe, is mortgaged to ideologically prescriptive disclosures of false consciousness or bad faith.[55] The unstable mooring of Argentina on the novel's predominantly realist register is perhaps the most prominent case in point, and there is more to be said about Argentina's peculiar resonance of at the novel's close. As it happens, the crucial event that complicates and challenges Alexandre's divided perception of the maternal body does not occur in the protagonist's represented social world. Instead, it occurs in the discursive modeling of two episodes that, from Alexandre's perspective, could not be more disparate in impact or import.

The negative exemplar, which I have already briefly touched on, details Alexandre's discovery of his mother's defection from the bourgeois ideal of domestic maternity in the exorcism's "savage" protocol (*PoS*, 161). The positive exemplar affords the boy one of the rare experiences of rapturous vertigo in his budding academic career. This is the moment in French class when Alexandre proves adept at penetrating not into the "heart of a primitive continent" (as his mother's participation in the exorcism seems to do), but rather into French literary classicism's rarefied essence. Alone among his peers, Alexandre produces the correct answer to the question posed by the instructor, Marrou, during a discussion of the "extraordinary scene" in Jean Racine's *Andromaque* "in which Pyrrhus admits his love" to Hector's widow, the prized captive among the spoils of war. The boy spontaneously identifies the line that is "most typical of Racine" (*PoS*, 112).

Recalling the event, the narrator does not dwell at length on the specifics of his unusual literary acumen. He handles the moment instead as though it were a treasure too delicate to withstand close scrutiny. Yet the furniture of the remembered episode rewards attention for the insights it holds into the shared but undeclared territory that joins two forms of proximity: Alexandre's horrified sense of his congenital intimacy with the "barbaric apparition" presented by his mother in the exorcism, and his cherished recall of his intuitive grasp of a signature moment in one of the pinnacles of tragic drama in the French literary canon. In both instances, Alexandre

comes into contact with the *face* of maternity that eludes his grasp. This is
the sense of maternity as something more than biological fact or naturalized cultural role. The surplus element is nothing other than the kenotic
bearing of ethical subjectivity, a bearing that remembers how natality is
never simply an accomplished fact or confirmation of social norms. It also
names (as Arendt proposes) the speculative grain of thought that blooms
into the unpredictable power to see, and thus act, otherwise.

Alexandre's inability or refusal to see the intimate connection between
what he witnesses in the exorcism and what he appears to have intuited
with astonishing precision in Racine's art amounts to a missed rendezvous in the boy's developing sense of the world and his place in it. Indeed, as Alexandre's memoir advances, it becomes clear that the irony of
the classroom exercise trumps the ecstatic but evanescent sense of *arrival*.
Thus, near the end of the chapter that closes the realist frame ("Examination," just before the final chapter, "Departure"), Alexandre bitterly recalls
the exercise as one of several symptoms of his monstrous and paralyzing
hybridity: "I am a Tunisian but of French culture ('You know, the art of
Racine, an art that is perfectly French, is accessible only to the French')"
(*PoS*, 331). By this point, Alexandre has forgotten what he had accessed in
the art of Racine, remembering only the apparent futility of disclosing his
immaculate assimilation of civilized Frenchness. He may have fled from
the exorcism ritual, but he himself has become a virtual exorcist. That is,
in the boy's mental theater, the drama of assimilation has been displaced
by the puppet show of mere impersonation. But Memmi's narrative craft
invites us to imagine what Alexandre *does not see* in the exorcism. We can
detect the shape of the blind spot by pausing longer than Alexandre does
to reflect on the signature moment he shows such instinctive affinity for in
Racine's play:

> We were analyzing Racine's *Andromaque* and he [Marrou] was a great
> enthusiast of the work of this poet; one morning, after we had read the
> extraordinary scene in which Pyrrhus admits his love, Marrou turned
> to the class and, in a tired and hopeless voice, asked:
> "Which line in this scene is most typical of Racine?"
> An embarrassed silence followed; to me, the class did not seem to
> have quite understood the question. I don't believe I had either, but
> somehow I felt what he was trying to say. Without raising my hand,
> I read aloud in the perplexed silence:
> "Je ne l'ai point encore embrassé d'aujourd'hui."
> Marrou gazed at me with his somewhat heavy look.

"That's right," he said slowly.

My heart cried with joy. I, son of an Italian-Jewish father and a Berber mother, had discovered in Racine's work the line that is most typical of Racine. (*PoS*, 112–13)

The words that Alexandre voices—and quite literally incorporates—belong to the most revered maternal figure in Racine's theater. It is telling that Memmi chooses Andromaque rather than Phèdre or Athalie.[56] In different ways, the careers of Phèdre and Athalie express the Racinian equivalent of what the boy sees in the exorcism: the shocking disclosure of depraved maternity. The choice of either the Athenian or the Judean queen, from equally celebrated plays, would thus undoubtedly make for a more straightforward invitation to consider a possible connection between the classroom exercise and the exorcism ritual. Such an invitation, however, would also convey the impression that Memmi's narrative design is everywhere consistent with the protagonist's perspective. Crucially, it would confuse the meaningful distinction between resemblance and proximity, and thus block access to the understanding of how Memmi's narrative articulates, in its own terms, Levinas's philosophical intuition of how the notion of proximity designates exposure to "the face of the approaching other"—in this case, the maternal gesture's ethical adventure.[57]

Consider the case of Andromaque. Superficially, she exemplifies the idealized portrait of benign maternity that Alexandre finds betrayed in his mother's actions. However, the coiled tension of the passional states that comprise the character—mourning widow of Hector; prisoner of war reduced to the status of political pawn; solicitous mother of her endangered son, Astyanax; appalled object and eventually astute, if also desperate, negotiator of the sacrificial wager engineered by the amorous and territorial designs of her captor, Pyrrhus—all of this discloses a preserve of thought and action that surpasses the dichotomized splitting of identity into idealized and degenerate poles. The line that Alexandre ventriloquizes—"I have not yet kissed my child today" (*Andromaque*, 1.4.264)—amply warrants being called the line "most typical of Racine" (*PoS*, 112), precisely for the economy and unnerving delicacy with which it navigates the conflicting claims closing in on the character.[58]

The line appears in the first exchange of words between Andromaque and Pyrrhus after she and Astyanax have been taken captive in the aftermath of the Trojan War. Already smitten, Pyrrhus greets her with an ingratiating invitation to pretend that she has floated into a parallel universe where she is free and amenable to amorous repartee. Andromaque replies with the same ingratiating tone, while raising the stakes in the game for mastery over the terms of the reality closing in on her. The simple expression "I have not yet kissed my child today" discloses her extreme emotional (and political) vulnerability even as it also radiates a preternatural insouciance before Pyrrhus's exigencies that negates their determinative force. Through her sheer resolve to survive with (and through) her son, the fact of Andromaque's carefully policed access to Astyanax dissolves into a casual report of the most ordinary and spontaneous display of maternal affection—in a world without Pyrrhus. This is freedom, she says. It has nothing to do with you, and you will never touch it.

The quintessentially Racinian character of the line comes, in part, from the extraordinary compaction of conflicting desires and self-states into a verbal gesture that is in equal parts conventional and unsettling, and the Racinian signature extends seamlessly into the narrative fallout from the scene. Andromaque's conversation with Pyrrhus both rebuffs him and further piques his interest, with lethal consequences for Pyrrhus. But there is more. French literary tradition harbors a famous interpretation of the play that sets for itself the same task proposed in Alexandre's classroom. I am thinking of François-René de Chateaubriand's *Génie du Christianisme* (1802). This text, unmentioned in Memmi's novel, isolates the connective tissue between Alexandre's voicing of the key line from *Andromaque* and his retreat into a different kind of archive in the exorcism scene.

The broad contours of Chateaubriand's argument are simple. Racine's Andromaque paradigmatically expresses the central distinction between "pagan" (Homeric) and "modern" (Christian) conceptions of maternity.[59] The "christian features" of the latter arise from the emphasis on "tender feelings" (*GoC*, 326).[60] The very line that Alexandre recognizes as most typical of Racine's art is also the line that for Chateaubriand exemplifies the key difference between Racine's Andromaque and the antique prototype: "The Andromaque of Homer sighs and sobs for the future misfortunes of Astyanax, but scarcely thinks of him for the present; the religious mother, more affectionate without being less provident, often forgets her own sorrows and afflictions in giving a sweet hearty kiss to her little child" (*GoC*, 327).

Chateaubriand identifies the apparent self-forgetfulness of Racine's Andromaque as one of the signal expressions of Christ-like kenosis in Christian moral tradition: humility. The "christian religion inculcates" the ethos of humility and is thus "directly opposed to pride and vanity," he observes. In this single regard, it effectively "changes the nature of our passions"

(*GoC*, 328). It is worth noting that Chateaubriand does not speak of subduing or repudiating passions, but of changing their nature. Transformation of this order is what "is visible in the whole of the modern Andromaque" (*GoC*, 328).

For all its importance in the aesthetic formation of French Romanticism, twenty-first century readers of Chateaubriand's treatise probably find it difficult to take the prestige accorded to humility—to say nothing of its specifically Christian, and tacitly gendered, trappings—at face value.[61] All the more reason to notice that Chateaubriand calls attention to something *unnatural* in Andromaque's maternal disposition. The "touching sentiments" on display, he asserts, "are not the language of nature; they contradict on the contrary the voice of the heart" (*GoC*, 328). For Chateaubriand, in other words, the antique Andromaque shows the degree to which deeds serve as the expression and confirmation of preexisting social identities (warrior, father, mother, son) and their corresponding emotive or affective habitat. The maternal solicitude of Racine's Andromaque, on the other hand, transfigures the entire field of operation, such that deeds no longer function primarily as proofs or symptoms of inherited contours of being, but instead as engines of becoming that produce and disclose unexpected dimensions of social identity.

It is precisely for this reason, in Chateaubriand's estimate, that Andromaque's "simple and amiable" expression of tender feeling ("I have not yet kissed my child today") is of a piece with the steely, quasi-Stoic resolve behind the advice she later instructs Céphise, her confidante, to give Astyanax in the wake of the endgame she now sees no way of avoiding (meaning the suicide she vows to commit following the forced marriage to Pyrrhus in exchange for her son's safety). Her advice amounts to a gift that opens a way for Astyanax to inhabit the memory of his Trojan ancestors without being enthralled to it: "Tell him the deeds that glorify their names,/And rather what they did than who they were."[62] Chateaubriand's commentary emphasizes how this moment discloses the radical dimension of "christian humility" as an ethical flashpoint. The radical dimension turns on what Andromaque's care for her endangered son achieves. It decouples humility from passive victimage and the Christianized legacy of Stoic *apatheia* by transposing these to the register of new beginnings. Andromache's extended province of maternal care, "christian humility," and political savvy instills a chance of delegitimizing Pyrrhus's claim over the meaning of her life and the future memories of her son.

This, in any event, is the gist of Chateaubriand's suggestion that Andromaque's career opens a window into the strangely subversive power of humility to liquidate received distinctions between "liberty or servitude, prosperity or adversity, the diadem or the shackles of poverty" in the service of a better, unseen, future (*GoC*, 329). Chateaubriand's idiom bears no obvious resemblance to Arendt's or, to be sure, Levinas's. Yet his understanding of the *unnatural* aspect of the "perpetual expansion towards an eternal beauty" that he discovers in Andromaque's nondistinction between resilience and care effectively points up the kenotic dimension of maternatality (*GoC*, 329). This dimension resides in the "dignity and delicacy" with which Andromaque's behavior subtracts itself from prevailing social and political partitions of reality (*GoC*, 328). It also suspends the law of noncontradiction, the very law that Alexandre is enthralled to in his understanding of what he observes in his mother's exorbitant dancing.

We can now appreciate the full measure of the Racinian echo in the exorcism ritual. Alexandre sees but does not grasp the kenotic sense of being-in-community that his mother's performance displays, in proximity to the maternal exemplar of Andromaque. In other words, he does not understand how his mother's participation in the exorcism suspends the law of noncontradiction in the interest of caring for an endangered member of her social and familial world. Attached to an abstractly idealized conception of home and its corresponding social roles, all he can see in his mother's behavior is evidence of an ontological depredation. In effect, what presents itself to his horrified gaze is an allegorical crisis—the disclosure of his origins' *essential* barbarity—whereas a very different type of disclosure actually takes place. What Alexandre's mother incarnates is an animated, kenotic image of ethical responsiveness: letting go of what is no longer needed (the attributes of the "sensible housewife") and, like a *bricoleur*, mobilizing the therapeutic resources at hand, including collective memories of local rituals' liturgical—that is, community-building and life-enhancing—properties. Just as Andromaque's "tender feelings" express resolute political agency (the intent to de-realize the authority of Pyrrhus's gaze), so too, by an inverse symmetry, Alexandre's mother's unexpected "barbaric" appearance expresses the ethico-poetic inventiveness of her response to urgent need. The collateral gift to Alexandre is the chance to relax his grasp of the rule of dichotomized essences. That chance, as we have seen, is not taken up, but the repeated narrative traces of the *onset* of the chance give witness to Memmi's investment in the prospect of *novitas*, new beginnings.

In the event, the undeclared proximity between the two episodes of maternal adventure places the stakes of Alexandre's increasingly immobilized perspective in relief. In view of the Racinian echo, his fear of congenital association with his mother's apparent barbarity makes for a perverse form of consolation, for the fear he can name buffers him from the nameless fear of dwelling in the uncertain meanwhile between "no-more' and "not-yet."[63] The full measure of Memmi's investment in the Sodom narrative resides here, in the narrowing distance between the French lesson scene and the exorcism ritual. For it is precisely here that Memmi's narrative design harbors an incubating counter-memory of Lot's wife that sees what the boy does not. The counter-memory sees the biblical figure's sheltering access to the ethical opening to be found within the ethical impasse.[64]

The most compact demonstration of this formal trait appears in the final episode of the chapter titled "The Camp," not far from the close of the novel and Alexandre's counterintuitive launch into an unknown land. "The Camp" chronicles the sobering aftermath of Alexandre's sudden and surprising (even to him) decision to join the interns in the local labor camp, despite the fact that his academic credentials have guaranteed his exemption: "I asked to go because it seemed intolerable to stay. Painfully but definitely, I was discovering that others really existed, and moreover that I would never be content merely with my own happiness" (*PoS*, 282). With ruthless precision, the chapter examines the cost of the boy's mistaking of the ideal of immersive identification with others for the goal of solidarity achieved through patient attunement to a co-implicated being with others.

The focal point addresses Alexandre's profound sense of alienation from his fellow interns after a prolonged dispute over how to care for a member of the group who has suddenly been stricken with a mysterious and violent illness. The dispute convinces him of the "vanity" and naiveté of his decision to enter the camp. He decides to search for means of escape, a decision hastened by signs that the Nazi forces, now facing imminent collapse, will likely exterminate the camp. While his decision propels the story's chronological momentum, the episode's heart resides in Alexandre's painful rumination over the contretemps produced by the intern's inexplicable illness. Equipped with a modicum of medical knowledge, Alexandre quickly guesses the nature of the ailment: appendicitis. The diagnosis rouses him to angry protestations when he sees some of the workers resorting to a traditional remedy—a stomach rub with hot ashes and oil—to calm the intestinal trouble, when ice rather than heat treatment is called for. Instantly—and, for Alexandre, irreversibly—barriers of class and educational distinction reassert themselves.

Yet the essential crux, and the episode's most penetrating narrative interest, turns on the initial therapy.

In the half-light on the parched grass, he was like a big animal strug-
gling in the grip of an unknown disease. How could one relieve such
an attack of appendicitis in a work-camp? Maddened by the pain, the
sick man had become a child again and was calling his mother. I knelt
beside him and tried to touch his stomach, but he pushed me away so
brutally that I got up, disconcerted by his violent refusal. All the workers left their tents and stood helplessly around him. At last the camp
tailor, an elderly man who had been forgotten here in spite of his large
family, took him gently on his knees and nursed him like a child. The
patient calmed down and I stood there, useless and humiliated, watch-
ing what I could not do myself, I mean take one of them in my arms
and nurse and comfort him. (*PoS*, 293)

The moment underscores Alexandre's difficulty in thinking of human
plurality as anything other than an obstacle to ethical responsiveness and
meaningful selfhood. There is, after all, no cause for him to take the sick
man's flailing gestures as a personal rejection, just as there is no reason for
him to assume that there is no continuity between what he has tried to do
and what the elderly man is able to give. The thought that prompted him
to act entered a field of contingencies that inflected the course of the act
without annulling the originating thought. The same is true for the elderly
man, who, as Alexandre himself observes in passing, "had been forgotten"
until the unforeseen circumstance claimed his attention.

Part of what troubles and indeed terrifies Alexandre is the action's contingency. In this regard, the depiction of Alexandre's traumatized response
to the episode is more than an instance of his perceived ethical failure.
It conveys the supernumerary effect of giving dramatic point to Arendt's
understanding of the "impossible" yet inescapable "burden" of action as
such.[65] "Men," she notes, "have always known . . . that he who acts never
quite knows what he is doing, that he always becomes "guilty" of consequences he never intended or even foresaw . . . that the process he starts
is never consummated unequivocally in one single deed or event, and that
its very meaning never discloses itself to the actor but only in the backward glance of the historian who himself does not act."[66] Arendt's fuller
argument presents a somewhat more agnostic view of what the "backward
glance of the historian" lays claim to, a point that is already suggested here
by the description of action as the beginning of a process that is "never
consummated unequivocally in one single deed or event."[67] Arendt's point
is particularly relevant to the matter at hand, because it invites us to re-
examine Alexandre's apparent failure to comfort the sick man in view in
the larger narrative context of Alexandre's repeated exposures to events—

ethically charged, face-to-face encounters—that mark him without resulting in a recognizable plot of self-accomplishment.

A moment's reflection on the several details of the therapeutic gambit—
the sudden onset of illness, the impulse to respond to urgent need, the
seeming standoff between modern medical regimens and traditional cu-
ratives—tells us that the episode is a refigured expression of the exorcism
ritual. Here, through the immediate gesture of care he offers the sick man,
Alexandre is closer than he has ever been to his mother—more precisely,
to the kenotic promptings of his mother's ethical responsiveness. Here, he
ventures into the coiled middle space between two neighboring views of
the ethico-political dimensions of love: Augustine's understanding of love
(*caritas*) as inherently *action-oriented*, which is to say inherently caught up
in the shared drama—the social and political and, for Augustine, spiritual
adventure—of human existence, and Arendt's more restrictive view of Augustinian *caritas* as essentially private, apolitical, and even antipolitical.[68]
For Memmi, the ethical provocation and kenotic resonance of love appear
in Alexandre's uncertain yet inquisitive sense of his identity's amphibious
character. The impacted ironies and disillusionments of Alexandre's career
have led him to the point where he comes face to face with himself as an
isolated individual irreducibly caught up with a "nameless singularity" attuned to the proposition that "*Anyone* is responsible for *any Other*."[69]

One further consideration presents itself, and it turns on the peculiar
temporality of Alexandre's intermittences of the heart. The recurrent pulse
of his habit of self-reflective rumination and his unguarded capacity for
spontaneity in navigating his social world convey a distinctly Levinasian
sense of the ungraspable but decisive interval in which the adventure of
ethical exposure begins. As Levinas puts it, this interval "lies behind the
distinction between rest and movement, between the being at home with
oneself (*chez soi*) and wandering, between equality and difference."[70] For
further measure, this interval "refers to a recurrence in the dead time or
the *meanwhile* which separates inspiration and expiration, the diastole and
systole of the heart beating dully against the walls of one's skin," and it
initiates, "improbably enough, a retreat into the fullness of the punctual."[71]
As we have seen, Alexandre repeatedly associates the "fullness of the punctual" with the paralyzing grip of the "meanwhile" of introspection. In the
book's final chapter, the name he gives to the experience is "Lot's wife."

Behind Alexandre's declared sense of paralysis, or rather subsisting
within it, is another, unnamed, association of the "meanwhile." Here,
Alexandre encounters the explosive generativity of the instant, through

which the present "rips apart and joins together again; it begins; it is beginning itself."[72] For Levinas, and to a certain extent for Arendt as well, the correlation of the present (what Arendt calls "the small inconspicuous track of non-time . . . within the time-space given to natal and mortal men") and the stirring of new beginnings has nothing to do with intentional perception or predictive knowledge (the "teleology of cognition"), but everything to do with the sheer contingency of the ethical relation.[73] This condition of openness to gratuity also makes itself felt in the disclosing of the face of the Other. As if by stealth, the event brings with it "the very collapse of phenomenality," and the interruption of being's otherwise "unrendable essence."[74]

I have invoked Levinas here because the intuition he describes underlies Memmi's orchestration of Alexandre's vigilance, resilience, and vulnerability in the labor-camp. Specifically, this intuition makes itself felt in the staccato of Alexandre's exposures to ethical claims and obligations that he can neither disavow nor translate into a satisfying story of personal accomplishment. By now it may be possible to see how the ensemble of Alexandre's disorienting experiences in the camp conveys, like the echo before the sound, the face of Lot's wife, in the Levinasian sense. Here, too, Alexandre makes contact with the counter-memory of Lot's wife as the imageless expression of *novitas*, the unheralded opening to be found, but not categorically known, in the kenotic instinct of mater-natality, with its abiding conviction that *"the one who is already assimilated can still surprise."*[75]

If we accept that Memmi's investment in the biblical legend of the flight from Sodom extends to the surprising turns to Alexandre's adventures in the camp, we can better understand how the final turn toward Argentina also belongs to Sodomscape. I want to advance the point by looking back to the claim I made at the outset. How does Memmi's narrative narrow the distance between desert and allegory? Memmi achieves this effect by repeatedly exposing his protagonist to the indefinite and fraught interval between allegory's two faces: "speaking other," with all that this locution implies as an ingredient of cosmopolitan dwelling and worldliness; and "speaking of the Other," with its attendant gesture of radical hospitality toward the infinitely improbable, as Arendt might say.

In Memmi's imagined world, this interval silently inheres in the lineaments of the everyday, even in the labor camp's regimented protocol. The interval expresses itself not only in Alexandre's recurring sense that he is not at home with himself. More profoundly, it expresses itself in his mounting sense that the rationales he has shored up to account for his feeling of homelessness, while not baseless, are neither therapeutic nor critically solvent. The impasse he faces is real enough. But the question is not whether the impasse is real. The question is whether Alexandre will find a way to assume a survivable relation with the tangle of contradictions that has shaped his world and his place in it. Memmi answers by asking us to think of the boy's turn to Argentina as a meaningful choice, not on historical or sociological grounds, but on figural grounds. Argentina's figural prospect—its imagined capacity to harbor a viable habitation between a "no-more" and a "not-yet"—holds open the promise that the entrenched social and political factors closing in on the boy do not hold the last word.[76]

Now is the time to recall the passage that composes the novel's last word. Alexandre is about to board ship when the memory of the labor camp suddenly returns: "I was taking only a bag on my back, like when I left home for the labor camp" (*PoS*, 342). There is reason to wonder whether the shadow of Lot's wife will fall across his path again. So it does, through a detour: "I stayed on deck till we were out a sea, leaning on the rail. I lost sight of the coastline as night descended on the ship. It seemed to ooze from the holds, to fill the hatch, and to stain the blue sky with gray. First one star shone, then a second, then thousands. I grew uneasy gazing at the violet sea, which attracted me like a sorceress while it heaved and settled, so I went down to the hold to sleep" (*PoS*, 342). Memmi writes Alexandre's voyage to Argentina into the allusive fabric of Odyssean wandering. The dangerously seductive appeal of the sea's sorcery recalls the legendary sirens of the *Odyssey*, with their false promise of calm sea and prosperous voyage. A nice touch: the finely gauged detail of the "violet sea" (*la mer violette*) recalls the famous Homeric locution of the "wine-dark sea," which serves as one of the scenographic signatures of adventure and risk in Homer's epics.[77] Alexandre may well be channeling one of the most famous invocations of the "wine-dark sea" in the *Odyssey*, the moment in which Odysseus resists the enticements of the goddess Calypso, who has given him safe harbor:

> Then Odysseus of many wiles answered her, and said: "Mighty goddess, be not wroth with me for this. I know full well of myself that wise Penelope is meaner to look upon than thou in comeliness and in stature, for she is a mortal, while thou art immortal and ageless. But even so I wish and long day by day to reach my home, and to see the day of my return. And if again some god shall smite me on the wine-dark sea, I will endure it, having in my breast a heart that endures affliction. For ere this I have suffered much and toiled much amid the waves and in war; let this also be added unto that."[78]

This particular intertext is apt, if ironic, because it reminds us that the Odyssey's overarching narrative scheme presents the protagonist's nomadic career as a means to an end, and the end is *nostos*, homecoming. Odysseus's homecoming, of course, has its complications. Yet, as Odysseus's leave-taking from Calypso's world suggests, the supreme value of *nostos* as a return to a place of familiar security is unquestioned.

The trajectory of Alexandre's career presents something other than an unqualified endorsement of this ethos. The sheer improbability of Alexandre's decision to bank on Argentina is the final testimony linking Memmi's novelistic world to the symposium of philosophical reflection where Augustine, Arendt, and Levinas contribute compatible insights into the profoundly figural dimension to the felt idea of home, in all the ways we have seen over the course of this book. More than any other region in Sodomscape, Memmi's novel gives visceral point to figure's migratory movement between memory and anticipation and, equally, to figure's sensitive registration of the folds of disappointment, regret, shame, well-being, and rapt attunement that give texture and shape to the course of what arrives, here and now, without assuring a predicted outcome. Memmi's novel reminds us that this is as true of the life remembered and lived as it is of the life held in the written gesture of words.

Memmi's place in the philosophical symposium is eloquent for yet another reason. *The Pillar of Salt* returns the question of home, and its negotiable boundaries, to the place where this book's argument began. In Memmi's fictional memoir, the assemblage work that goes into the forming of viable places to call home—in both local and extended senses of the word—gives narrative heft to Merleau-Ponty's generative insight into the relational configurations that make up the "flesh of the world."[79] Memmi's novel sees, and shows, the adventure, sorrow, and resilience of the flesh of figural being.

The closing moments of *The Pillar of Salt* bring flesh and figure into perfect alignment. Alexandre is embarked. The Homeric subtext to the choice of Argentina may literally have the novel's last word, but figuratively it has the navigational aptitude of the typographical index. The Homeric figure points toward the counter-memory of Lot's wife, with its seizure of the radical proximity of homelessness and home, desert and allegory, where hazard touches on something like hope. It's the *something like* that best remembers Lot's wife, in knowing that the turn is not abortive—it is merely unfinished.

Acknowledgments

This book began with a moment of wonder at an unlikely thing. Andrew Dickson White's monumental *History of the Warfare of Science with Theology in Christendom* (1896) is better known for its belligerent defense of scientific rationalism than for nuanced appraisal of the archive of religious myths. For all that, the chapter titled "From the Dead Sea Legends to Comparative Mythology" discloses something that frustrates White's Casaubon-like ambition. The exhaustive survey of legends and commentaries prompted by the biblical account of the flight from Sodom gives inadvertent testimony to the fabled pillar of salt's strangely captivating resistance to dogmatic translation. For me, the unacknowledged standoff between collector and quarry sparked an investigative journey aimed not at solving but at giving voice to the enigma White stumbled across. This book is the record of that journey.

Though mostly exhilarating, the interdisciplinary challenges of the project were also on occasion bewildering to the point of anguish. More than once, suggestive byways turned into a desert crossing. The fact that the book exists at all is testimony to the patience, generous good will, and support of many hands. First of all, the project was funded by a series of faculty research grants from the UCLA Committee on Research, which enabled several visits to archives in Germany and France. In addition, the Department of English and the Friends of English at UCLA provided invaluable assistance with funds that enabled color reproductions of many of the images included in these pages. The friendly advice of archivists at the Bibliothèque nationale de France, the Congregatio Jesu in Augsburg, Germany, and the National Library of Israel in Jerusalem enabled access to several visual and written materials that became central parts of the book. Special thanks to Sister Christina Kenworthy-Browne, CJ, Archivist at the Bar Convent, York, England, and the late Sister M. Gregory Kirkus, CJ, former Archivist at the Bar Convent, for their support. I am also grateful to Colleen Jankovic for her expert assistance in giving focus to key parts of the book manuscript.

I have been lucky in the intellectual community of colleagues and friends in my professional home, UCLA's Department of English. Words are poor to express the depth of my particular gratitude to the following people. Helen Deutsch's unique combination of brilliance, intellectual empathy, and down-to-earth candor has been a sustaining source of inspiration from the inception of this book, crucially so at hair-pin turns along the way. Arthur Little's sharp critical eye and keen sculptural sense of argument were invaluable guides in helping me navigate the Sodom legacy. Conversations with Karen Cunningham, one of the most acute wordsmiths I know, kept me mindful of the need to keep the big picture in sight. In 2011, Rachel Lee invited me to join the Life (Un)Ltd Research Colloquium she organized under the auspices of UCLA's Center for the Study of Women. During the several sessions of Life (Un)Ltd, Rachel's mercurial quickness of mind had a transformative impact on my understanding of the Dead Sea region's relevance to the developing argument of the book. Kenneth Reinhard's intellectual hospitality, especially during his tenure as director of UCLA's Center for Jewish Studies, offered a much-needed haven at a critical time. Many thanks to Ali Behdad, King-Kok Cheung, Christine Chism, Elizabeth DeLoughrey, Yogita Goyal, and Jinqi Ling for giving advice and moral support when I most needed it.

Throughout the many years of the book's gestation, I have had the great good fortune to benefit from the intellectual camaraderie and perceptive advice from numerous colleagues, friends, and mentors outside my department—more than I can name. I beg their indulgence for relying on the artifice of alphabetic sequence when a many-voiced song of gratitude is what is called for in thanking Carol Bakhos, Frances E. Dolan, Tamara Cohn

Eskenazi, Diana Henderson, Heather James, James Kearney, Mirta Kupferminc, Jayne Elizabeth Lewis, Jacques Lezra, Joan Pong Linton, Julia Reinhard Lupton, Howard Marchitello, Arthur F. Marotti, Jane O. Newman, Shankar Raman, Estelle Shane, Victoria A. Silver, Susanne Wofford, and Andreas Zachrau. Several former graduate students, who are now enjoying thriving academic careers, provided important ballast for the earliest stages of the book, and it gives me special pleasure to thank them here: Anthony Camara, Alice Dailey, David Long, Meredith Neuman, Holly Pickett, Jennifer R. Rust, Jan Stirm, and Julian Yates.

Many hands were indispensable to the final crafting of the book. The anonymous reader reports supplied wonderfully detailed, expert advice on both stylistic and conceptual matters. I owe an unpayable debt of gratitude to these thoughtful and patient readers, and no less to Thomas Lay for his discerning editorial eye, sage counsel, and vigilance in shepherding the book through the final stages of the publication process. Many thanks as well to my copy editor, Michael Koch, for his painstaking attention to the typescript.

The legacy of Lot's wife harbors abundant lessons. One is especially apt as I write these words, because it issues a call to remember the beloved dead. This book holds foremost in memory the untimely loss of Helen Tartar, esteemed former editorial director at Fordham University Press. Helen was one of my earliest interlocutors during the formative stages of this book. Her unswerving enthusiasm for the project, which extended over several years of e-mail correspondence and MLA cocktail hours, kept me from losing heart in more than one moment of adversity. The recent departures of three former professors who provided invaluable mentoring during my graduate studies long ago at Stanford University prompted the wish and need to mention their names here in belated yet grateful recognition of their shaping influence: J. Martin Evans (1935–2013), Ronald A. Rebholz (1932–2013), and René Girard (1923–2015). I hope these now-absent mentors, along with Helen Tartar, would be pleased to know that one of my guiding aspirations in writing this book was to honor them.

Finally, I wish to thank my husband, Jay H. Geller, for the countless ways in which he helped me remember that a desert crossing holds an oasis in sight. I am grateful for his expert photography during research trips to Israel in 2000 and 2007, his mock horror at listening to paragraph drafts riddled with academese, and above all his caring patience and boundless capacity for joy. He proves the hunch true that home is where hospitality settles in.

LG

PREFACE: ENTERING SODOMSCAPE

1. *The New Oxford Annotated Bible, New Revised Standard Version with the Apocrypha*, 4th ed., ed. Michael D. Coogan, Marc Z. Brettler, Carol A. Newsom, and Pheme Perkins (Oxford: Oxford University Press, 2010). This edition is used throughout, unless otherwise noted.

2. Rainer Maria Rilke, *The Complete French Poems*, trans. A. Pouline, Jr. (Minneapolis: Graywolf Press, 2002), 244–45.

3. "Another early reference to the curiosities preserved in the Anatomy School occurs in the manuscript diary of G[eorg] Christof Stirn of Nürnberg [Stirn, *Travel Diary*, MS. Bodley Adds. B. 67]. After he had visited the Bodleian Library, in 1638 . . . , he went down to the Anatomy School, where he saw 'in a lower room [. . .] some skeletons, a human skin, a basilisk, a piece of the pillar of salt (?=Lot's wife), two feet of a man who had been hanged with only two toes on each, a huge shell of a tortoise, and many similar objects.'" Robert Theodore Gunther, *Early Science in Oxford*, vol. 3 (Oxford: Oxford University Press, 1925), 252–53. An English translation of Stirn's full entry is in Herman Hager, *Englische Studien* 10, no. 1 (1887): 445–53.

4. The suffix *-scape* is related etymologically to the word *shape*, via the Germanic root *skap-*; see the *Oxford English Dictionary* (*OED*) entries for "-scape" and "-ship" and both substantive and verbal forms of "shape." Under the entry for "-ship" the *OED* gives multiple variants of the Old English "sciepe" and Old Teutonic "skai-z," from "skap-"—"to create, ordain, appoint."

5. I borrow (with caution) the term *dérive* from the field of psychogeography as developed by the Letterist International and Situationist International in the 1940s and 1950s, and associated with the work of Guy Debord. See Debord, "Theory of the Dérive," in *Situationist International Anthology*, ed. Ken Knabb (Berkeley, CA: Bureau of Public Secrets, 2007), 62–66. See also Jean-François Lyotard's interesting reflections on the notion in *Driftworks*, ed. Roger McKeon (New York: Semiotext[e], 1984), 9–18.

6. See *Oxford English Dictionary*, 3rd ed., s.v. "scape, n.1 and n.3."

7. Jean-François Lyotard, "Scapeland," in *The Inhuman: Reflections on Time*, trans. Geoffrey Bennington and Rachel Bowlby (Stanford, CA: Stanford University Press, 1991), 184.

8. Ibid., 186. Bracketed words are from the original French text, *L'Inhumain: Causeries sur le temps* (Paris: Éditions Galilée, 1988), 196.

9. Lyotard, "Scapeland," 186–87.

10. Ibid., 183. The roaming contours of Lyotard's thought express the point, inviting the reader to apprehend the essay itself as an encroaching instance of landscape—a textual incarnation of the intuition that "landscapes do not come together to make up a history and a geography" (ibid., 189).

11. Ibid., 183.

12. Ibid., 187.

INTRODUCTION: FIGURAL MOORINGS OF HOSPITALITY IN SODOMSCAPE

1. On this point, see Martin Harries, *Forgetting Lot's Wife: On Destructive Spectatorship* (New York: Fordham University Press, 2007), 76–102. See also, more broadly, Lisa Saltzman, *Anselm Kiefer and Art after Auschwitz* (Cambridge: Cambridge University Press, 2000) and Daniel Arasse, *Anselm Kiefer* (New York: Harry N. Abrams, 2001).

2. The Hebrew word *za'aqat*, translated as "outcry," broadly means "the cry of the oppressed, the plea of the victim of great injustice." Robert Ignatius Letellier, *Day in Mamre, Night in Sodom: Abraham and Lot in Genesis 18 and 19* (Leiden, Netherlands: Brill Academic Publishing, 1995), 119.

3. The Abraham and Lot cycle includes Genesis 13:2–13, 18:1–16, 19: 1–28, 30–37. Further discussion of the translation history of the episode of metamorphosis is in chapter 1.

4. "When morning dawned, the angels urged Lot, saying, 'Get up, take your wife and your two daughters who are here, or else you will be consumed in the punishment of the city.' . . . When they had brought them outside, they said, 'Flee for your life; do not look back or stop anywhere in the Plain; flee to the hills, or else you will be consumed'" (Gen. 19:15, 17).

5. Famously, Augustine identifies the principal transgression of Sodom as sexual acts between men ("stupra in masculos"). See Augustine, *The City of God* [*De civitate Dei*], Loeb Classical Library, vol. 5, trans. Eva M. Sanford and William M. Green (Cambridge, MA: Harvard University Press, 1965). Perhaps the most nuanced recent explication of the linguistic foundations for this view in the Genesis text, from a theologically conservative standpoint, is in Roger A. J. Gagnon, *The Bible and Homosexual Practice: Texts and Hermeneutics* (Nashville, TN: Abingdon Press, 2002), 71–90.

6. The most concise biblical formulation of this insight appears not in the Genesis text but in the Book of Ezekiel. Ezekiel's prophetic diatribe

against Jerusalem for her violations of covenantal principles includes a strategic summary of Sodom's self-regarding and dangerous indifference to others: "This was the guilt of your sister Sodom: she and her daughters had pride, excess of food, and prosperous ease, but did not aid the poor and needy" (Ezek. 16:49). On the link between inhospitality and homophobia, see Rictor Norton, *A History of Homophobia*, 2, "The Destruction of Sodom and Gomorrah," April 15, 2002, updated February 10, 2010, http://rictornorton .co.uk/homopho2.htm. See also Robert Alter, "Sodom as Nexus: The Web of Design in Biblical Narrative," *Tikkun* 1, no. 1 (1986): 30–38, repr. in *Reclaiming Sodom*, ed. Jonathan Goldberg (New York: Routledge, 1994), 28–42.

7. Suggestive treatments of the historical trajectory just described are in Goldberg, *Reclaiming Sodom*, as well as Jonathan Goldberg, *Sodometries: Renaissance Texts, Modern Sexualities* (New York: Fordham University Press, 2010). See also Glenn Burger and Steven F. Kruger, *Queering the Middle Ages* (Minneapolis: University of Minnesota Press, 2001), and Steven F. Kruger, *AIDS Narratives: Gender and Sexuality, Fiction and Science* (New York: Routledge, 1996).

8. See Alfred Lord Douglas, "Two Loves," originally published in *The Chameleon* (December 1894), http://www.fordham.edu/halsall/pwh/douglas .asp.

9. The vast critical literature on the theory and practice of hospitality draws much of its energy from the etymological ambiguities of the word: *hospitality* derives from the Latin *hostia* (sacrifice or victim) and the Latin *hospes* (guest, host, or stranger). A concise statement of the complex semantics is in J. Hillis Miller, "The Critic as Host," *Critical Inquiry* 3, no. 3 (Spring 1977): 439–47, at 442–43. Miller's observation that "there is no conceptual expression without figure, and no intertwining of concept and figure without an implied story, narrative, or myth" is axiomatic for this study (443). Inescapably, perhaps, the term *dwelling* conjures Martin Heidegger's influential pages on the notion in the essay "Building Dwelling Thinking." See *Poetry, Language, Thought*, trans. Albert Hofstader (New York: Harper and Row, 1971), 141–60; for a helpful commentary, see Robert Mugerauer, *Heidegger and Homecoming: The Leitmotif in the Later Writings* (Toronto: University of Toronto Press, 2008). I return to Heidegger's reflections in chapter 2.

10. Here I draw on Hannah Arendt's suggestive sense of artworks as "thought-things" borne of a twofold gesture, uprooting and repurposing: "Art therefore, which transforms sense-objects into thought-things, tears them first of all out of their context in order to de-realize and thus prepare them for their new and different function." Hannah Arendt, *The Life of the Mind* (New York: Harcourt Brace Jovanovich, 1978), 49.

11. Jacques Derrida, *Of Hospitality: Anne Dufourmantelle invites Jacques Derrida to respond*, trans. Rachel Bowlby (Stanford, CA: Stanford University Press, 2000), 135. I return to Derrida's writings on hospitality in chapter 4. An extensive discussion of Derrida's writings on hospitality is in Judith Still, *Derrida and Hospitality: Theory and Practice* (Edinburgh: Edinburgh University Press, 2012). An exemplary collection of approaches to the hospitality question is in *Mobilizing Hospitality: The Ethics of Social Relations in a Mobile World*, ed. Jennie Gurmann Moltz and Sarah Gibson (Aldershot, England: Ashgate, 2007). See also Richard Kearney, *Strangers, Gods, and Monsters: Approaching Otherness* (London and New York: Routledge, 2003), 63–82.

12. See Derrida's remarks on the Kantian emphasis on duty in *Of Hospitality*, 75–83.

13. Levinas conveys the term's essential provocation in *Totality and Infinity*: "The way in which the other presents himself, exceeding the idea of the other in me, we here name face. This mode does not consist in figuring as a theme under my gaze, in spreading itself forth as a set of qualities forming an image. The face of the Other at each moment destroys and overflows the plastic image it leaves me, the idea existing to my own measure . . . the adequate idea." Emmanuel Levinas, *Totality and Infinity: An Essay on Exteriority*, trans. Alphonso Lingis (Pittsburgh: Duquesne University Press, 1969), 50–51.

14. Levinas, *Totality and Infinity*, 229; Levinas, *Otherwise Than Being, Or Beyond Essence*, trans. Alphonso Lingis (Pittsburgh: Duquesne University Press, 1998), 127.

15. Richard Wolin, *The Frankfurt School Revisited and Other Essays on Politics and Society* (New York: Routledge, 2006), 131. A wide-ranging sample of approaches to Levinas in postcolonial and critical race studies is in *Levinas, Race, and Racism*, ed. John E. Drabinski, *Levinas Studies* 7 (2012). For a nuanced rejoinder to the charge of Levinas's apolitical tendency, see Timothy Secret, *The Politics and Pedagogy of Mourning: On Responsibility in Eulogy* (London and New York: Bloomsbury Academic, 2015), 63–108.

16. "Being-Toward-Death and 'Thou Shall Not Kill,'" *Is It Righteous to Be?: Interviews with Emmanuel Lévinas*, ed. Jill Robbins (Stanford, CA: Stanford University Press, 2001), 133.

17. In the passage cited, Levinas makes us of the term "the third" to indicate this opening of ethics into political concern: "For me, [the other] is singular. When the third appears, the other's singularity is placed in question. I must look him in the face as well. One must, then, compare the incomparable" (ibid.).

18. Derrida, *Adieu to Emmanuel Levinas*, trans. Pascale-Anne Brault and Michael Naas (Stanford, CA: Stanford University Press, 1999), 35.

19. For an overview of the career of Maître François, see *The Grove Encyclopedia of Medieval Art and Architecture*, ed. Colum Hourihane (Oxford: Oxford University Press, 2012), 2:612–14.

20. Maurice Blanchot, "Prophetic Speech," in *The Book to Come*, trans. Charlotte Mandell (Stanford, CA: Stanford University Press, 2003), 79–85, at 79.

21. In this regard, the concluding statement in Auerbach's 1938 essay "Figura" might well apply, with a different emphasis, to the aspirations of *ressourcement* theology in its search to understand forgotten resources of patristic thought: "Our purpose was to show how on the basis of its semantic development a word may grow into a historical situation and give rise to structures that will be effective for many centuries." Auerbach, "Figura," in *Scenes from the Drama of European Literature* (Gloucester, MA: Peter Smith, 1973), 76.

22. Arendt, *Life of the Mind*, 204. Here Arendt is describing the activity of thinking, yet there is an undertow of messianic urgency to her claim that the "activity of thinking can be understood as a fight against time itself"—that is, against the "continuity of everyday life in a world of appearances" (ibid.).

23. Peg Birmingham, *Hannah Arendt and Human Rights: The Predicament of Common Responsibility* (Bloomington: Indiana University Press, 2006), 33–34.

24. Mika Ojakangas, "On the Pauline Roots of Biopolitics: Apostle Paul in Company with Foucault and Agamben," *Journal for Cultural and Religious Theory* 11, no. 1 (Winter 2010): 92–110, at 93.

25. Hans Blumenberg, *Work on Myth*, trans. Robert M. Wallace (Cambridge, MA: MIT Press, 1985), 4.

26. Ibid., 9.

27. Hannah Arendt, *Between Past and Future* (New York: Penguin, 1977), 13.

28. See Levinas, "Judaism and Kenosis," in *The Time of Nations*, trans. Michael B. Smith (London: Athlone Press, 1994), 101–18; and Levinas, "A Man-God?," in *Entre Nous: Thinking-of-the-Other*, trans. Michael B. Smith and Barbara Harshav (New York: Columbia University Press, 1998), 53–60.

29. See David R. Law, *Kierkegaard's Kenotic Christology* (Oxford: Oxford University Press, 2013), 34–63.

30. Albert Memmi, *La statue de sel* (Paris: Corrêa, 1953); translated by Edouard Roditi as *The Pillar of Salt* (Boston, MA: Beacon Press, 1992). *The Pillar of Salt* appeared in print four years before Memmi's more widely read study, *The Colonizer and the Colonized* (*Portrait du colonisé, précédé par Portrait du colonisateur*, 1957).

31. "Hence, it was for the sake of *novitas*, in a sense, that man was created. Since man can know, be conscious of, and remember his 'beginning' or his

origin, he is able to act as a beginner and enact the story of mankind." Hannah Arendt, *Love and Saint Augustine* (Chicago: University of Chicago Press, 1996), 55.

32. Martin Harries, *Forgetting Lot's Wife: On Destructive Spectatorship* (New York: Fordham University Press, 2007). Taking the theatrical theory of Antonin Artaud as its point of departure, Harries's book ranges across a wide range of twentieth-century media, including the apocalyptic strand of American film and the post-Holocaust aesthetics of German artist Anselm Kiefer. See also Madeline Caviness, *Visualizing Women in the Middle Ages: Sight, Spectacle, and Scopic Economy* (Philadelphia: University of Pennsylvania Press, 2001); and Mitchell Breitwieser, *American Puritanism and the Defense of Mourning: Religion, Grief, and Ethnology in Mary White Rowlandson's Captivity Narrative* (Madison: University of Wisconsin Press, 1990). Caviness traces the associative resonance between the representational formats of Lot's wife in medieval art and the lethal drive of the scopic economy as mapped in the Lacanian system of desire. Breitwieser's application of the Derridean supplement in combination with Hegel's reading of *Antigone* in *Phenomenology of Spirit* calls attention to the "anti-exemplaristic power of grief" in Rowlandson's captivity narrative (Breitwieser, *American Puritanism*, 97).

33. Martin Jay, *Downcast Eyes: The Denigration of Vision in Twentieth-Century French Thought* (Berkeley: University of California Press, 1994), 17.

34. Maurice Merleau-Ponty, *The Visible and the Invisible*, trans. Alphonso Lingis (Evanston, IL: Northwestern University Press, 1968), 248.

35. Maurice Merleau-Ponty, *Signs*, trans. Richard C. McCleary (Evanston, IL: Northwestern University Press, 1964), 22.

36. Ibid.

37. Merleau-Ponty, *The Visible and the Invisible*, 224.

38. The paradigm: Paul's Adam-Christ typology. In essence, typological temporality pivots on the fine edge between, on the one hand, the ethos of Adam, which is correlated with "sinful flesh" (Rom. 8:3) and, more broadly, routinized absorption in the familiar contours of the everyday; and, on the other hand, the ethos of Christ, which is correlated with the "spirit of life" (Rom. 8:2) and its attendant sense of "eschatological awakening to new creation," or salutary wounding. On this point, see William Schweiker, *Dust That Breathes: Christian Faith and the New Humanisms* (Chichester, England: Wiley-Blackwell, 2010), 169.

39. For a helpful account of the semantic complications attending Paul's use of the word *sarx*, see James D. G. Dunn, *The Theology of Paul the Apostle* (Grand Rapids, MI: Wm. B. Eerdmans Publishing, 1998), 62–75.

40. Merleau-Ponty, *The Visible and the Invisible*, 139–40.

41. Ibid., 155.

42. Ibid., 138.

43. See, for example, Jean-François Lyotard's assessment of Merleau-Ponty's chiasm in "Philosophy and Painting in the Age of their Experimentation: Contribution to an Idea of Postmodernity," in *The Merleau-Ponty Aesthetics Reader*, ed. Galen A. A. Johnson (Evanston, IL: Northwestern University Press, 1993), 323–35, at 330–31. An impressive treatment of the debates among feminist thinkers over the alleged normative implications of Merleau-Ponty's idiom is in Dorothea Olkowski and Gail Weiss, eds., *Feminist Interpretations of Maurice Merleau-Ponty* (Philadelphia: Pennsylvania State University Press, 2006). My use of Merleau-Ponty's notion of the flesh has a glancing relation to the notion's application in Roberto Esposito's project to diagnose the territorializing reach of the biopolitical field in late modernity as a structural outworking of early Christian intuitions of the tensile relation between the governable body and the labile flesh. My approach, while sympathetic to the inherent aporias Esposito finds in Merleau-Ponty's thought of the flesh, is less committed to the inherent overcoming of the fissured legacy of incarnational theology, as suggested by Esposito's assertions that "[t]he flesh is neither another body nor the body's other; it is simply the way of being in common of that which seeks to be immune" or that "the notion of the flesh needs to be rethought outside of Christian language, namely, as the biopolitical possibility of the ontological and technological transmutation of the human body." Roberto Esposito, *Immunitas: The Protection and Negation of Life*, trans. Zakiya Hanafi (Cambridge, England: Polity Press, 2011), 118–21, at 121; and *Bios: Biopolitics and Philosophy*, trans. Timothy Campbell (Minneapolis: University of Minnesota Press, 2008), 159–69, at 168. Though compelling, such judgments tacitly subscribe to the immanent unfolding of a grand narrative. My approach is more interested in the operative fecundity of flesh's capacity to express the converging claims of localized place (*topos*), exposure to an unassimilable outside (*typos*), and omnidirectional change in structures of attachment (*tropos*).

44. Merleau-Ponty, *The Visible and the Invisible*, 144.

45. Bernhard Waldenfels, "The Paradox of Expression," in *Chiasms: Merleau-Ponty's Notion of the Flesh*, ed. Fred Evans and Leonard Lawlor (Albany: State University of New York Press, 2000), 89–102, at 92.

46. Ibid. As Merleau-Ponty puts it, all expression takes place, enfleshes itself, in the in-between, endlessly "reorganizing things-said, affecting them with a new index of curvature, and bending them to a certain enhancement of meaning" (*Signs*, 19).

47. Waldenfels, "The Paradox of Expression," 97.

48. Merleau-Ponty, *The Visible and the Invisible*, 144–45.

49. Ibid., 115.

50. Ibid., 133, 123, 153.

51. A helpful account of the utopian aspect of Merleau-Ponty's phenomenology is in Greg Johnson, "Merleau-Pontian Phenomenology as Non-Conventionally Utopian," *Human Studies* 26, no. 3 (2003): 383–400.

52. Merleau-Ponty, *The Visible and the Invisible*, 153.

53. Symptomatic efforts to harness the word's semantic lability are in Sara Ahmed, *Queer Phenomenology: Orientations, Objects, Others* (Durham, NC, and London: Duke University Press, 2006), and *Queer Theology: Rethinking the Western Body*, ed. Gerard Loughlin (Hoboken, NJ: Wiley-Blackwell, 2007). For a helpful overview of the development of queer studies, see Mary Klages, *Literary Theory: A Guide for the Perplexed* (New York: Bloomsbury Publishing, 2007), 111–20.

54. The complicated semantic history of the word *Sodom* (and affiliated terms *sodomy* and *sodomite*) gives a good picture of how the divergent senses of "queer" have played out in recent arguments in queer theory. See, for example, the cumulative perspective offered by the essays in *Reclaiming Sodom*, ed. Jonathan Goldberg (New York: Routledge, 1994). In brief, historians and cultural theorists of sexuality and correlative models of the sex/gender system, following Michel Foucault's insights, have amply shown how the word *sodomy*, for example, did not always refer exclusively or necessarily to a set of sexual practices or a targeted sexual identity. Following the biblical proof text of Ezekiel 16:49 ("Look! This was the sin of your sister Sodom and her daughters: Pride, too much food, undisturbed peace, and failure to help the poor and needy"), homiletic and pastoral discourse from the medieval era well into the twentieth century conjured the phrase "sins of Sodom" to address problems of moral blindness and hardness of heart rather than specific marks of homosexual practice or identity, even though the latter associations gradually eclipsed the older and broader view after the ascendancy of the modern invention of the homosexual as a category of species identity.

55. Valerie Traub, "The New Unhistoricism in Queer Studies," *PMLA* 128, no. 1 (January 2013): 21–39, at 35.

56. Sigmund Freud, *Civilization, Society and Religion*, trans. James Strachey, ed. Albert Dickson (New York: Penguin, 1991), 131, 305.

57. I'm borrowing the term "scopic trauma" from Kaja Silverman, *The Acoustic Mirror: The Female Voice in Psychoanalysis and Cinema* (Bloomington: Indiana University Press, 1988).

58. Paul Claudel, *The Eye Listens* [*L'oeil écoute*], trans. Elsie Pell (New York: Philosophical Library, 1950). See also Jean-Louis Chrétien, "The Visible Voice," in *The Call and the Response*, trans. Anne A. Davenport (New York: Fordham University Press, 2004), 33–43, at 33–34.

1. EXODUS, INTERRUPTED: LOT'S WIFE AND THE ALLEGORICAL INTERVAL

1. Emmanuel Levinas, "Reality and Its Shadow," trans. Alphonso Lingis, 1987; repr. in *The Levinas Reader*, ed. Séan Hand (Oxford: Basil Blackwell, 1989), 129–43, at 141.

2. Blaise Pascal, *Pensées*, 3:§233, quoted in Graeme Hunter, *Pascal the Philosopher: An Introduction* (Toronto: University of Toronto Press, 2013), 117. As Hunter observes, the "nautical metaphor was already dead in seventeenth-century French, as it is in the English equivalent 'embarked.' But in both languages, the cognate associations retain their metaphorical associations with a *journey begun*" (119).

3. On the career of Raoul de Presles, see Anne Jourdan, "A propos de Raoul de Presles. Documents sur l'homme," *Bibliothèque de l'école des chartes* 139, no. 2 (1981): 191–207. On the career of Maître François, see François Avril and Nicole Reynaud, *Les manuscrits à peintures en France, 1420–1520* (Paris: Flammarion, 1993), 45–52.

4. Auerbach, "Figura," 29, 33.

5. Ibid., 53. For a helpful discussion of Auerbach's misreading of the relation between *allegoria* and *figura*, see Jesse M. Gellrich, "Figura, Allegory, and the Question of History," in *Literary History and the Challenge of Philology: The Legacy of Erich Auerbach*, ed. Seth Lerer (Stanford, CA: Stanford University Press, 1996), 107–13.

6. Auerbach, "Figura," 58–59. For a more temperate assessment of Auerbach's notion of figura, see David Dawson, *Christian Figural Reading and the Fashioning of Identity* (Berkeley: University of California Press, 2001).

7. Quintilian, *Institutio oratoria*, vol. 3, trans. H. E. Butler, Loeb Classical Library (Cambridge, MA: Harvard University Press, 1920), 9.2.46.

8. Ibid., 9.2.47.

9. Gordon Teskey, "Irony, Allegory, and Metaphysical Decay," *PMLA* 109, no. 3 (May 1994): 397–408, at 399.

10. Ibid.

11. This feature recalls Merleau-Ponty's "paradox of expression," described in the introduction.

12. Teskey, "Irony, Allegory, and Metaphysical Decay," 407.

13. As Teskey points out, because irony "never establishes limits that could give it definite form," irony is "unlimited in its scope but powerless before real power" (ibid.).

14. Ibid. My phenomenologically oriented treatment of allegory shares Sayre N. Greenfield's skepticism toward the rigid distinction between allegory and allegoresis. See Greenfield, *The Ends of Allegory* (Newark: University of Delaware Press, 1998). The distinction typically asserts that the "interpretive strategy" of allegory is a formal feature of the work and the immanent

allegorical intention is signposted as such, whereas allegoresis is a second-order interpretive strategy applied to the work. A secondary feature of the distinction is that allegory "expands meaning" while allegoresis "suppresses meaning." As Greenfield points out, however, "generic allegory is allegoresis, a way of reading a text": just as "allegoresis (or what we judge to be such) invokes a metaphoric structure of reading to divert attention from certain meanings, so an 'intentional' allegory simply by invoking that metaphoric structure of reading will divert attention from certain meanings, even if the reader tries to preserve them all" (58).

15. Thus, for Levinas, "every artwork is in the end a statue" ("Reality and Its Shadow," 141).

16. Augustine, *The City of God* [*De civitate Dei*], Loeb Classical Library, vol. 5, trans. Eva M. Sanford and William M. Green (Cambridge, MA: Harvard University Press, 1965). A helpful discussion of Augustine's view in the context of Jewish and Christian traditions of reading Genesis 19 is in J. A. Loader, *A Tale of Two Cities: Sodom and Gomorrah in the Old Testament, Early Jewish and Early Christian Traditions* (Kampen, Netherlands: J. H. Kok, 1990), 136.

17. Augustine, *City of God*, 16:30.

18. For a fuller discussion of the genealogy of the "old/new" figure, see Arthur D. Nock, *Conversion: The Old and the New in Religion from Alexander the Great to Augustine of Hippo* (Baltimore, MD: Johns Hopkins University Press, 1998). Unless otherwise indicated all references to biblical texts are from *The New Oxford Annotated Bible with Apocrypha: New Revised Standard Version*, 4th ed., ed. Michael Coogan, Marc Z. Brettler, Carol Newsom, and Pheme Perkins (Oxford: Oxford University Press, 2010).

19. See Deborah L. Madsen, *Rereading Allegory: A Narrative Approach to Genre* (Houndmills, England: Basingstoke, 1995), 55. Augustine's own fourfold method appears in *De utilitate credendi* [*On the Profit of Believing*], 5–8.

20. On the Ovidian analogs to the account of metamorphosis in Genesis 19, see Ralph Hexter, "The Metamorphosis of Sodom: The Ps-Cyprian De Sodoma as an Ovidian Episode," *Traditio* 44 (1988): 1–35.

21. On this point, see Albert van der Heide, "Midrash and Exegesis," in *The Book of Genesis in Jewish and Oriental Christian Interpretation: A Collection of Essays*, Traditio Exegetica Graeca, ed. J. Frishman and L. Van Rompay (Leuven, Belgium: Peeters Publishers, 1997), 44–56.

22. *Confessions*, 7.10.16. Augustine, *Confessions*, ed. and trans. Carolyn J. B. Hammond, vol. 1 (Cambridge, MA: Harvard University Press, 2014), 329. Helpful assessments of Augustine's use of the Neoplatonic phrase are in Pierre Courcelle, *Les 'Confessions' de Saint Augustin dans la tradition littéraire: Antécédents et postérité* (Paris: Etudes Augustiniennes, 1963), 623–640; and

Margaret W. Ferguson, "Saint Augustine's Region of Unlikeness: The Crossing of Exile and Language," *Georgia Review*, no. 29 (1975): 842–64.

23. See Madsen, *Rereading Allegory*, 30. My remarks on allegory in this
paragraph are indebted to Madsen's argument. I concur with Madsen's basic
claim that the "shift within the allegorical genre . . . when classical and Ju-
daistic allegorisms were adapted to the newly discovered needs of Christian
exegesis, is obscured by an essential conception of allegory as one only of
'other speaking' or 'speaking of the Other.' But when considered as a mixed
genre that is sensitive to the shifting nature of temporality, allegory articulates itself as both an agent and record of cultural change" (ibid., 133). The
overarching term I use in this book for Madsen's "mixed genre" is *figure*.
Gerald L. Bruns considers the suggestive analogy between the work of allegory and the Heideggerian "rift" (*Riss*) in *Hermeneutics Ancient and Modern*
(New Haven, CT: Yale University Press, 1995), 203–8.

24. As Seyla Benhabib suggests, "rather than being at home in *every* city,"
cosmopolitan beings "were *indifferent* to them all." Benhabib, "Cosmopolitanism and Democracy: Affinities and Tensions," *Hedgehog Review* 11, no. 3
(2009): 30–41, at 32. See also, more broadly, Benhabib, *Another Cosmopolitanism* (New York: Oxford University Press, 2006).

25. For a careful inspection of Augustine's ambivalent perception
of the Theodosian imperial establishment of the Church, see Robert A.
Markus, *Saeculum: History and Society in the Theology of Augustine* (Cambridge: Cambridge University Press, 1988), 39–53. See also Daniel Frank-
lin Pelario, *Back to the Rough Grounds of Praxis: Exploring Theological Method
with Pierre Bourdieu* (Leuven, Netherlands: Peeters Publishers, 2006),
487–88.

26. Paul's use of allegory here is virtually indistinguishable from what
later schools of exegesis will call typology or figural interpretation (*figura*).
Paul's use of the term also harbors a covenantal ethos. For Paul, the events
recorded in scripture present an evolving stage of memories and anticipa-
tions of God's providential interventions in the unfolding drama of salvation
history. My comments in this chapter assume the commonplace understanding that two Pauls are at issue here: the "radical Jew" whose voice of reform is
intelligible within existing patterns of Jewish mystical and messianic thought;
and the retrospectively constituted theorist and founder of a distinctively
Christian and universalizing *ecclesia*. On this point, see Alan F. Segal, *Paul
the Convert: The Apostolate and Apostasy of Saul the Pharisee* (New Haven, CT:
Yale University Press, 1992), and Daniel Boyarin, *A Radical Jew: Paul and the
Politics of Identity* (Berkeley: University of California Press, 1997). A brilliant
examination of the secularizing implications of the latter view of Paul—Paul
as theorist of not only ecclesial but also civic identity—is in Julia Reinhard

Lupton, *Citizen Saints: Shakespeare and Political Theology* (Chicago: University of Chicago Press, 2005).

27. On this point, see especially Alan F. Segal, *Rebecca's Children: Judaism and Christianity in the Roman World* (Cambridge, MA: Harvard University Press, 1989) and Paula Fredriksen, "What 'Parting of the Ways?': Jews, Gentiles, and the Ancient Mediterranean City," in *The Ways That Never Parted: Jews and Christians in Late Antiquity and the Early Middle Ages*, ed. Adam H. Becker and Annette Yoshiko Reed (Tübingen, Germany: Mohr Siebeck, 2003), 35–63.

28. On this point, see the succinct account in Henry Duméry, *Phenomenology and Religion: Structures of the Christian Institution* (Berkeley: University of California Press, 1975), 18–32.

29. Amos Funkenstein, "Basic Types of Christian Anti-Jewish Polemics in the Later Middle Ages," *Viator* 2 (1971): 373–382, at 375.

30. See Sanford Budick, "Cross-Culture, Chiasmus, and Manifold of Mind," in *The Translatability of Cultures: Figurations of the Space Between*, ed. Sanford Budick and Wolfgang Iser (Stanford, CA: Stanford University Press, 1996), 224–44, at 239–42.

31. Auerbach, "Figura," 53.

32. Levinas, "Reality and Its Shadow," 141.

33. "Now Hagar is Mount Sinai in Arabia and corresponds to the present Jerusalem, for she is in slavery with her children. But the other woman corresponds to the Jerusalem above; she is free, and she is our mother" (Gal. 4:25–26).

34. Robert Alter, *The Art of Biblical Narrative*, 2nd ed. (New York: Basic Books, 2011), 27–29.

35. Alter, "Sodom as Nexus: The Web of Design in Biblical Narrative," *Tikkun* 1, no. 1 (1986): 30–38, at 32, repr. in *Reclaiming Sodom*, ed. Jonathan Goldberg (New York: Routledge, 1994), 28–42.

36. Alter, "Sodom as Nexus," 36.

37. Alter's formalist argument speaks to the technique of "mnemohistory" that Jan Assmann calls "normative inversion," the retention of a cultural element "not for its own sake, but as the counter-image of one's own identity." Assmann, *Moses the Egyptian: The Memory of Egypt in Western Monotheism* (Cambridge, MA: Harvard University Press, 1998), 216.

38. Sodom here resembles the canceled middle term of the enthymeme, which harbors undeclared assumptions informing the syllogistic train of thought in a given argument. See Jeffrey Walker, "The Body of Persuasion: A Theory of the Enthymeme," *College English* 56, no. 1 (January 1994): 46–65.

39. A good survey of controversies associated with Gnostic movements in biblical antiquity is in Karen L. King, *What Is Gnosticism?* (Cambridge, MA: Harvard University Press, 2003).

40. The Moabite line is also crucial in messianic genealogy; the Davidic Messiah descended from Ruth the Moabite. Midrashic attention to this detail is noted in Daniel C. Matt, *The Zohar: Pritzker Edition* (Stanford, CA: Stanford University Press, 2003), 2:160–61. For a broadly compatible examination of the Sarah-Hagar-Lot's wife nexus in the covenantal drama of hospitality, see Tracy McNulty, *The Hostess: Hospitality, Femininity, and the Expropriation of Identity* (Minneapolis: University of Minnesota Press, 2007), 15–20.

41. The apocryphal book of Wisdom defines the pillar of salt as a "monument to an unbelieving soul" (*apistousè psyche*, Wis. 10:6–7).

42. My hunch here is that the semiotics of color prevail over the ambiguity of the depicted gesture of uplifted hands in the city. The so-called *orans* gesture, used in many ancient religions to mark rites of supplication and prayer, migrated to early Christian devotional practices and formed the basis for iconographic renderings of the gesture in catacomb art, for example. See Walter Lowrie, *Art in the Early Church* (New York: Pantheon, 1947).

43. "Lot looked about him, and saw that the plain of the Jordan was well watered everywhere like the garden of the LORD, like the land of Egypt, in the direction of Zoar; this was before the LORD had destroyed Sodom and Gomorrah. So Lot chose for himself all the plain of the Jordan, and Lot journeyed eastward; thus they separated from each other. Abram settled in the land of Canaan, while Lot settled among the cities of the Plain and moved his tent as far as Sodom" (Gen. 13:10–12).

44. Alter, "Sodom as Nexus," 33.

45. Assmann, *Moses the Egyptian*, 1.

46. An early expression of this view appears in the commentary of Philo of Alexandria, which dwells on the "deeper meaning" of Abraham's gaze: "the mind is firm, as the one God is firm," *Questions and Answers on Genesis* [*Quaestiones et Solutiones in Genesin et Exodum*], 4.53, Loeb Classical Library, vol. 380, trans. Ralph Marcus (Cambridge, MA: Harvard University Press, 1953), 333–34.

47. For nuanced discussion of Philo's exegetical procedure, see Jean Daniélou, *Philo of Alexandria*, trans. James G. Colbert (Eugene, OR: Wipf and Stock Publishers, 2014).

48. Philo, *Questions and Answers on Genesis*, 4:52, 330: "The literal meaning is very clear. For the angels had commanded (them) not to turn backward, and she transgressed the command, wherefore she paid the penalty."

49. For an account of Philo's relation to Middle Platonism, see John M. Dillon, *The Middle Platonists: 80 B.C. to A.D. 220* (Ithaca, NY: Cornell University Press, 1996).

50. Philo, *Questions and Answers*, 4:52, 332.

51. Philo, *De ebrietate*, 164–66, quoted in Loader, *Tale of Two Cities*, 94–95.

52. Philo, *De fuga et inventione*, 121–22, quoted in Loader, *Tale of Two Cities*, 94–95.

53. Michael Camille, *The Gothic Idol: Ideology and Image-Making in Medieval Art* (Cambridge: Cambridge University Press, 1991), 94.

54. The earliest example of the word "statue" in English given in the OED occurs in a description of Lot's wife from the alliterative poem *Cleanness*: "For his make [Lot's wife] was myst, þat on þe mount lenged In a stonen statue þat salt sauor habbes" (l. 995).

55. Among the extensive critical literature on this topic, see especially Alain Besançon, *The Forbidden Image: An Intellectual History of Iconoclasm*, trans. Jane Marie Todd (Chicago: University of Chicago Press, 2009) and Kenneth Gross, *The Dream of the Moving Statue* (University Park: Penn State University Press, 2006). The closing pages of the *Confessions* encapsulate Augustine's sense of the hospitable "interval" between the essential goodness of the created order and the ambivalent orientation of the human sensorium: "Your works proclaim your glory, and because of this we love you. . . . They have their beginning and their end in time, their rising and their setting, their progress and decline, their beauty and defect. . . . For the matter of heaven and earth is one thing, their form another. You created the matter from absolutely nothing and the form of the world from this formless matter. But you created both in one act, so that the form followed upon the matter with no interval of delay. . . . We see the things which you have made, because they exist. But they exist only because you see them. Outside ourselves we see that they exist, and in our inner selves we see that they are good. . . . It was only after a lapse of time that we were impelled to do good, that is, after our hearts had received the inspiration of the Holy Spirit. Before then our impulse was to do wrong, because we had deserted you. But you, who are the one God, the good God, have never ceased to do good. . . . What man can teach another this truth? . . . We must ask it of you, seek it in you; we must knock at your door. Only then shall we receive what we ask and find what we seek; only then will the door be opened to us" (*Confessions*, 12.33, 38).

56. "That is why Scripture says of them, after they had violated God's command by an overt transgression, 'The eyes of both of them were opened and they recognized that they were naked'" (Augustine, *City of God*, 14.17, trans. Bettenson, 578). See Camille's discussion of this passage in *The Gothic*

Idol: Ideology and Image-Making in Medieval Art (Cambridge: Cambridge University Press, 1991), 87–101.

57. Madeline Caviness examines the psychoanalytical formulations of this problem in *Visualizing Women in the Middle Ages: Sight, Spectacle, and Scopic Economy* (Philadelphia: University of Pennsylvania Press, 2001), 45–82.

58. On this point, see James Wetzel, "Body Double: Saint Augustine and the Sexualized Will," in *Weakness of Will from Plato to the Present*, ed. Tobias Hoffmann (Washington, DC: Catholic University of America Press, 2008), 58–81.

59. See John T. Spike, *Masaccio* (New York: Abbeville Press, 1996); and James Clifton, "Gender and Shame in Masaccio's *Expulsion from the Garden of Eden*," *Art History* 22, no. 5 (December 1999): 637–55.

60. The disputed authorship of Ephesians is not immediately relevant to my argument; for an account of the central issues in the debate, see H. J. Cadbury, "The Dilemma of Ephesians," *New Testament Studies* 5 (1959): 91–102.

61. See Derrida, *Of Hospitality*, 135.

62. The Hellenistic discourse on *phronesis*, which is indebted to the moral pedagogy found in Plato's *Republic* and Aristotle's *Ethics*, is not quite what Paul endorses in Ephesians or elsewhere in the Pauline canon. Nonetheless, the ethical as well as interpretive risk at the heart of classical *phronesis* resurfaces in postbiblical encounters with Lot's wife. Hannah Arendt's sense of classical *phronesis*, which challenges Heidegger's solipsistic sense of the practice, is particularly relevant to the figural history of Lot's wife. I return to this point in chapter 7. A helpful discussion of Arendt's handling of *phronesis* is in Jacques Taminiaux, "The Interpretation of Aristotle's Notion of *Aretê* in Heidegger's First Courses," in *Heidegger and Practical Philosophy*, ed. François Raffoul and David Pettigrew (Albany: State University of New York Press, 2002), 13–28.

63. The iconography of prudence includes several visual codes in addition to the *contrapposto* effect. These include the trope of gazing into a looking glass, the *vultus trifons* (three-faced figure), and the death's head. See Martin Porter, *Windows of the Soul: Physiognomy in European Culture, 1470–1780* (Oxford: Oxford University Press, 2005), 229–44, as well as the classic study by Erwin Panofsky, "Titian's *Allegory of Prudence*: A Postscript," in *Meaning in the Visual Arts* (Garden City, NY: Doubleday Anchor Books, 1955), 149–51.

64. See Clayton J. Drees, ed., *The Late Medieval Age of Crisis and Renewal, 1300–1500: A Biographical Dictionary* (Santa Barbara, CA: Greenwood, 2000), 334–35.

65. Caviness, *Visualizing Women in the Middle Ages*, 56. Caviness also notes that the twelfth-century *Glossa Ordinaria* presents Lot's wife as an elaboration of the fault of Eve, repeating the primordial disobedience (ibid., 56n26.).

66. "Sal enim prudentiae loco ponitur, quae ei defuit," Origen, *Homélies sur la Genèse*, trans. Louis Doutreleaux (Paris: Éditions du Cerf, 1976), 169.

67. See Jay, *Downcast Eyes*, 21–82.

68. "For all that is in the world, the lust of the flesh, and the lust of the eyes, and the pride of life, is not of the Father, but is of the world" (1 John 2:16, KJV).

69. Lot's wife, he reports, was "continually turning round towards the city, curious to observe its fate, notwithstanding God's prohibition of such action." *Flavius Josephus: Translation and Commentary*, vol. 3, ed. Steve Mason, trans. Louis H. Feldman (Leiden, Netherlands: Brill, 2000), 203. A helpful overview of Josephus's account is in Thomas W. Franxman, *Genesis and the "Jewish Antiquities" of Flavius Josephus* (Rome: Gregorian and Biblical Press, 1979).

70. Transposing the matter into two of the key figures of hospitality in Levinasian ethics, we could say that Josephus's practice of benign curiosity corresponds to the thought that the ethical "subject is a host," whereas the insidious vein of curiosity opens onto the thought that "subjectivity is being hostage" (Levinas, *Totality and Infinity*, 229; and *Otherwise Than Being, Or Beyond Essence*, 127). I return to this topic in chapters 2 and 4.

71. See especially Augustine, *Confessions* 10.35.54; Plutarch, *De curiositate* (included in the *Moralia*); and Tertullian, *De praescriptione haereticorum*, chap. 14. For a penetrating analysis of the premodern dossier on curiosity, see Maria Tasinato, *La curiosité: Apulée et Augustin* (Paris: Éditions Verdier, 1999).

72. Jean-Claude Fredouille, *Tertullien et la conversion de la culture antique* (Paris: Études Augustiniennes, 1972), 417.

73. On this point, see ibid., 412–26.

74. Philo, *Questions and Answers*, 4:32, 330–32.

75. Ibid., 4:32, 331–32.

76. On this point, see the classic account of the narrative logic of secrecy in Mieke Bal, "The Point of Narratology," *Poetics Today* 11, no. 4 (Winter 1990): 727–53.

77. Foucault, *The History of Sexuality*, vol. 1, *An Introduction*, trans. Robert Hurley (New York: Random House, 1978), 21.

78. *Genèse Rabba*, trans. Bernard Maruani and Albert Cohen-Arazi (Paris: Verdier, 1987), 540–41: "Rabbi Itshaq dit: C'est qu'elle fauta avec le sel. La nuit même où les anges arrivèrent chez Loth, que fit-elle? Elle se rendit chez tous les voisins, en disant: Donnez-moi un peu de sel car nous avons des invités. Elle voulait que les gens de la ville apprennent leur présence. Voilà pourquoi elle devint une colonne de sel." See also *Genesis Rabbah: The Judaic Commentary to the Book of Genesis*, ed. Jacob Neusner, vol. 2, *Parashiyyot Thirty-Four through Sixty-Seven on Genesis 8:15 to 28:9*, Brown Judaic Studies (Atlanta, GA: Scholars Press, 1985), 540–41.

79. For a detailed examination of salt symbolism in biblical textuality and ecclesiastical tradition, see James E. Latham, *The Religious Symbolism of Salt* (Paris: Beauchesne, 1982).

80. A useful account of the range of targumic and midrashic interpretations of Genesis 19 is in Michael Carden, *Sodomy: A History of a Christian Biblical Myth* (New York: Routledge, 2004), 105–8. Carden helpfully traces the complex textual history of the above-cited commentary in *Genesis Rabbah* (ibid., 106–7). See also Jill Hammer, *Sisters at Sinai: New Tales of Biblical Women* (Philadelphia: Jewish Publication Society, 2004), 253–54.

81. The text also introduces an eschatological component: "And she remains a pillar of salt until the time of the resurrection of the dead" (*Targum Neophyti*, Gen. 19:26), quoted in James L. Kugel, *Traditions of the Bible: A Guide to the Bible as It Was at the Start of the Common Era* (Cambridge, MA: Harvard University Press, 2009), 337.

82. "The pity of 'Edith [Idit] the wife of Lot was stirred for her daughters, who were married in Sodom, and she looked back behind to see if they were coming after her or not. And she saw behind [her] the Shekinah, and she became a pillar of salt," *Pirḳê de Rabbi Eliezer*, chap. 25, trans. Gerald Friedlander (New York: Hermon Press, 1965), 186. See also the commentary in Martin I. Lockshin, *Rabbi Samuel Ben Meir's Commentary on Genesis: An Annotated Translation* (Lewiston, NY: E. Mellen Press, 1989), 76–77. Hammer notes that the name given Lot's wife in *Pirḳê de Rabbi Eliezer*, Idit, means "witness" (Hammer, *Sisters at Sinai*, 254).

83. Alan F. Segal's commentary is helpful: "the word that the Gospel of John uses to describe the incarnation is *eskenosen* signifying encampment. Its Hebrew equivalent is the root *sh-k-n* which designates both setting up a tent and dwelling. It is the same as the normal Arabic root for 'residing' . . . Jewish tradition will call this divine presence the Shekhina, the 'Indwelling.' Later mystical Judaism will even identify this figure with the lowest of the *spheroth*, the metaphysical divine emanations: this one is the spiritual Israel, the way in which God normally makes his presence known to the world." Segal, "The Incarnation: the Jewish Milieu," in *The Incarnation: An Interdisciplinary Symposium on the Incarnation of the Son of God*, ed. Stephen T. Davis, Daniel Kendall, and Gerald O'Collins (Oxford: Oxford University Press, 2004), 116–42, at 137.

84. Philo, *De fuga*, 265n2. See also Daniel Boyarin's important qualification to the antiscopic bias attributed to biblical and rabbinic textuality in Boyarin, "The Eye in the Torah: Desire in Midrashic Hermeneutic," *Critical Inquiry* 16, no. 3 (Spring, 1990): 532–50.

85. See, for example, the terms of the prohibition in Numbers and the *Pirḳê de Rabbi Eliezer*: "Those who touch the dead body of any human being

shall be unclean for seven days" (Num. 19:20); "one made unclean through a corpse (needs) seven (days of purification)" (*Pirk̥ê de Rabbi Eliezer*, chap. 53, 435). Mary Douglas's comments on the structural logic of ritual purity codes remain useful; see Douglas, *Purity and Danger* (1970, repr. New York: Routledge, 2005). Michel Serres detects the misrecognized place of the cadaver in Genesis 19: "Natural miracles, here, the rain of stones, reveal how human atrocities are concealed. Flesh transformed into stone is a lapidated body." Serres, *Statues: The Second Book of Foundations*, trans. Randolph Burks (London and New York: Bloomsbury Publishing, 2015), 181.

2. THE RISE OF PROPHECY: FIGURAL NEUTER, DESERT OF ALLEGORY

1. Maurice Blanchot, *The Work of Fire*, trans. Lydia Davis (Stanford, CA: Stanford University Press, 1995), 328.

2. Among the extensive critical literature on this point, see in particular Alain P. Tournayan, *Encountering the Other: The Artwork and the Problem of Difference in Blanchot and Levinas* (Pittsburgh: Duquesne University Press, 2004).

3. Walter Benjamin, "Theses on the Philosophy of History," in *Illuminations: Essays and Reflections*, ed. Hannah Arendt (New York: Harcourt Brace, 1968), 253–64, at 255.

4. Lynn Hunt, "History as Gesture; or, The Scandal of History," in *Consequences of Theory*, ed. Jonathan Arac and Barbara Johnson (Baltimore, MA: Johns Hopkins University Press, 1991), 91–107, at 103. For a sustained mediation on the hermeneutical premise of Hunt's point, see Hayden White, *The Content of the Form: Narrative Discourse and Historical Representation* (Baltimore, MA: Johns Hopkins University Press, 1990).

5. Hunt, "History as Gesture," 103.

6. Ibid., 91.

7. Waldenfels, "The Paradox of Expression," 92.

8. In other words, the later Heideggerian project figurally links to Tertullian's fascination with the dangerous scruple of curiosity when it comes to the postmetaphysical subject's heroic assumption of authentic existence. For Heidegger, the "two factors constitutive for curiosity, *not staying* in the surrounding world taken care of and *distraction* by new possibilities, are the basis of the third essential characteristic of this phenomenon, which we call *never dwelling anywhere*. Curiosity is everywhere and nowhere. This mode of being-in-the-world reveals a new kind of being of everyday *Da-sein*, one in which it constantly uproots itself." Heidegger, *Being and Time*, trans. Joan Stambaugh (Albany: State University of New York Press, 1996), 36/161. See also Tasinato's comment on Heidegger's debt to Augustine in *La curiosité*, 36–42.

9. Augustine, *Confessions*, trans. R. S. Pine-Coffin (New York: Penguin, 1961), 242 [*Confessions*, 10.35: *In hac tam immensa silva plena insidiarum et periculorum*].

10. In the *Confessions*, Augustine worries over the contaminating effects of curiosity in religious matters: "it even infects our religion, for we put God to the test when we demand signs and wonders from him, not in the hope of salvation, but simply for the love of the experience" (ibid.).

11. A helpful overview of these matters is in Bart D. Ehrman, *Lost Christianities: The Battles for Scripture and the Faiths We Never Knew* (Oxford: Oxford University Press, 2003), 95–112.

12. I address the Lukan treatment of the Sodom story in chapter 3.

13. See Loader, *Tale of Two Cities*, 131.

14. "Lot's wife is seen as an example of the danger of harking back to what lies in the past (*Adv Mar* 4:23:499, 22). In the light of the implication that the leaders of the established church are 'Sodomites,' this probably refers to the Catholic past as opposed to the Montanist future rather than to the pre-Christian/Christian eras in an individual's life" (Loader, *A Tale of Two Cities*, 131). The relevant passage in the *Adversus Marcionem* comments on the closing verses of Luke 9, which describe varieties of lukewarm observance of Jesus's eschatological mission: "To another he said, 'Follow me.' But he said, 'Lord, first let me go and bury my father.' But Jesus said to him, 'Let the dead bury their own dead; but as for you, go and proclaim the kingdom of God.' Another said, 'I will follow you, Lord; but let me first say farewell to those at my home.' Jesus said to him, 'No one who puts a hand to the plow and looks back is fit for the kingdom of God'" (Luke 9:59–62). Tertullian's commentary on the last verse reads: "In the third case as well, concerning the man who wished to bid farewell to his family [before following the messianic call], Jesus follows the pattern of the Creator, who forbade the same action of those whom he had rescued from Sodom." Tertullien, *Contre Marcion*, vol. 4, trans. René Braun (Paris: Editions du Cerf, 2001), 303; my translation.

15. See the detailed account of Tertullian's relationship with ecclesial orthodoxy in William Tabbernee, *Fake Prophecy and Polluted Sacraments: Ecclesiastical and Imperial Reactions to Montanism* (Leiden, Netherlands: Brill, 2007), esp. 161–64.

16. Tabbernee's comment on this issue is relevant: "the Spirit's final revelation contained in the oracles and books of the New Prophecy was a progressive, interpretive, and dependent ethical revelation, revealing only how spiritual Christians were to act in an age of Christian maturity. Montanist fasts, sexual abstinence, monogamy, and other practices, such as the veiling of virgins and the refusal to pardon serious sins, were but acts expressing the full

ethical implications of previously revealed truth and, hence, did not constitute [heretical] novelty" (ibid., 162–63).

17. The bishop of Rome did not recognize the Montanist proclamations. This contretemps seems to have reinforced Tertullian's suspicion (or scruple) that the established orthodoxy had become too secular, too concerned with protecting its administrative authority, as evidenced by its turning a deaf ear to prophetic interventions in church business. In any event, after the Montanist sect fell into a state of virtual schism, Tertullian himself was cut off from the presiding church of Carthage; he later founded his own sect. The precise status of the sect in the ecclesial order is uncertain. See David Rankin, *Tertullian and the Church* (Cambridge: Cambridge University Press, 1995). Rankin's assessment—building on the revisionist projects of noted scholars such as Jean-Claude Fredouille, T. D. Sider, and T. D. Barnes—goes far toward rehabilitating Tertullian's place in canonical ecclesiastical history, insisting that the state of documentary evidence does not warrant the traditional view of Tertullian's ultimate separation from the church. The prevailing view in church tradition since Augustine, however, places Tertullian in a far less ambiguous position, and it is this aspect of Tertullian's cultural identity that pertains to my argument. The difficulty of ascertaining whether and when Tertullian turned from the recognized course of episcopal authority places him figuratively under the sign of the turning figure in the Sodom narrative.

18. Ian Balfour, *The Rhetoric of Romantic Prophecy* (Stanford, CA: Stanford University Press, 2002), 5.

19. Gerhard von Rad, *The Message of the Prophets*, trans. D. M. G. Stalker (London: SCM Press, 1968), 37.

20. Blanchot, "Prophetic Speech," in *The Book to Come*, trans. Charlotte Mandell (Stanford, CA: Stanford University Press, 2003), 79–85. Hereafter cited in text as *BtC* and page number. Blanchot's essay is nominally a review of André Neher's *L'essence du prophétisme* (1955). An illuminating treatment of Blanchot's thought on prophecy, applied to Romantic poetics, is in Balfour, *Rhetoric of Romantic Prophecy*.

21. Thus the prophetic character of the tensed dialogue of Sodom's fate (Gen. 18) begins with God's need to "hear his own speech—thus become response—repeated in the man in whom it can only assert itself and who becomes responsible for it" (Blanchot, "Prophetic Speech," 83). Interestingly, Blanchot passes over the detail of Abraham's strenuous questioning of God's decision.

22. For a discussion of "counter-history" see Amos Funkenstein, *Perceptions of Jewish History* (Berkeley: University of California Press, 1993), 36–40, 169–201; and David Biale, "Counter-History and Jewish Polemics against

Christianity: The *Sefer toldot yeshu* and the *Sefer zerubavel*," *Jewish Social Studies* 6, no. 1 (Autumn 1999), 130–45. Funkenstein's influential use of the term emphasizes the dangerous distortions associated with the polemical function of counter-histories in Jewish-Christian rivalries. Biale explores the experimental dimension of counter-historical imagination. Counter-history may also articulate "a new form of the polemical exploitation of history for ideological purposes: history not as past but as imagined future, that singular reorientation of time with which an apocalypse puts historical events into the prophetic mouth of an ancient source" ("Counter-History," 142). See also Assmann's discussion of this point in *Moses the Egyptian*, 12.

23. My reading of the symbolic associations of the snail draws on the superb analysis of the basic motifs in Yves and Françoise Cranga, "L'escargot dans le Midi de la France: Approche iconographique," *Mémoires de la Société Archéologique du Midi de la France*, no. 57 (1997): 70–90. See also the wide-ranging study by François-Xavier Gleyzon, *Shakespeare's Spiral: Tracing the Snail in King Lear and Renaissance Painting* (Lanham, MD: University Press of America, 2010).

24. The biblical proof-text is Psalms 58:8: "Let them be like the snail that dissolves into slime; like the untimely birth that never sees the sun" (NRSV). The Hebrew word *shabbelul* (snail or slug) is translated as "wax" in the Septuagint and Latin Vulgate (*kēros, cera*). English vernacular bibles use "snail" (excepting the Douay-Rheims, which maintains the word "wax"). As Cranga and Cranga point out, the perceived asexuality of the snail also encouraged its application as figure of the Annunciation ("L'escargot," 89).

25. See *Les Très Riches Heures du duc de Berry*, ed. Raymond Cazelles and Jean Longnon, trans. Victoria Benedict (1969; repr. New York: George Braziller, 1989), 13, 124, 180, 219.

26. Cranga, "L'escargot dans le Midi de la France," 90; my translation. The original text reads: "Être de l'intermèdiaire, il chemine entre Dieu et diable, tragédie et comédie."

27. Patricia Cox Miller, "On the Edge of Self and Other: Holy Bodies in Late Antiquity," *Journal of Early Christian Studies* 17, no. 2 (Summer 2009): 171–93, at 185. Miller's point elaborates the argument of Michael A. Williams, *The Immovable Race: Gnostic Designation and the Theme of Stability in Late Antiquity* (Leiden, Netherlands: Brill, 1997), 8–34.

28. Levinas, *Totality and Infinity: An Essay on Exteriority*, trans. Alphonso Lingis (Pittsburgh: Duquesne University Press, 1969), 50–51.

29. Levinas, "Reality and Its Shadow," in *The Levinas Reader*, ed. Séan Hand (Oxford: Basil Blackwell, 1989), 129–43, at 138. Hereafter cited in text as *RIS* and page number. The essay "La réalité et son ombre" first appeared in *Les temps modernes*, no. 38 (1948): 771–89.

30. Levinas, *Existence and Existents*, trans. Alphonso Lingis (The Hague: Martinus Nijhoff, 1978), 57. See Robbins's careful reading of the relation between Blanchot and Levinas on the ethicity of the artwork, *Altered Reading*, 133–54. See also Sarah Hammerschlag, *The Figural Jew: Politics and Identity in Postwar French Thought* (Chicago: University of Chicago Press, 2010), 166–200.

31. Gerald L. Bruns, *Maurice Blanchot: The Refusal of Philosophy* (Baltimore, MD: Johns Hopkins University Press, 1997), 52.

32. The ethical provocation of the *il y a* derives in part from the suggestion in Heidegger's *Letter on Humanism* that the abode of *Dasein* (the "there" or place of human being) entails exposure to "existence without any existing entity: being's anonymous form." Alain Finkielkraut, *The Wisdom of Love*, trans. K. O'Neill and D. Suchoff (Lincoln: University of Nebraska Press, 1997), 6.

33. "The Poet's Vision" addresses primarily Blanchot's 1955 collection *L'espace littéraire*. See Blanchot, *The Space of Literature*, trans. Ann Smock (Lincoln: University of Nebraska Press, 1982). As I suggest in this chapter, the imagistic repertoire in Blanchot's earlier collection *La part du feu* (1949) silently informs Levinas's account of Blanchot's enterprise as well, especially the essay "Literature and the Right to Death." See *Work of Fire*, 300–44, at 327–28.

34. Levinas, "The Poet's Vision," in *Proper Names*, trans. Michael Smith (Stanford University Press, 1997), 127–39, at 137. Subsequent citations in this paragraph are to this text.

35. Blanchot, *Space of Literature*, 76–77 and 236–37.

36. The essay first appeared in *Critique* 18 (November 1947) and 20 (January 1948). A nuanced explication of the triangulation of Blanchot's critical responses to Levinas, Heidegger, and Alexandre Kojève's reading of Hegel is in Leslie Hill, *Blanchot: Extreme Contemporary* (London and New York: Routledge, 1997), 103–57.

37. Blanchot, *Work of Fire*, 332. Hereafter cited in text as *WoF* and page number.

38. See also Levinas's early essay "There Is: Existence without Existents," in *The Levinas Reader*, 29–36. Blanchot's meditation on the dispossessive core of literature welcomes Levinas's perspective into its purview by insisting that the "one subject" of literature is the making present of "the process through which whatever ceases to be continues to be . . . whatever seeks to attain the beyond is always still here," in a circuit of "consciousness whose light is no longer the lucidity of the vigil but the stupor of lack of sleep, it is existence without being" (*Work of Fire*, 334).

39. Blanchot's major formulation of this link is in "René Char and the Thought of the Neutral," in *The Infinite Conversation*, trans. Susan Hanson (Minneapolis: University of Minnesota Press, 1992), 298–306.

40. Blanchot, "Reading Kafka," in *Work of Fire*, 9.

41. Levinas, *Otherwise Than Being or Beyond Essence*, trans. Alphonso Lingis (The Hague: Nijhoff, 1981), 90. On Levinas's use of the notion of trauma see the excellent analysis by Simon Critchley, "The Original Traumatism: Levinas and Psychoanalysis," in *Ethics-Politics-Subjectivity: Essays on Derrida, Levinas, and Contemporary French Thought* (London: Verso, 1999), 183–97. It is important to recall here that the Levinasian notion of "face" refers not to the phenomenal appearance of the Other, but to the urgent proximity of the Other in an encounter that compels attention and demands a response.

42. The question of how Levinas's notion of the "face" of the other applies to nonhuman life forms is an ongoing topic of debate in Levinas studies. A helpful overview of the question is in Kelly Oliver, *Animal Lessons: How They Teach Us to Be Human* (New York: Columbia University Press, 2009), 25–50.

43. Thus Blanchot on the equivocality of literature: "Literature is language turning into ambiguity. . . . Here ambiguity struggles with itself. It is not just that each moment of language can become ambiguous and say something different from what it is saying, but that the general meaning of language is unclear: we do not know if it is expressing or representing, if it is a thing or means of that thing; if it is there to be forgotten or if it only makes us forget it so that we will see it . . . obscure because it says too much, opaque because it says nothing" (*Work of Fire*, 341–42).

44. Blanchot cites Hegel's remark in the preface to the *Phenomenology of Spirit*; see *Phenomenology of Sprit*, trans. A. V. Miller (Oxford: Oxford University Press, 1977), 19, para. 32.

45. Blanchot, "Orpheus's Gaze," in *Space of Literature*, 171–76, at 174. For a helpful analysis of the four main mythopoetic figures in Blanchot's writing—Orpheus, Jesus, Lazarus, and Narcissus—see John Gregg, *Maurice Blanchot and the Literature of Transgression* (Princeton, NJ: Princeton University Press, 1994).

46. Norbert Elias, *The Civilizing Process: Sociogenetic and Psychogenetic Investigations*, trans. Edmund Jephcott, rev. ed. (Oxford: Basil Blackwell, 2000).

47. Blanchot, *Book to Come*, 80.

48. See Assmann, *Moses the Egyptian*, 67, 1.

49. Blanchot, "Our Clandestine Companion," 1980; repr. in *Face to Face with Levinas*, ed. Richard A. Cohen (Albany: State University of New York Press, 1986), 41–50.

50. Levinas, "The Poet's Vision," 329.

51. In the 1966 essay "The Servant and Her Master," Levinas turns explicitly to the Sodom narrative in the course of parsing his careful appreciation of the narrative tactics of disorientation that shape Blanchot's novel *L'attente l'oubli*. The allusion to Lot's wife serves as an index of proximity between Blanchot's aesthetic enterprise and Levinas's concept of diachrony. As defined in *Otherwise as Being or Beyond Essence*, diachrony indicates "a disjunction of identity where the same does not rejoin the same: there is non-synthesis, lassitude. The for-oneself of identity is now no longer for itself. . . . The subject is for another; its own being turns into for another, its being dies away turning into signification. . . . It signifies in the form of the proximity of a neighbor and the duty of an unpayable debt, the form of a finite condition." Levinas, *Otherwise than Being or Beyond Essence*, trans. Alphonso Lingis (Duquesne University Press, 1998), 52. The passage from "The Servant and Her Master" reads as follows: "Reflection brings up the old foundation stones and mixes them with current things. That simultaneity of conditioning and conditioned is known as coherent discourse. But, looking back to examine their condition, words are immobilized, become pillars of salt. Here again, Forgetting restores diachrony to time. A diachrony with neither pretention nor retention. To await nothing and forget everything—the opposite of subjectivity—'absence of any center' [*L'attente l'oubli*, 45]" (146).

52. Blanchot, "Prophetic Speech," 84.

53. In the cited passage, the word *figure* appears only once; in the preceding phrases Blanchot uses the word *visage*. The latter is Levinas's preferred term to indicate the ethical expressivity or "face" of the Other. Arguably, Blanchot's choice of the word *figure* makes a case for designating prophetic speech as an exceptional mediation of the expressive power of art (its figural dimension) and the ethicity of the "face." For the French text, see Blanchot, *Le livre à venir* (Paris: Gallimard, 1959), 117. Though Blanchot insists on the radical distinction between allegory and prophecy, Augustinian tradition broods over the two modes' co-implication. As Giuseppe Mazzotta argues, Dante's poetics of the desert in the *Divine Comedy* grippingly expresses the drama of "Augustine's view of meaning," which "places us outside of the text," an outside where "to decide means that something is always left out, that the poem . . . has no simple truth to give . . . that the language of man always prevaricates, follows a crooked path and cannot snatch the secrets that lie deep in a dark cave." Giuseppe Mazzotta, *Dante, Poet of the Desert* (Princeton, NJ: Princeton University Press, 1979), 270–71.

54. Blanchot, "Prophetic Speech," 85.

55. Ibid., 79.

56. Ibid., 85.

3. REMEMBERING LOT'S WIFE: THE STRUCTURE
OF TESTIMONY IN THE *PAINTED LIFE* OF MARY WARD

An earlier version of this chapter is in *Religious Diversity in Early Modern English Texts: Judaic, Catholic, Feminist and Secular Dimensions*, ed. Arthur F. Marotti and Chanita Goodblatt (Detroit, MI: Wayne State University Press, 2013), 77–104.

1. Hans Urs von Balthasar, *A Theology of History* (New York: Sheed and Ward, 1963), 45.

2. Luigi Pulci, *Il Morgante* (Florence, Italy: Bartolomeo Sermartelli, 1574), 198. For an account of Sermartelli's typographical designs, together with bibliographical details of the letter "L," see Franca Petrucci Nardelli, *La lettera e l'immagine: le iniziali parlante nella tipografia italiana, secc. XVI–XVII* (Florence, Italy: Leo S. Olschki, 1991), 74–75. I thank Paul Gehl for pointing out this reference.

3. For a discussion of the relation between talking letters, rhetorical techniques of *copia*, and mnemonic arts in the sixteenth century, see Lina Bolzoni, *Gallery of Memory: Literary and Iconographic Models in the Age of Printing*, trans. Jeremy Parzen (Toronto: University of Toronto Press, 2001), 98–105.

4. For a relevant discussion of this point, see Tracy McNulty, *The Hostess: Hospitality, Femininity, and the Expropriation of Identity* (Minneapolis: University of Minnesota Press, 2007), 15–20.

5. Ward's critics used the term "Jesuitress" as code to signal contempt for her apparent ambition to emulate the organizational ethos of the Jesuit order. See Lowell Gallagher, "Mary Ward's 'Jesuitresses' and the Construction of a Typological Community," in *Maids and Mistresses, Cousins and Queens: Women's Alliances in Early Modern England*, ed. Susan Frye and Karen Robertson (New York: Oxford University Press, 1999), 203–6.

6. See Erich Auerbach, "Figura," in *Scenes from the Drama of European Literature: Six Essays* (New York: Meridian, 1959), 11–76. For an account of the relation between typology and Hegelian dialectic, see Cyril O'Regan, *The Heterodox Hegel* (Albany: State University of New York Press, 1994).

7. See John A. Gallagher, *Time Past, Time Future: An Historical Study of Catholic Moral Theology* (New York: Paulist Press, 1990), 123–61. For a helpful account of the key figures and issues associated with the *nouvelle théologie*, see Jürgen Mettepenningen, *Nouvelle Théologie—New Theology Inheritor of Modernism, Precursor of Vatican II* (London: T&T Clark International, 2010).

8. Gallagher, *Time Past*, 144–46.

9. For a lucid account of de Lubac's sense of the *complexio oppositorum*, or "complex of opposites held in tension," see Dennis M. Doyle, "Henri de Lubac and the Roots of Communion Ecclesiology," *Theological Studies* 60,

no. 2 (June 1999): 209–12. Such an orientation explains why the notion of catholicity for de Lubac could imply, as Doyle suggests, "not only an encompassing of various dimensions of truth held in tension, and not only a socially conscious embrace of all that is good and worthy, but also a radical inclusion of all human beings in all of their depth and mystery" (212).

10. I refer here to the engaged pastoralism of de Lubac's project generally, as distinct from his magisterial recuperation of biblical intertextuality and Christian exegetical practice in his three-volume survey, *Exégèse médiévale* (Paris: Aubier, 1959–1964).

11. For an account of the theological controversy prompted by de Lubac's revisionist arguments, see John Milbank, *The Suspended Middle: Henri de Lubac and the Debate Concerning the Supernatural* (Grand Rapids, MI: Wm. B. Eerdmans, 2005). For an authoritative reading of the ferment of *ressourcement* thought, which includes a nuanced appreciation of de Lubac's commitment to revitalizing a sense of sacramental ontology in the church, see Hans Boersma, *Nouvelle Théologie and Sacramental Ontology: A Return to Mystery* (Oxford: Oxford University Press, 2009), 4–12, 88–99.

12. In the phenomenological and ethical sense developed by *ressourcement* theologians, *figura* stands for exposure to the trace or passage of the infinite within the material embodiment of events. In a phrase fully cognizant of its figural resonance, de Lubac argues that knowledge of God is irreducible to propositional language, because it is already, primordially, the existential trace of "an 'image,' an 'imprint,' a 'seal' . . . the mark of God upon us," multiply disseminated throughout the envelope of creaturely existence. Henri de Lubac, *Discovery of God*, trans. Alexander Dru (London: Darton, Longman and Todd, 1960), 7. The phrase recalls the etymological scope of figura's Greek antecedent, *tupos*, which signifies a blow or wounding gesture as well as the impression left by invasive or intimate contact and, by extension, the material representation of an idea, concept, or absent thing. See Mark Taylor, *Erring: A Postmodern Theology* (Chicago: University of Chicago Press, 1984), 56–57. The act of exposure corresponds to what Auerbach identifies as the pivotal function of figura in patristic writing as a "middle term" between the literal sense of a described event (*historia* or *littera*) and the spiritual "fulfillment" of event (*veritas*). See Auerbach, "Figura," 47. For a succinct account of de Lubac's nuanced sense of the sacramental character of the church, see Doyle, "Henri de Lubac."

13. Gallagher, *Time Past*, 149–50. See also Joseph O'Malley, *What Happened at Vatican II* (Cambridge, MA: Harvard University Press, 2008), 36–43, 75–76.

14. The incest scene involving Lot and his two surviving daughters provokes ambivalent responses from rabbinic and Christian commentators alike,

but from the standpoint of providential history as construed in Christian exegesis, the fact that the house of David grew out of the incest could not be ignored. For a wide-ranging account of the afterlife of the story of Lot's daughters, see Robert M. Polhemus, *Lot's Daughters: Sex, Redemption, and Women's Quest for Authority* (Stanford, CA: Stanford University Press, 2005).

15. Robert Alter, "Sodom as Nexus: The Web of Design in Biblical Narrative," in *Reclaiming Sodom*, ed. Jonathan Goldberg (New York: Routledge, 1994), 28–42. For the text of the encyclical, see http://www.papalencyclicals .net/Pius12/P12HUMAN.HTM.

16. Although the encyclical's mention of deadly fruit bears Edenic associations, postbiblical Sodom lore also makes much of the so-called "apples of Sodom," first documented in Josephus, *Bellum Judaicum*, IV, viii, 4. Alluring in appearance, the fabled apples were believed to dissolve into smoke and ashes upon touch.

17. The Hebrew text of Genesis 19:26 reads: *vatabet ishto me'aharav vatehi netziv melah*. The semantic range of *netziv* is covered in Francis Brown, S. R. Driver, and Charles A. Briggs, eds., *A Hebrew and English Lexicon of the Old Testament* (1907; repr. Oxford: Oxford University Press, 1977), 662. The unstable exemplarity of Lot's wife is partly registered, if not caused, by a problem in translation that entered Christian biblical cultures quite early. The Vulgate translates *netziv* (pillar) as *statuam* (standing figure or object, statue). In Continental and English vernacular bibles based on the Vulgate, Lot's wife becomes either a statue or an "ymage." Thus we read in a thirteenth-century French vernacular bible: "La fame Loth regarda arrieres soi, si fu muee en une ymage de sel." *La bible française du XIIIe siècle: édition critique de la Genèse*, ed. Michel Quereuil (Geneva: Droz, 1988), 200. William Tyndale's Pentateuch, which follows the Hebrew, introduces the figure of Lot's wife into early modern English as a pillar, and so she remains in virtually all the vernacular bibles printed in England, up to and including the King James Version. Visual representations of the episode in the early modern period continued the practice established in medieval illuminations and authorized by the Vulgate, figuring Lot's wife as a statue. Gradually, however, the object that the Hebrew text indicates came into view. For example, the woodcut from the celebrated *Nuremburg Chronicle* (1493) shows Lot's wife either in the process of becoming a pillar or, the transformation completed, as a hybrid figure, part pillar, part statue. See Heinrich Schedel, *Chronicle of the World, 1493: The Complete and Annotated Nuremburg Chronicle* (Cologne, Germany: Taschen, 2001).

18. Balthasar, *Theology of History*, 44. For Balthasar, Christic time "assumes into itself the growing emptiness and desolation of the unreal time of sin"; and its "truth and validity" contain "the modality of untrue, non-valid

time; not only in order to know it and having known it to overcome it, but in order to fill it with valid meaning" (42–43). For a relevant account of the symbolic crisis provoked by the death of Jesus in Christian testament writings, see Roy A. Harrisville, *Fracture: The Cross as Irreconcilable in the Language and Thought of the Biblical Writers* (Grand Rapids, MI: Wm. B. Eerdmans, 2006).

19. Maurice Blanchot, *The Writing of the Disaster*, trans. Ann Smock (Lincoln: University of Nebraska Press, 1995), 75. Published in 1980, Blanchot's text resumes a constellation of themes that germinated in the postwar years, during the time of his early contact and friendship with Emmanuel Levinas, whose impact on Blanchot's thought is readily discernible in *The Writing of the Disaster*. An unwritten page in the cultural history of *ressourcement* theology concerns its tacit conversation with the developing thought of Blanchot and Levinas in the postwar years and during the ecumenical period of Vatican II.

20. Blanchot's ruminations on passivity in *The Writing of the Disaster* (16–34) make the impact of Levinas's thought explicit.

21. For a suggestive opening into the relation between Blanchot and the theological culture animating the *ressourcement* movement, see Kevin Hart, *The Dark Gaze: Maurice Blanchot and the Sacred* (Chicago: University of Chicago Press, 2004), 22–49.

22. "This is what is strange: passivity is never passive enough. It is in this respect that one can speak of an infinite passivity: perhaps because passivity evades all formulations—yet it seems that there is in passivity something like a demand that would require it to fall always short of itself. There is in passivity not passivity, but its demand, a movement of the past toward the insurpassable. Passivity, passion, past, *pas* (both negation and step—the trace or movement of an advance): this semantic play provides us with a slippage of meaning, but not with anything to which we could entrust ourselves, not with anything like an answer that would satisfy us" (Blanchot, *Writing of the Disaster*, 16–17).

23. See Janice Haaken, *Pillar of Salt: Gender, Memory, and the Perils of Looking Back* (New Brunswick, NJ: Rutgers University Press, 1998), 18. The most famous use of Lot's wife in art relating to the Shoah is perhaps Anselm Kiefer's 1989 multimedia work *Lots Frau* (Cleveland Museum of Art). See my discussion in this book's introduction. See also Martin Harries's astute account of Kiefer's painting in *Forgetting Lot's Wife: On Destructive Spectatorship* (New York: Fordham University Press, 2007), 76–102. An extensive treatment of Kiefer's developing aesthetics of traumatic witnessing is in Daniel Arasse, *Anselm Kiefer*, trans. Mary Whittal (New York: Harry N. Abrams, 2001).

24. "And while these things were taking place, his wife remained in [the region of] Sodom, no longer corruptible flesh, but a pillar of salt [*statua salis*] which endures forever; and by those natural processes which appertain to the human race, indicating that the Church also, which is the salt of the earth, has been left behind within the confines of the earth [*sal terrae*], and subject to human sufferings [*patiens quae sunt humana*]; and while entire members are often taken away from it, the pillar of salt still endures, thus typifying the foundation of the faith which fortifies and advances children toward their Father. . . . For the Church alone sustains with purity the reproach of those who suffer persecution for righteousness' sake, and endure all sorts of punishments, and are put to death because of the love which they bear to God, and their confession of His Son; often weakened indeed, yet immediately increasing her members, and becoming whole again, after the same manner as her type, Lot's wife, who became a pillar of salt. Thus, too, [she passes through an experience] similar to that of the ancient prophets, as the Lord declares, 'For so persecuted they the prophets who were before you,' inasmuch as she does indeed, in a new fashion, suffer persecution from those who do not receive the word of God, while the self-same spirit rests upon her [as upon these ancient prophets]." Irenaeus, *Adversus haereses*, ed. Adelin Rousseau and Louis Doutreleau (Paris: Éditions du Cerf, 1982), 4.31.3, 4.33.9. My translation is from the preferred modern critical edition by Rousseau and Doutreleau.

25. For a pertinent discussion of the second-century debates about bodily resurrection in the emergent orthodoxy of the church, see Caroline Walker Bynum, *The Resurrection of the Body in Western Christianity, 200–1336* (New York: Columbia University Press, 1995), 27–58. For an account of Balthasar's debt to Irenaeus, see Kevin Mongrain, *The Systematic Thought of Hans Urs von Balthasar: An Irenaean Retrieval* (Chestnut Ridge, NY: Crossroads, 2002), 27–50.

26. Martin Luther, *Lectures on Genesis*, vol. 3, trans. George V. Schick, ed. Jaroslav Pelikan (St. Louis, MO: Concordia, 1961), 299. Like most of the polemical applications of Genesis 19:26 in the decades to follow, Luther takes his moorings from the note of eschatological urgency attributed to Jesus's conjuring of Lot's wife in the End Times segment of the Gospel according to Luke: "Remember Lot's wife" (Luke 17:32). Luther's commentary: "From this we readily understand what it means to look back, namely, to depart from God's command and to be occupied with other matters—matters outside one's calling. . . . For everyone should stick to his own calling and not concern himself with what others are doing. At the present time the papists beset us a great deal with the example of a former age during which everything lay in darkness. 'Your doctrine,' they say, 'is new and unknown to our ancestors;

therefore if it is true, all our ancestors have been condemned.' They, too, are looking back and thus disregard the word they have before them. . . . Thus the church is never without a trial, for the world does not continue on the proper and steady course of its calling but looks back like Lot's wife. . . . To be drawn away from the Word by new and strange ideas is . . . no joke or slight trial. . . . Such were the beginnings of nearly all heresies."

27. "From one end of the Bible to the other there is scarcely a woman of prominence who is not in some way a figure of that Church. The ingenuity of the first commentators, encouraged by the speculations of the rabbis, saw her in Lot's wife; following Paul, they recognized her in Sara; she it was, too, that they found in Rachel and Rebbeca, in Deborah, and in Samuel's mother Anne, in the widow of Sarepta and in Esther." Henri de Lubac, *Catholicism: Christ and the Common Destiny of Man*, trans. Lancelot C. Shepherd and Sister Elizabeth Englund (San Francisco: Ignatius Press, 1988), 187–88. De Lubac's catalog does not mention Irenaeus's text, however, nor does it pause to consider the impact of the "ingenuity" involved in recasting Lot's wife as a figure of the church.

28. The proof-text is Genesis 18:20–33, which describes Abraham's strenuous effort to ratchet up the prospects for Sodom's survival under the imminent threat of extinction in God's incendiary judgment.

29. On the mutable contours of the papist community, see, for example, Michael Questier, *Conversion, Politics, and Religion in England, 1580–1635* (Cambridge: Cambridge University Press, 1996); and Alexandra Walsham, *Church Papists: Catholicism, Conformity, and Confessional Polemic in Early Modern England* (Woodbridge, England: Boydell, 1993). Homiletic interest in Lot's wife is a subset of broader investment in the Sodom story for ecclesial boundary drawing in early modern sermon literature; see Mary Morrissey's brief discussion of this point in the context of puritan preaching at Paul's Cross in the early seventeenth century, in *Politics and the Paul's Cross Sermons, 1558–1642* (Oxford: Oxford University Press, 2011), 216–17.

30. Karl Marx, *The Eighteenth Brumaire of Louis Bonaparte* (New York: International Publishers, 1964), 15.

31. The preface to the first English sermon commemorating Gunpowder Plot calls attention to the generic amphibiousness of the event by conjuring the "discovery of this late Tragi-comical treason [Tragical, in the dreadeful intention: Comical in the happye and timely Detection thereof]." William Barlow, *The Sermon preached at Paules Cross, the Tenth day of November, being the next Sunday after the Discoverie of this late Horrible Treason* [1606], *STC²* 1455, sig. A3. Mark Nicholls's recent inspection of the complex tissue of motives and loyalties among the known conspirators leads to the judgment that the plot should be understood as a "failed rebellion" rather than a

terrorist action. See Nicholls, "Strategy and Motivation in the Gunpowder Plot," *Historical Journal* 50, no. 4 (2007): 787–807, at 806. For an account of the Gunpowder Treason rhymes, see Ronald Hutton, *Stations of the Sun: A History of the Ritual Year in Britain* (Oxford: Oxford University Press, 2001), 403–5.

32. Peter McCullough, ed., *Lancelot Andrewes: Selected Sermons and Lectures* (Oxford; Oxford University Press, 2006), xxvi. Among the many pieces of critical historiography on the Gunpowder Plot, see especially David Cressy, *Bonfires and Bells: National Memory and the Protestant Calendar in Elizabethan and Stuart England* (Berkeley: University of California Press, 1989); Antonia Fraser, *Faith and Treason: The Story of the Gunpowder Plot* (New York: Doubleday, 1996); and James Sharpe, *Remember, Remember: A Cultural History of Guy Fawkes Day* (Cambridge, MA: Harvard University Press, 2005).

33. Morrissey observes that "[w]hat is most surprising about the Gunpowder Plot sermons at Paul's Cross is how heterogeneous they are. Exhortations to thanksgiving, reassertions of God's providential care for England, and, most emphatically, denunciations of Catholicism are the only characteristics that these sermons share with each other and with other political anniversary sermons" (*Politics and the Paul's Cross Sermons*, 150). My remarks on the sermon literature in this paragraph are indebted to Morrissey's assessment. Though most of the Sodom sermons of the era play up the apocalyptic hazard incurred by Lot's wife, the biblical figure makes an interestingly burlesqued appearance in the famous trial of one of the alleged Gunpowder Plot conspirators, the Jesuit Henry Garnet. Henry Howard, first earl of Northampton and one of the architects of Garnet's conviction, turned the paired chemical and mineral associations of the Sodom legend—sulfur and saltpeter, the principal ingredients of gunpowder—into a biting typological satire on the conspirators' seditious intentions. Just as "Sodom [was] destroyed by sulphur and the wife of Lot transmuted into salt," so, too, the "Devil in his last project of powder" was defeated by providential interference. See *Trial of Guy Fawkes and Others (The Gunpowder Plot)*, ed. Donald Carswell (London and Edinburgh: William Hodge and Company, 1934), 180–81.

34. Barlow, *The Sermon preached at Paules Crosse, the Tenth day of November* (1606), *STC²* 1455.

35. As Morrissey observes, virtually all the Gunpowder Plot sermons "painted lurid pictures of the death and chaos that might have resulted had God not prevented the plotters" (*Politics and the Paul's Cross Sermons*, 149).

36. Robert Wilkinson, "Lot's Wife. A Sermon Preached at Paules Crosse" (London, 1607). On Wilkinson's career, see McCullough, *Sermons at*

Court: Politics and Religion in Elizabethan and Jacobean Preaching (Cambridge: Cambridge University Press, 1998), 189.

37. Wilkinson's attunement to the ambiguities of papist survivalism is consistent with the broad tenor of the Paul's Cross sermons' rhetorical apparatus, which both rallied eschatological expectation and conveyed an elegiac, quasi-Stoic sense of entropy. "On the one hand," argues Millar Maclure, "the preachers espoused a nationalistic type of messianism . . . [b]ut the preachers also brooded upon the twilight close at hand. Humane learning, however by times discountenanced in comparison with clear revelation, gave them some sense of the long reaches of the past and the mutability of all earthly things." Maclure, *The Paul's Cross Sermons, 1534–1642* (Toronto: University of Toronto Press, 1958), 118–19.

38. Wilkinson, "Lot's Wife," 49–56.

39. Ibid., 51, 52–53.

40. Michael Quester, "Loyalty, Religion and State Power in Early Modern England: English Romanism and the Jacobean Oath of Allegiance," *Historical Journal* 40, no. 2 (June 1997): 311–29, at 321.

41. Ibid., 321–22.

42. Assman, *Moses the Egyptian*, 44.

43. Frances E. Dolan, *Whores of Babylon: Catholicism, Gender, and Seventeenth-Century Print Culture* (Ithaca, NY: Cornell University Press, 1999), 50. See also Marie B. Rowlands, "Recusant Women, 1560–1640," in *Women in English Society, 1500–1800*, ed. Mary Prior (London: Methuen, 1985), 149–80; Susannah Monta, "Uncommon Prayer? Robert Southwell's *Short Rule for a Good Life* and Catholic Domestic Devotion in Post-Reformation England," in *Redrawing the Map of Early Modern English Catholicism*, ed. Lowell Gallagher (Toronto: University of Toronto Press, 2012), 245–71; and, more broadly, Alexandra Walsham, *Catholic Reformation in Protestant Britain* (Aldershot, England: Ashgate, 2014).

44. Wilkinson, "Lot's Wife," 49.

45. Ibid., 54.

46. Ibid., 37.

47. Ibid.

48. See Henriette Peters, *Mary Ward: A World in Contemplation* (Leominster, England: Gracewing, 1994), 55–67.

49. For a discussion of the several ways in which Ward's ambitions violated prevailing ecclesial norms for female religious orders, see Lowell Gallagher, "Mary Ward's 'Jesuitresses,' and the Construction of a Typological Community," 202. See also Laurence Lux-Sterritt, "Mary Ward's English Institute: The Apostolate as Self-Affirmation?" *Recusant History* 28 (2006): 192–208; as well as Lux-Sterritt's account of Ward's pedagogic and apostolic

ambitions in *Redefining Female Religious Life: French Ursulines and English Ladies in Seventeenth-Century Catholicism* (Aldershot, England: Ashgate, 2005).

50. The assessment is based on the phenomenal success of the educational programs Ward initiated and deployed across Europe, modeling her enterprise after the protocols for the Jesuit order. The most detailed modern account of Ward's career is Peters, *Mary Ward*. For an illuminating account of Ward's practice in Germany, see Ulrike Strasser, *State of Virginity: Gender, Religion, and Politics in an Early Modern State* (Ann Arbor: University of Michigan Press, 2004).

51. Cited in Margaret Mary Littlehales, *Mary Ward: Pilgrim and Mystic* (London: Burns and Oates, 2001), 253–57.

52. In 2004 the Vatican further acknowledged the institute's close ties to the Jesuit order by giving official approval to the institute's new name: The Institute of the Blessed Virgin Mary is now known as the Congregation of Jesus.

53. See Christina Kenworthy-Browne, ed., *Mary Ward (1585–1645): A Brief Relation . . . with Autobiographical Fragments and a Selection of Letters*, Catholic Record Society, vol. 81 (Woodbridge, England: Boydell and Brewer, 2008). Although not exhaustive, Kenworthy-Browne's edition provides a well-balanced group of foundational documents, including the *English Vita*, attributed to Mary Poyntz, one of Ward's first companions. For a survey of trends in scholarship on Ward before Kenworthy-Browne's fine edition, see David Wallace, "Periodizing Women: Mary Ward (1585–1645) and the Premodern Canon," *Journal of Medieval and Early Modern Studies* 36, no. 2 (Spring 2006): 397–453. See also David Wallace, "Holy Amazon: Mary Ward of Yorkshire, 1585–1645," in *Strong Women: Life, Text, and Territory, 1347–1645* (Oxford: Oxford University Press, 2011), 133–200.

54. For an overview of the visual narrative correlated with details from Ward's life, see M. Gregory Kirkus, *The Painted Life of Mary Ward* (York, England: Bar Convent, n.d.). Lux-Sterritt (*Redefining Religious Life*, 186–89) offers sensitive readings of a few of the panels, using a hermeneutic guided by a logic of correspondence between scenographic details in the panels and Ward's devotional meditations on traditional ideals of martyrdom and sacrificial selflessness. Without discounting the paintings' evident commemorative and quasi-hagiographic elements, I am arguing that the paintings also harbor a polemical edge prompted by the community's memory of the radically ambivalent reception of Ward's project. The paintings are reproduced online at http://www.congregatiojesu.org/en/maryward_painted_life.asp. I wish to thank Christina Kenworthy-Browne for her generous assistance in obtaining permissions for images of the *Painted Life*. Many thanks also to Andreas

Zachrau and the members of the Congregation of Jesus for their assistance in the archives at the Geistliches Zentrum Maria Ward in Augsburg.

55. M. C. E. Chambers, *The Life of Mary Ward (1585–1645)*, 2 vols. (London: Burnes and Oates, 1882–1885), 1:xlvi, 2:554.

56. Chambers, *Life of Mary Ward*, 1:xlvi.

57. Maurice Blanchot, *The Instant of My Death* / Jacques Derrida, *Demeure: Fiction and Testimony*, trans. Elizabeth Rottenberg (Palo Alto, CA: Stanford University Press, 2000), 45.

58. Derrida, *Demeure*, 41.

59. Ibid.

60. "The exemplarity of the 'instant,' that which makes it an 'instance,' is that it is singular, like any exemplarity, singular *and* universal, singular *and* universalizable. The singular must be universalizable; this is the testimonial condition" (ibid., 41).

61. Ibid., 45.

62. Blanchot, *Writing of the Disaster*, cited in Derrida, *Demeu*re, 49.

63. Derrida, *Demeure*, 49.

64. Ibid., 75.

65. English translations of the German captions are in Kirkus, *Painted Life*.

66. Derrida, *Demeure*, 50.

67. The notion of papal infallibility was already implicit in Irenaeus's argument that all the churches participating in the Christian dispensation must conform to the teaching of the church of Rome, the bearer of the "certain gift of truth" (*Adversus haereses*, IV, 26, 2).

68. My point is not that the anonymous authors of the *Painted Life* were deliberately following iconographic precedent in the tactical use of red chairs to depict a discursive privilege associated with papal authority. Not enough is known about the authorship of the painted narrative to make such a claim. My point is that the pictorial grammar of the *Painted Life* is partly constructed as an ad hoc assemblage of available semantic associations attached to the color red and the hieratic significance of chairs. Coincidentally, one of the most famous papal portraits of the era, Diego Velázquez's portrait of Pope Innocent X (ca. 1650), shows the pontiff seated in a red chair, as does Pietro da Cortona's 1627 portrait of Urban VIII, a pontiff with more immediate relevance to Ward's career. Neither of these works could possibly have been a reference point for the authors of the *Painted Life*, although each testifies to the contemporary legibility of the associative index presented in the painted narrative.

69. From this vantage point the tableau represents a provocative extension of Richard Crashaw's expression of the mystical experience of Teresa of Avila

in "The Flaming Heart": "Love's passives are his activ'st part./The wounded is the wounding heart" (ll. 73–74).

70. Ward reported the visionary instructions to follow the Jesuit protocol in a 1619 letter to John Gerard, her confessor, and again in a 1621 letter to Antonio Albergati, the papal nuncio in Cologne; see Kenworthy-Browne, *Mary Ward*, 141–48.

71. For an account of Ward's illness, see Littlehales, *Mary Ward*, 64.

72. For an account of Ward's variable success in gaining the support of Jesuit advisers and authorities, see Peters, *Mary Ward*, 211–95.

73. Cited in Littlehales, *Mary Ward*, 67. Mary Cramlington's compilation provided material for one of the earliest accounts of Ward's institute: Marcus Fridl, *Englische Tugend-Schul* (1732).

74. Littlehales, *Mary Ward*, 9.

75. The process on behalf of Ward was officially opened in 1929 and, after eight decades, resulted in Ward's recognition as "venerable" (and thus "heroic in virtue") by the church in December 2009. See http://www.congregatiojesu .org/en/maryward_canonization.asp. In order for the process to proceed to the next stage, beatification, a reported miracle must be evaluated and authenticated by the Congregation of Rites.

4. AVANT-GARDE LOT'S WIFE: NATALIA GONCHAROVA'S *SALT PILLARS* AND THE REBIRTH OF HOSPITALITY

1. Hannah Arendt, *The Origins of Totalitarianism* (New York: Harcourt Brace, 1973), 479.

2. Traditionally attributed to the fourth-century BCE Megarian philosopher Eubulides, the sorites paradox foregrounds the perceptual difficulties resulting from vague predicates. The paradox goes like this: "One grain does not form a heap. Adding one grain to what is not yet a heap does not make a heap. Consequently, there are no heaps." Petr Hájek and Vilém Novák, "The Sorites Paradox and Fuzzy Logic," *International Journal of General Systems* 32, no. 4 (August 2003): 373–83. See also Jason Stanley, "Context, Interest Relativity and the Sorites," *Analysis* 63, no. 4 (October, 2003): 269–80.

3. Exhibition data for *Salt Pillars* may be found in *Amazons of the Avant Garde*, ed. John E. Bowlt and Matthew Drutt (New York: Guggenheim Museum, 2000), 351.

4. Guillaume Apollinaire, *Apollinaire on Art: Essays and Reviews, 1902–1918*, trans. Susan Suleiman, ed. LeRoy C. Breunig (New York: Viking Press, 1972), 394.

5. Ibid., 413–14. Apollinaire also wrote the preface to the exhibition catalog. The reprint in Bruenig's edition "is essentially the same as the preface, with a few variants and five new paragraphs added at the end" (510n45).

6. Apollinaire, *The Cubist Painters: Aesthetic Meditations* [1913], trans. Lionel Abel (New York: Wittenborn, 1944), quoted in Mark C. Taylor, *Disfiguring: Art, Architecture, Religion* (Chicago: University of Chicago Press, 1992), 60. Taylor's source is the anthologized text in *Theories of Modern Art: A Source Book by Artists and Critics*, ed. Herschel B. Chipp (Berkeley: University of California Press, 1968), 227.

7. Taylor, *Disfiguring Art*, 59.

8. Goncharova, quoted in *Amazons of the Avant-Garde*, 310. The text is Goncharova's redaction of advice from Larionov, to which she subscribes.

9. For a detailed assessment of these matters, see Jane Ashton Sharp, *Russian Modernism Between East and West: Natal'ia Goncharova and the Moscow Avant-Garde* (Cambridge: Cambridge University Press, 2006), 148–64.

10. Bruenig, *Apollinaire on Art*, 394.

11. Diaghilev's production of *Le Coq d'Or* opened at the Opéra May 24, 1914. Accounts of Goncharova's work for the stage are in Mary Chamot, *Goncharova: Stage Designs and Paintings* (London: Oresko Books, 1979), and John E. Bowlt, *Russian Art of the Avant-Garde: Theory and Criticism, 1902–1934* (New York: Viking Press, 1976).

12. For an account of Russian Futurism see Susan P. Compton, "Italian Futurism and Russia," *Art Journal* 41, no. 4 (1981): 343–48.

13. Sharp, "Natalia Goncharova," in *Amazons of the Avant-Garde*, 162.

14. See Sharp, *Russian Modernism*, 221–53.

15. Ibid., 4–5. See also Sharp's useful account of the complications that the peculiar hybridity of Russia's cultural identity introduces into the critique of Orientalism as defined by Edward Said (ibid., 6–7).

16. Quoted in Sharp, *Amazons*, 162.

17. For a detailed account of Goncharova's place in Zdanevich's theory of "everythingism," see Sharp, *Russian Modernism*, 254–60.

18. Ibid., 257.

19. Ibid., 208.

20. Goncharova, letter to the editor of *Russkoe slovo*, quoted in ibid., 272.

21. Accounts of the debates over the statuettes' provenance are in Katherine Lahti, "On Living Statues and Pandora, *Kamennye baby* and Futurist Aesthetics: The Female Body in *Vladimir Mayakovsky: A Tragedy*," *Russian Review* 58, no. 3 (July 1999): 432–55, esp. 449–53; and Sharp, *Russian Modernism*, 161. For an account of the equivocal gender of the *kamennye baby*, see Stamen Michailov, "Les figurations dites 'Kamennye baby' et leur survivance tardive dans le culte funéraire chez les Bulgares," *Bulgarian Historical Review* 16, no. 4 (1988), 55–68.

22. Reported speech from Goncharova's conversations between 1959 and 1962 with Ehrhard Steneberg, "Gontcharova se penche sur son passé,"

in *Gontcharova et Larionov: cinquante ans à Saint Germain-des-Prés*, compiled and introduced by Tatiana Loguine (Paris: Éditions Klincksieck, 1971), 213; my translation. The conversation was conducted in German, with French translation by Olga Erbes, adapted by Tessa Radjine and Tatiana Loguine. Loguine's text: "L'Art en Russie est si particulier! On dit que, maintenant les archéologues y font des fouilles. Enterrées dans la steppe à côté des squelettes, on a découvert des figurines d'un temps lointain, très lointain. Ces petites créatures avaient comme fonction la protection des morts."

23. Maurice Halbwachs, *On Collective Memory*, ed. and trans. Lewis A. Coser (Chicago: University of Chicago Press, 1992), 116.

24. Patrick H. Hutton, *History as an Art of Memory* (Hanover, NH: University Press of New England, 1993), 79.

25. Halbwachs, *On Collective Memory*, 194–95.

26. Jacques Derrida, *Demeure* (Paris: Galilée, 1998), 49.

27. Sharp, *Russian Modernism*, 211.

28. Ibid.

29. Derrida, *Of Hospitality: Anne Dufourmantelle Invites Jacques Derrida to Respond*, trans. Rachel Bowlby (Stanford, CA: Stanford University Press, 2000), 75.

30. Ibid., 76–77.

31. Ibid., 135. The phrase "obsidional situation," alluding to the Latin *obsidium* (state of siege, associated with sovereign power), occurs in Derrida's rumination over the "obscure environs of a semantic, if not etymological, kinship between *host* and *hostage*" in Levinas's writings (*Adieu to Emmanuel Levinas*, 57).

32. Derrida, *Of Hospitality*, 153.

33. Derrida, *Adieu*, 35–36. See also *Adieu à Emmanuel Levinas* (Paris: Editions Galilée, 1997), 69–70.

34. Ibid.

35. The language of "ordeal" and "temptation" is Kierkegaard's, in *Fear and Trembling*, 60. On the semantic nexus of "test," "temptation," "ordeal," and "try" in Kierkegaard's idiom, see the explanatory note to the Exordium in Hong and Hong's edition, 341n2. Søren Kierkegaard, *Fear and Trembling*, ed. and trans. Howard V. Hong and Edna H. Hong (Princeton, NJ: Princeton University Press, 1983).

36. Emmanuel Levinas, *Proper Names*, trans. Michael B. Smith (Stanford, CA: Stanford University Press, 1996), 77. Levinas's earlier essay on the subject, "Kierkegaard: Existence and Ethics," makes a similar point (ibid., 74). Kierkegaard does in fact use the episode to underscore Abraham's hospitality. In the "Eulogy on Abraham" he imagines a counternarrative to the *akedah* in which Abraham commits suicide rather than kill his son—an outcome that

would have guaranteed his heroic status. His capacity to believe "the preposterous" explains his fidelity to the first command, and his earlier intercession on behalf of Sodom illustrates the point: "But Abraham had faith. He did not pray for himself, trying to influence the Lord; it was only when righteous punishment fell upon Sodom and Gomorrah that Abraham came forward with his prayers" (*Fear and Trembling*, 20, 21).

37. Levinas, *Proper Names*, 75.

38. Ibid., 77–78.

39. Ibid., 78. As Hent de Vries remarks in his commentary on the difficult negotiation between Derrida's and Levinas's readings of the *akedah*, "Abraham shows that in every genuine decision the ethical *must* be sacrificed" (*Religion and Violence*, 158). See also John D. Caputo's careful reflections on this scene, in *The Prayers and Tears of Jacques Derrida: Religion Without Religion* (Bloomington: Indiana University Press, 1997), 188–211.

40. Jacques Derrida, *The Gift of Death*, trans. David Wills (Chicago: University of Chicago Press, 1996), 80.

41. In her pioneering study of Goncharova, Mary Chamot calls the columnar figures in *Salt Pillars* and the contemporaneous work titled *God of Fertility (Bozhestvo plodorodiia)* "comic monstrosities": "Ces deux formes, monstrueusement comiques, avec d'énormes têtes et des jambes en fuseau paraissent n'avoir aucun précédent et rien de semblable ne se manifeste dans le reste de son œuvre." Chamot, *Gontcharova* (Paris: La Bibliothèque des Arts, 1972), 32.

42. Agamben, *Time That Remains*, 69.

43. Ibid., 68.

44. Ibid., 71–72. Agamben takes the image of the hairsbreadth from *Genesis Rabbah* (vol. 1, chap. 10, sec. 9, quoted in ibid.).

45. "Messianic presence lies beside itself, since, without ever coinciding with a chronological instant, and without ever adding itself onto it, it seizes hold of this instant and brings it forth to fulfillment" (ibid., 70–71).

46. Derrida, *Acts of Religion*, 362. The vigilance described here is not to be confused with the strong form of decisionism that characterizes, for example, Carl Schmitt's influential concept of the "state of exception" as the linchpin for the totalizing mandate of sovereign political authority. In this matter, Schmitt's debt to the Pauline notion of kairos is well established, but Schmittian kairos identifies a specific tropism of the term, not its semantic destiny. For an illuminating account of the "loving strife" (*liebender Streit*) between Jacob Taubes and Carl Schmitt over the notion of kairotic time, see Bruce Rosenstock, "Palintropos Harmoniê: Jacob Taubes and Carl Schmitt 'im liebenden Streit,'" *New German Critique* 44, no. 1 (2014): 55–92.

47. Sharp, *Russian Modernism*, 236. "Goncharova's approach to religious subjects," Benois admitted, "is clearly aesthetic; right now, it cannot be anything else. Yet of all the various aesthetic approaches to religious themes to appear in recent years, Goncharova's is probably the freest and most captivating." *Natalia Goncharova: The Russian Years*, exhibition catalog (State Russian Museum, St. Petersburg, 2002), 294, quoted in Andrew Spira, *The Avant-Garde Icon: Russian Avant-Garde Art and the Icon Painting Tradition* (Aldershot, England: Lund Humphries, 2008), 138.

48. John D. Caputo, "The Messianic: Waiting for the Future," in *Deconstruction in a Nutshell: A Conversation with Jacques Derrida*, ed. John D. Caputo (New York: Fordham University Press, 1997), 160–62.

49. Ibid., 162, 164.

50. Mary Chamot notes that "most of [Goncharova's] extant paintings with religious themes date from 1909–1911" (*Gontcharova*, 36), my translation.

51. Bowlt, "Orthodoxy and the Avant-Garde: Sacred Images in the Work of Goncharova, Malevich, and Their Contemporaries," in *Christianity and the Arts in Russia*, ed. William C. Brumfield and Milos M. Velimirovic (Cambridge: Cambridge University Press, 2008), 146.

52. Ibid.

53. My discussion of the controversy surrounding Goncharova's religious works is indebted to Sharp's account (*Russian Modernism*, 238–53).

54. "Dubl'-ve," "Futurizm i Koshchunstvo," 5, quoted in Sharp, *Russian Modernism*, 240.

55. Ibid., 242.

56. "By imitating these masters in the context of a tradition based on transmitting a prototype through a continuous series of copies, Goncharova neutralizes the West European distinction between originality and derivation in high art inasmuch as the two are shown to be mutually defining" (ibid., 194).

57. Ibid., 249.

58. Quoted in ibid., 253. A helpful discussion of Goncharova's role in developing the Rayist manifestos is in Anthony Parton, "Russian 'Rayism,' the Work and Theory of Mikhail Larionov and Natalya Goncharova 1912–1914: Ouspensky's Four-Dimensional Super Race?" *Leonardo* 16, no. 4 (Autumn 1983): 298–305.

59. As Sharp points out, the word *bezobrazna* means "literally that which is without form; hideous, shapeless, or disfigured" (*Russian Modernism*, 242).

60. The theme of the Coronation was not canonical either; on this point see ibid., 191. Nevertheless, Goncharova's *Coronation of the Virgin* proved

sacrilegious because of the unambiguous Marian reference and seeming parody of iconic images of the Virgin.

61. In essence, Irenaeus's Christic transvaluation of Lot's wife refigures the salt pillar as the paradigmatic expression of Christ's "mystical body," where *corpus* means communal event, a sacramental disposition borne out of the vigilance of affective attunement to the needs of the other. As Dominic J. Unger points out, "St. Irenaeus does not treat of the Mystical Body *ex professo*, but the idea of the idea of the Church as a Mystical Body was in his blood" (186), in *St. Irenaeus of Lyons Against the Heresies*, book 1, trans. and ed. Dominic J. Unger with John J. Dillon (Mahwah, NJ: Paulist Press, 1992).

62. I am not proposing that *Salt Pillars* reflects Goncharova's specific acquaintance with Irenaeus's unusual reading of Lot's wife or the prestige of the church father's thought in Eastern Orthodox theology. My point is that the painting's figural assemblage presents an occasion to imagine the symbolic intimacy between two otherwise dissociated regions in Irenaeus's own mapping of the expressive range of Christic embodiment in the ecclesial community—Sodom and Annunciation. A classic example of Eastern Orthodox speculation on Mary's role in salvation economy is in Sergius Bulgakov, *The Burning Bush: On the Orthodox Veneration of the Mother of God*, trans. Thomas Allan Smith (Grand Rapids, MI: Wm. B. Eerdmans, 2009). For an account of Irenaeus's influence in Eastern Orthodox tradition, see Daniel B. Clendenin, *Eastern Orthodox Christianity: A Western Perspective* (Ada, MI: Baker Academic, 2003).

63. In the *Adversus haereses* 3.22.4, Irenaeus delivers a succinct account of the Eve-Mary typology. For Irenaeus, the "purity" associated with Mary's virginal state functions as testimony to the radical character of the new: "those [prophets] who proclaimed Him as Immanuel, [born] of the Virgin, exhibited the union of the Word of God with His own workmanship, [declaring] that the Word should become flesh, and the Son of God the Son of Man (the pure One opening purely that pure womb which regenerates men unto God, and which He Himself made pure); and having become this which we also are, He [nevertheless] is the Mighty God, and possesses a generation which cannot be declared" (*Adversus haereses* 4.33.11). See *Contre Les Hérésies*, Livre IV, Edition critique, ed. Adelin Rousseau, Bertrand Hemmerdinger, Louis Doutreleau, Charles Mercier (Paris: Éditions du Cerf, 1965), 2:813. A helpful discussion of Irenaeus's treatment of Mary as "the source of our regeneration" is in Eric Osborn, *Irenaeus of Lyons* (Cambridge: Cambridge University Press, 2005), 118.

64. For the Thomist emphasis on Mary as *conciliatrix*, see James T. O'Connor, *The Hidden Manna: A Theology of the Eucharist* (San Francisco: Ignatius Press, 2005), 349–61.

65. An account of the various theological and ecclesial aspects of Marian veneration is in Hans Urs von Balthasar, *Mary for Today* (San Francisco: Ignatius Press, 1988). See also the treatment of von Balthasar's writings on this topic in Francesca Aran Murphy, "Immaculate Mary: The Ecclesial Mariology of Hans Urs von Balthasar," in *Mary: The Complete Resource*, ed. Sarah Jane Boss (London: Continuum, 2007), 300–13, at 313.

66. Sharp, *Russian Modernism*, 248.

67. For a pertinent discussion of the theological association of Mary's procreative virginity and the Abrahamic parsing of the question of hospitality, see Cleo McNelly Kearns's insightful reading of Derrida's debt to this nexus as it appears in the writings of Louis Massignon: "Mary, Maternity, and Abrahamic Hospitality in Derrida's Reading of Massignon," in *Derrida and Religion: Other Testaments*, ed. Yvonne Sherwood and Kevin Hart (New York: Routledge, 2005), 73–94.

68. For a detailed account of the varied symbolic senses of salt in Judeo-Christian tradition, see James E. Latham, *The Religious Symbolism of Salt* (Paris: Beauchesne, 1982).

69. As James G. D. Dunn points out, the Pauline experience of "being saved" entails "the tension between a work 'begun' but not 'complete,' between fulfillment and consummation, between a decisive 'already' and a still to be worked out 'not yet.'" Dunn, *The Theology of Paul the Apostle* (Grand Rapids, MI: Wm. B. Eerdmans, 1998), 465. Dunn's argument elaborates Oscar Cullmann's use of the phrase "eschatological tension" in *Salvation in History*, trans. Sidney G. Sowers (London: SCM Press, 1967).

70. The rich patristic tradition of desert asceticism testifies to the allure of the figural coupling of virgin and desert. On this point, see Lynda L. Coon, *Sacred Fictions: Holy Women and Hagiography in Late Antiquity* (Philadelphia: University of Pennsylvania Press, 1997), 71–94. For an account of the figural allure of the desert as ascetic space, see Gavin Flood, *The Ascetic Self: Subjectivity, Memory, and Tradition* (Cambridge: Cambridge University Press, 2004), 144–74.

71. Blanchot, *Book to Come*, 80. Hereafter cited in text as *BtC* and page number.

72. See especially Leslie Hill's recent examination of the development of Blanchot's thoughts on messianic temporality in *Maurice Blanchot and Fragmentary Writing: A Change of Epoch* (London: Bloomsbury Publishing, 2012), 368–91. A helpful account of the messianic dimension to Levinas's thought is in Bettina Bergo, "Levinas's Weak Messianism in Time and Flesh, or The Insistence of Messiah Ben David," in *The Messianic Now: Philosophy, Religion, Culture*, ed. Arthur Bradley and Paul Fletcher (New York: Routledge, 2011), 45–68.

73. Agamben, *Time That Remains*, 72.

74. Hannah Arendt, *The Human Condition*, 2nd ed. (Chicago: University of Chicago Press, 1998), 9.

75. The epigraph to this chapter supplies one of the most famous of Arendt's citations of Augustine's definition of human being in *The City of God*: "'Initium ut esset homo creatus est'—'that a beginning be made, man was created,' said Augustine. This beginning is guaranteed by each new birth; it is indeed every man" (*Origins of Totalitarianism*, 479). Arendt's creative appropriation of Augustine's identification of human being and beginning has received abundant attention in Arendt scholarship. An extensive treatment is in Stephan Kampowski, *Arendt, Augustine, and the New Beginning: The Action Theory and Moral Thought of Hannah Arendt in the Light of Her Dissertation on St. Augustine* (Grand Rapids, MI: Wm. B. Eerdmans, 2008).

76. Arendt, *Human Condition*, 178.

77. Ibid., 177.

78. Ibid., 176. A strongly argued case for the enduring critical value of Arendt's notion of natality is in Anne O'Byrne, *Natality and Finitude* (Bloomington: Indiana University Press, 2010), 78–106.

79. Oliver Marchart refers to the "quasi-transcendental status" of natality in Arendt's work, which is another way of recognizing the term's nomadic, rather than internally consistent, aspect. See Marchart, "Time for a New Beginning: Arendt, Benjamin, and the Messianic Conception of Political Temporality," *Redescriptions: Yearbook of Political Thought and Conceptual History* 10 (2006): 134–47, at 135.

80. Franz Kafka, "Notes from the year 1920," in *The Great Wall of China: Stories and Reflections*, trans. Willa and Edwin Muir (New York: Schocken, 1946), quoted in Arendt, *Between Past and Future*, rev. ed. (1961; New York: Penguin Books, 2006), 7, hereafter cited in text as *BPF* and page number.

81. Arendt, *Life of the Mind*, 2:207. Tellingly, Arendt's discussion of Kafka's parable opens with a reflection on an aphorism by René Char: "*Notre heritage n'est précédé d'aucun testament*—'our inheritance was left to us by no testament'" (*Between Past and Future*, 3). The Provençal poet also figures significantly in Blanchot's ruminations on the advent of the neuter in literary space; see Blanchot's essay "René Char and the Thought of the Neuter" in *The Infinite Conversation*, trans. Susan Hanson (Minneapolis: University of Minnesota Press, 1993), 298–310.

82. An astute commentary on the legacies of Arendt's coinage is in Julia Reinhard Lupton, "Hannah Arendt's Renaissance: Remarks on Natality," *Journal for Cultural and Religious Theory* 7, no. 2 (Spring 2006): 7–17.

83. Arendt, *Human Condition*, 169. In the section on "Labor," Arendt rehearses the aesthetic truism that "Greek opinion, which ranked painters

higher than sculptors, certainly did not rest upon a higher regard for paintings" (93).

84. Ibid., 168.

85. Ibid., 187. Arendt not only repeats Aristotle's preferential treatment of drama as the "political art par excellence," she also questions the aptness of Aristotle's treatment of staged drama as a viable exemplar of the types of mimetic activity at work in other genres: "it is obvious that Aristotle's model for 'imitation' in art is taken from the drama, and the generalization of the concept to make it applicable to all arts seems rather awkward" (ibid., 187n11).

86. Arendt, *Between Past and Future*, 10. All remaining quotes in this paragraph are ibid, 14.

87. Arendt, *Human Condition*, 168–69. In a footnote, Arendt identifies the description of fire burning to ashes as a paraphrase of a poem by Rainer Maria Rilke on art, "Magic," which describes a similar transfiguration (168n19).

88. "Such is the confidence that we have through Christ toward God. Not that we are competent of ourselves to claim anything as coming from us; our competence is from God, who has made us competent to be ministers of a new covenant, not of letter but of spirit; for the letter kills, but the Spirit gives life" (2 Cor. 3:4–6)

89. Arendt's remarks on the transfigurative potency of artworks carry an implicit debt to Martin Heidegger's phenomenological readings of Paul. For an account of Heidegger's engagement with Paul's writings, see Ward Blanton, "Paul's Secretary: Heidegger's Apostolic Light from the Ancient Near East," in *Displacing Christian Origins: Philosophy, Secularity, and the New Testament* (Chicago: University of Chicago Press, 2007), 105–28.

90. Sharp, *Russian Modernism*, 211.

91. Ibid.

5. SOUNDINGS IN SODOMSCAPE: BIBLICAL PURITY CODES, SPA CLINICS, AND THE ENDS OF IMMUNITY

1. François-René de Chateaubriand, *Itinéraire de Paris à Jérusalem et de Jérusalem à Paris*, ed. Jean-Claude Berchet (Paris: Éditions Gallimard, 2005), 317; my translation.

2. Chateaubriand, *Itinéraire*, 315–19; see also the excerpted passage in chapter 2.

3. Josephus, *The Wars of the Jews* 7.8–9, in *The Life and Works of Flavius Josephus*, trans. William Whiston (Philadelphia: John C. Winston Company, 1957), 847–55.

4. Yael Zerubavel, "The Death of Memory and the Memory of Death: Masada and the Holocaust as Historical Metaphors," *Representations* 45 (Winter 1994): 90. For an analysis that emphasizes the peculiar choreography

of narrative design and collective memory in the use of Josephus's account of Masada, see Pierre Vidal-Naquet, *The Jews: History, Memory, and the Present*, trans. David Arnes Curtis (New York: Columbia University Press, 1996), esp. 20–56.

5. Zerubavel, "The Death of Memory," 91. For a broadly complementary account of the informing ambivalences of Palestinian landscape, see Gary Fields, "Enclosure Landscapes: Historical Reflections on Palestinian Geography," *Historical Geography* 39 (2011): 182–207. My point here draws on Jan Assmann's concept of mnemohistory. "Mnemohistory," writes Assmann, "is reception theory applied to history," but Assmann's sense of "reception" emphasizes its dialectical nature: "'reception' is not to be understood here merely in the narrow sense of transmitting and receiving. The past is not simply 'received' by the present. The present is 'haunted' by the past and the past is modelled, invented, reinvented, and reconstructed by the present" (Assmann, *Moses the Egyptian*, 9). A lucid account of the affinity between Assmann's mnemohistory and Nora's *lieux de mémoire* is in Marek Tamm, "History as Cultural Memory: Mnemohistory and the Construction of the Estonian Nation," *Journal of Baltic Studies* 39, no. 4 (2008): 499–516.

6. See Gordon Waitt and Kevin Markwell, *Gay Tourism: Culture and Context* (New York and London: Haworth Press, 2006), 168–72, at 169. The Gay Tel Aviv website describes the city as "one of the world's finest and friendliest GLBT travel destinations" (http://www.gaytlvguide.com/). The gay tourism industry in Israel also promotes the luxury resort and spa facilities near the Dead Sea. Tellingly, the Pride Tours site's account of Masada, for example, converts the geopolitical association of the desert fortress into a "story of liberty, freedom, and most importantly—a story of pride!" while ignoring the legendary trauma associated with the lost Cities of the Plain (http://www.pridetours.com/tours/deadseaandmasada). The site's account of Dead Sea tourism emphasizes the region's sybaritic and therapeutic resources, which offer "ultimate relaxation"—"the time to forget all your worries and connect with nature's historic fountain of youth" (ibid.). I thank Colleen Jankovic for the above two references.

7. For background relevant to the disputed locations (the Early Bronze III sites of Bab edh-Dhra' and Numeira vs. Mount Sedom), see David Neev and K. O. Emery, *The Destruction of Sodom, Gomorrah, and Jericho: Geological, Climatological, and Archaeological Background* (New York and Oxford: Oxford University Press, 1995), 130–31.

8. What bears noting in all this is that the political, ethical, medico-cultural, and ontological implications of the idea of the sodomitic are typically geared toward either reinforcing or repudiating the pathological designation of the sexual practices or sexualities found on the map of what

Jonathan Goldberg calls "sodometries," those "relational structures precariously available to prevailing discourses." Jonathan Goldberg, *Sodometries:
Renaissance Texts, Modern Sexualities* (Stanford, CA: Stanford University Press,
1992), 20.

9. Here I recall Robert Alter's useful narratological account of the
Sodom story, "Sodom as Nexus" (see chapter 2). For a useful account of
the specific contexts in biblical antiquity for understanding the presumed
sexual practices depicted in the Sodom narrative, see Richard Elliott Fried-
man and Shawna Dolansky, *The Bible Now* (Oxford: Oxford University Press,
2011), 2–9.

10. Assmann, *Moses the Egyptian*, 216.

11. Derrida, *Of Hospitality*, 153.

12. Blanchot, *Book to Come*, 80.

13. Ibid.

14. Ibid. The silence of Lot's wife in this regard adds resonance to the
expression "the silence of Sodom," used by Mark D. Jordan to identify the
strange cohabitation of unacknowledged hospitality toward and formal repudiation of homosexuals in the institutional rhythms of the Catholic priest-
hood. See Mark D. Jordan, *The Silence of Sodom: Homosexuality and Modern
Catholicism* (Chicago: Chicago University Press, 2000). See also the important
recapture of the Sodom-Eden nexus as a figure for contemporary gay rights
in Israel, in Lee Waltzer, *Between Sodom and Eden: A Gay Journey Through
Today's Changing Israel* (New York: Columbia University Press, 2000).

15. As both Levinas and Derrida observe in their meditations on hospitality, the notion of "dwelling" is both a place and an event. In Rosalyn
Diprose's succinct formulation, "For Levinas, as for Derrida, 'the dwelling' or 'home' that conditional hospitality presupposes is at once the *place*
of one's dwelling (self, home, and so on) and the 'event' or *temporality* of
dwelling. That is, dwelling is the ongoing event (apparent in every activity,
although exemplified for Levinas by the activity of labor) that lifts the self,
home, nation, and so on, above an immediate, affective relation to the world"
(Diprose, "Women's Bodies Giving Time for Hospitality," *Hypatia* 24, no. 2
(Spring 2009), 142–63, at 147. See Levinas's meditation on dwelling and
hospitality in *Totality and Infinity*, especially the following exemplary passage:
"To exist henceforth means to dwell. To dwell is not the simple fact of the
anonymous reality of a being cast into existence as a stone one casts behind
oneself; it is a recollection, a coming to oneself, a retreat home with oneself
as in a land of refuge, which answers to a hospitality, an expectancy, a human
welcome" (156).

16. See *Egeria's Travels to the Holy Land*, ed. and trans. John Wilkinson
(Warminster, England: Aris and Phillips, 1981). For a useful analysis of this

text, see Leo Spitzer, "The Epic Style of the Pilgrim Aetheria," *Comparative Literature* 1, no. 3 (1949): 225–58.

17. Felix Fabri, *Evagatorium in Terrae Sanctae, Arabiae et Egypti peregrinationem*, ed. C. D. Hassler, 3 vols. (Stuttgart, Germany: n.p., 1843); translated into English in *Palestine Pilgrims' Text Society* VII–IX (1893–97), 1893:235a–247b. Useful background to Fabri's texts is in Joan E. Taylor, "The Dead Sea in Western Travellers' Accounts from the Byzantine to the Modern Period," *Strata: Bulletin of the Anglo-Israel Archaeological Society*, no. 27 (2009): 9–29. A concise review of the competing rationales for locating Sodom on the northern or southeastern shores is in *Theological Dictionary of the Old Testament*, vol. 10, ed. G. Johannes Botterweck et al. (Grand Rapids, MI: Wm. B. Eerdmans, 2000), 153–55.

18. Max Blanckenhorn, *Das Tote Meer und der Untergang von Sodom und Gomorrha* (Berlin: Dietrich Reimer, n.d.), cited in Y. Braslavy, *Around the Dead Sea* (in Hebrew) (Tel Aviv: Hakibutz Hameuchad Publishing House, 1956), 96. For a discussion of this reference see David Neev and K. O. Emery, *The Destruction of Sodom, Gomorrah, and Jericho: Geological, Climatological, and Archaeological Background* (New York and Oxford: Oxford University Press, 1995), 130–31.

19. See Gal Karniel and Yehouda Enzel, "Dead Sea Photographs from the Nineteenth Century," in Special Paper 401: New Frontiers in Dead Sea Paleoenvironmental Research (Boulder, CO: Geological Society of America, 2006), 231–40, at 239.

20. For accounts of this early sense of leisure, see Roger Scruton, "Introduction: The Philosophy of Leisure" in *Loisir et liberté en Amérique du Nord*, ed. Pierre Lagayette (Paris: Presses de l'université Paris-Sorbonne, 2008), 11–27; and the classic Catholic-humanist argument by Josef Pieper in *Leisure: The Basis of Culture*, trans. Alexandre Dru (San Francisco: Ignatius Press, 2009), 19–74. Both essays draw on Aristotle's famous aphorism, "happiness is thought to reside in leisure from business; for we busy ourselves in order to have leisure, and go to war in order to live at peace" (*Nicomachean Ethics*, 1177b, 4–6). See Aristotle, *Nicomachean Ethics*, trans. Christopher Rowe, ed. Christopher Rowe and Sarah Broadie (Oxford: Oxford University Press, 2002), 251.

21. Joan-Lluís Marfany points out that the earliest recorded appearance of the saying appears in 1866. Marfany, "Debate: The Invention of Leisure in Early Modern Europe," *Past and Present* 156 (August 1997): 174–91, at 179. But the nineteenth-century record is not as revelatory as it may seem. Marfany cautions against the temptation to "construe the silence and the biases of the sources [in social history] as proof of the absence of leisure or the idea of it. The historian of leisure, like the historian of sex, should always bear in

mind an old Catalan saying: *sempre han tingut bec les oques* (geese have always had beaks). Unfortunately, nobody knows how old the saying is either" (191).

22. Heraclitus, Fragment 112 (Diehls), quoted in Pieper, *Leisure*, 28.

23. Thomas Aquinas, *Quaestiones disputatae de virtutibus cardinalibus*, 5.1, quoted in Pieper, *Leisure*, 29.

24. See Brian Vickers, "Leisure and idleness in the Renaissance: The ambivalence of *otium*," *Renaissance Studies* 4, nos. 1 and 2 (1990): 1–37 (pt. 1) and 107–54 (pt. 2). See also Peter Burke, "The Invention of Leisure in Early Modern Europe," *Past and Present*, no. 146 (February 1995): 136–50. The question of leisure interestingly informs the critical dimension of asceticism as well; on this point see Geoffrey Harpham, *The Ascetic Imperative in Culture and Criticism* (Chicago: University of Chicago Press, 1992).

25. "Ecce haec fuit iniquitas Sodomae sororis tuae, superbia, saturitas panis, et abundantia et otium ipsius et filiarum eius et manum egeno et pauperi non porrigebant" (Latin Vulgate, Ezek. 16:49, http://vulgate.org/ot/ezekiel_16.htm).

26. The sense of skin I have in mind draws on Michel Serres's discussion of the critical force of the term in *The Five Senses: A Philosophy of Mingled Bodies*, trans. Margaret Sankey and Peter Cowley (New York: Continuum, 2008). For Serres, the porous membrane called skin is both a material thing and a material process; he treats this porous membrane as "itself a *sensorium commune*, a sense common to all the senses, forming a link, bridge and passage between them: an ordinary, interconnecting, collective, shared plain" (70).

27. See Wendy Elliman, *The Living Dead Sea* (Jerusalem: Israel Ministry of Foreign Affairs, April 1999), http://www.mfa.gov.il/mfa/mfa-archive/1999/pages/focus%20on%20israel-%20the%20living%20dead%20sea.aspx; Thilo Gambichler, "Balneophototherapy for Psoriasis Using Saltwater Baths and UV-B Irradiation, Revisited," *Archives of Dermatology* 143, no. 5 (May 2007): 647–49; and A. I. Kudish et al., "The Analysis of Ultraviolet Radiation in the Dead Sea Basin, Israel," *International Journal of Climatology*, no. 17 (1997): 1697–704.

28. A summary of the Levitical prescriptions is in Margaret Lloyd Davies, "Levitical Leprosy: Uncleanness and the Psyche," *Expository Times*, no. 99 (May 1988): 136–39. For a recent ethno-medical account of the Levitical prescriptions that is sensitive to the life-affirming character of the covenantal subtexts, see Mary Douglas, *Leviticus as Literature* (Oxford: Oxford University Press, 1999), especially chap. 9, "Atonement for Sick Bodies."

29. Note that the biblical purity codes infer a relation between the onset of *ṣāra'at* and violations of hospitality—"slander, tale-bearing, infringing on the rights of one's neighbors, and fraud." Joseph Zias, "Lust and Leprosy: Confusion or Correlation?," *Bulletin of the American Schools of Oriental*

Research, no. 275 (August 1989): 27–31, at 27. Descriptions of *elephantiasis* in ancient Greek medical writings attribute some instances of the disorder not simply to a contagious factor but to venereal disease as well. See Michael W. Dols, "Leprosy in Medieval Arab Medicine," *Journal of the History of Medicine and Allied Sciences* 34, no. 3 (1979), 315–16. These two strands of thought were intermingled in the medieval association of the contagion of leprosy.

30. John G. Andersen, "Studies in the medieval diagnosis of leprosy in Denmark," *Danish Medical Bulletin*, no. 16 (1969), suppl. 9, 14–54, quoted in Dols, "Leprosy in Medieval Arab Medicine," 317. My account of lexical transformations in this paragraph and the next is indebted to several accounts in biblical and medical scholarship. The earliest I have consulted remains a useful general resource: Ernest L. McEwen, "The Leprosy of the Bible in Its Medical Aspect," *Biblical World* 38, no. 3 (September 1911): 194–202. For a straightforward discussion of the anthropological significance of ritual purity codes in Leviticus and the Christian gospel narratives, see John Dominic Crossan, *Jesus: A Revolutionary Biography* (New York: HarperOne, 2009), 77–85. Crossan's argument is indebted to the conceptual models proposed by Mary Douglas, *Purity and Danger: An Analysis of the Concepts of Pollution and Taboo* (New York: Routledge, 2002); Arnold Kleinman, *Patients and Healers in the Contest of Culture* (Berkeley: University of California Press, 1980); and the series of articles written by John Pilch in the 1980s on the symbolic economy of healing in the New Testament, gathered together in *Healing in the New Testament: Insights from Medical and Mediterranean Anthropology* (Minneapolis: Augsburg Fortress, 2000).

31. See especially Carole Rawcliffe, *Leprosy in Medieval England* (Rochester, NY: Boydell Press, 2006), Luke Demaitre, *Leprosy in Premodern Medicine: A Malady of the Whole Body* (Baltimore, MD: Johns Hopkins University Press, 2007), and Susan Zimmerman, "Leprosy in the Medieval Imaginary," *Journal of Medieval and Early Modern Studies* 38, no. 3 (2008): 559–87. For a wide-ranging account of leprosy as a cultural signifier, see Rod Edmond, *Leprosy and Empire: A Medical and Cultural History* (Cambridge: Cambridge University Press, 2007). See also Tony Gould, *A Disease Apart: Leprosy in the Modern World* (New York: St. Martin's Press, 2005).

32. For a detailed account of the wide range of application of the word *lepra* in late antiquity, see Dols, "Leprosy in Medieval Arabic Medicine," 314–33. Ian Johnston notes two cognate terms for *lepra* in Galen's writings, *alphoi* and *leuke*, which are occasionally grouped with "other conditions exemplifying 'excess' as something that may damage function." *Galen: On Diseases and Symptoms*, ed. and trans. Ian Johnston (Cambridge: Cambridge University Press, 2006), 57.

33. Medieval Arabic writings describe lymphatic filariasis as the "the malady of the elephant" (*dā'al-fīl*); the expression was translated into Latin as *elephantiasis arabum*. For an account of the translation process, see Dols, "Leprosy in Medieval Arabic Medicine," 321–22. Unlike the word *lepra*, which covered (and obscured) several diseases, the word *elephantiasis* followed different semantic career. See B. R. Laurence, "'Barbadoes Leg': Filariasis in Barbados, 1625–1900," *Medical History* 33, no. 4 (October 1989): 480–88; Hirak Behari Routh and Kazal Rekha Bhowmik, "History of Elephantiasis," *International Journal of Dermatology* 32, no. 12 (1993): 913–16; and B. R. Laurence, "The Curse of St. Thomas" *Medical History* 14, no. 4 (October 1970): 352–63.

34. See, for example, Floyd Merrell's application of Peircean semiotics to articulate a shared field of biosemiotics between life sciences and social sciences, in *Signs Grow: Semiosis and Life Processes* (Toronto: University of Toronto Press, 1996). See also Thomas A. Sebeok, *Global Semiotics* (Bloomington: Indiana University Press, 2001).

35. See Zvi Even-Paz and Jashovam Shani, "The Dead Sea and Psoriasis: Historical and Geographic Background," *International Journal of Dermatology* 28, no. 1 (January–February 1989), 1–9. For an account of the uses of bitumen in antiquity, see James Forbes, *Studies in Ancient Technology*, vol. 1 (Leiden, Netherlands: Brill, 1993).

36. See Alissa Cowden and Abby S. Van Voorhees, "Introduction: History of Psoriasis and psoriasis therapy," in *Treatment of Psoriasis*, ed. Jeffrey M. Weinberg (Cambridge, MA: Birkhäuser, 2008), 1–3. See also Peter C. M. van de Kerkhof, ed. *Textbook of Psoriasis*, 2nd ed. (Hoboken, NJ: Wiley-Blackwell, 2003), 3–4.

37. If the notion of the "last leper colony" harbors a queue of candidates, this is so primarily because the disease is correlated with specific regions of endemic poverty and inadequate public health resources. A recent medical report claims: "[As of 2007] leprosy was virtually eradicated in all but 4 of 122 countries where the disease was believed to be a public health problem in 1985 (*Weekly Epidemiological Record* 82 [2007]: 225–32; *Wkly Epidemiol Rec.* 82 [2007]: 388). Leprosy cases in these 4 countries—Brazil, the Democratic Republic of the Congo, Mozambique, and Nepal—accounted for nearly one quarter of all new cases globally in 2006 and one third of all registered cases at the beginning of 2007, according to WHO" (http://bmartinmd. com/2008/02/whos-leprosyelimination-progra.html). Notable candidates for "last leper colony" status outside the above-mentioned regions include Carville, Louisiana; Tichilesti, Romania; Kalaupapa, Molokai; and Sorok Island, South Korea.

38. The opening statement in the 2007 review article by Andrew Blau-velt is representative of recent medical opinion: "Psoriasis is a chronic inflammatory skin disease that affects 2–3% of the population world-wide, causing significant morbidity in affected individuals. The etiology of psoriasis is unknown, although it is generally believed to be a complex autoimmune inflammatory disease with a genetic basis." Blauvelt, "New Concepts in the Pathogenesis and Treatment of Psoriasis: Key Roles for IL-23, IL 17A and TGF-ß1," *Expert Review of Dermatology* 2, no. 1 (2007): 69–78, at 69.

39. Judith Butler, *Frames of War: When Is Life Grievable?* (London and New York: Verso, 2010), 4–5. Butler's argument provides a helpful over-view of the Hegelian derivation of the concept of recognition and its criti-cal history. Butler's brief account of apprehension covers ground similar to that found in Deleuze's phenomenological account of the critical difference between the rationalizing ethos of "recognition" and the estranging advent of the "encounter." Recognition, for Deleuze, produces the impression of self-identity in the intended object and presupposes a symmetrical relation between "the form of identity in objects" and the foundational "unity of a thinking subject, of which all the other faculties must be modalities" (*Differ-ence and Repetition*, 133).

40. Butler, *Frames of War*, 5.

41. See Agamben's discussion of the "anthropological machine" in *The Open: Man and Animal*, trans. Kevin Artell (Stanford, CA: Stanford Univer-sity Press, 2004), 33–38. Famously, Michel Foucault gave the name "biopoli-tics" to the process, begun in the seventeenth century, of assigning to *bios* the task of regulating *zoe* by exercising administrative and institutional means "to *foster* life or *disallow* it" (*History of Sexuality*, 139). The ascendancy of *bios*, of course, has a long prehistory, beginning with the territorializing logic of im-munity found in Roman jurisprudence; on this point, see Ed Cohen, *A Body Worth Defending: Immunity, Biopolitics, and the Apotheosis of the Modern Body* (Durham, NC: Duke University Press, 2009), 40–45.

42. Henk Oosterling, "From Interests to Inter-esse: Jean-Luc Nancy on Deglobalization and Sovereignty," *SubStance* 34, no. 1 (2005): 81–103, at 99. With Oosterling's reading of Nancy's interest in the "in between" in mind, one has to wonder whether Giorgio Agamben insists overmuch on calling the distinction a "zone of indifference" that is also "perfectly empty," through which "the articulation between human and animal, man and non-man, speaking being and living being, must take place" (*The Open*, 37–38).

43. See Jean-Luc Nancy, *Being Singular Plural*, 96: "Any being that one would like to imagine as not distinguished, not dis-posed, would really be indeterminate and unavailable: an absolute vacancy of Being. This is why the

ontological moment or the very order of ontology is necessary. *'To be' is not the noun of consistency; it is the verb of disposition'"* (emphasis in text).

44. Gilles Deleuze, *Pure Immanence: A Life*, trans. Anne Boyman (New York: Zone Books, 2001).

45. "This indefinite life does not itself have moments, close as they may be one to another, but only between-times, between-moments; it doesn't just come about or come after but offers the immensity of an empty time where one sees the event yet to come and already happened, in the absolute of an immediate consciousness" (ibid., 29).

46. Levi R. Bryant, *Difference and Givenness: Deleuze's Transcendental Empiricism and the Ontology of Immanence* (Evanston, IL: Northwestern University Press, 2008), 187. This is precisely what Levinas recoils from in his condemnation of the artwork as scandalous perpetuation of the "impersonal and anonymous" instant ("Reality and Its Shadow," 138).

47. As Deleuze reminds us, that suspension is not a void but rather is the "form of everything that changes and moves," which is not to say that it is an eternal form but rather "the form of that which is *not* eternal, the immutable form of change and movement" (*Kant's Critical Philosophy*, vii–viii, quoted in Bryant, *Difference and Givenness*, 186). Deleuze's scheme carries a distant echo of Augustine's famous rumination over the subjective paradoxes of temporality in Book 11 of the *Confessions*. Paul Ricoeur elegantly summarizes Augustine's understanding of the threefold character of the present as "the present of the past which is memory, the present of the future which is expectation, and the present of the present which is intuition (or attention)." Paul Ricoeur, *Memory, History, Forgetting*, trans. Kathleen Blamey (Chicago: University of Chicago Press, 2004), 347. For Augustine, however, the subjective paradoxes of temporality are epiphenomena of a divinely created order that reaches its eschatological fulfillment in God's aeon, outside time. Deleuze's scheme dispenses with Augustine's metaphysical telos, replacing it with the idea of infinite immanence, a dynamic field of multiple becomings. On this point, see Rosa Braidotti, "The Ethics of Becoming Imperceptible," in *Deleuze and Philosophy*, ed. Constantin Boundas (Edinburgh: Edinburgh University Press, 2006), 133–59.

48. Here we should recall the critical reflex that the Greek word for "presence" introduces into Paul's messianic vocabulary. *Parousia*, literally "being beside," captures the disjointedness of the now as well as the subject's unsettled residence in the now. This is not to say, of course, that anything can happen but rather that the borderline between the possible and the impossible cannot be secured simply by deducing it from the constraints of the empirical sense of actualized events. On the latent critical sense of *parousia*, see Agamben, *Time That Remains*, 69–72.

49. See Ed Cohen, "My Self as an Other: On Autoimmunity and 'Other' Paradoxes" and "Metaphorical Immunity: A Case of Biomedical Fiction," and the more expansive argument in *A Body Worth Defending*. Cohen presents a wide-ranging critical reflection on the cultural legacies of the word's etymology. See the etymological definition in the *Oxford English Dictionary*: "classical Latin *immūnitās* exemption from tax or tribute, exemption from duties or obligations, in post-classical Latin also inviolability, sanctity of hallowed ground (from 8th cent. in British sources; from 11th cent. in continental sources), right of sanctuary, asylum (from 12th cent. in British sources), place of sanctuary (from 13th cent. in British sources), benefit of clergy (13th cent. in a British source)."

50. See Giorgio Prodi, "Signs and Codes in Immunology," in *Essential Readings in Biosemiotics*, ed. Donald Favareau (Dordrecht, Heidelberg, London, and New York: Springer, 2009) 323–35, at 328.

51. The expression "white stigma" owes a debt to Derrida's well-known meditation in "White Mythology" on the call to "take the risk of a continuity between metaphor and concept, as between animal and man, instinct and knowledge" (262–63). See Ed Cohen's discussion of Derrida's essay in the context of Nietzsche's rehabilitation of the metaphoric lineaments of truth, in "Metaphoric Immunity," 144–47. Substituting the word *stigma* for "metaphor" emphasizes the social (and institutionalized) integument of the risk Derrida describes. It also pays to recall that the word *stigma* is related conceptually (not etymologically) to the wounding and marking actions denoted by the Greek word *typos* and the Latin *figura*. This neighborly relation suggestively points up the power of stigmas to activate forgotten and unanticipated linkages between seemingly disparate domains of social life or thought.

52. It bears noting that the rise of the immune theory of psoriasis followed shortly after clinical observation of the correlation between the onset of psoriasis symptoms and HIV progression. The genocidal subtext of HIV disease, of course, is now widely understood to be ecumenical—attached to regions marked by poverty and racialized inequities in addition to the continued association with same-sex communities. Psoriasis tends to be associated with more developed countries.

53. The Mayo Clinic website offers the following précis: "Mild cases of psoriasis may be a nuisance. But more severe cases can be painful, disfiguring and disabling. Most types of psoriasis go through cycles, flaring for a few weeks or months, then subsiding for a time or even going into complete remission. In most cases, however, the disease eventually returns" (http://www.mayoclinic.com/health/psoriasis/DS00193/DSECTION=symptoms). See also Linda Papadopoulos and C. Walker, "Personality, Coping and Sex

as Psychosocial Aspects of Psoriatic Arthropathy," *Dermatology and Psychosomatics* 4, no. 1 (2003): 27–32, and "Coping and Adaptation," in *Psychological Approaches to Dermatology* (Hoboken, NJ: Wiley-Blackwell, 1993), 23–30; and Corina Ioana Vladut, "Psychosocial Implications of Psoriasis: Theoretical Review," *Cognition, Brain, Behavior; An Interdisciplinary Journal* 14, no. 1 (March 2010): 23–35, http://www.faqs.org/periodicals/201003/1997374711 .html#ixzz14EdAtf5h.

54. Three of the five basic types of psoriasis (plaque, pustular, and erythrodermic) exhibit scaling lesions to varying degrees. For an account of the psychological impact of the disorder, see Iona H. Ginsburg and Bruce G. Link, "Feelings of stigmatization in patients with psoriasis," *Journal of the American Academy of Dermatology* 20, no. 1 (1989): 53–63.

55. John Updike comments on the "normal" aspect of the lesions for the person with psoriasis; see Updike, "At War with My Skin," *New Yorker*, September 2, 1985, 39–57.

56. "The disease is usually manifested as raised, well-demarcated erythematous oval plaques with adherent silvery scales. The scales are a result of a hyperproliferative epidermis with premature maturation of keratinocytes and incomplete cornification with retention of nuclei in the stratum corneum (parakeratosis). The mitotic rate of the basal keratinocytes is increased as compared with that in normal skin. As a result, the epidermis is thickened. . . . The redness of the lesions is due to increased numbers of tortuous capillaries that reach the skin surface through a markedly thinned epithelium." F. Nestle et al., "Mechanisms of Disease: Psoriasis," *New England Journal of Medicine* 361, no. 5 (July 30, 2009): 496, 498.

57. To recall the basic terms of the sorites paradox as inherited from Stoic logic: if you remove grains of corn from a heap, one by one, when does the heap cease to be a heap?

58. A discussion of the relationship between the sorites problem and fuzzy logic is in Peter Hajek and Vilem Novak, "The Sorites Paradox and Fuzzy Logic," *International Journal of General Systems* 32, no. 4 (August 2003): 373–83.

59. John Updike, "At War with My Skin," 56. The essay was reprinted in Updike's memoir collection, *Self-Consciousness* (New York: Random House, 1989), 42–80. In the later version, the phrase "in its eccentric chemistry" is deleted and replaced with "which has no aesthetic criteria" (78).

60. Cohen, *Body Worth Defending*, 41. My summary of the evolving semantics of immunity is indebted to Cohen's detailed account.

61. Cohen, "Metaphorical Immunity: A Case of Biomedical Fiction," 159.

62. Cohen gives a useful account of the Nietzschean and Derridean contributions to this story; see *Body Worth Defending*, 23–26, 36–38.

63. As Michel de Certeau reminds us, the word *metaphor* harbors a memory of errancy, transport, and exposure; see de Certeau, *The Practice of Everyday Life* (Berkeley: University of California Press, 1984), 91–110. William Corlett emphasizes the critical implication of this point: "Metaphor is not always easily noticed; but metaphor is never innocent. It orients research and fixes results." Corlett, *Community without Unity: A Politics of Derridean Extravagance* (Durham, NC: Duke University Press, 1993), 35.

64. Cohen, *Body Worth Defending*, 281.

65. Ibid.

66. Ibid.

67. Ibid., 43–44.

68. See Corlett, *Community without Unity*, 18. Cohen also notes the ambiguity: "Denoting obligations or responsibilities performed with others, whether within a state formation or not, community can refer both to a 'municipal corporation' and to a sharing 'in common' without specific regard to the province of the state, as in 'communication' or 'communion' (*OED*)" (*Body Worth Defending*, 43).

69. See Jean-Luc Nancy, *Being Singular Plural* (Stanford, CA: Stanford University Press, 2000).

70. See *Lawrence et al. v. Texas*, 539 U.S. 558 (2003), 586–605, https://supreme.justia.com/cases/federal/us/539/558/case.html. For a succinct discussion of the slippery slope argument, see Eugene Volokh, "The Mechanics of the Slippery Slope," *Harvard Law Review* 116 (2003): 1026–134, at 1029–30: "the most useful definition of a slippery slope is one that covers all situations where decision A, which you might find appealing, ends up materially increasing the probability that others will bring about decision B, which you oppose." A critical assessment of Scalia's use of the slippery slope argument is in Ruth Sternglantz, "Raining on the Parade of Horribles: Of Slippery Slopes, Faux Slopes, and Justice Scalia's Dissent in *Lawrence v. Texas*," *University Pennsylvania Law Review* 153 (2005): 1097–120. Referring to *Lawrence*, 123 S. Ct. at 2490, Sternglantz notes Scalia's warning that *Lawrence* was "the first step onto a slippery slope that would lead courts to legalize a parade of sexual-conduct horribles" (1098). For a helpful account of minor differences between the sorites paradox and the slippery slope argument, see Douglas Walton, "The Argument of the Beard," *Informal Logic* 18, nos. 2 and 3 (1996): 235–59, at 252.

71. Jane Bennett, *Vibrant Matter: A Political Ecology of Things* (Durham, NC, and London: Duke University Press, 2010), 23.

72. Ibid., ix–x.

73. Ibid., 23–24.

74. Merleau-Ponty, *The Visible and the Invisible*, 133.

75. Deleuze, *Cinema 2: The Time-Image*, trans. Hugh Tomlinson and Robert Galeta (Minneapolis: University of Minnesota Press, 1989), 98. Deleuze's phrase appears in the following context: "The past is not to be confused with the mental existence of recollection-images which actualize in us. It is preserved in time: it is the virtual element into which we penetrate to look for the 'pure recollection' which will become actual in a 'recollection-image' . . . Memory is not in us; it is we who move in a Being-memory, a world-memory. In short, the past appears as the most general form of an already-there, a pre-existence in general, which our recollections presuppose, even our first recollection if there was one, and which our perceptions, even the first, make use of" (ibid.). On the face of it, Deleuze's notion of an enveloping "world-memory" bears no relation to Merleau-Ponty's notion of the flesh, particularly if one considers Deleuze's complaint that Merleau-Ponty's argument converts too easily to "a pious and sensual notion, a mixture of sensuality and religion." Deleuze and Felix Guattari, *What Is Philosophy?*, trans. Hugh Tomlinson and Graham Burchell (New York: Columbia University Press, 1994), 178. Deleuze's objection returns in Jean-Luc Nancy's and, more recently, Roberto Esposito's critiques of Merleau-Ponty's thought. On this point, see Esposito, *Bios*, 162–65. The perspective I am advancing takes issue with these critiques' unstated assumption that residual implications of an idea denote inherent obstacles to the idea's application or development. For example, consider Esposito's vision of modernity's biopolitical grid as the inherent and inherently ambivalent outworking of the flesh. The claim silently discounts the possibility that the vexed association it draws between "flesh" and "body" may also be seen as a particular bricolage of the flesh rather than its historical destiny. As Esposito suggests, "biotechnology" must be thought of as "a non-Christian form of incarnation," but it does not follow from this that the expressive fecundity of the flesh converts unilaterally to "the biopolitical possibility of the ontological and technological transmutation of the human body" (*Bios*, 168).

6. THE FACE OF THE CONTEMPORARY: LOST WORLD FANTASIES OF FINDING LOT'S WIFE

1. Giorgio Agamben, "What Is the Contemporary?," in *Nudities*, trans. David Kishik and Stefan Pedatella (Stanford, CA: Stanford University Press, 2011), 10–19, at 11.

2. See Francesca Orestano, "Pictures of Modernity, the Modernity of the Picturesque: A Chiasmus," in *Pictures of Modernity: The Visual and the Literary in England, 1850–1930*, ed. Loretta Innocenti, Franco Marucci, Enrica Villari (Venice: Cafoscarina, 2008), 111–26, at 125. For a helpful overview of the link between early photographic technology and the aesthetics of the

picturesque, see James S. Ackerman, "The Photographic Picturesque," *Artibus et Historiae* 24, no. 48 (2003): 73–94.

3. For an account of geological evidence suggesting analogues to the biblical Cities of the Plain in the southeastern region of the Dead Sea, see David Neev and K. O. Emery, *The Destruction of Sodom, Gomorrah, and Jericho: Geological, Climatological, and Archaeological Background* (New York: Oxford University Press, 1995).

4. Agamben, "What Is the Contemporary?," 18.

5. Ibid., 11; emphasis in text.

6. Ibid. 17. All remaining excerpts in this paragraph are ibid.

7. Ibid., 18.

8. Herzl's most influential works, *Der Judenstaat* (1896) and *Altneuland* (1902), laid out a multilateral project a Jewish state whose autonomy would be supported by revenues from the harvesting of natural resources of the Dead Sea. For an account of the project described in *Altneuland*, see S. Ilan Troen, *Imagining Zion: Dreams, Designs, and Realities in a Century of Jewish Settlement* (New Haven, CT: Yale University Press, 2008), 87.

9. See the official environmental policies of Dead Sea Works Ltd. and Dead Sea Magnesium Ltd. at http://www.iclfertilizers.com/Fertilizers /DSW/Pages/BUHomepage.aspx and http://www.dsmag.co.il/.

10. Projected for completion in 2018, the plan entails construction of a one-hundred-mile long pipeline extending from the Gulf of Aqaba to the Dead Sea. A massive desalination plant in Jordan, near the Gulf of Aqaba, would produce significant supplies of drinking water to be shared equitably by Israel and drought-ridden Jordan, in exchange for which Israel would correspondingly increase the amount of water it sells to the Palestinian Authority from the Sea of Galilee. The desalination brine from the Aqaba plant would be pumped into the north basin of the Dead Sea in order to mitigate the shrinkage of the water level. Alternatively—no agreement on this point has yet been reached—the brine would be dumped into the Gulf of Aqaba, where it would likely endanger the Yahmanieh coral reef system.

11. Yifa Yaakov, "Israel, Jordan, PA Agree to Build Red Sea-Dead Sea Link," *Times of Israel*, December 9, 2013, http://www.timesofisrael.com /israel-jordan-pa-agree-to-build-red-sea-dead-sea-link/.

12. On this point, see Rob Holmes, "the dead sea works," *mammoth*, 2010, http://m.ammoth.us/blog/2010/02/the-dead-sea-works/. *mammoth* is an architectural research and design platform directed by Stephen Becker and Rob Holmes.

13. Yossi Ron, quoted in John Donnelly, "Environmentalists challenging Dead Sea industry," *Rome News-Tribune*, May 11, 1997. The plant in fig. 14 and plate 10 was built by A.D.Y.R. Constructions; see http://www

.adyr.co.il/projects.asp?lang=eng&isHistory=true. Ron's position comports well with the DSW's official environmental policy to "[b]lend in with nature with minimum adverse effects" (http://www.iclfertilizers.com/Fertilizers /Knowledge%20Center/DSW_Policy_Environment.pdf).

14. For an account of the nineteenth-century Jewish settlements in Palestine, see Yaron Perry and Elizabeth Yodim, *British Mission to the Jews in Nineteenth-Century Palestine* (London: Frank Cass Publishers, 2003). A helpful overview of the interest in Sodom as an object of archaeological study in the nineteenth century is in Astrid Swenson, "Sodom," in *Cities of God: The Bible and Archaeology in Nineteenth-Century Britain* (Cambridge: Cambridge University Press, 2013), 197–227.

15. Clark was not the only Victorian-era novelist to appropriate the figure of Lot's wife. The figure also served as a resource in the anti-Protestant polemical novels of the Irish-American writer Mary Anne Sadler (1820–1903). See Janelle Peters, "Lot's Wife in the Novels of Mary Anne Sadler," *Postscripts* 5, no. 2 (2009): 185–204.

16. *Saturday Review*, March 10, 1894, 283.

17. *Book Buyer* 13, no. 7, August 1896, 426.

18. *Book Buyer* 13, no. 8, September 1896, 469.

19. See http://members.cox.net/comingattractions/index.html.

20. For an account of White's career and the reception of *The Warfare of Science*, see Glenn C. Altschuler, *Andrew D. White—Educator, Historian, Diplomat* (Ithaca, NY: Cornell University Press, 1979), esp. 202–16.

21. Two accounts of Lynch's expedition were published (Kreiger, *Dead Sea*, 77–93). For a nuanced account of Lynch's narratives in the context of nineteenth-century American adventurism in the Holy Land, see Bruce A. Harvey, *American Geographics: U.S. National Narratives and the Representation of the Non-European World, 1830–1865* (Stanford, CA: Stanford University Press, 2001), 97–149.

22. See Robert P. Multhauf, *Neptune's Gift: A History of Common Salt* (Baltimore, MD: Johns Hopkins University Press, 1978), 154.

23. Andrew D. White, *A History of the Warfare of Science with Theology in Christendom* (Amherst, NY: Prometheus Books, 1993), 2:251–52.

24. Ibid., 2:252.

25. Ibid.

26. Ibid., 2:394.

27. The controversies attending such congress were not lost on White. The chapter on the Dead Sea legends calls attention to two highly publicized heresy trials, in Scotland and in North Carolina, in which the defendants' interest in evolutionary theories figured in the cases for prosecution. William Robertson Smith and James Woodrow, White reminds his readers, were

"both recently driven from their professorships for truth-telling" (White, 259). For an account of Robertson Smith's heresy trial (1878–1880) and dismissal from his professorial chair (1881) see David Livingstone, "Public Spectacle and Scientific Theory: William Robertson Smith and the Reading of Evolution in Victorian Scotland," *Studies in History and Philosophy of Biological and Biomedical Sciences* 35, no. 1 (2004): 1–29.

28. See Albert Schweitzer, *The Quest of the Historical Jesus: The First Complete Edition*, trans. W. Montgomery et al., ed. John Bowden (Minneapolis: Fortress Press, 2000). For Bultmann, to demythologize is "to deny that the message of Scripture and of the Church is bound to an ancient worldview which is obsolete. . . . Therefore, it is mere wishful thinking to suppose that the ancient world-view of the Bible can be renewed." The central aim of demythologizing is rather to seek the "deeper meaning which is concealed under the cover of mythology." Rudolf Bultmann, *Jesus Christ and Mythology* (New York: Scribner, 1958), 36, 38, 18. For a measured account of Schweitzer's and Bultmann's contributions to twentieth-century biblical studies, see Paul Ricoeur, "From Proclamation to Narrative," *Journal of Religion* 64, no. 4 (October 1984): 501–12.

29. White, *History of the Warfare*, 394, 393.

30. Ricoeur, "Preface to Bultmann," in *Paul Ricoeur: The Conflict of Interpretations*, ed. Don Ihde (Evanston, IL: Northwestern University Press, 1974), 381–401, at 394.

31. See "Myth as the Bearer of Possible Worlds" [dialogue with Richard Kearney], in *On Paul Ricoeur: The Owl of Minerva* by Richard Kearney (Aldershot, England: Ashgate, 2004), 121.

32. Ibid., 122.

33. Vida Pavesich, "Hans Blumenberg's Philosophical Anthropology: After Heidegger and Cassirer," *Journal of the History of Philosophy* 46, no. 3 (2008): 421–48, at 438, 437. My discussion of Blumenberg is indebted to Pavesich's analysis. See also Chiara Bottici, *A Philosophy of Political Myth* (New York: Cambridge University Press, 2007), 123–25.

34. Blumenberg, *Work on Myth*, 4.

35. Ibid.

36. Blumenberg's argument on this point differs markedly from Cassirer's theory of symbolic form; see Blumenberg, "An Anthropological Approach to the Significance of Rhetoric," in *After Philosophy: End or Transformation?*, ed. Kenneth Baynes et al. (Cambridge, MA: MIT Press, 1986), 429–58, at 438–39; and *Work on Myth*, 166–72. See also Pavesich's illuminating discussion of Blumenberg's critiques of Cassirer and Heidegger on the anthropological moorings of "significance" ("Hans Blumenberg's Philosophical Anthropology," 421–48).

37. The concept of human "eccentricity" is Helmut Plessner's; for an account of Blumenberg's assimilation and modification of Plessner's philosophical anthropology, together with that of Max Scheler and Arnold Gehlen, see Pavesich, "Hans Blumenberg's Philosophical Anthropology," 427–29.

38. Blumenberg, *Work on Myth*, 9.

39. Ibid., 633.

40. Hayden White, *Figural Realism: Studies in the Mimesis Effect* (Baltimore, MD: Johns Hopkins University Press, 1999), 67.

41. Ibid.

42. Ibid.

43. For a useful discussion of the preference for the phrase "lost world" rather than "lost race" fiction as a descriptor of the main emphasis in the proliferating Victorian genre of fictionalized travel writing, see Bradley Deane, "Imperial Barbarians: Primitive Masculinity in Lost World Fiction," *Victorian Literature and Culture*, no. 36 (2008): 205–25.

44. See in particular Stephens's description of Petra in John Lloyd Stephens, *Incidents of Travel in Egypt, Arabia Petræa, and the Holy Land* (Cambridge: Cambridge University Press, 2015), 2:50–78. Aptly, the man whose travel narratives provided ready passport to lost or exotic worlds was also instrumental in the development of more literal means of rapid transit: the first American transatlantic steamship company and the first railroad across the Isthmus of Panama. Stephens's expedition narratives also presented a prose analogue to David Roberts's enormously popular and widely reproduced lithographs of exotic locales, with their delicately cantilevered aesthetics of the picturesque and the sublime. A helpful discussion of Roberts's tacit mapping of the difference between the presumed scopic privilege of the spectator and the more engaged, potentially self-critical, position of the engaged observer is in Manu Samriti Chander, "Framing Difference: The Orientalist Aesthetics of David Roberts and Percy Shelley," *Keats-Shelley Journal*, no. 60 (2011): 77–94.

45. Alfred Clark, *The Finding of Lot's Wife* (New York and London: Frederick A. Stokes Company, 1896), 107. Hereafter cited in text as *FLW* and page number. Isha takes pains to correct Aylward's impression that her name is a variant of the Arabic "Ayesha" (108), thus securing her identity within the Judaeo-Christian rather than Islamic archive.

46. See Blackstone's *Commentaries on the Laws of England*, III.10, at the Yale Law School Avalon Project, http://avalon.law.yale.edu/18th_century /blackstone_bk3ch10.asp.

47. The political marginalization of Catholics living in Clark's England had been significantly attenuated with the passage of the Roman Catholic Relief Act in 1829, but this fact does not legislate erasure of the enduring resonance in cultural memory of the name "Yorke" as a mark of catholicizing

otherness in the felt perception of Englishness. See Edward Royle, *Noncon-formity in Nineteenth-Century York*, Borthwick papers, no. 68 (York, England: University of York, 1985).

48. Clark's account of the Monastery of St. Lot relies on ancient lore; the site was discovered and excavated in 1986. See Konstantinos Politis, "Exca-vations at Deir Ain 'Abata 1988," *Annual of the Department of Antiquities of Jordan*, no. 33 (1989): 227–33, 404–40; Konstantinos Politis, "The Sanctuary of Agios Lot, the City of Zoara and the Zared River," *Madaba Map Centenary* (Jerusalem 1999): 225–27.

49. See *Jerusalem and the Holy Land Rediscovered: The Prints of David Rob-erts*, ed. W. D. Davies, Eric M. Myers, and Sarah Walker Schroth (Durham, NC: Duke University Press, 1997).

50. The key reference point is Picasso's notorious *Les Demoiselles d'Avignon* (1907). As Patricia Leighten argues, "*Les Demoiselles d'Avignon* was the most outrageous artistic act conceivable at that time," partly because its evident primitivism—notably the edgy admixture of Iberian and African elements—subverted "canons of beauty and order in the name of 'authenticity,' as a way of contravening the rational, liberal, "enlightened" political order in which they are implicated." Leighten, "The White Peril and *L'Art nègre*: Picasso, Primitivism, and Anti-Colonialism," *Art Bulletin* 74, no. 4 (December 1990): 609–30, at 627. See also Patricia Leighten, *Re-Ordering the Universe: Picasso and Anarchism, 1897–1914* (Princeton, NJ: Princeton University Press, 1989).

51. The depiction of the tribal judgment and execution of Selim appears in chap. 12, titled "A Young Martyr" (*FLW*, 168–88).

52. For Levinas, let us recall, the "face" of the Other eclipses its phenom-enal appearance: "The Other does not only *appear* in his face, as a phenom-enon subject to action and domination of a freedom; infinitely distant from the very relation he enters, he presents himself there from the first as an absolute. . . . The face with which the Other turns to me is not reabsorbed in a representation of the face. To hear his destitution which cries out for justice is not to represent an image to oneself, but is to posit oneself as responsible, both as more and as less than the being that presents itself in the face" (*Total-ity and Infinity*, 215).

53. For an account of the differences between Sándor Ferenczi's and Sigmund Freud's emphases in treating the Medusa myth as a mythic archive of castration anxiety and traumatic subjectivity, see Ruth Leys, *Trauma: A Genealogy* (Chicago: University of Chicago Press, 2000), 134–38.

54. Blumenberg, *Work on Myth*, 4.

55. Ibid., 34–35.

56. Ibid., 16. For Blumenberg, the functional adaptability of myth and the operation of reason are regional expressions of a generalized meaning-

making propensity. The jewel-like sheen of Blumenberg's playful assertion—
"Myth itself is a piece of high-carat 'work of logos'"—quietly acknowledges
the arresting character of the claim (ibid., 12). Blumenberg's quasi-image of
"high-carat 'work'" calls attention to how the achievements in both domains,
myth and reason, persist as variably pressurized *figural* states of thought and
feeling that are irreducible to totalized comprehension, though with different degrees of urgency at different historical moments. A concise account
of the "therapeutic" dimension of Blumenberg's argument is in William J.
Bouwsma, review of Hans Blumenberg, *Work on Myth*, in *Journal of the History of Ideas* 48, no. 2 (1987): 347–54, at 349.

57. For an account of Muslim demographics in Victorian England, see
Humayun Ansari, *The Infidel Within: The History of Muslims in Britain, 1800 to
the Present* (London: C. Hurst and Co., 2004).

58. Leslie Hill argues persuasively for the signature trait of unreadability
in Blanchot's aesthetic program. For Blanchot, "reading is haunted by the
spectre of the unreadable. That spectre is a necessary one. . . . To read at
all, it may be argued, is to encounter the unfamiliarity, the strangeness, the
otherness of the unreadable. In other words, to read is by necessity to strain
towards the point at which its own possibility is put into crisis." Leslie Hill,
"'Affirmation without Precedent': Maurice Blanchot and Criticism Today," in *After Blanchot: Literature, Criticism, Philosophy*, ed. Leslie Hill, Brian
Nelson, and Dimitris Vardoulakis (Newark: University of Delaware Press,
2005), 58–79, at 70. Hill also reminds us that for Blanchot, importantly, "to
affirm the future is to affirm exposure to that which is without name, without
example, and cannot be evaluated in advance—but without which justice
itself cannot be affirmed in its turn. It is a decision that decides on behalf of
undecidability" (ibid., 73).

59. An illuminating account of the several strands of the debate over
miracles in the nineteenth and twentieth centuries is in Robert Bruce Mullin,
Miracles and the Modern Religious Imagination (New Haven, CT: Yale University Press, 1996).

60. The critical literature on the topic is vast; see especially Horst Brede-
kamp, *The Lure of Antiquity and the Cult of the Machine*, trans. Allison Brown
(Princeton, NJ: Markus Wiener Publishers, 1995); Ken Arnold, *A Cabinet
for the Curious: Looking Back at Early English Museums* (Aldershot, England:
Ashgate, 2006), and Lorraine J. Daston and Katharine Park, *Wonders and the
Order of Nature, 1150–1750* (New York: Zone Books, 2001).

61. For a succinct account of the scientific cult of "information transfer"
with vanishing mediators, see Bruno Latour, "How to be Iconophilic in Art,
Science, and Religion?" in *Picturing Science, Producing Art*, ed. Caroline A
Jones and Peter Galison (New York and London: Routledge, 1998), 427.

62. See Sean Silver, *The Mind Is a Collection: Case Studies in Eighteenth-Century Thought* (Philadelphia: University of Pennsylvania Press, 2015), 51.

63. Agamben, "What Is the Contemporary?," 11; italics in text.

64. Ibid., 17.

65. In essence, the painting's quiet provocation speaks to Jean-Luc Marion's insight into the theo-aesthetic drama lodged in the encounter with the icon. Drawing on the kenotic strand to Levinas's thought, Marion identifies the dispossessive yet transformative agency of the icon as "the kenosis of the image." Marion, "The Blind at Shiloh," in *The Crossing of the Visible*, trans. James K. A. Smith (Stanford, CA: Stanford University Press, 2004), 46–66, at 62.

66. Levinas, "Reality and Its Shadow," 141.

7. OUT OF AFRICA: ALBERT MEMMI'S DESERT OF ALLEGORY IN *THE PILLAR OF SALT*

1. Emmanuel Levinas, "Judaism and Kenosis," in *In the Time of Nations*, trans. Michael B. Smith (Bloomington: Indiana University Press, 1994), 126.

2. Elio Kapszuk, *Shalom Argentina: Huellas de la colonización judía / Tracing Jewish Settlement* (Buenos Aires: Ministerio de Turismo, Cultura y Deporte, 2001), 274. See also Morton D. Winsberg, "Jewish Agricultural Colonization in Entre Rios, Argentina, I: Some Social and Economic Aspects of a Venture in Resettlement," *American Journal of Economics and Sociology* 27, no. 3. (July 1968), 285–95.

3. Memmi, *The Pillar of Salt*, trans. Edouard Roditi (Boston, MA: Beacon Press, 1992), 335. Hereafter cited in text as *PoS* and page number. Unless otherwise noted, I use Roditi's translation throughout.

4. I take the word *eventfulness* in the phenomenological sense concisely described by François Dastur: "The event in the strong sense of the word is therefore always a surprise, something which takes possession of us in an unforeseen manner, without warning, and which brings us towards an unanticipated future. The *eventum*, which arises in the becoming, constitutes something which is irremediably excessive in comparison to the usual representation of time as flow. It appears as something that dislocates time and gives a new form to it, something that puts the flow of time out of joint and changes its direction" ("Phenomenology of the Event: Between Waiting and Surprise," *Hypatia* 15, no. 4 (2000): 178–89, at 182).

5. Levinas, "No Identity," in *Collected Philosophical Papers*, trans. Alphonso Lingis (Dordrecht, Netherlands: Nijhoff, 1987), 148–49.

6. Ibid., 149. Levinas also discusses the biblical notion of kenosis as a figure of "the proximity of God to human suffering" and the understanding of the human as "the possibility of a being-for-the other," in "Judaism and

Kenosis," 114–35, at 115 and 126. Cogent overviews of the theological and philosophical legacies of Pauline kenosis are in Graham Ward, "Kenosis: Death, Discourse, and Resurrection," in *Balthasar at the End of Modernity*, ed. Lucy Gardner, David Moss, Ben Quash, and Graham Ward (Edinburgh: T&T Clark, 1999), 15–68; and "Kenosis and Naming: Beyond Analogy and Towards *Allegoria Amoris*," in *Religion, Modernity and Postmodernity*, ed. Paul Heelas (Oxford: Blackwell, 1998), 233–57.

7. On the "worklessness" of art, see Blanchot, *The Infinite Conversation*, trans. Susan Hanson (Minneapolis: University of Minnesota Press, 1993), 424.

8. Blanchot, "Prophetic Speech," in *Book to Come*, 80.

9. See chapter 2.

10. Judith Roumani, *Albert Memmi* (Philadelphia: Celfan Edition Monographs, 1987), 37, 20.

11. Ibid., 19, 38.

12. See Suzanne Gearhart's account of the sociopolitical emphasis in Fanon's and Bhabha's respective negotiation of Marxist and psychoanalytical methods, in "Colonialism, Psychoanalysis, and Cultural Criticism: The Problem of Interiorization in the Work of Albert Memmi," in *"Culture" and the Problem of the Disciplines*, ed. John Carlos Rowe (New York: Columbia University Press, 1998), 171–97.

13. Edouard Glissant, *La relation poétique* (Paris: Seuil, 1992), 46–47.

14. I follow Gearhart's suggestion of a partial overlap between Glissant's notion of *créolisation* and Memmi's idiosyncratic application of the psychoanalytic notion of interiorization; see Gearhart, "Colonialism," 177. Gearhart's central claim is apposite to my argument: "a portrait of colonial society such as Memmi has provided can serve as the basis for a powerful critique of (neo) colonialsm and racism and also elucidate the processes of interiorization-as-*métissage* that are inherent in all cultures, and that even the most repressive of colonial regimes cannot suppress" (ibid., 191).

15. Memmi, *The Colonizer and the Colonized*, trans. Howard Greenfield (Boston, MA: Beacon Press, 1984), xiii.

16. Ibid., xii.

17. Gearhart ("Colonialism," 181) rightly points out that Memmi's critical gaze "does not substitute cultural factors for economic determinants; instead its ultimate effect is to undermine both the cultural and the economic as principles of identity."

18. Ibid., 182. Thus Memmi's portrait of what he calls the "Nero complex" emphasizes how the stain of disavowed usurpation and illegitimacy in the colonial situation produces an enveloping, toxic ethos of perpetually being on trial—in different yet complementary ways for both colonizer

and colonized. But Nero is not a mask or substitute for Oedipus. The figure demonstrates Memmi's tactical mining of the psychoanalytical archive to interrupt and critique both the sociopolitical and economic metric's empirical gravitas and prestige, and the unintended reduction of a given conflict or crisis' particularities to the status of a case study through the omnibus application of the psychoanalytical repertoire. On this point see Henry Louis Gates, "Critical Fanonism," *Critical Inquiry* 17, no. 3 (1991): 457–70.

19. On the distinction between Levinas's and Deleuze's notions of infinity in the *à-venir*, see Leonard Lawlor, "God and Concept: On the Love of the Neighbour in Levinas and Bergson," in *Emmanuel Levinas: Levinas in the History of Philosophy*, Critical Assessments of Leading Philosophers, vol. 2, ed. Claire Elise Katz and Lara Trout (New York and London: Routledge, 2005), 175–94, at 179–81. Giorgio Agamben uses the phrase "being outside, yet belonging" to pinpoint the paradoxical phenomenon of the state of exception grounded in the sovereign's decision. As Agamben's writings also indicate, however, the paradox has its origins in Paul's innovative sense of kairotic possibility. See Agamben, *State of Exception*, trans. Kevin Attell (Chicago: University of Chicago Press, 2005), 35; and Agamben, *The Time That Remains: A Commentary on the Letter to Romans*, trans. Patricia Dailey (Stanford, CA: Stanford University Press, 2005), 62–75.

20. Camus, "Preface to *The Pillar of Salt*," trans. Scott Davidson, *Journal of French and Francophone Philosophy* 19, no. 2 (2011), 15. See also Memmi, *La statue de sel* (Paris: Gallimard, 1966) 10.

21. Gearhart, "Colonialism," 188.

22. For a detailed account of the early critical reception of the novel, see Guy Dugas, "Réception critique des premiers ouvrages d'Albert Memmi (1952–1962)," in *Lire Albert Memmi: Déracinement, exil, identité*, ed. David Ohana, Claude Sitbon, and David Mendelson (Paris: Éditions Factuel, 2002), 15–28. Dugas also places Memmi's early novels in the context of contemporary Maghrebian fiction by Claude Benady, Irma Ychou, and Jean Daniel.

23. "*La Statue de sel* est tout à la fois un roman, une autobiographie, un documentaire et une étude sociologique, et bien d'autres choses encore," Wurmser, *Les lettres françaises*, July 31, 1953, quoted in Dugas, "Réception critique," 18; my translation.

24. For an account of the widespread critical perception that the narrator's departure for Argentina amounts to "a flight, a refusal, in the face of choices prematurely cut off [tronqués] which are proposed to him," see Anny Dayan Rosenman, "Les représentations de l'histoire dans l'œuvre romanesque d'Albert Memmi," in *Lire Albert Memmi*, 59; my translation. See also Isaac Yetiv's observation that the narrator's choice to leave for Argentina is inauthentic because he "leaves without having understood, without

having truly chosen." Yetiv, *Le theme de l'aliénation dans le roman maghrebin d'expression française, 1952–1956* (Quebec: CELEF, Université de Sherbrooke, 1972), 162.

25. Touitou-Benitah, "Memmi le passeur," 82.

26. My translation. Memmi's text: "Cette fois, il s'était découvert un oncle planteur, en Argentine, pays neuf, plein de richesses vierges" (*La statue de sel*, 347).

27. The symmetry is attenuated in the English translation, where the chapter titles are "Prologue" and "Examination." For a rewarding narratological analysis of Memmi's novel, see Jacqueline Levi-Valensi, " 'La Statue de sel': étude narratologique," in *Albert Memmi, écrivain et sociologue: actes du colloque de Paris X-Nanterre, 15–16 mai 1988*, ed. Jean-Yves Guérin (Paris: L'Harmattan, 1990), 31–47.

28. German occupying forces established a Tunisian *Judenrat* (Jewish council under Nazi supervision) in December 1942, shortly after German troops entered the country. German control ended with the Allied liberation of Tunisia in May 1943. See Emil Kerenji, *Jewish Responses to Persecution*, vol. 4, *1942–1943* (London: Rowman and Littlefield, 2015), 283.

29. Memmi, "Vous voyez bien que l'aubiographie est un genre faux: une vie ne se raconte pas. On la rêve, on la réinvente à mesure qu'on la raconte, on la revit sans cesse d'une manière différente." Memmi, *La terre intérieure* (Paris: Gallimard, 1976), 11; my translation. Memmi's skepticism is abundantly documented in interviews and autobiographical remarks. In the Malka interview, for example, Memmi elaborates on his philosophical training at the Sorbonne and the resulting skeptical habit he maintained in his literary career; see *La terre intérieure*, 88–91.

30. In his memoir, Memmi identifies the real-life version: the impasse Tronja at rue Vielle-Tronja was a *"no man's land*, between the Arab quarter and the Jewish quarter" and the family lived cheek by jowl, in a condition of ambient poverty, with other Jews and Arabs as well as working-class Sicilians and Maltese (*Nomade immobile*, 12–13; my translation).

31. Yetiv reports Memmi's accounts of his Jewish background as "la matrice de son oeuvre" and discusses the complex character of Memmi's relation to the religious, cultural, social, and political dimensions of Judaism. See Yetiv, "La dimension juive dans l'oeuvre d'Albert Memmi," in *Albert Memmi: Écrivain et sociologue*, ed. Jean-Yves Guerin (Paris: L'Harmattan, 1990), 79–90, at 80–82.

32. See Memmi, *La terre intérieure*, 181.

33. Augustine, *The City of God*, trans. M. Dods, ed. Whitney J. Oates, in *Basic Writings of Saint Augustine*, 2 vols., XII.20 (Grand Rapids, MI: Baker Book House, 1992), 2:203. An important leitmotif of Arendt's phenomeno-

logical and political thought, the notion of natality appears in several guises throughout her writing career; on this point see Patricia Bowen-Moore, *Hannah Arendt's Political Philosophy of Natality* (New York: St. Martin's, 1989). A succinct formulation appears in Arendt's essay "What is Freedom?" in *Between Past and Future: Eight Exercises in Political Thought* (New York: Penguin, 2006), 166: "In this birth of each man this initial beginning is reaffirmed, because in each instance something new comes into an already existing world which will continue to exist after each individual's death. Because he *is* a beginning, man can begin; to be human and to be free are one and the same. God created man in order to introduce into the world the faculty of beginning: freedom."

34. Bowen-Moore, *Hannah Arendt's Political Philosophy*, 1.

35. Miguel Vatter, "Natality and Biopolitics in Hannah Arendt," *Revista de Ciencia Política* 26, no. 2 (2006): 136–59, at 151.

36. Derrida, *Demeure*, 75.

37. Arendt, *Between Past and Future*, 166.

38. Levinas, *Otherwise Than Being*, 75. See Astell's discussion of the proximity of Levinas's notion of maternity to Arendt's notion of natality, in "Mater-Natality," 381–83.

39. Blanchot, *Book to Come*, 80.

40. Arendt, *Between Past and Future*, 168.

41. Memmi's recollection of the ghetto in the Malka interviews is instructive in this regard: "I admit that the idea of a just society—socialist, not to mince words—to which I aspired and continue to strive for—is the memory of the City of God of my childhood, and the social and historical harmony for which I still fight is but the retrieval of the moral and cosmic harmony of the ghetto. In the ghetto, you know the rules of the game, which are human, familial, social, and divine, all at the same time; you submit, but in submitting, you discover great peace of mind, great comfort, great joy. . . . That was the ghetto, at least as I remember it, or imagine it, I'm not sure which" (*La terre intérieure*, 16; my translation).

42. Peg Birmingham, "Political Affections: Kristeva and Arendt on Violence and Gratitude," in *Revolt, Affect, Collectivity: The Unstable Boundaries of Kristeva's Polis*, ed. Tina Chanter and Ewa Płonowska Ziarek (Albany: State University of New York, 2005), 127–46, at 129. Birmingham argues that Arendt later "splits the event of natality," effectively dissociating the two meanings of the event from each other, which renders her subsequent arguments unable "to incorporate gratitude for the given into the space of the political" (ibid., 129).

43. Arendt, *Between Past and Future*, 167.

44. Later in the chapter, the narrator tries to contain his horror at the frenzied dancing by giving it a medical diagnosis: "But how is one to stop this collective seizure of epilepsy?" (*PoS*, 162).

45. Joëlle Bahloul observes that both Jewish and Muslim households in colonial Algeria paid tribute, in different ways, to the *djnoun*; see Bahloul, *The Architecture of Memory: A Jewish-Muslim Household in Colonial Algeria, 1937–1962* (Cambridge: Cambridge University Press, 1996), 95–96.

46. Famously, Lévy-Bruhl proposed that one of the distinctive features of primitive mentality was its indifference to the logical principle of noncontradiction: "in the collective representations of primitive mentality, objects, beings, phenomena, can be, though in a way incomprehensible to us, both themselves and something other than themselves." Lucien Lévy-Bruhl, *How Natives Think*, trans. Lilian A. Clare, 1926 (Princeton, NJ: Princeton University Press, 1985), 76–77.

47. For a helpful account of Lévy-Bruhl's nonevolutionary concept of participation, see Ugo Bianchi, *The History of Religions* (Leiden, Netherlands: Brill, 1975), 79–83.

48. See Ann Pellegrini's account of the depiction of the maternal body as the locus of dread in the colonial machine as anatomized in *The Pillar of Salt*, in *Performance Anxieties: Staging Psychoanalysis, Staging Race* (London and New York: Routledge, 1996), 112–13.

49. See Memmi, *Pillar of Salt*, 276–79.

50. Anne W. Astell, "Mater-Natality: Augustine, Arendt, and Levinas," *Analecta Husserliana*, no. 89 (2006): 373–98, at 382–83.

51. Sara Ahmed, *Strange Encounters: Embodied Others in Post-Coloniality* (London and New York: Routledge, 2000), 152. Ahmed mounts a critique of the ontologically stable "home"/"away" opposition and its silent partner, the fetishization of the "stranger" (ibid., 77–94). Her critique draws on the complex relationship between Levinas and Derrida on the question of ethics and hospitality and includes a brief account of Blanchot's poignant and jarring account of alterity in *The Writing of the Disaster* (Ahmed, *Strange Encounters*, 137–60).

52. Memmi, *Pillar of Salt*, 164; *La statue de sel*, 183.

53. Memmi, *Pillar of Salt*, 111; *La statue de sel*, 126.

54. On this point, see Pellegrini, "Between Men: Fanon, Memmi, and the Colonial Encounter," in *Performance Anxieties*, 109–30; and Debra Kelly, "Albert Memmi: Fictions of Identity and the Quest for Truth," in *Autobiography and Independence: Selfhood and Creativity in North African Postcolonial Writing in French* (Liverpool: Liverpool University Press, 2005), 131–203.

55. To recall one of Bruno Latour's recent coinages, the narrative coherence of Alexandre's career testifies to the diminishing returns of the "salvo of

anti-fetishism" in critical discourse; see Bruno Latour, "Why Has Critique Run Out of Steam? From Matters of Fact to Matters of Concern," *Critical Inquiry* 30, no. 2 (Winter 2004): 225–48, at 239.

56. Memmi's selection of *Andromaque* no doubt reflects the fact that this play is the most common representative of French classical theater in the curriculum of the *lycée* system. In the event, Racine's *Phèdre* appears elsewhere in the novel, in the episode detailing Alexandre's attempt to seduce his classmate Ginou while tutoring her in French literature (185–91).

57. Benjamin Hutchens, *Levinas: A Guide for the Perplexed* (London: Bloomsbury Academic, 2004), 47.

58. Racine, *Andromaque*, ed. Yves Brunsvick and Paul Ginestier (Paris: Didier, 1970). All further references to the play are from this edition. An online bilingual edition of the play is at http://www.tclt.org.uk/racine /Racine_2011.pdf.

59. Chateaubriand, *Genius of Christianity, or The Spirit and Beauties of the Christian Religion*, trans. E. O'Donnell (Paris: E. Thunot and Co., 1854), 326. Hereafter cited in text as *GoC* and page number. See also the French text (1828 edition from the Bibliothèque Nationale) at http://visualiseur.bnf.fr /CadresFenetre?O=NUMM-101356&M=tdm.

60. "[T]he spirit of Christianity has a profound sympathy with the affectionate sentiments of mothers" (Chateaubriand, *Genius of Christianity*, 326).

61. Contemporary feminist theologians have labored mightily to disentangle the Pauline notion of kenosis from the vexed chronicle of humility in Christian ethics. For an illuminating discussion of how advocacy of humility may perform an unwitting or blinkered rearguard action in perpetuating gendered inequities in both social and moral life, see the exchange between Sarah Coakley and Daphne Hampson in *Swallowing a Fishbone? Feminist Theologians Debate Christianity*, ed. Daphne Hampson (London: SPCK, 1996).

62. Racine, *Andromaque*, 4.1.1115–16

63. Arendt's use of these terms is apposite: "The legendary hiatus between a no-more and a not-yet clearly indicated that freedom would not be the automatic result of liberation, that the end of the old is not necessarily the beginning of the new, that the notion of an all-powerful time continuum is an illusion" (*Life of the Mind*, 204).

64. I use the term *counter-memory* following George Lipsitz's tempered application of Foucault's sense of the term: "Counter-memory is a way of remembering and forgetting that starts with the local, the immediate, and the personal. Unlike historical narratives that begin with the totality of human existence and then locate specific actions and events within that totality, counter-memory starts with the particular and the specific and then builds toward a total story. . . . [It] forces revision of existing histories by supplying

new perspectives about the past." Lipsitz, *Time Passages: Collective Memory and American Popular Culture* (Minneapolis: University of Minnesota Press, 1990), 213.

65. Arendt, *Human Condition*, 233.

66. Ibid.

67. Ibid.

68. For an illuminating account of Arendt's misreading of Augustine's notion of *caritas* as essentially apolitical, see Stephan Kampowski. *Arendt, Augustine, and the New Beginning: The Action Theory and Moral Thought of Hannah Arendt in the Light of Her Dissertation on St. Augustine* (Grand Rapids, MI: Wm. B. Eerdmans, 2008).

69. The phrase is Lisa Guenther's; it appears in her subtle account of Levinas's notion of the hypostasis of the ethical subject as a recurrent tension between becoming and being ("*coming-to*-be" versus "coming-*to-be*"), in "'Nameless Singularity': Levinas on Individuation and Ethical Singularity," *Epoché* 14, no. 1 (Fall 2009): 167–87, at 170 and 173–74.

70. Levinas, *Otherwise Than Being*, 108.

71. Ibid., 108–9.

72. Levinas, *Time and the Other*, 52.

73. Arendt, *Life of the Mind*, 210; Levinas, *Otherwise Than Being*, 96.

74. Levinas, *Otherwise Than Being*, 88, 89. This feature makes itself felt in the prepositional emphasis to the expression "the-one-for-the-other" in Levinas's philosophy: "the *for* of the-one-for-the-other, outside of any correlation and any finality, is a *for* of total gratuity, breaking with interest: *for* characteristic of the human fraternity outside of any preestablished system" (ibid., 96–97).

75. Ahmed, *Strange Encounters*, 152.

76. Arendt, *Life of the Mind*, 204.

77. Memmi, *La statue de sel*, 292. The best history of the Homeric phrase is in R. Rutherford-Dyer, "Homer's Wine-Dark Sea," *Greece and Rome* 30, no. 2 (October 1983): 125–28. The common French rendering of "wine-dark sea" (*oînops póntos*) is "la sombre mer." See, for example, *L'odyssée*, trans. Leconte de Lisle (Paris: Alphonse Lemerre, 1877), 76.

78. Homer, *The Odyssey*, trans. A. T. Murray, Loeb Classical Library, vol. 1 (Cambridge, MA: Harvard University Press, 1919), 5.214–24.

79. Merleau-Ponty, *The Visible and the Invisible*, 248.